The Lafayette Flying Corps
Volume 1

MANOEUVRING FOR THE ATTACK

The Lafayette Flying Corps Volume 1
During the First World War

Edited by
James Norman Hall
&
Charles Bernard Nordhoff

The Lafayette Flying Corps Volume 1
During the First World War
Edited by James Norman Hall & Charles Bernard Nordhoff

First published under the titles
The Lafayette Flying Corps Volumes 1 & 2

Leonaur is an imprint of Oakpast Ltd
Copyright in this form © 2014 Oakpast Ltd

ISBN: 978-1-78282-329-2 (hardcover)
ISBN: 978-1-78282-330-8 (softcover)

http://www.leonaur.com

Publisher's Notes

The views expressed in this book are not necessarily those of the publisher.

Contents

Preface	9
The Origin of the Escadrille Américaine	13
The Escadrille Lafayette at the Front	28
The Lafayette Flying Corps	62
Enlistment and Early Training	82
Adventures in Action	149
Life on the Front	251
Combats	343
Prisoners of War	414

THE LAFAYETTE FLYING CORPS

To
WILLIAM K. VANDERBILT
GENEROUS AND LOYAL FRIEND OF THE
LAFAYETTE FLYING CORPS

Far above the squalor and the mud, so high in the firmament as to be invisible from earth, they fight out the eternal issues of right and wrong. Their daily and nightly struggles are like Miltonic conflicts between winged hosts. They fight high and low. They skim like armed swallows along the Front, attacking men in their flights, armed with rifle and machine gun. They scatter infantry on the march; they destroy convoys; they wreck trains. Every flight is a romance, every record an epic. They are the knighthood of this war, without fear and without reproach; and they recall the legendary days of chivalry, not merely by the daring of their exploits, but by the nobility of their spirit.
—(From a speech of David Lloyd George before the House of Commons, October 29, 1917)

Preface

In offering this record of the Lafayette Flying Corps to the families and friends of the men who served in it, and to the public at large, the editors feel that a few words of explanation are necessary. Their purpose has been twofold: to furnish a record as complete and authentic as possible, and to reconstruct an atmosphere. To accomplish the first has not been easy, for the work of collecting and arranging the material was not begun until after the signing of the armistice, when the pilots in the corps had become widely scattered. Some were still on duty in France; others had been sent to aviation schools and depots throughout America; yet others had returned to civilian life. The task of getting in touch with them has been difficult and in some cases impossible.

In preparing the service records and biographical sketches, to be found in Volume 2, the general policy has been followed of including only those of the men who served at the Front. A few exceptions have been made in the case of men killed in accidents, those who served with distinction in other than combatant capacities, and those who were released because of wounds received in some other branch of war service. The service records are as complete as painstaking care could make them. Dates are occasionally wanting and copies of citations, for the reason that they could be secured neither from the men themselves nor from the French records. It was likewise impossible always to decide upon the exact dates of American commissions. Those given here are sometimes the date of granting, sometimes that of accepting the commission, and sometimes that of the pilot's active duty orders in U.S. Aviation.

The biographical sketches have not been written to the satisfaction of the editors. It was inevitable, perhaps, that there should be a good deal of similarity in them, written, as they were, of men whose experiences as aviators were so largely similar. Furthermore, detailed information of the service of many of the volunteers has been lacking. The editors had personal knowledge of only those men who were in their own squadrons or *groupes de combat*. The length or quality of a man's service is not, therefore, to be judged wholly by the length or character of his biographical sketch.

Members of the Lafayette Corps who were not breveted, or who were released from the French service before being sent on active duty, are included in a separate list. Most of the names in this supplementary list are of men who served honourably and faithfully, and who were released because of illness, as the result of injuries received in flying accidents, or because of inaptitude. While always a matter of regret to a pilot, inaptitude is no cause for shame. In the air service of any country, the number of men released before receiving the military brevet was always large, sometimes one half of the number enlisted.

Owing chiefly to limits of space, the formal history has been made as concise as possible. The editors have contented themselves with preparing a brief narrative of the origin of the *Escadrille Américaine*, its service at the Front, and its development into the Lafayette Flying Corps, carrying the story through the winter of 1917-18, when the members of the Escadrille Lafayette, as well as most of the American volunteers in other French squadrons, were transferred to the U.S. Air Service. Access has been had to the files of the Lafayette Corps as well as to those of the French *Service Aéronautique*, and every effort has been made to give an accurate account as well as to include in it all essential facts.

The more important history, the narrative of life in French aviation schools and at the Front, has been told by the volunteers themselves. This volume contains their letters written under the emotional stress of a great experience. In order to obtain many of the letters, it was necessary to promise that the name of the writer would be withheld. It was decided, therefore, to print all anonymously. In choosing those for publication the editors have kept in mind the fact that the Lafayette Corps was a cosmopolitan one. It is to be hoped that its members will be seen here as they actually were, boys fresh from school or college, men just entering business or professional life; men from the east and the west, the north and the south; those who enlisted from a high sense of duty and those who came at the irresistible call of adventure. In reading over their letters, one seems to relive the old heroic days, to hear the distant mutter of the guns, and the pulsing of the motors of the midnight Gothas; to see the return of the patrol remote against the evening sky; to feel the thrill and the terror of combat; to breathe again the unforgettable fragrance of an aerodrome—the sweet, pungent odour of gasoline and burnt castor oil.

The Lafayette Corps has played its part in history—how great a part the future will decide. One hundred and ten of America's six hundred and fifty aviators who served at the Front were Lafayette men. In addition thirty-three pilots remained in the French service, fighting in French squadrons until the end of the war. Others were acting as instructors at aviation schools both in France and in America. It seemed necessary that some record of the accomplishment of the Lafayette Corps be set down, not only for the pleasure of the men who were a part of it, but that others in later days might not forget these volunteers who were among the first Americans to go to the aid of France at a time of great need.

J. N. H.
C. B. N.

Squibnocket, Martha's Vineyard
Massachusetts

[FACSIMILE]

7. 11. 19.

Le Maréchal Foch

Le 26 avril 1777, La Fayette s'embarquait à la Pointe-de-Grave, pour mettre son épée et celles de ses compagnons au service de Washington. Son acte spontané fut la cause initiale de la participation de la France à la guerre de l'Indépendance.

En janvier 1915, Norman Prince et plus tard les 267 compatriotes aviateurs volèrent au secours de la France et de la Liberté du monde. Leur action glorieuse, qui devança l'entrée officielle de leurs pays dans la guerre, fut le signal de la mise en mouvement des États-Unis vers la France.

Honneur à ces héros, dont j'ai connu la bravoure, pour avoir si noblement rendu la visite que La Fayette fit à leurs ancêtres.

F. Foch
Mal de France.

1
The Origin of the Escadrille Américaine

As one considers the historical significance of the Lafayette Flying Corps, it becomes evident that the outstanding accomplishment of the volunteers was their influence on public opinion in America at a time when we were neutral and under heavy pressure to maintain our neutrality. The position of the United States in regard to the war was at once the greatest obstacle confronting the founders of the corps, and their most forceful argument used in urging the French to permit enlistments in the Aviation Service.

France was forced to exercise ceaseless vigilance against German spies masquerading as American subjects. Before admitting a neutral to her flying schools, depots, and squadrons, where there were daily opportunities to acquire information of importance to the enemy, it was necessary to make a painstaking examination of the candidate. This was no small obstacle to enlistment, and added to it was the fact that there existed a superabundance, rather than a shortage, of flying personnel. France and the United States, on the other hand, were traditional friends, united for more than a hundred years by the bond of a common idealism. The best element in America was already in open sympathy with France, and the French authorities, with ready understanding of our race, realised that the presence of a band of young Americans in French uniform, fighting the spectacular battles of the sky, would be certain to arouse a widespread interest and sympathy at home. To appreciate the importance of the movement, therefore, one must bear in mind that the motive which actuated France in permitting the establishment of the Lafayette Flying Corps was largely political.

To Norman Prince, of Pride's Crossing, Massachusetts, belongs the credit of first conceiving the idea of a squadron of American volunteer pilots to serve with the French. In November, 1914, Prince was at Marblehead, learning to pilot hydro-aeroplanes at the Burgess school. He hoped to offer his services to France as soon as he had perfected himself in flying, believing that other Americans with experience as aviators would like to join with him, and that the French Government would be willing to accept a squadron of volunteer airmen for service at the Front. He suggested the idea to Frazier Curtis, who was in training with him, and the two men spent much time in discussing it. Curtis had just returned from England, where he had offered his services to the Royal Flying Corps, but had been refused on account of his American citizenship. While strongly approving of Prince's plan, he decided that he would take no active part in it until he had made another attempt at enlistment in England. In case of a second failure there, he promised his active support in the attempt to organise an *Escadrille Américaine* in France.

Deciding to offer his plan to the French Government at the earliest opportunity, Prince sailed for France on January 20, 1915, and set to work at once to enlist the aid of several Americans residing in Paris. Some could not be convinced that the project was feasible, and others thought it unwise to organise a squadron of American volunteers because of the neutrality of the United States. In Mr. Robert W. Bliss and Mr. Robert Chanler, however, Prince found helpful and enthusiastic allies who not only gave him the encouragement of a profound belief in his plan, but gave practical support by arranging for introductions and interviews with members of the French War Department.

On December 24, 1914, Curtis sailed for England, where he found it impossible to join the Royal Flying Corps without giving up his American citizenship—a step he was unwilling to take; and early in February, 1915, he went to France to make application for enlistment in the French Aviation. At the Hôtel Palais d'Orsay in Paris he met Prince, who told him that he had taken up his plan with the Ministry of War through his friends Jacques and Paul de Lesseps—members of the Air Guard of Paris—and that the outcome was still uncertain. At a dinner given by the de Lesseps brothers to the two Americans, the situation was discussed from every point of view, and a letter drawn up addressed to M. Millerand, then Minister of War, offering to France the services of a squadron of American airmen. This letter met with a very discouraging response. The Americans were told that no volunteers could be admitted to the Aviation, owing to the popularity of this branch with the French soldiers, hundreds of whom—far more than could be used—were applying for training as pilots.

JAROUSSE DE SILLAC

The situation seemed almost hopeless, but Prince was not to be discouraged. Another avenue of approach was opened through the courtesy of Mr. Robert Bliss, who arranged a meeting with M. Jarousse de Sillac,—a meeting fruitful in result for the future Corps. It was chiefly through the sympathy and active interest of M. de Sillac that permission for the formation of an American squadron was finally obtained. On February 20, 1915, the following letter was sent by him to his friend Colonel Bouttieaux, of the Ministry of War:

I beg to transmit to you herewith attached the names of six young men, citizens of the United States of America, who desire to enlist in the French Aviation—an offer which was not accepted by the Minister of War. Permit me to call your attention to this matter, insisting upon its great interest. It appears to me that there might be great advantages in the creation of an American Squadron. The United States would be proud of the fact that certain of her young men, acting as did Lafayette, have come to fight for France and civilization. The resulting sentiment of enthusiasm could have but one effect: to turn the Americans in the direction of the Allies. There is a precedent in the Legion of Garibaldi, which has had an undeniably good influence on Franco-Italian relations. If you approve these considerations, I am confident that it will be possible to accept these young men and to authorise their enlistment in such a manner that they may be grouped under the direction of a French chief. In doing this you will contribute to the happiness of these six Americans.

This letter brought the following reply from Colonel Bouttieaux, dated February 24, 1915:

I think that your candidates will be welcomed. They should contract an engagement in the French Army for the duration of the war, and should agree to fly only the aeroplanes customarily used in the French Aviation Service.

Many thanks and very cordially yours

The six Americans to whom M. de Sillac alluded were: Norman Prince, Frazier Curtis, Elliot Cowdin, William Thaw, Bert Hall,[1] and James Bach. The three latter were already enlisted in the French Army as *engagés volontaires*, and had effected their transfer to the Aviation after serving from August to December, 1914, in the Foreign Legion. All three had commenced their training at Buc (Seine-et-Oise). Cowdin, who had been in the Ambulance Service, was ready to transfer at once to Aviation, and during the week following the receipt of Colonel Bouttieaux's letter, Prince, Curtis, and Cowdin signed their enlistment papers (March 9, 1915) and were sent to Pau (B.P.) to begin their training. They were soon joined by Bach and Hall, whose transfer from Buc had been requested by Prince. Thaw, who was already an

---

1. *En l'air! (In the Air)* by Bert Hall is also published by Leonaur.

American Légionnaires. 1914 Thaw seated (centre). Bach seated (right). Bert Hall standing (right)

The Bureau de Pilotage. Buc

experienced airman and about to be sent to the Front, naturally preferred this opportunity for gaining actual experience as a war pilot to the alternative of going to Pau, where he would have to wait until the other Americans had completed their training. He therefore requested to go on active duty as a member of a French squadron, planning to join the other volunteers later, if the *Escadrille Américaine* should become a reality.

Meanwhile another American, Dr. Edmund L. Gros (later Lieutenant-Colonel, U.S. Air Service), then one of the heads of the American Ambulance, had been thinking, quite independently, of the possibility of forming a squadron of American volunteer airmen. In the Foreign Legion, Americans had already distinguished themselves as combatants, and in the Ambulance[2] there were dozens of young men eager for a more active branch of service. It occurred to Dr. Gros that both in the Legion and in the Ambulance there was splendid material which might be used to good advantage in the French Aviation Service. Curtis, who was now as keenly interested as Prince, spent much of his leisure time in searching for volunteers. Early in July, while making a canvass of Ambulance men at Neuilly, he learned of Dr. Gros's activity in the same direction, and wrote the following letter:

Dear Dr. Gros:
I went to the Ambulance today to see if I could find any drivers who wanted to join the French Aviation Service. The government is willing to train 100 American flyers and to keep them together in one corps. Men of flying experience would be preferred, but those of apparent aptitude (knowledge of French, gas engines, etc.) will be acceptable. Mr. Fréchon tells me you are keen on getting up a big corps, so we ought to be able to work together. I would like to introduce you to one of my friends who is pretty much running this enlarged Corps. I am here on sick-leave, three accidents having left me pretty well jarred up. I expect to go to the seaside for a good rest in a day or two, but am very anxious to see you first. Sincerely yours
(Signed) Frazier Curtis

Meeting Curtis shortly after this, and through him M. de Sillac, Dr. Gros discussed with them his ideas and the three found themselves in hearty accord. As his duties lay in Paris, and he knew thoroughly the language and customs of the French, Dr. Gros was peculiarly fitted to

2. *"Ambulance 464" Encore Des Blessés* by Julien H. Bryan is also published by Leonaur.

COWDIN AND PRINCE, PAU, MARCH, 1915

CURTIS. BACH, COWDIN. AND BERT HALL. PAU, MARCH, 1915

push forward the work begun by Prince, who was then at the flying school at Pau and busy with his duties. It was left for M. de Sillac and Dr. Gros to interview the French authorities, arouse the interest of prominent Americans, and to keep the project moving forward toward realisation. A committee was formed, consisting of M. de Sillac President, Dr. Gros Vice-President, and Mr. Frederick Allen; these three men kept in close touch with the Ministry of War.

Many difficulties, which at times seemed almost insurmountable, were encountered, but finally, on July 8, 1915, General Hirschauer, Chief of French Military Aeronautics, accepted an invitation to meet the supporters of the proposed *escadrille* at a luncheon at the house of Senator Menier. There were present: General Hirschauer, Colonel Bouttieaux, Senator Menier, Leon Bourgeois, Mr. Robert Bacon, M. de Sillac, Dr. Gros, and Dr. William White, of Philadelphia. Hitherto the French had been uniformly averse to grouping American flyers on the Front, but at this luncheon General Hirschauer was persuaded of the feasibility and benefits of such a plan, and agreed to give orders for the formation of an American squadron, to be known as the *Escadrille Américaine*.

Military business moves with proverbial slowness; many details remained to be settled, and eight months were to elapse before the

Residence of
Dr. Edmund L. Gros.
23 Avenue du Bois de
Boulogne, Paris

commander-in-chief finally authorised the formation of the American Squadron. On August 21, 1915, it was arranged between the Ministry of War and the Ministry of Foreign Affairs that all matters concerning the *Escadrille Américaine* should be dealt with by the Franco-American Committee mentioned above.

The efforts of the committee were beginning to bear fruit, as is shown in the correspondence between M. René Besnard, Sub-Secretary of State for Military Aeronautics, and the president of the committee. On October 28, M. Besnard wrote that the initiative of the committee would be greatly appreciated by the commander-in-chief. And a few days later:

> The letter which I sent you on October 28, showed you the great interest which the commander-in-chief, as well as I, attach to a prompt solution of the question. I therefore ask you to send me as soon as possible the details of your plan of action.

In accordance with M. Besnard's request, the president of the committee wrote on December 1, 1915:

> You are kind enough to ask me what measures are proposed in order to facilitate our plan. A committee composed of Americans has been formed, with the object of making known to their compatriots the conditions under which they may enlist in the French Aviation, and to select the more desirable candidates from among those who offer themselves. The Americans who will lend their efforts to recruiting, and among whom are Mr. Bacon, Mr. Vanderbilt, Mr. Allen, Colonel Mott, and Dr. Gros, prefer, for the time being, to avoid publicity. In order to facilitate their work, they should be able to assure their compatriots that they will be well treated in the French Aviation, and not subjected to useless moving about or change of units. Permit me to call to your attention a case in point.
> Dudley L. Hill enlisted in September, 1915, passed the medical examination at Paris, and was sent to Pau. It was discovered there that he suffered from defective vision of one eye, and it was proposed, not to release him, but to employ him as a mechanic at Dijon. Allow me to ask you, therefore, if it would be possible to give to Americans who desire to enlist the following assurances:
> 1. That every care will be taken to settle definitely at Paris their

medical fitness for flying.

2. That if, once enlisted, they show inaptitude for flying, it be made possible to release them.

3. That they be treated, in so far as possible, with courtesy inspired by their generosity in offering their lives in the service of France.

In answering this letter, M. Besnard stated that the medical examination at Paris would be final in so far as possible, and that he appreciated the generous sentiments actuating the volunteers and would personally see that they received just treatment. The matter of release had been taken up with the Direction of Infantry. On December 25, 1915, the President of the Committee received from M. Besnard the following letter, which marked an important and generous concession on the part of the French authorities:

> It gives me pleasure to inform you, as a sequel to my letter of the 13th, that the Direction of Infantry has admitted the possibility of releasing Americans serving in the French Aviation . . . if they do not satisfy the conditions demanded of the flying personnel. . . . The following solution, which should be satisfactory to those interested, has been authorised: The letter sent to Americans, authorising their engagement, in the French Aviation, will contain the following clause: "It is guaranteed to you that this act of engagement may be rescinded, either on your demand, or on demand of the military authorities, in case of proven inaptitude for service in the flying personnel of the Military Aviation."

In July, General Hirschauer had agreed to give orders for the formation of an American squadron, but the summer and autumn passed, and 1915 gave place to 1916 without definite steps toward the grouping of Americans on the Front. The fine determination of the Committee is shown by the fact that discouragement was never for a moment permitted to interfere with its efforts, which found expression in the following letter sent by the committee to M. Besnard on January 24, 1916:

> The members of the Franco-American Committee wish to express to you their sincere thanks for the approval which you have given to their plan, which gives them encouragement

to continue their efforts. We therefore propose to spread our booklet with which you are already familiar. In order to second this action, I would be grateful if you could obtain through General Headquarters the grouping of American pilots in the same squadron. This has often been promised us, and it is of the greatest importance that such a squadron be constituted. Most of the pilots are already familiar with Nieuport planes, and would be happy to have the honour of being assigned to a fighting squadron equipped with Nieuports.

Among those who are breveted, and of whom several have distinguished themselves, permit me to recall to you the names of the following pilots who could be grouped immediately: Lieutenant Thaw; Sergeants Cowdin, Prince, and Masson; Pilots Guérin, Hall, Balsley, Chapman, Rockwell, Rumsey, and Johnson. Captain Thenault,[3] of the C. 42, D.A.L., has already made a request to be commanding officer of the American Squadron, and the Committee would be grateful for your approval of his appointment. In addition to the fully trained pilots, there are a few American volunteers, particularly qualified to make flyers, who have sent in requests to be transferred to the Aviation. They are:

Soubiran, Robert (170th Infantry)
Dugan, William E. (170th Infantry)
Boal, Pierre (1st Cuirassiers)
Rocle, Marius (170th Infantry)
Zinn, Frederick (Foreign Legion)

We would be happy, in the interests ... of the Franco-American Corps, if you would be kind enough to take measures to transfer these Americans to the Aviation as soon as possible.

During the month of February, Colonel Regnier was made Director of Aeronautics, and no time was wasted in winning the new director to the cause of the American volunteers. On March 3, 1916, the committee wrote him:

Following our letter of January 24, addressed to M. René Besnard, and of which a copy is attached, allow us respectfully to call your attention to the situation of the Americans enlisted in the French Army. M. Millerand, General Hirschauer,

---

3. *The Story of the Lafayette Escadrille* by Georges Thenault is also published by Leonaur.

Sergent Vignon

Sergent de Guingon and Lieutenant Bougaud

Lieutenant Henriot

Sergeant Anson

and M. Besnard, after careful study of the question, decided that the American pilots should be united in one squadron. General Headquarters also took this view, and it was furthermore decided that Americans should fly the Nieuport fighting planes. Notwithstanding this, . . . only four have been grouped at Plessis-Belleville. The others are scattered, and most of them have not been assigned to Nieuports. . . . The Franco-American Committee, which has taken upon itself the task of selecting volunteers from the United States . . . would be very grateful if you could find it possible to carry out the decisions taken after careful reflection by your predecessors.

Colonel Regnier's reply to this letter was both courteous and satisfactory. He said that on February 20 he had taken up the matter of an American squadron with General Headquarters, and had been informed that such a squadron was to be organised from a list of pilots communicated to him. He also stated that all American student-pilots who seemed to be capable of piloting the Nieuport were to be given a chance to learn to fly that machine. On March 23, 1916, he wrote M. de Sillac again regarding the disposition of Americans, suggesting that men who did not show enough aptitude to justify assigning them to Nieuport training be formed into a Caudron squadron, analogous to the Nieuport squadron now finally authorised by General Headquarters. (As nearly all of the Americans did well in the schools, it did not become necessary to act on this suggestion.) The important passages of Colonel Regnier's letter of March 14, 1916, announcing to the president of the committee that the efforts of the committee had finally met with success, are as follows:

> Replying to your letter of March 3, 1916, I have the honor to communicate to you the following information. I had already considered the question of an American squadron, and as early as February 20, 1916, I asked the Commander-in-Chief to advise me of his intentions in this matter. General Headquarters has just replied, informing me that an American squadron will be organised, with the pilots whose names follow: William Thaw, Elliot Cowdin, Kiffin Rockwell, Norman Prince, Charles C. Johnson, Clyde Balsley, Victor Chapman, Lawrence Rumsey, and James R. McConnell. . . . I have every reason to believe that the . . . squadron will be constituted rapidly . . . and I will keep you posted as to what is done in this matter.

ADJUDANT PRIEUD   ADJUDANT DECKERT

ADJUDANTS CARON AND PARIS

Shortly after this the pilots, some of whom were then in service with French squadrons, were assembled at Le Plessis-Belleville, the great Aviation depot a short distance north of Paris, and on April 20, 1916, the *Escadrille Américaine*, officially the N 124, was placed on duty at the Front.

2
The Escadrille Lafayette at the Front

On the evening of April 17, 1916, a dinner was held at a Paris restaurant to celebrate the final and definite organisation of the *Escadrille Américaine*. There were present: Norman Prince, the founder of the Squadron; William Thaw, Victor Chapman, Kiffin Rockwell, James McConnell, Clyde Balsley, Chouteau Johnson, and Lawrence Rumsey, all breveted pilots; Michel, Norman Prince's *mécanicien*; and Paul Rockwell, Kiffin Rockwell's brother, who had been with him in the Legion. Five of the men were on their way to the Front as pilots of the newly formed American Squadron, N.124. Prince, Chapman, Rockwell, and McConnell left the same evening for Luxeuil-les-Bains, where the unit was to begin active service. They were joined, a few days later, by Thaw, Elliot Cowdin, and Bert Hall, these seven men being the original members of the *Escadrille Américaine*. The following account of the early history of N. 124 is taken from James McConnell's book, *Flying for France*,[1] which was written in the autumn of 1916.

★★★★★★

On our arrival at Luxeuil we were met by Captain Georges Thenault, the French commander of the *Escadrille Américaine*—officially known as N. 124—and motored to the aviation field in one of the staff cars assigned to us. I enjoyed that ride. Lolling back against the soft leather cushions, I recalled how in my apprenticeship days at Pau I had had to walk six miles for my laundry.

The equipment awaiting us at the field was even more impressive than our automobile. Everything was brand-new, from the fifteen Fiat

---

1. *Eagles Over the Trenches* a double edition which includes *Flying for France* by James R. McConnell and *Our Pilots in the Air* by William B. Perry is also published by Leonaur.

trucks to the office, *magasin*, and rest tents. And the men attached to the *escadrille!* At first sight they seemed to outnumber the Nicaraguan army—mechanicians, chauffeurs, armourers, motor-cyclists, telephonists, wireless operators, Red-Cross stretcher-bearers, clerks! Afterward I learned they totalled seventy-odd, and that all of them were glad to be connected with the American *Escadrille*.

Rooms were assigned to us in a villa adjoining the famous hot baths of Luxeuil. We messed with our officers, Captain Thenault and Lieutenant de Laage de Meux, at the best hotel in town. An automobile was always on hand to carry us to the field. I began to wonder whether I was a summer resorter or a soldier.

Among the pilots who had welcomed us, we discovered the famous Captain Happe, commander of the Luxeuil bombardment group. After we had been introduced, he pointed to eight little boxes arranged on a table.

"They contain *Croix de Guerre* for the families of the men I lost on my last trip," he explained, and he added: "It's a good thing you're here to go along with us for protection. There are lots of Boches in this sector."

I thought of the luxury we were enjoying; our comfortable beds, baths, and motor cars, and then I recalled the ancient custom of giving a man selected for the sacrifice a royal time of it before the appointed day.

To acquaint us with the few places where a safe landing was possible, we were motored through the Vosges Mountains and on into Alsace. It was a delightful opportunity to see that glorious countryside, and we appreciated it the more because we knew its charm would be lost when we surveyed it from the sky. From the air the ground presents no scenic effects.

The ravishing beauty of the Val d'Ajol, the steep mountain-sides bristling with a solid mass of giant pines, the glittering cascades tumbling downward through fairylike avenues of verdure, the roaring, tossing torrent at the foot of the slope—all this loveliness, seen from an airplane at 12,000 feet, fades into flat splotches of green traced with a tiny ribbon of silver.

The American *Escadrille* was sent to Luxeuil primarily to acquire the team work necessary to a flying unit. Then, too, the new pilots needed a taste of anti-aircraft fire to familiarise them with the business of aviation over a battlefield. They shot well in that sector, too. Thaw's machine was hit at an altitude of 13,000 feet.

The *Escadrille's* First Sortie

The memory of the first sortie we made as an *escadrille* will always, remain fresh in my mind because it was also my first trip over the lines. We were to leave at six in the morning. Captain Thenault pointed out on his aerial map the route we were to follow. Never having flown over this region before, I was afraid of losing myself. Therefore, as it is easier to keep other airplanes in sight when one is above them, I began climbing as rapidly as possible, meaning to trail along in the wake of my companions. Unless one has had practice in flying in formation, however, it is hard to keep in contact. The diminutive *avions de chasse* are the merest pin-points against the great sweep of landscape below and the limitless heavens above. The air was misty and clouds were gathering. Ahead there seemed a barrier of them. Although as I looked down, the ground showed plainly, in the distance everything was hazy. Forging up above the mist, at 7000 feet, I lost the others altogether. Even when they are not closely joined, the clouds seen from immediately above, appear as a solid bank of white. The spaces between are indistinguishable. It is like being in an Arctic ice-field.

To the south I made out the Alps. Their glittering peaks projected up through the white sea about me like majestic icebergs. Not a single plane was visible anywhere, and I was growing very uncertain about my position. My splendid isolation had become oppressive, when, one by one, the others began bobbing up above the cloud level, and I had company again.

We were over Belfort and headed for the trench lines. The cloud-banks dropped behind, and below us we saw the smiling plain of Alsace stretching eastward to the Rhine. It was distinctly pleasurable, flying over this conquered land. Following the course of the canal that runs to the Rhine, I sighted, from a height of 13,000 feet over Dannemarie, a series of brown, woodworm-like tracings on the ground—the trenches!

My attention was drawn elsewhere almost immediately, however. Two balls of black smoke had suddenly appeared close to one of the machines ahead of me, and with the same disconcerting abruptness similar balls began to dot the sky above, below, and on all sides of us. We were being shot at with shrapnel. It was interesting to watch the flash of the bursting shells, and the attendant smoke puffs—black, white, or yellow, depending on the kind of shrapnel used. The roar of the motor drowned the noise of the explosions. Strangely enough, my feelings about it were wholly impersonal.

GENERAL HIRSCHAUER

PATROL TIME: THE ESCADRILLE LAFAYETTE AT LUXEUIL, 1916

We turned north after crossing the lines. Mulhouse seemed just below us, and I noted with a keen sense of satisfaction our invasion of real German territory. The Rhine, too, looked delightfully accessible. As we continued northward I distinguished the twin lakes of Gérardmer sparkling in their emerald setting. Where the lines crossed the Hartmannsweilerkopf there were little spurts of brown smoke as shells burst in the trenches. One could scarcely pick out the old city of Thann from among the numerous neighbouring villages, so tiny it seemed in the valley's mouth. I had never been higher than 7000 feet, and was unaccustomed to reading country from a great altitude. It was also bitterly cold, and even in my fur-lined combination I was shivering. I noticed, too, that I had to take long, deep breaths in the rarefied atmosphere. Looking downward at a certain angle, I saw what at first I took to be a round, shimmering pool of water. It was simply the effect of the sunlight on the congealing mist. We had been keeping an eye out for German machines since leaving our lines, but none had appeared. It wasn't surprising, for we were too many.

Only four days later, however, Kiffin Rockwell brought down the *escadrille's* first plane in his initial aerial combat. He was flying alone when, over Thann, he came upon a German on reconnaissance. He dived and the German turned toward his own lines, opening fire from a long distance. Rockwell kept straight after him. Then, closing to within thirty yards, he pressed on the release of his machine gun, and saw the enemy gunner fall backward and the pilot crumple up sideways in his seat. The plane spun downward and crashed to earth just behind the German trenches. Swooping close to the ground Rockwell saw the debris burning brightly. He had turned the trick with but four shots and only one German bullet had struck his Nieuport. An observation post telephoned the news before Rockwell's return, and he had a great welcome. All Luxeuil smiled upon him—particularly the girls. But he couldn't stay to enjoy his popularity. The *escadrille* was ordered to the Verdun sector.

While in a way we were sorry to leave Luxeuil, we naturally didn't regret the chance to take part in the aerial activity of the world's greatest battle. The night before our departure, some German aircraft destroyed four of our tractors and killed six men with bombs, but even that caused little excitement compared with going to Verdun. We would get square with the Boches over Verdun, we thought—it is impossible to chase airplanes at night, so the raiders made a safe retreat.

As soon as we pilots had left in our machines, the trucks and trac-

CHANGING SECTORS

NORMAN PRINCE, LIEUTENANT NUNGESSER (CENTRE), AND
DIDIER MASSON AT BAR-LE-DUC. AUGUST. 1916

tors set out in convoy, carrying the men and equipment. The Nieuports carried us to our new post in a little more than an hour. We stowed them away in the hangars and went to have a look at our sleeping-quarters. A commodious villa halfway between the town of Bar-le-Duc and the aviation field had been assigned to us, and comforts were as plentiful as at Luxeuil.

Our really serious work had begun, however, and we knew it. Even as far behind the actual fighting as Bar-le-Duc, one could sense one's proximity to a vast military operation. The endless convoys of motor trucks, the fast-flowing stream of troops, and the distressing number of ambulances brought realisation of the near presence of a gigantic battle.

Within a twenty-mile radius of the Verdun Front aviation camps abound. Our *escadrille* was listed on the schedule with the other fighting units, each of which has its specified flying hours, rotating so there is always an *escadrille de chasse* over the lines. A field wireless to enable us to keep track of the movements of enemy planes became part of our equipment.

Lufbery joined us a few days after our arrival. He was followed by Chouteau Johnson and Clyde Balsley, who had been on the air guard over Paris. Dudley Hill and Lawrence Rumsey came next, and after them Didier Masson and Paul Pavelka. Nieuports were supplied them from the nearest depots, and as soon as they had mounted their instruments and machine guns, they were on the job with the rest of us.

Before we were fairly settled at Bar-le-Duc, Bert Hall brought down a German observation craft and Thaw a Fokker. Fights occurred on almost every sortie. The Germans seldom crossed into our territory, unless on a bombarding jaunt, and thus practically all the fighting took place on their side of the line. Thaw dropped his Fokker in the morning, and on the afternoon of the same day there was a big combat far behind the German trenches. Thaw was wounded in the arm, and an explosive bullet detonating on Rockwell's windshield tore several gashes in his face. Despite the blood which was blinding him, Rockwell managed to reach an aviation field and land. Thaw, whose wound bled profusely, landed in a dazed condition just within our lines. He was too weak to walk, and French soldiers carried him to a field dressing-station, whence he was sent to Paris for further treatment. Rockwell's wounds were less serious and he insisted on flying again almost immediately.

A week or so later Victor Chapman was wounded. Considering the number of fights he had been in and the courage with which he attacked, it was a miracle he had not been hit before. He always fought against odds and far within the enemy's country. He flew more than any of us, never missing an opportunity to go up, and never coming down until his gasoline was giving out. His machine was a sieve of patched-up bullet holes. His nerve was almost superhuman and his devotion to the cause for which he fought sublime. The day he was wounded he attacked four machines. Swooping down from behind, one of them, a Fokker, riddled Chapman's plane. One bullet cut deep into his scalp, but Chapman, a master pilot, escaped from the trap, and fired several shots to show he was still safe. A stability control had been severed by a bullet. Chapman held the broken rod in one hand, managed his machine with the other, and succeeded in landing on a nearby aviation field. His wound was dressed, his machine repaired, and he immediately took the air in pursuit of some more enemies. He would take no rest, and with bandaged head continued to fly and fight.

The *escadrille's* next serious encounter took place on June 18. Captain Thenault, Rockwell, Balsley, and Prince were surrounded by a large number of Germans, who, circling about them, commenced firing at long range. Realising their numerical inferiority, the Americans and their commander sought the safest way out by attacking the enemy machines nearest the French lines. Rockwell, Prince, and the captain broke through successfully, but Balsley found himself hemmed in. He attacked the German nearest him, only to receive an explosive bullet in his thigh. In trying to get away by a vertical dive, his machine went into a corkscrew and swung over on its back. Extra cartridge rollers dislodged from their case hit his arms. He was tumbling straight toward the trenches, but by a supreme effort he regained control, righted the plane, and landed without disaster in a meadow just behind the firing line.

Soldiers carried him to the shelter of a nearby fort, and later he was taken to a field hospital, where he lingered for days between life and death. Ten fragments of the explosive bullet were removed from his stomach. He bore up bravely, and became the favourite of the wounded officers in whose ward he lay. When we flew over to see him, they would say: *Il est un brave petit gars, l'aviateur américain.* On a shelf by his bed, done up in a handkerchief, he kept the pieces of bullets taken out of him, and under them some sheets of paper on which he was trying to write his mother, back in El Paso.

Balsley was awarded the *Médaille Militaire* and the *Croix de Guerre*, but the honours scared him. He had seen them decorate officers in the ward before they died.

Then came Chapman's last fight. Before leaving, he had put two bags of oranges in his machine to take to Balsley, who liked to suck them to relieve his terrible thirst. There was an aerial struggle against odds, far within the German lines, and Chapman, to divert their fire from his comrades, engaged several enemy airmen at once. He sent one tumbling to earth, and had forced the others off when two more attacked him. Such a fight is a matter of seconds, and one cannot clearly see what passes. Lufbery and Prince, whom Chapman had defended so gallantly, regained the French lines. They told us of the combat, and we waited on the field for Chapman's return. He was always the last in, so we were not much worried. Then a pilot from another *escadrille* telephoned us that he had seen a Nieuport falling. A little later the observer of a reconnaissance plane called up and told us that he had witnessed Chapman's fall. The wings of the plane had buckled, he said, and it had dropped like a stone.

We talked in lowered voices after that: we could read the pain in one another's eyes. If only it could have been some one else, was what we all thought, I suppose. To lose Victor was not an irreparable loss to us merely, but to France, and to the world. I kept thinking of him lying over there, and of the oranges he was taking to Balsley. As I left the field, I caught sight of Victor's mechanician leaning against the end of our hangar. He was looking northward into the sky where his *patron* had vanished, and his face was very sad.

By this time Prince and Bert Hall had been made adjutants, and we corporals promoted sergeants. The next impressive event (June 28, 1916) was the awarding of decorations. We had assisted at that ceremony for Cowdin at Luxeuil, but this time three of our messmates were to be honoured for the Germans they had brought down. Rockwell and Hall received the *Médaille Militaire* and the *Croix de Guerre*, and Thaw, being a lieutenant, the *Legion d'Honneur* and another palm for the ribbon of the *Croix de Guerre* he had won previously. Thaw, who came up from Paris for the presentation, still carried his arm in a sling. There were also decorations for Chapman, but poor Victor, who so often had been cited in the Orders of the Day, was not on hand to receive them.

Verdun to the Somme

We had been fighting above the battlefields of Verdun from the 20th of May, 1916, until orders came the middle of September for us

THE SQUADRON IN AUGUST. 1916
Lieutenant de Laage de Meux, Johnson, Rumsey, McConnell. Thaw,
Lufbery, Kiffin Rockwell, Masson Norman Prince, Bert Hall

WHISKEY AND SODA, THE SQUADRON MASCOTS

WHISKEY AND SODA CHANGING SECTORS

to leave our planes, for a unit which was to replace us, and to report at Le Bourget, the great Paris aviation centre.

The mechanics and the rest of the personnel left, as usual, in the *escadrille's* trucks with the material. For once the pilots did not take the aerial route, but they boarded the Paris express at Bar-le-Duc with all the enthusiasm of schoolboys off for a vacation. They were to have a week in the capital! Where they were to go after that, they did not know, but presumed it would be the Somme. As a matter of fact the *escadrille* was to be sent to Luxeuil in the Vosges to take part in the Mauser raid.

Besides Captain Thenault and Lieutenant de Laage de Meux, our French officers, the following American pilots were in the escadrille at this time: Lieutenant Thaw, who had returned to the Front, even though his wounded arm had not entirely healed; Adjutants Norman Prince, Bert Hall, Raoul Lufbery, and Didier Masson; and Sergeants Kiffin Rockwell, Dudley Hill, Paul Pavelka, C. C. Johnson, and Lawrence Rumsey. I had been sent to a hospital at the end of August, because of a lame back resulting from a smash-up in landing, and couldn't follow until later.

Every aviation unit boasts several mascots. Dogs of every description are to be seen around the camps, but the Americans managed, during their stay in Paris, to add to their menagerie by the acquisition of a lion cub named "Whiskey." The little chap had been born on a boat crossing from Africa and was advertised for sale in France. Some of the American pilots bought him. He was a bright-eyed baby lion who tried to roar in a most threatening manner, but who was blissfully content the moment one gave him one's finger to suck. "Whiskey" had a good view of Paris during the few days he was there. Like most lions in captivity, he became acquainted with bars, but the sort "Whiskey" saw were not for purposes of confinement.

The orders came directing the *escadrille* to Luxeuil, and we boarded the Belfort train with bag and baggage—and the lion. Lions, it developed, were not allowed in passenger coaches. The conductor was assured that "Whiskey" was quite harmless and was going to overlook the rules when the cub began to roar and tried to get at the railwayman's finger. That settled it, so two men had to stay behind in order to crate up "Whiskey" and take him along the next day.

The *escadrille* was joined in Paris by Robert Rockwell, of Cincinnati, who had finished his training as a pilot, and was waiting at the Reserve.

When the squadron arrived at Luxeuil, it found there a large British aviation contingent. This detachment from the Royal Navy Flying Corps numbered more than fifty pilots and a thousand enlisted men. New hangars harboured their fleet of bombardment machines. Their own anti-aircraft batteries were in emplacements near the field. Though detached from the British forces and under French command, this unit followed the rule of His Majesty's armies in France by receiving all of its food and supplies from England. It had its own transport service.

Our *escadrille* had been in Luxeuil during the months of April and May. We had made many friends among the townspeople and the French aviators stationed there, so the older pilots were welcomed with open arms and their new comrades made to feel at home in the quaint Vosges town. It was not long, however, before the Americans and the British got together. At first there was a feeling of reserve on both sides, but once acquainted they became fast friends. The naval pilots were quite representative of the United Kingdom, hailing as they did from England, Canada, New South Wales, South Africa, and other parts of the Empire. Most of them were soldiers by profession. All were officers, but they were as democratic as it is possible to be. As a result there was a continuous exchange of dinners.

There was trouble in getting new airplanes. Only five arrived. They were the new model Nieuport. Instead of having only 140 square feet of supporting surface, they had 160, and the forty-seven-shot Lewis machine gun had been replaced by the Vickers. This gun is mounted on the hood and by means of a timing-gear shoots through the propeller. The 160-foot Nieuport mounts at a terrific rate, rising to 7000 feet in six minutes. It will go to 20,000 feet handled by a skilful pilot.

It was some time before these planes arrived and every one was idle. There was nothing to do but loaf at the hotel, where the American pilots were quartered, visit the British in their barracks at the field, or go walking. It was about as much like war as a Bryan lecture. While I was in the hospital I received a letter written at this time from one of the boys. I opened it expecting to read of an air combat. It informed me that Thaw had caught a trout three feet long, and that Lufbery had picked two baskets of mushrooms.

Kiffin Rockwell and Lufbery were the first to get their new machines ready, and on the 23rd of September went out for the first flight since the *escadrille* had arrived at Luxeuil. They became separated in the air, but each flew on alone, which was a dangerous thing to do in the Alsace sector. There is but little fighting in the trenches there, but great activity in the air. Due to the British and French squadrons at Luxeuil, and the threat their presence implied, the Germans had to oppose them by large forces. I believe there were more than forty Fokkers alone in the camps of Colmar and Habsheim. Observation machines protected by two or three fighting planes would venture far into our lines. It is something the Germans dared not do on any other part of the Front. They had a special trick that consisted in sending a large, slow observation machine into our lines to invite attack. When a French plane would dive after it, two Fokkers, that had been hovering high overhead, would drop on the tail of the Frenchman and he stood but small chance if caught in the trap.

Just before Kiffin Rockwell reached the lines he saw a German machine under him flying at 11,000 feet. Rockwell had fought more combats than the rest of us put together, and had shot down several German machines that had fallen in their lines, but this was the first time he had had an opportunity of bringing down a Boche in our territory.

A captain, the commandant of an Alsatian village, watched the aerial battle through his field-glasses. He said that Rockwell approached so close to the enemy that he thought there would be a collision. The German craft, which carried two machine guns, had opened a rapid fire when Rockwell started his dive. He plunged through the stream of lead and only when very close to his enemy did he begin shooting. For a second it looked as though the German was falling, so the captain said, but then he saw the French machine turn rapidly nose down, the wings of one side broke off and fluttered in the wake of the airplane, which hurtled earthward in a rapid drop. It crashed into the ground in a small field—a field of flowers—a few hundred yards back of the trenches. It was not more than two and a half miles from the spot where Rockwell, in the month of May, brought down his first enemy machine. The Germans immediately opened up on the wreck with artillery fire. In spite of the bursting shrapnel, gunners from a nearby battery rushed out and recovered poor Rockwell's broken body. There was a hideous wound in his breast where an explosive bullet had torn through. A surgeon, who examined the body, testified that if it had been an ordinary bullet, Rockwell would have had an even chance of landing with only a bad wound. As it was, he was killed the instant the unlawful missile exploded.

Lufbery engaged a German craft, but before he could get to close range two Fokkers swooped down from behind and filled his aeroplane full of holes. Exhausting this ammunition he landed at Fontaine, an aviation field near the lines. There he learned of Rockwell's death and was told that two other French machines had been brought down within the hour. He ordered his gasoline tank filled, procured a full band of cartridges, and went out to avenge his comrade. He sped up and down the lines, and made a wide detour to Habsheim where the Germans have an aviation field, but all to no avail. Not a Boche was in the air.

The news of Rockwell's death was telephoned to the *escadrille*. The captain, lieutenant, and a couple of men jumped into a staff car and hastened to where he had fallen. On their return, the American pilots were convened in a room of the hotel and the news was broken to them. With tears in his eyes the captain said: "The best and bravest of us all is no more."

No greater blow could have befallen the *escadrille*. Kiffin was its soul. He was loved and looked up to not only by every man in our corps, but by everyone who knew him. Kiffin was imbued with the spirit of the cause for which he fought and gave his heart and soul to the performance of his duty. The old flame of chivalry burned brightly in this boy's fine and sensitive being. With his death France lost one of her most valuable pilots. When he was over the lines the Germans did not pass—and he was over them most of the time.

The night before he was killed, he had stated that if he were brought down he would like to be buried where he fell. It was impossible, however, to place him in a grave so near the trenches. His body was draped in a French flag and brought back to Luxeuil. He was given a funeral worthy of a general. His brother, Paul, who had fought in the Legion with him, and who had been rendered unfit for service by a wound, was granted permission to attend the obsequies. Pilots from all nearby camps flew over to render homage to Rockwell's remains. Every Frenchman in the Aviation at Luxeuil marched behind the bier. The British pilots, followed by a detachment of five hundred of their men, were in line, and a battalion of French troops brought up the rear. As the slow-moving procession of blue- and khaki-clad men passed from the church to the graveyard, airplanes circled at a feeble height above and showered down myriads of flowers.

Rockwell's death urged the rest of the men to greater action, and the few who had machines were constantly after the Boches. Prince brought one down. Lufbery, the most skilful and successful fighter

CAPTAIN THÉNAULT AND FRAM

in the *escadrille*, would venture far into the enemy's lines and spiral down over a German aviation camp, daring the pilots to venture forth. Prince, out in search of a combat, ran into a crowd of them Lufbery had aroused. Bullets cut into his machine, and one exploding on the front edge of a lower wing broke it. Another shattered a supporting mast. It was a miracle that the machine did not give way. As badly battered as it was, Prince succeeded in bringing it back from over Mulhouse, where the fight occurred, to his field at Luxeuil.

The same day Lufbery missed death by a very small margin. He had taken on more gasoline and made another sortie. When over the lines again he encountered a German with whom he had a fighting acquaintance. Lufbery manoeuvred for position, but, before he could shoot, the Teuton would evade him by a clever turn. They kept after one another, the Boche retreating into his lines. When they were nearing Habsheim, Lufbery glanced back and saw French shrapnel bursting over the trenches. It meant a German plane was over French territory and it was his duty to drive it off.

Swooping down near his adversary he waved goodbye, the enemy pilot did likewise and Lufbery whirred off to chase the other German. He caught up with him and dove to the attack, but he was surprised by an enemy he had not seen. Before he could escape, three bullets entered his motor, two passed through the fur-lined combination he wore, another ripped open one of his woollen flying boots, his airplane was riddled from wing tip to wing tip, and other bullets cut the elevating plane. Had he not been an exceptional aviator, he never would have brought safely to earth so badly damaged a machine. It was so thoroughly shot up that it was junked as being beyond repairs. Fortunately Lufbery was over French territory or his forced descent would have resulted in his being made prisoner.

The uncertain wait at Luxeuil finally came to an end on the 12th of October, for the bombardment of Oberndorf was on. British, French, and American machines were to take part in it. The pilots were given their orders just before the start. The English in their single-seater Sopwiths, which carried four bombs each, were the first to leave followed by the French Breguets and Farmans with their tons of explosive destined for the Mauser works. The fighting machines, which were to convoy them as far as the Rhine, rapidly gained height and circled above their charges. Four of the battleplanes were from the *Escadrille Américaine*. They were piloted by Lieutenant de Laage, Lufbery, Norman Prince, and Masson.

The Germans were taken by surprise, and as a result few of their machines were in the air. The bombardment fleet was attacked, however, and six of its planes shot down, some of them falling in flames. Baron, the famous French night bombarder, lost his life in one of the Farmans. Two Germans were brought down by machines they attacked and the four pilots from the *Escadrille Américaine* accounted for one each. Lieutenant de Laage shot down his Boche as it was attacking another French machine, and Masson did likewise.

As the fuel capacity of a Nieuport allows but little more than two hours in the air, the *avions de chasse* were forced to return to their own lines to take on more gasoline, while the bombardment planes continued on into Germany. The Sopwiths arrived first at Oberndorf. Dropping low over the Mauser works they discharged their bombs and headed homeward. All arrived, save one, whose pilot lost his way and came ,to earth in Switzerland. When the Breguets and Farmans arrived, they saw only flames and smoke where once the rifle factory stood. They unloaded their explosives on the burning mass.

The Nieuports, having refilled their tanks, went up to clear the air of Germans hovering in wait for the returning raiders. Prince found one and shot it down. Lufbery came upon three. He dove for one, making it drop below the others, then forcing a second to descend, attacked the one remaining above. The combat was short, and at the end of it the German tumbled to earth. This made the fifth enemy machine which was officially credited to Lufbery, and he was thereafter mentioned by name in the official *communiqués*.

Darkness came rapidly on, but Prince and Lufbery remained in the air to protect the bombardment fleet. Just at nightfall, Lufbery made for a small aviation field near the lines, known as Corcieux. Slow-moving machines, with great planing capacity, can be landed in the dark, but to try and feel for the ground in a Nieuport is to court disaster. Ten minutes after Lufbery landed, Prince decided to make for the field. He spiralled down and skimmed rapidly over the trees bordering the Corcieux field. In the dark he did not see a high-tension electric cable that was stretched just above the tree-tops. The landing gear of his airplane struck it. The machine snapped forward and hit the ground on its nose. It turned over and over.

The belt holding Prince broke and he was thrown far from the wrecked plane. Both of his legs were broken and he suffered internal injuries. In spite of the terrific shock and his intense pain, Prince did not lose consciousness. He even kept his presence of mind and gave

STANDING: SOUBIRAN, A. C. CAMPBELL, PARSONS, BRIDGMAN, DUGAN, MACMONAGLE, LOVELL, WILLIS, HENRY JONES PETERSON, LIEUTENANT MAISON-ROUGE
SEATED: HILL, MASSON, THAW, CAPTAIN THENAULT, LUFBERY, C. C. JOHNSON, BIGELOW, ROBERT ROCKWELL

STANDING: DOOLITTLE, CAMPBELL, PARSONS, BRIDGMAN, DUGAN, MACMONAGLE, WILLIS, JONES, PETERSON
SEATED: MASSON, THAW, THENAULT, LUFBERY, JOHNSON, BIGELOW, ROBERT ROCKWELL

THE ESCADRILLE AT CHAUDUN (AISNE), JULY, 1917

orders to the men who had run to pick him up. Hearing the hum of a motor, and realising a machine was in the air, Prince told them to light gasoline fires on the field. "Don't let another fellow come down and break himself up the way I've done," he said.

Lufbery went with Prince to the hospital in Gérardmer. As the ambulance rolled along, Prince sang to keep up his spirits. He spoke of getting well soon and returning to service. It was like Norman. He was always energetic about his flying. Even when he passed through the harrowing experience of having a wing shattered, the first thing he did on landing was to busy himself about getting another fitted in place and the next morning he was in the air again.

No one thought that Prince was mortally injured, but the next day he went into a coma. A blood clot had formed on his brain. Captain Happe, in command of the aviation groups of Luxeuil, accompanied by our officers, hastened to Gérardmer. Prince, lying unconscious on his bed, was named a second lieutenant and decorated with the Legion of Honor. He already held the *Médaille Militaire* and *Croix de Guerre*. He died on the 15th of October. He was brought back to Luxeuil and given a funeral similar to Rockwell's. It was hard to realise that Norman had gone. He never let his own spirits drop, and was always ready with encouragement for others.

Two days after Prince's death, the *escadrille* received orders to leave for the Somme. The night before the departure the British gave the American pilots a farewell banquet and toasted them as their "Guardian Angels." They keenly appreciated the fact that four men from the *Escadrille Américaine* had brought down four Germans, and had cleared the way for their squadron returning from Oberndorf. When the train pulled out the next day, the station platform was packed by khaki-clad pilots waving goodbye to their friends the "Yanks."

The *escadrille* passed through Paris on its way to the Somme Front. The few members who had machines flew from Luxeuil to their new post. At Paris the pilots were reinforced by three other American boys who had completed their training. They were Fred Prince, who ten months before had come over from Boston to serve in aviation with his brother Norman; Willis Haviland, of Chicago; and Robert Soubiran, of New York.

Before its arrival on the Somme, the *escadrille* had always been quartered in towns, and the life of the pilots was all that could be desired in the way of comforts. We had, as a result, come to believe that we should wage only a *de luxe* war, and were unprepared for any other sort of campaigning. The introduction to the Somme was a rude awakening. Instead of being quartered in a villa or hotel, we were directed to a portable barracks newly erected in a sea of mud.

It was set in a cluster of similar barns nine miles from the nearest town. A sieve was a water-tight compartment in comparison with that elongated shed. The damp cold penetrated through every crack, chilling one to the bone. There were no blankets, and until they were procured the pilots had to curl up in their flying-clothes. There were no arrangements for cooking and the Americans depended on the other escadrilles for food. Eight fighting units were located at the same field and our ever-generous French comrades saw to it that no one went hungry. The thick mist, for which the Somme is famous, hung like a pall over the birdmen's nest dampening both the clothes and spirits of the men.

Something had to be done, so Thaw and Masson, who is our *Chef de Popote* (President of the Mess), obtained permission to go to Paris in one of our light trucks. They returned with cooking-utensils, a stove, and other necessary things. All hands set to work, and as a result life was made bearable. In fact I was surprised to find the quarters as good as they were when I rejoined the *escadrille* a couple of weeks after

SAMPSON.
THE COOK OF THE N. 124

its arrival in the Somme. Outside of the cold, mud, and dampness, it wasn't so bad. The barracks had been partitioned off into little rooms leaving a large space for a dining-hall. The stove was set up there, and all animate life from the lion cub to the pilots centred around it.

The eight *escadrilles* of fighting machines formed an interesting colony. The large canvas hangars were surrounded by the house tents of their respective *escadrilles*; wooden barracks for the men and pilots were in close proximity, and between the encampments of the various units were the tents of the commanding officers. In addition there was a bath-house and the power plant which generated electric light for the tents and barracks; and in one very popular tent was the community bar, the profits from which were sent to the Red Cross.

We had never before been grouped with so many combat squadrons, nor at a field so near the Front. We sensed the war to better advantage than at Luxeuil or Bar-le-Duc. When there is activity on the lines, the rumble of heavy artillery reaches us in a heavy volume of sound. From the field one can see the line of observation balloons, and beyond them distant patrols, darting like swallows in the sharpnel puffs of anti-aircraft fire. The roar of motors that are being tested is punctuated by the *staccato* barking of machine guns, and at intervals the hollow, whistling sound of a fast plane diving to earth is added to this symphony of war notes.

★★★★★★

The squadron arrived at the aerodrome at Cachy on the Somme, six months after its original muster at Luxeuil. Its work at the Front during this period may be summarized briefly: one hundred and fifty-six combats had been fought and seventeen of the enemy machines shot down had been officially confirmed as destroyed. These victories came in the following order:

1. May 18, 1916   Kiffin Rockwell
2. May 23, 1916   Bert Hall
3. May 24, 1916   William Thaw
4. July 21, 1916   Sous-Lt. Nungesser
5. July 23, 1916   Bert Hall
6. July 27, 1916   Lt. de Laage de Meux
7. July 31, 1916   Raoul Lufbery
8. August 4, 1916   Raoul Lufbery
9. August 4, 1916   Raoul Lufbery
10. August 8, 1916   Raoul Lufbery

11. August 28, 1916		Bert Hall
12. September 9, 1916.		Norman Prince
13. September 9, 1916		Kiffin Rockwell
14. October 10, 1916		Norman Prince
15. October 12, 1916		Norman Prince
16. October 12, 1916		Raoul Lufbery
17. October 12, 1916		Didier Masson

In the autumn of 1916, as a result of the activities of the American Squadron, there occurred an incident which aroused great interest in the United States and did much to enlist American sympathies on the side of France. On November 16, Colonel Barres, Chief of French Aviation at General Headquarters, informed Dr. Gros that the squadron could no longer be known as the *Escadrille Américaine*, but must henceforth be called simply the N. 124, its official military number. The following day at the Ministry of War, Dr. Gros learned the reason. Herr Bernstorff, the German Ambassador at Washington, called the attention of the American Government to the fact that Americans were fighting with the French and that the French communiqués often contained mention of an American *escadrille*. He protested in the name of the German Government. This protest gave rise, presumably, to a dispatch from Washington to the French Ministry of War, and this, in turn, to the following letter from French General Headquarters:

> The Commander-in-chief
> To the General Commanding the Armies of the North
> Villers-Bretonneux.
> By decision No. 9,763D, the Ministry of War has decided that for diplomatic reasons the Escadrille N.124 should be called the *Escadrille des Volontaires*, and that name *Escadrille Américaine*, in use at present, must be given up. Will you be kind enough to communicate this decision to the commanding officer of the 13th Combat Group, and to give orders that only the name *Escadrille des Volontaires* be used.
>
> (Signed) Poindron

Calling at the Ministry of War a few days later, Dr. Gros had an interview with Captain Bertaud, who told him that the title "*Escadrille des Volontaires*" was being considered for the squadron. Dr. Gros found this too colourless, and finally, at his suggestion, the name "Escadrille Lafayette" was agreed upon. This is the origin of the title which will go down in history as the name of the American Squadron which

AT THE AERO CLUB OF FRANCE, JUNE 14, 1917
SEATED: LIEUT. DEUILLIN, CAPT. HEURTEAUX, CAPT. GUYNEMER,
SOUS-LIEUT. TARASCON, CAPT. WATEAU.
STANDING: ADJ. JAILLER, SERGENT LOVELL, LIEUT. LUFBERY,
SERGENT JOHNSON, SERGENT HAVILAN, CAPT.
THENAULT, SERGENT WILLIS, SOUS-LIEUT. LANGUEDOC,
LIEUT. TOURTAY, SOUS-LIEUT. VARCIN, LIEUT. THAW

LOVELL, GENET, LUFBERY, AND MCCONNELL, SAINT-JUST,
FEBRUARY, 1917

fought under the French flag for nearly two years, and which afterward became the 103rd Pursuit, the first squadron at the Front, of the U.S. Air Service.

The squadron was now incorporated in *Groupe de Combat 13*, which comprised the following *escadrilles de chasse*: N. 15, N. 65, N. 84, and N. 124. N.88 was afterward added to the *groupe*. The letter "N" was the designation of all French combat squadrons, an abbreviation for "Nieuport," which was the name of the single-passenger pursuit machine then in use. In the winter of 1916, the Nieuport began to be superseded by the Spad (an abbreviation for *Société pour l'Aviation et ses Dérivés*, the company which perfected this new craft) until, by the spring of 1917, many French squadrons were entirely equipped with the new planes. Even before the change in plane equipment, there had been a change in armament. The Lewis guns, mounted on the top plane, gave place to the Vickers, mounted on the hood over the motor, and firing directly through the circle made by the revolving blades of the propeller.

By the middle of the summer of 1917, the Escadrille Lafayette was wholly a Spad squadron. The 13th Combat Group moved from sector to sector following the needs of the military situation, so that the pilots of the Spad 124 had a wide experience of war-time aviation on all parts of the Western Front. From the date of its organisation until its transfer to the U.S. Air Service, it has operated on the following sectors:

April 20 to May 19, 1916
    Luxeuil (Haute Saone)   Vosges Sector
May 20 to Sept. 14, 1916
    Bar-le-Duc (Meuse)   Verdun Sector
Sept. 15 to Oct. 18, 1916
    Luxeuil (Haute-Saone)   Vosges Sector
Oct. 19, 1916 to Jan. 26, 1917
    Cachy (Somme)   Somme Sector
Jan. 27 to April 7, 1917
    Saint-Juste (Oise)   Oise & Aisne Sectors
April 8 to June 3, 1917
    Ham (Somme)   Somme Sector
June 4 to July 17, 1917
    Chaudun (Aisne)   Aisne Sector
July 18 to Aug. 12, 1917
    Saint-Pol-sur-Mer (Nord)   Flanders Sector
Aug. 13, to Sept. 28, 1917
    Senard (Meuse)   Verdun Sector

SAINT POL-SUR-MER

CACHY (SOMME)

HAM (SOMME)

LA FERME DE LA NOBLETTE, CHAMPAGNE

LUXEUIL (VOSGES)

SAINT-JUST (SOMME)

AERODROMES OF THE ESCADRILLE LAFAYETTE

Sept. 29 to Dec. 5, 1917
        Chaudun (Aisne)   Aisne Sector
Dec. 6, 1917 to Feb. 18, 1918.
    La Cheppe and La Ferme de la Noblette (Marne) Champagne Sector

On August 3, 1917, while Group 13 was at Saint-Pol-sur-Mer, cooperating with the British in their Flanders offensive, Commandant Féquant made the following report on the work of the Escadrille Lafayette, in a proposition sent to General Headquarters, favouring the citation of the squadron as a unit:

> The Escadrille N. 124, first called the *Escadrille Américaine*, then the *Escadrille des Volontaires*, and finally the "Escadrille Lafayette," was formed under the command of Captain Georges Thenault on the 15th day of March, 1916.
>
> All of the pilots, excepting only the captain and a french lieutenant, are American citizens serving as volunteers for the duration of the war. The total flying personnel (including the commanding officer) has been in the neighbourhood of
>
> 9 pilots from April 20 to May 1, 1916.
> 12 pilots from May, 1916, to March, 1917.
> 15 to 20 pilots, from March, 1917, to the present time.
>
> Moved by the finest spirit of sacrifice, the squadron has rendered effective service, first in Alsace where it participated in protecting large bombardment expeditions sent beyond the Rhine; then, at Verdun where it was called upon to take part in the heaviest fighting. In October, 1916, it was sent to the Somme to fight against the most powerful aerial forces which the German High Command could levy. On the Oise it played an active role during the German retreat toward Saint-Quentin. The long-distance reconnaissances made by its pilots kept the French command in close touch with the enemy. It was engaged on the Aisne during the Soissons offensive of 1917 and is now operating on the Front in Flanders.
>
> Without mentioning the valuable reconnaissance flights or photographic missions, made in their single-passenger machines, or the daily combats of less importance, the pilots of the squadron have had 325 combats under conditions so hard and trying that they have often returned from them with their machines riddled with bullets.
>
> Twenty-eight enemy machines have been shot down in our

COMMANDANT FÉQUANT, CAPTAIN THENAULT
LIEUT. THAW, AND SOUS-LIEUT. LUFBERY

THE FIRST CITATION
OF THE ESCADRILLE LAFAYETTE

lines or destroyed in their own. A much larger number have been forced to land in the enemy lines after combat, in badly damaged condition. Up to the present four *Croix de Legion d'Honneur*, seven *Médailles Militaires*, thirty citations *à l'Ordre de l'Armée* and one *à l'Ordre de l'Aéronautique* have been awarded to the pilots for their exploits.

They have paid dearly for their successes. Nine pilots have been killed, five wounded, and several others, worn out in service, have had to be evacuated. These losses have increased, rather than diminished their ardour. The vacant places have been filled by other Americans eager to avenge their comrades. The splendid spirit of the Escadrille Lafayette and its devotion to duty has been a matter for pride to all Americans and has helped to bring their country to our aid in the war. The spirit of sacrifice of these men, who came as volunteers to fight for us, is revealed in the last words of those who have been killed. All of them said that they would gladly give their lives in the service of France. Their example has raised the morale even of the pilots in the French squadrons who have fought at their side. In order, then, to reward in some measure, the Escadrille Lafayette for the valour of its pilots and for its success as a squadron, I ask that it be cited to the order of the army.

On the 15th of August, 1917, the squadron was cited in the following terms:

Grand Quartier Général, État-Major   *Le 15 août, 1917*
Le General Commandant en Chef cite à l'Ordre de l'Armée, l'Escadrille N. 124 (Escadrille Lafayette).
Escadrille composée de volontaires américains, venus se battre pour la France avec le plus pur esprit de sacrifice.
A mené sans cesse, sous le commandement du Capitaine Thenault, qui la formée, une lutte ardente contre nos ennemis.
Dans des combats très durs et au prix de pertes qui, loin de l'affaiblir, exaltaient son morale, a abattu 28 avions adverses.
A excité l'admiration profonde des Chefs qui l'ont eue sous leurs ordres et des escadrilles françaises qui, combattant à ses côtés, ont voulu rivaliser de valeur avec elle.

        (Signé)   Pétain

After America's declaration of war, the Executive Committee of the Lafayette Corps decided that the pilots of the Escadrille Lafayette, as well as all of those Americans serving in other French squadrons, should be asked to offer their services to the United States Government. The final decision was left wholly to the men themselves, and it was a difficult one to make. While all of them were eager to serve their own country, they were reluctant to leave the service of France. They had formed lasting friendships with their French comrades, and had come to think of France as a second mother country, almost as dear to them as their own. After many long conferences held in barracks on rainy days, and between patrol hours, the pilots of the Lafayette Squadron decided that their first duty was to their own land; and that, inasmuch as the French Government had expressed its willingness to release them, they would offer their services as a unit to the United States.

This was done in the late autumn of 1917. They were officially released from the French Army in December, but as many of them did not receive notification of their American commissions until January or February, 1918, they continued to serve at the Front as civilians, still wearing their French uniforms. During this time the Squadron, which was then stationed at La Ferme de la Noblette on the Champagne Front, remained with *Groupe de Combat* 13 as a French unit.

On February 18, 1918, under the provisions of a curious and interesting agreement between the French and American armies, the Escadrille Lafayette became the 103rd Pursuit Squadron of the U.S. Air Service, retaining a detachment of French mechanics to instruct the newly arrived American non-flying personnel in their duties. A clause in the agreement, which states that the average annual cost of keeping one Spad in service at the Front was 313,865 *francs*, illustrates the enormous expense of military aviation.

The squadron, still under French orders, was attached to the *Groupe de Combat* 15, for at that time there were no other American squadrons ready for service. The pilots were: Ray C. Bridgman, Charles H. Dolan, Jr., William E. Dugan, Jr., Christopher W. Ford, James N. Hall, Dudley L. Hill, Henry S. Jones, Kenneth Marr, David McK. Peterson, Robert L. Rockwell, and Robert Soubiran, under command of Major William Thaw. To this number were added Phelps Collins, Paul F. Baer, Charles J. Biddle, C. Maury Jones, George E. Turnure, Jr., and Charles H. Wilcox, who had received their American commissions and had been sent from their French squadrons for further duty with the Escadrille Lafayette.

Arrival of the American Mechanics, Escadrille Lafayette,
February 17. 1918

The quarters of the American mechanics.
La Ferme De La Noblette (Champagne Sector)

It had been the hope of the pilots of the squadron that they might be kept together as a unit, but this was not to be. By the early summer of 1918, many of them were scattered through the new American squadrons, as commanding officers and flight leaders. A few of them were left with the 103rd, which became a training squadron at the Front for new pilots. Many Americans, who afterward became flight and squadron commanders gained their first experience and their first successes in combat in the old Escadrille Lafayette.

From February 18 to April 9, 1918, the squadron operated first with the 15th and then with the 21st Combat Group, with the Fourth French Army. From April 10 to April 30, with the Sixth French Army, and from May 1 to June 30, with the French D.A.N. From July 1 to August 6, it was incorporated in the 2nd Pursuit Group attached to the First Army, A.E.F., and from August 7 until the Armistice, in the 3rd Pursuit, First Army, A.E.F. During the period of its service as an American squadron, forty-five enemy planes and two observation balloons were shot down and their destruction officially confirmed; and eighty-two others were probably destroyed. Twenty-five of these officially confirmed victories were gained by pilots who formerly belonged to the Lafayette Corps.

On October 28, 1918, the squadron was again cited in French Army Orders for its work during the final summer of the war. The text of the citation is as follows:

Grand Quartier Général des Armées
    du Nord et du Nord-Est,
        État-Major   Ordre No. 10,805 'D' (Extrait)
Après approbation du Général Commandant en Chef les Forces Expéditionnaires américaines en France, le Général Commandant en Chef les Armées françaises du Nord et du Nord-Est, cite à l'Ordre de l'Armée:

                Escadrille Américaine "Lafayette"
Brillante unité, commandee par le Major Thaw, qui s'est montrée au cours des opérations dans les Flandres, digne de son glorieux passé. Sans se laisser arrêter par des pertes atteignant le tiers de son effectif, a assuré dans un secteur difficile une sécurité parfaite à nos avions de corps d'armée, un service de reconnaissance à haute et à basse altitude des plus complets et la destruction, tant près de nos lignes qu'a grande distance chez l'ennemi, d'un très grand nombre d'avions et de ballons captifs allemands.

Au Grand Quartier Général, le 22 Octobre, 1918.
Le Général Commandant en Chef
(Signé) Pétain

After the signing of the Armistice the 103rd Pursuit Squadron was chosen as one of those to be sent into Germany with the Army of Occupation. This announcement was made in General Order No. 17:

Headquarters, First Pursuit Wing Air Service,
A.E.F. General Order
November 16, 1918

General Order

1. The 103rd Aero Squadron, Third Pursuit Group, will hold itself in readiness to move at any moment to join the First Pursuit Group and proceed into Germany.

2. This honor has been conferred upon the 103rd Aero Squadron for its long and faithful service with French and American armies.

3. The Wing Commander takes this opportunity of expressing his pleasure at having this squadron under his command. The Lafayette Escadrille, organised long before the entry of the United States into the European war, played an important part in bringing home to our people the basic issues of the war. To the French people of future generations the names of its organisers and early pilots must mean what the names of Lafayette and Rochambeau mean to us Americans of this generation. To mention only a few, the names of Norman Prince, Kiffin Rockwell, James McConnell, Victor Chapman, Captain James Norman Hall, Major Kenneth Marr, Major David McK. Peterson, Major Raoul Lufbery, and Lieut. Colonel William Thaw, are never to be forgotten.

In February last the Lafayette Escadrille of the French Army was transferred to the 103rd Aero Squadron, United States Army. It was the first, and for nearly two months it was the only American Air Service organisation on the Front. Since that time it is not too much to say that pilots who served in this squadron have formed the backbone of American Pursuit Aviation on the Front. The squadron produced two of America's four Pursuit Group Commanders as well as a very large proportion of the Squadron and flight commanders. While giving thus liberally of its experienced personnel to new units the standard of merit of this squadron has not been lowered. No task was too arduous or too hazardous for it to perform successfully. In the recent decisive operations of the First American Army the 103rd Aero Squadron has done it's share.

4. The Wing Commander congratulates Captain Soubiran, Squadron Commander, 103rd Aero Squadron and all of his personnel, commissioned and enlisted. No other organisation in the American Army has a right to such a high measure of satisfaction in feeling it's difficult task has been performed. So long as the personnel bears in mind the record the Squadron has established there can be no other prospect for it than that of a splendid future.

B. M. Atkinson
Lt. Col., Air Service, U.S.A.
Commanding

The order was rescinded, however. It was decided that the Lafayette Squadron which had been continuously on active duty since April 20, 1916, fighting under the flags of both France and America, had earned the right to be released from further service abroad. It was therefore placed under orders to return to America.

3

The Lafayette Flying Corps

Before the *Escadrille Américaine* had been on the Front six weeks, the exploits of the volunteers began to attract world-wide attention, and it became evident to the committee that with hard work and the necessary funds there were great possibilities ahead. It was at this time that the Franco-American Flying Corps (later the Lafayette Flying Corps) came into being. Around the original committee of three a larger Executive Committee had already been formed, to handle the finances and other business of the corps. It was composed as follows:

Honorary President:	Mr. William K. Vanderbilt
President:	M. Jarousse de Sillac
Vice-President, Director for France, and Examining Physician:	Dr. Edmund L. Gros
Treasurers:	Mr. Lawrence Slade / Colonel Bentley Mott
Assistant Treasurer:	Mr. Arthur G. Evans
Secretary:	Mrs. Edward P. Ovington
Bankers:	Bonbright & Company
Director for America:	Mr. (later Lieutenant-Commander) Frederick Allen
American Representatives:	Mr. F. J. McClure / Mr. Philip Carrol / Mr. Henry Earle / Mr. George F. Tyler / Mr. Charles Greene
Honorary Members:	M. Léon Bourgeois / M. Gaston Menier / General Hirschauer / Colonel Bouttieaux / Mr. Robert Bacon

Theodore Roosevelt, Astor Chanler, Robert Glendinning, Pierre Étienne Flandin, René Besnard, and Louis Dumesnil completed the group which assisted in the work, and prepared a pamphlet with the view of calling to the attention of the Americans the requirements for enlistment in the French Aviation.

Headquarters for the corps at 15 avenue des Champs Élysées were provided through the generosity of the Countess Greffulhe, and this became the meeting-place for the American volunteers passing through Paris.

Money was required for many purposes. Many of the volunteers needed help to pay their passages from America, and their hotel bills while waiting in Paris for enlistment papers to go through. French army pay was not sufficient for even the most necessary personal expenses, so a monthly allowance was given each volunteer during his period of training and while at the Front. As the cost of living increased with the progress of the war, this allowance was raised from one hundred *francs* to one hundred and fifty, and finally to two hundred *francs* per month. At the time of his *brevet*, each man was presented with a uniform. Funds were also necessary for the printing and distribution of pamphlets, setting forth the work of the corps and the justice of the French cause.

Finally—and this became an increasingly heavy as well as a pleasant obligation—the committee established a system of awards for citations and decorations given the Americans for victories at the Front. It was to Mr. William K. Vanderbilt, that the Lafayette Flying Corps owed the financial support without which an organisation of this kind cannot exist. There were other contributors inspired by the same unselfish and far-sighted motives—but it may be said that Mr. Vanderbilt shouldered the responsibility almost single-handed. Through the entire existence of the corps he supported it with the utmost generosity, his contributions reaching a total of more than 500,000 *francs*.

The earlier recruits of the corps were, in most cases, Americans who had enlisted in the Foreign Legion [1] (Infantry), or in the American Ambulance, in the early days of the war. As time went on and the organisation was perfected, many volunteers came direct from America, after being passed upon by the representative of the corps in New York. Every candidate for enlistment, upon arrival in Paris, presented himself to Dr. Gros, who examined him physically, looked into his credentials, and sent him on to the *Bureau de Recrutement* at the Invali-

1. *Vide En l'air! (In the Air)* by Bert Hall also published by Leonaur.

des, where he signed his papers of enlistment in the Foreign Legion, to be detached to the Aviation. As already mentioned, the committee, acting through M. de Sillac, had persuaded the French authorities to provide a special form of enlistment, whereby Americans who proved inapt at flying could be released outright, if they so desired, without the customary transfer to some other branch of military service. All candidates recommended by Dr. Gros, acting on behalf of the committee, were accepted without question by the military authorities, so that the prospective pilot had only to sign his engagement and take the train for the flying school to which he had been assigned. It speaks well for the painstaking care and discrimination of those in charge, that in the days when the United States was a hotbed of German agents seeking access to France, no serious suspicion of this kind has ever been attached to a member of the Lafayette Flying Corps.

In connection with the terms of enlistment a question of citizenship arose. There was naturally some worry about loss of nationality through enlistment in a foreign army, and at last the matter was taken up with the United States Consul-General who referred it to Washington. It was there decided that as the volunteer did not swear allegiance to France, only promising to obey orders and submit to discipline, he did not lose his American citizenship.

In the autumn of 1916 occurred the diplomatic incident which led to the name "Escadrille Lafayette," and some time afterward it was decided that the name "Franco-American Flying Corps" should likewise be changed, and that henceforth it should be known as the "Lafayette Flying Corps." The new name was adopted and at first gave rise to some confusion in America, as all men enlisted in the corps were thought to be serving in the *escadrille*, which of course was not the case. Like all French squadrons, the Escadrille Lafayette was limited to a flying personnel of from twelve to fifteen pilots. As the corps increased in size, it became necessary to send the great majority of the men to French squadrons, until, by the close of 1917, there were Americans scattered, singly and in twos and threes, among the French squadrons all the way from the Channel coast to the Swiss frontier. When hostilities ceased, Lafayette pilots had served in sixty-six *escadrilles de chasse*, and twenty-seven army corps and bombardment squadrons of the French Aviation Service.

The Lafayette was from the beginning a *chasse*, or pursuit, squadron. Originally provided with the thirteen-metre Nieuports, armed with a Lewis gun on the top plane, it changed successively to the

Vickers-armed fifteen-metre Nieuport, and to the Spad. Although it was customary to recruit fighting pilots from among the veterans of bombing and observation work, the record of the N 124 encouraged the French to send Americans direct to the single-seaters, a high compliment to skill and initiative. For this reason, most of the Lafayette men enjoyed a peculiarly interesting form of training—the old Blériot system. It is true that in the summer of 1917 a certain number were trained on Caudrons, but the Blériot will always be remembered as the characteristic training machine of the corps. Primary training on the Blériot was given originally at Pau, later at Buc, and after January, 1917, at Avord. In this method, one was always alone in the machine. Beginning with the tiny, three-cylinder penguins, incapable of flight, the student was taught to roll in a straight line at full speed. This difficult art mastered, he passed to the six-cylinder *rouleurs*, and from them to a machine capable of low flights, in which he did straightaways, rising to a height of three or four yards. From this point it was an easy step to real flying—banks, spirals, serpentines, and finally the cross-country and altitude tests for the military *brevet*.

After passing the *brevet*, Americans were usually given a brief preliminary training on Nieuport at Avord, and sent to Pau, where they were taught to fly the service type of Nieuport, to do acrobatic flying, and to practice combat tactics. Two or three weeks sufficed for the course at Pau, after which the pilot was considered ready for the Front and sent on to the G.D.E. (*Groupe des Divisions l'Entrainement*), at Le Plessis-Belleville. While there he was given an opportunity to perfect himself in handling service types of machines. Within a short time he received his assignment to a squadron on the Front—in some cases the Lafayette, but usually, as the Corps increased in size, to a Spad squadron, with a flying personnel of French pilots in one of the various *groupes de combat*.

The American volunteers enlisted as privates (*soldats de deuxieme classe*), were made corporals on receiving the pilot's license, and sergeants after flying thirty hours over the lines. Some, after one hundred hours, and a certain number of combats and victories, were made *adjudants*, and a very few attained commissioned rank. The great majority, however, were N.C.O.'s, and lived with the non-commissioned pilots who constitute the bulk of the French flyers. Side by side with the French, in the mess, in billets, and in scores of combats over the lines, the Americans proved themselves good comrades and first-class fighting men, as a long list of citations and decorations shows. There have been,

AMERICANS AT BUC. SUMMER OF 1916

M. DE SILLAC AND DR. GROS VISITING THE AMERICAN PILOTS AT
AVORD, MARCH, 1917

among the Lafayette men, a certain number of brilliant combat pilots. Prince, Chapman, and Kiffin Rockwell, though killed before their lists of victories had grown long, would have gone far had they lived.

Lufbery, the greatest figure of the corps, was recognised as one of the keenest and most skilful flyers in France. Baylies, a member of the famous *Cigognes*, the squadron of Dorme and Guynemer,[2] was considered a prodigy, even in that band of aces. He was a wonderful shot, and attacked at such close quarters and so bitterly that each combat was a duel to the death. Putnam, favourite pupil of the great Madon, was another famed for the reckless bitterness of his attack. Always on the offensive, he cruised far within the enemy lines, attacking with a ruthlessness and a disregard of odds which ran up his victories like magic, and in the end led to his death.

There are others, too numerous for individual mention here, whose records of service on the Front are more eloquent than any words of praise. Among the ninety-three pilots who transferred to the U.S. Air Service, and those who entered our Naval Air Service, were men of wide experience and ability, who served as a framework about which the Pursuit Branch of our Aviation was built up, and contributed, in no small degree, to the fine record of our Air Service on the Front.

In April, 1917, the dearest wish of every American in France was realised—our country declared war. On April 7, the following proclamation was posted at Avord:

Paris, le 7 avril, 1917

Le Lieutenant Colonel, Inspecteur Général des
Dépôts et Écoles d'Aviation, à Pilotes américains à Avord
Je suis sûr d'être l'interprète des sentiments de tout le personnel sous mes ordres en saluant, à l'heure où elle se range aux côtés des Alliés dans la Bataille mondiale, votre grande et belle Patrie. Déjà, vous aviez devancé cette heure historique en apportant à la France le concours de vos volontés, de vos audaces, et de vos cœurs; je vous en remercie, et avec l'Aviation française, l'Armée, et toutes les Nations debout contre le crime, je m'incline devant le Drapeau américain. Ses couleurs, mêlées aux nôtres, iront porter le triomphe au ciel de la Patrie.
Nous sommes fiers de vous instruire. Vous serez fiers, avec nous, de vaincre.

(Signé)   *Girod*

---

2. Guynemer: *Chevalier of the Air*, a double edition, (*George Guynemer, Knight of the Air*) by Henry Bordeaux (*The Chevalier of Flight: Captain Guynemer*) by Mary R. Parkman is also published by Leonaur.

COLONEL GIROD,
COMMANDING OFFICER OF THE FRENCH
AVIATION SCHOOLS

In June, General Pershing, with the first contingent of Americans, arrived in Paris, and many a Lafayette man went absent without leave to cheer himself hoarse at sight of his country's uniform. It was. soon rumoured that Americans in the French Service were to be transferred to the United States Army, but it was not until September that the following orders were issued to examine Americans in the schools.

Headquarters Air Service Line of Communications
American Expeditionary Forces
Paris, France, September 11, 1917
(Extract)

Special Order No. 34

Par. 9. Major Edmund Gros, S.O.R.C, Major R. H. Goldthwaite, M.C., Lieut. R. S. Beam, M.O.R.C. will proceed from Paris, France, to French Aviation Schools at Avord and Tours, and to the American Aviation School at Issoudun, for the purpose of examining Americans now enlisted in French Army with the view of their transfer to the United States Army, and obtaining medical history of the personnel of the American School at Issoudun. Upon completion of this duty they will return to Paris, France.

The travel directed is necessary in the military service.

By command of Major-General Blatchford
W. C. Langfitt, Brig. Gen. U.S.A.
Chief of Staff

Major Gros, Major Goldthwaite, and Lieutenant Beam visited Avord, Juvisy, and Tours, taking the names of Americans who desired to transfer, and subjecting the candidates to a physical and mental examination to ascertain their fitness to hold a United States Commission. On October 1, 1917, the following orders were issued, creating a special Board to examine Americans in the French Service:

Headquarters American Expeditionary Forces,
France, October 1, 1917

Special Order No. 113 (Extract)
Par. 3. A Board of officers to consist of:

Major Ralph H. Goldthwaite, M.C.

Major Robert Glendinning, A.S.S.O.R.C.

Major Edmund L. Gros, A.S.S.O.R.C.

Major William W. Hoffman, A.S.S.O.R.C.

is hereby convened for the examination of such American citizens, now commissioned or enlisted in the French Aviation Service, as may desire to obtain their release from that Service for the purpose of entering the Service of the United States. The Board will make specific recommendations in each case, covering suitability of the applicant for service in the Air Service, American Expeditionary Forces, and the grade in which he should be accepted at such time as it shall be agreeable to the French Government to release him.

The Board is authorised to proceed to: Chaumont, Nancy, Jonchéry, Souilly, Châlons, Soissons, Plessis-Belleville, Paris (France), and Hoodekoute (Belgium). Upon completion of this duty the members of the Board will return to their proper stations.

The travel directed is necessary in the military service.

By Command of Major General Pershing
James G. Harbord, Col. General Staff
Chief of Staff

To do its work, the Board travelled by motorcar along the Front from Verdun to Dunkirk, stopping at every aerodrome where Americans were to be found. Each candidate was examined and classified, as shown by the following report made by the Board on completion of its work:

Report to Brigadier-General William Kenly

1. This Board was appointed to examine such American citizens, now commissioned or enlisted in the French Aviation Service, who desire to obtain their release from that Service for the purpose of entering the Service of the United States; to make recommendations in reference to their suitability and grade in which they should be accepted at such time as it shall be agreeable to the French Government to release them. The Board was much impressed by the class of men examined, the fine reports of their work given by their officers, and their great desire to serve under their own colours. The material is valuable as a nucleus of aviators, experienced at the Front, around whom can be grouped the less experienced pilots recently trained or undergoing training here. It is capital with which to build and should be preserved.

Many of the pilots are flying in machines which are not modern, which involves large risks—and the nature of the work itself is necessarily highly dangerous. The Americans are not receiving any outside assistance, which they have had hitherto, cannot live on the French pay, and most have no independent source of income. It is the opinion of the Board and also of the French officers commanding these Americans, that their position should be settled as soon as possible; that they should be allowed to remain at the Front until required by the A.E.F.; and that as soon as they are required they should immediately undertake the new duties assigned them.

2. In compliance with Special Order No. 113, paragraph 3, Headquarters A.E.F., October 1, 1917, this Board proceeded in accordance with the itinerary directed in the order, and examined certain American citizens, now commissioned or enlisted

in the French Aviation Service, who desired to obtain their release for the purpose of entering the Service of the United States. On October 9, 1917, the Board met at the Aviation Headquarters, Paris, all members of the Board being present. All applicants examined were considered and classed in one of the following six classes:

1. Capable of commanding a squadron—rank, Major.
2. Capable of commanding a flight of six airplanes—rank, Captain.
3. Capable of command, but not to be commissioned as flight commander until later, owing to present lack of experience—rank, 1st Lieutenant.
4. Capable of being pilots—rank, 1st Lieutenant.
5. Capable of being an instructor, 1st class—rank, Captain.
6. Capable of being an instructor, 2nd class—rank, 1st Lieutenant.

The recommendations are being based upon reports from *escadrille* commanders, group commanders, and from Plessis-Belleville (Instruction); also on personal impression and past history. The Board was impressed by the fine class of Americans serving with the French Aviation, their seriousness, and their desire to serve under their own colours.... There remain a few others to be examined—not seen because of leave, illness, or other reasons. These will be reported on in a supplementary report after examination.

Men who desired to transfer to the American Air Service were required to fill out the following form, stating rank, name, and unit, and requesting release from the French service:

À Monsieur le Sous-Secrétaire d'État de l'Aéronautique
Étant citoyen américain, et m'étant engagé dans l'Armée française, comme (pilote, or observateur) j'ai l'honneur de vous demander de bien vouloir résilier mon engagement pour me permettre de passer dans l'Aviation de l'Armée américaine.

The Board sent in its recommendations on October 20, 1917, and the French authorities were informed that the Lafayette men desirous of transferring would soon be commissioned in the American Army, and that their releases, at the earliest possible date, would be appreciated. Release is naturally an unusual procedure in the French Army, but in view of the urgent nature of the request, the various *bureaux* made a special effort to hasten the process. It seemed, at last, that the untiring efforts of Colonel Bolling and Major Gros, supported by General Kenly, always a stanch friend of the Lafayette Corps, were to meet with success, in the acquisition, for the United States Air Service, of more than one hundred pilots, fully trained and experienced on the latest types of European service machines.

Unfortunately, however, for the corps and for the Air Service at large, General Kenly's policy was not followed by the officers who superseded him and who seemed to appreciate neither the value of the material offered nor the critical need of pilots. There seemed to be a feeling that hundreds of American pilots were ready to come overseas, just as there was the illusion that hundreds of American planes would soon be flying over the lines. In neither the one case nor the other was this confidence justified: it was many months before American-trained pilots were ready to go to the Front, and it was not until August, 1918, that the first American-built planes crossed the lines.

Very little interest was shown in the Lafayette Flying Corps, and although it was repeatedly brought to the attention of those responsible that serious complications would arise unless the men were commissioned as recommended by the Board, no heed was paid to the warning. The Board made one mistake—in recommending for a commission one man, whose record in the schools, was excellent, and who had not flown over the lines at the time of his examination.

A short time afterward, his French commander sent to the Air Service an unfavourable report of his conduct in the face of the enemy—suggesting that his commission, if authorised, be revoked. On this pretext, the whole report of the Board was questioned, and the French commanders of squadrons on the Front were asked to send in new reports—a serious and absolutely unnecessary cause of delay, as in all cases, except the one mentioned above, the new reports were found to correspond with the recommendations of the Board.

Meanwhile, complying with the expressed desire of the Air Service, the French Army was slowly but steadily releasing the Lafayette pilots then in the schools and on the Front, making civilians of men who had come great distances, and put up with weary months of training, in order to take an active part in the fighting. Some remained in Paris, expecting each day to learn that they had been commissioned—and finally, after weeks of waiting, joined the navy. Others, like Baylies, refused to leave their squadrons, and had the curious experience of flying and fighting, for weeks and even months, as civilians, though still in French uniform. In the end, the transfers were effected, but only after inexcusable loss of time, lowering of morale, and annoyance to the French Aviation Service, at a time when every pilot was needed on the Front.

Throughout the affair, Colonel Bolling and Major Gros worked unceasingly for the transfer—at first to persuade the French to release the men, and later urging the Americans to accept them as rapidly as possible. On December 14, 1917, Major Gros wrote to all members of the corps who had applied for transfer:

> Knowing how impatiently you must be awaiting the time of your release, I want to tell you that everything is being done to hasten the delay, which is entirely due to slowness in the ministerial *bureaux*. Your papers are now going through the *bureau* of the Minister of War, and we expect that in a very few days your official release will be granted. At that time you will be notified, and asked to come in to take the oath as an officer of the American Expeditionary Forces. I want you to know that the delay in your transfer is entirely beyond my control, and that I am doing everything in the world to hasten these steps.

A RAINY DAY IN CAMP

THE PLUMED
KNIGHT

THE DRAGON

THE FOX

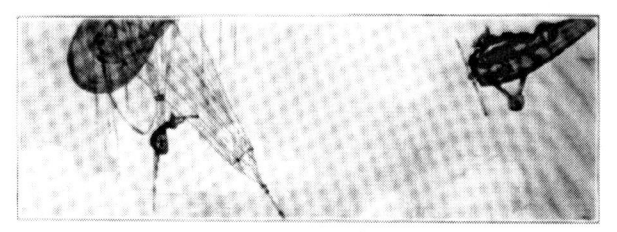

THE SNAKE

THE INDIAN

GROUPE DE COMBAT

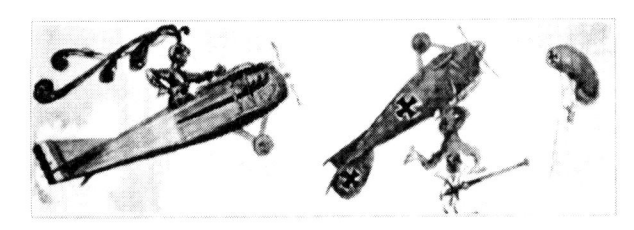

SPA.15

SPA.65

SPA.84

SPA.88

SPA.124

13 IN ACTION

A few days later, in urging the French to hasten the releases, Major Gros said:

> The Lafayette Escadrille and the members of the Lafayette Flying Corps are very much in the public eye of America. They have played a great part in forming public opinion, and at this moment the American newspapers contain pointed articles, asking why we have not looked more carefully after the interests of these young men, several of whom have died for France.

The following telegram, sent by General Pershing on November 5, 1917, recommended for commissions the first men to be transferred from the Lafayette Flying Corps. It is of considerable historical interest and not without an element of unconscious humour, for these senile and defective veterans, for whom it was necessary in so many cases to recommend waivers, became the mainstays of the American Pursuit.

> No. 272. S.
> Agwar—Washington   November 5, 1917
> Par. 14. Recommend following American citizens with Lafayette Escadrille of French Army be commissioned in Aviation Reserve as follows: As Majors John F. Huffer and Victor Raoul Lufbery, 32 years of age, recommend waiver. As Captains, Charles J. Biddle, Phelps Collins, Kenneth P. Littauer, David McK. Peterson, Robert Soubiran whose age is 31, recommend waiver. Robert L. Rockwell and Kenneth Marr whose age is 32, recommend waiver. As First Lieutenants, Paul F. Baer, Willis B. Haviland, Charles M. Jones, Henry S. Jones, Granville A. Pollock, Leland L. Rounds, Joseph C Stehlin, George E. Turnure, Jr., Frank W. Wells, Charles H. Wilcox, and Charles C. Johnson. Also recommend William Thaw as Major, waiving defective vision left eye, 20/80 opthalmoscopic left shows atrophy plus pigmentation in focal area, hearing defective 15/20, and recurrent knee injury with limitation of motion, 3 years' experience at the Front with French Army; Walter Lovell, age 33, as Captain, very slight defect in hearing, definitely colour blind, got his *brevet* one year ago and has been flying seven months at the Front after completion of course at Pau. In view of his experience waiver is recommended so that his services may be utilised in instruction. Dudley L. Hill as Captain, vision right eye limited to finger perception, on account three years flying with French army it is thought he would make a very useful officer in spite

COMMANDANT BROCARD

JACQUES-LOUIS DUMESNIL
Sous-Secrétaire d'État de l'Aéronautique Militaire et Maritime, 1917-1919

of marked vision defect. Charles H. Dolan, Jr., as First Lieutenant, vision both eyes corrected to 20-30 myopia, on account of experience of 14 months flying in French Army waiver of defect is recommended.   Pershing

The Lafayette Squadron, as already mentioned, became an American unit in February, 1918. The American pilots, scattered through other French squadrons, were transferred slowly throughout the winter and spring. Some remained for several weeks or months on detached service with their former units; others were sent as instructors to the American training schools at Tours or Issoudun, until American squadrons were ready for active duty. The Lafayette pilots, who were the last to join the corps, and who had not yet completed their training in French Aviation schools, were taken over as soon as they were ready for active duty. By June 1, 1918, nearly all of those who had applied for transfer had received their American commissions.

A brief consideration of statistics will serve to summarise the accomplishments of the corps. The total enlistment was 267, of whom 43 were released, before receiving the military *brevet*, because of illness, inaptitude, or injuries received in flying accidents. Those who served at the Front in French uniform numbered 180, and fought with 66 Pursuit, and 27 Observation and Bombardment Squadrons of the French Aviation Service. After our country declared war, 93 of these trained pilots transferred to the U.S. Air Service, and 26 to the U.S. Naval Aviation. Five died of illness, and 6 by accident in the aviation schools; 15 were taken prisoners (of whom 3 escaped to Switzerland), 19 were wounded in combat, and 51 were killed at the Front. The members of the Lafayette Flying Corps shot down, and had officially confirmed by the military authorities, 199 enemy machines.

On November 3, 1918, a few days before the Armistice which proclaimed our final victory, the French Ministry of War showed its appreciation of the work of the corps by conferring on the volunteers a decoration in the form of a commemorative Service Ribbon. Each member also received an engraved certificate, signed by M. Dumesnil, which reads as follows:

Ministère de la guerre
Sous-Secrétariat d'État
de l'Aéronautique Militaire et Maritime.   *République Française*
Le Président du Conseil, Ministère de la Guerre, a décidé, sur ma proposition, d'accorder un souvenir aux quatre officiers directeurs et aux

The Moselle at Trèves

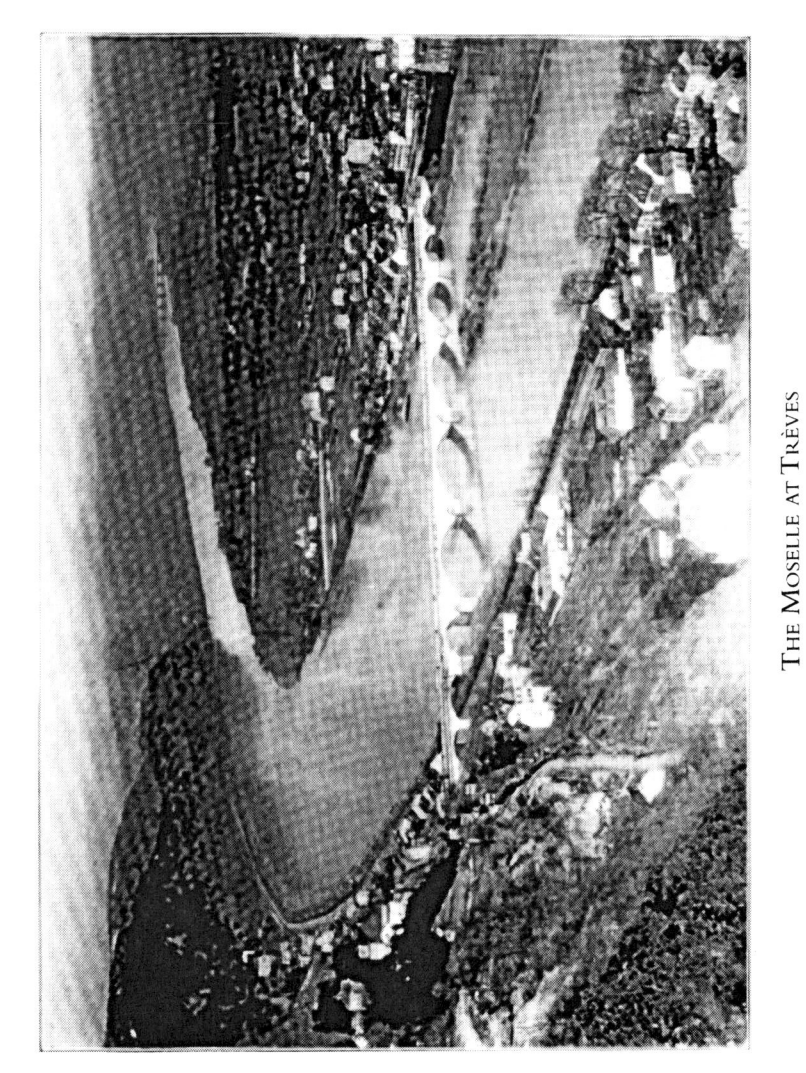

214 pilotes du Lafayette Flying Corps, qui, devançant l'élan de tout un peuple, sont venus prendre fraternellement dans les rangs français une belle part de périls et de la gloire.

Ce souvenir consiste en un ruban bleu, semé d'étoiles, bordé des couleurs de France et d'Amérique, orné en relief de la tête de Sioux en argent, qu'ont glorieusement portée sur nos champs de bataille les avions de la première Escadrille Lafayette.

Je suis particulièrement heureux de vous faire parvenir cet insigne, qui demeurera le témoignage reconnaissant de l'Aviation française fière de vous avoir compté parmi ses pilotes, et de la France tout entière, que vous avez bien servie.

This brief outline of the history of the Lafayette Flying Corps would not be complete without an expression of deep gratitude for the never-failing friendship of the French people. Lafayette men will not forget the brothers Jacques and Paul de Lesseps, who gave such timely aid in the early days; the tireless work, on behalf of the corps, of M. de Sillac, or his interest in the welfare of the pilots. As President of the Executive Committee, he was in close touch with the needs of the Corps. There were loyal friends in every department of public administration, civil and military: M. René Besnard, M. Léon Bourgeois, M. Daniel Vincent, M. Jacques Dumesnil, M. Pierre E. Flandrin, Senator Gaston Menier, M. Millerand, M. Viviani, were among those in the civil government most actively concerned in the organisation and the development of the *Escadrille Américaine* and the Lafayette Corps.

Among the military were General Hirschauer, Colonel Bouttieaux, Colonel Regnier, Lieutenant-Colonel Girod, Commandant Brocard, Commandant Féquant, Captain Berteaux. These and countless others, in both public and private life, revealed their friendship in generous and kindly ways, making the American volunteers more than ever debtors of France, and grateful for their privilege of serving her.

Captain Guynemer of the Cigognes winning a double victory in the Parvilliers Sector during a gas attack, (May, 1917)

THE LAFAYETTE FLYING CORPS LETTERS

4

Enlistment and Early Training

TRANSFERRED FROM THE LEGION

1

August 8, 1915

You ought to know, by the time this reaches you, that I have finally changed corps. A typical instance of the way things are done in the army is the way I was told the news. I was sitting in the sunshine playing mumble-the-peg with three or four others before mounting squad. Ames came up and whispered in my ear that a sergeant had just told him I was going to the Aviation. An hour or so later the sergeant, in an offhand way, said that I was to leave. That evening I met the lieutenant, who begged me not to forget to drop him a line. When or whither I was leaving no one seemed to know. The next day I almost collared the lieutenant, and we went together to the *bureau*. Oh, yes, the demand had come for me to be sent without delay to the Gare Régulatrice de Gray. I was leaving at seven the next morning. With many *adieux* and five fellows helping me on with my sack, I got off, and presented myself in due course at the station of Champagny with a sealed letter of the *Commissionnaire Militaire.*

The contents of the letter proved that it was quite unnecessary to go to Gray, since my destination was Nancy. "Change at Lure": a jolly, unmodern town with a Grande Rue, Louis Quinze windows, keystones, a pond and trees, and a provincial brown-stone Louis XIV *château*—now the *sous-préfecture*. At Ailleures I waited again three hours. It was some time before I could find the town here. Finally I saw it across the track on a hill a mile off, with stone church, the image of a New England eighteenth-century structure. Less amusing town than Lure, but with very pretty children (to whom I gave the cake which a drummer had forced upon me in a cafe of Lure), and chickens perched on the window-sills. Groups of old women and young girls were industriously stuffing green litre bottles with new string beans; and I found an old farmer before the tobacco shop with a handsome yoke of oxen actually tied together with nothing more or less than his umbrella!

With difficulty I boarded the express. "Guilty of something underhand until proved to the contrary," seems the attitude of all the military officials. And they only let one by with a kind of despairing, resigned air, as though saying: "I suppose I'll have to. You beat me this time." A pale, olive-complexioned woman, with a fair-haired little girl of two, sat opposite me. It was easy to see, by her calm, resolute, yet sad face, that she had lost her husband in the war, even if she were not dressed in black. A grandmother and two uninteresting *backfisch* studiously read inferior funny-sheets and *deux-sous* novels. A tall, respectable gentleman was resentfully given a place by the females.

I reached Nancy at 8.30, and, after the usual examination, started on a train to Malzeville. Hardly a street lamp anywhere, yet in the dark I saw a handsome, mediaeval town-gate with towers and rows of gargoyles on the eaves of the houses we passed. At Nancy the train goes no farther. "Twenty-five minutes' walk up a hill and with a sack! Are you mad?" This the advice of a couple of men who had just joined the Corps as mechanics. I turned to the *café* on the street corner and asked for information about hotels. "*Eh toi! Poilu! D'oul viens-tu? Viens prendre un bock.*" In the semi-darkness sat two fantassins, two girls and an old man. They were all in exuberant spirits as though they had just met, and pressed me with questions. Where did I come from? going where? seen fighting? etc., all mixed in with adoring by-play between the sexes. I launched forth on the Legion, the Aviation, *engagé volontier*, and incidentally let them know that I came from some regiment—of which not much was left now, but which showed its temper at Carency, de Bettrau, de Lorette, etc.

"And where do you come from?"

"Bois-le-Prêtre." Oh, I change my tone. Bois-le-Prêtre—the Germans call it the Forest of Death—is about the most famous and dangerous section on all the Front, and the only place really on a par with Arras because of the heavy fighting there since last autumn. "Yes, we have been there a year now and I tell you we were glad to get off."

"On *permission?*"

"No, we just beat it. It's only twenty kilometres off. M. here is a telephonist, and we got across the Moselle bridge by pretending to be mending the line." The beer was very, very good.

"*Tiens, je connais un Américain de l'ambulance. Son nom de famille ne me revient pas, mais tout le monde l'appelle 'Villie.' C'est le type le plus charmant, le plus gentil que j'ai jamais vu*" Of course it was Willie Iselin. The long and short of it, I was taken to the house of the larger *poilu*. The prettiest girl was his wife, the other the wife of his foreman—he being a rubber manufacturer and engineer. His friend, the telephonist, who wore the regimental blue tie as though it were a silk cravat at a wedding, was in the Peugeot automobile business. Everything in the house was higgledy-piggledy; two days' unwashed dishes in the kitchen; but who cared? Cold meats were produced from somewhere, lima beans heated, much time and discussion were expended on a mayonnaise which looked splendid when finally created, but later we discovered it to be devoid of vinegar. Red wine and champagne, and then a fellow in blue jeans came in, very solemn, like a boy in *Pickwick* grown older, and explaining how he had found the house first try, sat down at the end of the table. "One of my workmen," said M. B.—"in the artillery, wounded twice, has a *Croix de Guerre*" The round-faced man remained very quiet all through dinner; but I suspected he consumed his share of the seductive white *liqueur* which I was introduced to, called Mirabelle—a great friend for trench life, but there is such a thing as pushing it too far.

They told me how from time to time they had private truces with the German sentinels, traded cigars and magazines, even had signals—three shots in the air for a change of guards—so that the other fellow should know that he must not show himself any more. "Odd, the way it works, this mobilisation of labour and recall of mechanics from the front," said the rubber manufacturer, showing me a wad of what appeared to be mattress-stuffing; "the beard I shaved this morning. They have requisitioned my shop and pay me one *franc* a day; besides, they intend to remove lathes, etc. (Not if I know it.) Now being a patron I recall my men, but I can't recall myself. Hence I remain at Bois-le-Prêtre." Finally the old man with the drooping gray moustache took me to his house, where I slept on a feather bed with a Mauser and a Bavarian casque on the wall beside me. I took coffee with the *poilus* next morning and presented each girl with a little aluminium ring.

Here I find myself in the *escadrille* of Cowdin and Prince; but for the moment they are both away, Cowdin getting another machine at Paris and Prince in the north with a *canon de* 35.

84

2

Buc, June 5, 1916

My letter from the Roosevelt at Paris on May 31 should be a big surprise for you, for that will be the first news you will receive that I have even been trying to enter the French Aviation Corps, let alone being actually in it. I had been trying through every possible source, ever since last October, and have kept it to myself and the few good friends over here who have helped me do it only because I wanted to surprise you all. Well, I'm in now and today arrived at the camp here to begin flying. That ought to take me from three to five months of good, earnest, steady work, and I'm in to "do or die." I officially entered the Aviation Corps the 22nd of May, but the papers were delayed, etc., so that I didn't even know of my success until the 29th, when the orders came to the Legion for me to leave for the Aviation depot at Dijon the next morning.

My happiness at that news I can't describe. It seemed all like a dream—too good and sudden to be true; but it was, dear mother, and my long, hard service in the Legion came to an end the next day. Another fellow from New York by the name of Chatkoff, who has been in the Legion since the start of the war, was changed at the same time and we met and have been together ever since. We stopped off at Paris, as you know from my letter, on our way to Dijon, and I saw Dave and Mrs. Wheeler and some of the others. We left for Dijon that afternoon getting there early the following morning. I would have written from there, but we were too busy. Last Saturday noon we were sent to Buc (only a short distance from Paris), and we had to go through Paris to get here, so stayed over at Truchet's hotel.

It was an Under-Secretary in the French Office of Foreign Affairs, a M. de Sillac, Dr. Gros, head of the American Ambulance, Dave, and various others who helped push me through to this. I saw Dr. Gros when I was on leave in April and he was extremely amiable, said he had heard about me, and helped me make my second demand to the Minister of War for my transfer. It needed a big effort and plenty of influence to get out of the Legion. That was our chief obstacle, but thanks to Dr. Gros and M. de Sillac, it was overcome. There are ten of us here in Buc. There are about twenty actually at the Front, with five or six others at other training-camps, so we're thirty-five in all. Lots of fellows have come in from the American Ambulance, a few from civil life, and about half are, like myself, from the Legion or the 170th Regiment.

THE BARRACKS AT BUC

    There's one mighty fine young fellow by the name of Boal from Pennsylvania and Washington, D.C., who got into the French cavalry early last year. He is, next to Dave, the best one I 've met over here of the American fighters. This is the most dangerous branch of the service, but it's the best as far as future is concerned, and if anything does happen to me, you all surely can feel better satisfied with the end than if I was sent to pieces by a shell or put out by a bullet in the infantry, where there are seventy-five out of one hundred possibilities of your never hearing of it. The glory is well worth the loss. I'd far rather die as an aviator over the enemy's lines than find a nameless shallow grave in the infantry, and I'm certain you'd all feel better satisfied too. We won't look for trouble, though.

    There's a possibility that all Americans serving here in France will get forty-eight hours off over the Fourth of July and be given a big banquet by the American Chamber of Commerce at Paris. We're looking forward to it and the American newspapers there are planning to help us get it. There ought to be a mighty big lot of us—many more than there were last year. Last year, we of the 1st Regiment got there two days too late to attend the banquet on the night of the Fourth. It will be far better planned this time, so that shouldn't occur.

A *Franc* Twenty-Five per Day

Avord, France, April 15, 1917

My application for permission to enlist in the French Foreign Legion, Aviation Section, went in on March 24. It takes several weeks for this to go through, however, and it was not until last Tuesday that Dr. Gros notified me that I had been accepted. The next day I went to a dingy recruiting office near the Invalides and was examined by the French doctors. The office reminded me very much of an old print of an ancient police station from Dickens. A dark little place with barred windows, adorned with numerous cobwebs, on each side of the main room a rough bench, and in the corner a huge old-fashioned barrel stove. The examination was not severe; none of that business of shooting off pistols unexpectedly that we used to hear was part of an aviator's preliminary examination.

There were a number of men being examined at the same time for the infantry of the Foreign Legion. We all stripped to our bare skins, negroes, Frenchmen, another American, and myself, and some gentlemen at whose nationality one could only guess. One of the latter who spoke a little English was much perturbed because he forgot and signed his real name. He had all his papers made up in an alias, and then got excited at the last minute. The officer in charge noticed the mistake, but laughed and passed it over. They are used to such things in the Legion. Of course the Aviation Division of *La Légion Étrangère* is entirely separate from the infantry so far as our seeing anything of the latter is concerned. On Thursday I went to the Invalides, enlisted, and received my orders, which were to proceed to the aviation school at Avord the following morning. This I did, arriving here Friday afternoon, and here I am.

This school is a most extremely interesting place and more enormous than anything one who had not seen it could possibly imagine. The aviation fields and hangars literally stretch for miles, and I can hardly guess how many machines there are here. I should say about six hundred. At the Curtiss school at Newport News there were about fifteen. This is the largest school in France, but there are many other very large ones scattered all over the country. Any morning or afternoon when the weather permits, the machines look like the crows flying home to roost from the marshes on the Delaware.

I started work on Saturday morning in the beginners' class. I will write you all about the various steps as I go along. At all events, it will probably be from one to two months before I get off the ground and six before I get to the Front, so there is nothing to worry about just yet. In this school a pupil is so thoroughly trained in the rudiments that by the time he is ready to fly, he is capable of doing so with the least possible danger. The French machines are beautifully made; nothing that we have so far in America can compare with them.

You would laugh to see your cute little son dressed up in the blue uniform of a French *poilu*. The government gives us everything from the skin out, and the committee for the Franco-American Flying Corps provides us with a really good uniform. I have just ordered mine from the tailor. I am going to take some pictures with my Kodak and will send them to you as soon as they are finished. We live in a barracks, about twenty men in a room, and eat in a great mess-shack. There are about three thousand men in the camp counting mechanics and quantities of Annamites. These latter act as servants, make roads, and do the dirty work generally. They come from Indo-China, and look much like Chinese. They all shellac their teeth until they are coal black which gives their faces a most extraordinary expression.

The food is wholesome enough, although extremely rough; nothing like as good as the U.S. Army gets. There are canteens where we buy things to help out; we receive two hundred *francs* a month from the Franco-American Committee for this purpose. I am therefore not exactly living in luxury, but am getting so fat and healthy you won't know me when I come home.

P.S. I enclose two notes, one for one *franc* and the other for fifty *centimes*. They are part of my first pay as a soldier of France, and I thought that you or mother might care to keep them. We get one *franc* twenty-five *centimes* per day, which is five times what the infantry gets.

Breaking the News

Paris, June 7, 1917

Please do forgive me for not writing during the past few days; now I will try and tell all that has happened....

I am waiting for my papers to come back from the French War Department, changing me from Ambulance to Aviation. Please do not be alarmed and worry. Dr. Edmund Gros, an American doctor here, an officer and medical advisor of the Field Service and Aviation, is a man who has the respect of all who know him. I respect his advice, and he is trying to help us leave and enter the Aviation. In fact, Bill Ponder, Wallie York, Cliff Thompson, Herm Whitmore, and myself have already left the Ambulance, and after our papers are returned, we shall be sent to the aviation school for at least three months, perhaps more.

I can understand that this will be a shock to all of you dear folks at home. Yet I am trying to do the best in my power and I know you will realise that I am trying to be unselfish in this time of crisis.

Please do not tell my friends of this latest act until you hear that all my papers have been returned. I am on my way to the aviation school; I shall have a man's job then, and if God lets me live through it all I shall be much more of a man than if I loafed behind the trenches without doing my share.

A Full-Fledged Frenchman

Paris, France

Dear Folks:

Well, how are you all today? I have not heard from you since the 8th of the month. I am a full-fledged Frenchman now as far as citizenship goes. How do you like your French son? You may wonder why I did not join the American service. That service is not organised here as yet, and then the French planes are so much better, and the instruction almost perfect, so it looked best. They do not permit one to go to the Front till he is an expert in every way and can perform almost any old stunt.

You cannot realise what it means to know that I am now doing the most I can do. I did not feel right in driving an ambulance.

The Flying Corps is filled with the best sons of France, and that means a lot.

How strange it will be to settle down to college life after the war. I wonder if we will get credit for what we missed this year? Ask Dr. Hinitt if he will graduate us if the war lasts over next spring.

Paris is the most beautiful place you could imagine; the pretty old gardens; the splendid buildings; the Notre Dame Cathedral with its rose-colored windows with the light effect gives one a feeling of awe.

The mystic service is over my head, but everyone has a right to worship according to his own convictions.

The kiddies here in their *chic* costumes play on the Champs Élysées and in the wonderful gardens all day. The little girls play with dolls and the boys sail boats just as all children do. The little beggars! They make me homesick at times. It makes one's heart ache to see them cling to daddy when he comes home on a six days' leave every four months. He is as happy as he can be, and goes along the street with as many holding to him as can get near him. They are a lovable bunch, these French. Six months after the war, they will have forgiven Germany for all she has done.

I must close, I hope to hear from you soon. The days go slow when there is no mail.

Getting Started

Avord, June 15, 1917

I am sitting under a tree in a hayfield outside the aviation school grounds near Avord, Cher, France, trying to keep cool, as it is a very hot, sunny day. We arrived here yesterday afternoon after several days of seemingly unnecessary delay in signing up and getting our military railroad passage from Paris, and I got very impatient to get away.

We were two full weeks in Paris, as it took several days between each of the various official steps. Finally, however, we signed up in *La Légion Étrangère*, were assigned to the Aviation Corps and sent to the school at Avord. We are enlisted for the duration of the war, but have a letter from the Minister of War guaranteeing that we shall only have to serve as aviators, and if I understand French correctly, can be released if incompetent or if we should for any reason wish to resign.

We left Paris yesterday morning at 8.35 and came down to Bourges where we had to wait two hours. Bourges is a considerable town and we had an excellent lunch there, then came on to Avord, only eighteen kilometres. We were met at the station by a large motor truck and came right out to the *École Militaire d'Aviation,* about three miles from Avord. Avord itself is a very small village. The aviation school is one of the largest in France and is beautifully laid out. There are great numbers of barracks arranged in rows—mess-houses, offices, bath-houses, etc. All the buildings are of substantial construction, with red-tile roofs, and between them are crushed rock and gravel paths, and the whole camp is clean and neat to a wonderful degree.

The aviation field is an immense flat field covered with green grass—possibly three miles long and a half-mile wide, and in several places around it there are groups of hangars containing hundreds of aeroplanes. The whole thing is on a scale much larger than I imagined, and is really very impressive. I am so glad to be here at last, training, that I can hardly contain myself. We had heard in Paris that this was a barren region, but the countryside looks delightful to me. It is much like parts of Hennepin County in its natural features, and white roads, hedges, cherry trees, and attractive little villages make it delightful.

ON LEAVE AT BOURGES
Holden, Bassett, Skinner, McKerness, Terres, Rousseau, H. Whitmore, Stanley, de Roode, Moore, Buffum, Brown, Chapman, Read

THE GATE AT AVORD

First Impressions of Avord

Avord, July, 1917

I have been sitting for the last hour or so in front of a little hotel about four miles from Camp d'Avord. All is very peaceful and seems far from war. The hotel is on the village square. In the centre is the well, to which the peasants come for water. The women are all dressed in black and wear spotless white caps. The wooden shoes one hears about really exist and are much worn, since the war has advanced the price of leather so greatly. The children are very well-mannered, the little boys always touching their hats when spoken to, and wishing you a pleasant *"Bonjour, monsieur."* The contrast between this place and Paris is very sharp. There, a certain gayety may seem to prevail. It is superficial and not supplied by the French. The saddest of all to me in Paris were the women, perhaps because they are so brave. To see the mourning in the streets, each bit of black representing the loss of some loved one, to see these same women bearing the burden cheerfully, having given all they had to the cause—the greatest struggle between right and wrong in the history of the world—makes a person feel that what he has to offer is only too little.

As for myself it's simply that I have lived some twenty-two years in peace and comfort, one reason for which is that, when the crisis came generations ago between right and wrong, some of my forebears shouldered their guns. Now—well, it's just up to me to do my bit. At last America and France stand hand in hand, and it is for us all to do our best and give our best, regardless of the cost.

Near here is a great munitions plant, and every day the shells are tested. As I sit here, the blue, cloudless sky is traced from zenith to horizon with streamers of white, resembling confetti thrown across a room, but infinitely more beautiful. It seems more like the fireworks of the Gods than the product of the brains of man for the destruction of other men.

I am much interested in the cosmopolitan character of Camp d'Avord. There are men from many countries, and for the most part representing the so-called "better classes." I wonder, when the real test comes, which will prove the better men, the soldiers of fortune who are here for various reasons, but always the underlying one of love of adventure, or the university men, who as a rule are rather unresponsive, but cool-headed, and usually come up to the scratch when the necessity arises.

EN REPOS

Avord, July 1, 1917

The whole school has had *repos* today for some reason and I have taken advantage of it by sleeping most of the day. I have gotten behind on sleep lately, and don't expect to get much next week. I have just been notified that I report tomorrow at the Blériot field, which means that I am through with the penguins, and start on the next class, using planes that will make short flights. Also it means that I shall be working both mornings and evening. A truck will pick us up here at 4.30 in the morning and take us out to the Blériot field, which is about one and one half miles from the barracks. We work there from 5 until about 9, and from 5.30 or 6 p.m. until 8.30. I have been included in a group of fifteen Americans who are going up tomorrow to the next class. Some of the boys who came here at the time I did, in fact most of them, will not go ahead for a week or two, so I conclude I have done a little better than the average, which is encouraging.

Now that there are so many of us, and also because the United States is in the war, we hear that there will be some weeding out of the Americans, and it is therefore important to do well all the time. Up to this time they have scarcely ever eliminated any Americans no matter how slowly they learned. We hear that there is a new aviation school being started somewhere in this region of France exclusively for United States army aviators, but it will not affect our completing our course here, I believe. You probably have read that a part of our regular army has landed in France. The French papers are featuring news of the American Army, and every one seems to attach a great deal of importance to the United States' entry into the war. We are coming in at a very critical time, and I hope we shall do it in such a way as to exert a decisive influence on the outcome.

I wonder if I have given you any idea of the life here. We are perfectly comfortable in every way. There are some bugs, but I am gelling used to them. The eating arrangements are inconvenient, but I get very good food by going to little inns and restaurants at various places around the country. I have some coffee and hard-boiled eggs early in the morning, and after the morning work usually go to Farges, two or two and a half miles up the road for a big breakfast—eggs, chocolate, bread, *confiture*, and cheese. After getting back at 10.30 or so, I shave, and attend the conference if there is one, take a French lesson at 12.30, and then sleep or take a walk. At about 4.30 I usually go to the *Café des Aviateurs*, about a half-mile from the camp and have a good

PENGUINS

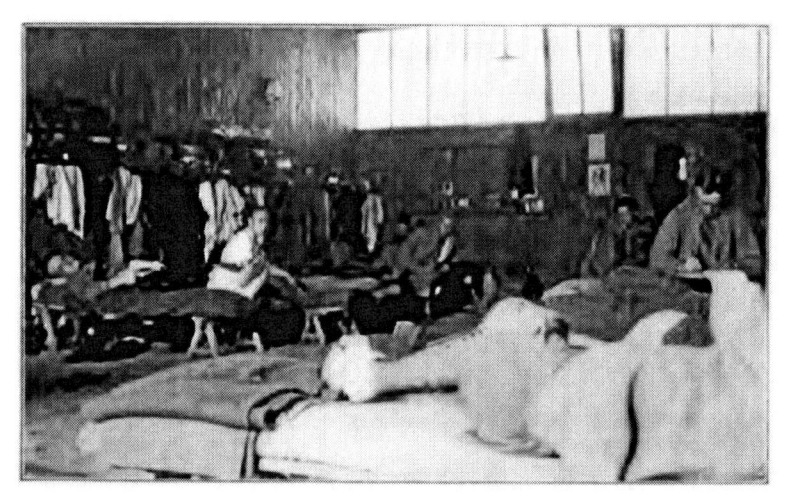

AMERICAN BARRACKS AT AVORD

dinner—soup or omelette, the eternal veal in some form, peas, potatoes or string beans, salad and cheese or *confiture* and coffee. At 9.30 we usually have a bit of something at the camp canteen. Eating takes a lot of time in France, as it is impossible to get more than one dish at a time, with long waits between courses.

Also everything is quite expensive. We have a washroom with running water in our barracks and there is a bath-house with hot showers a few steps away. The barracks are electric lighted, and as I brought my own blankets and a canvas cot down from Paris I am very comfortable. I wear, most of the time, a light khaki uniform I got in Paris, sometimes the complete leather suit furnished us here, or corduroy breeches and puttees with a leather coat. I hope to have an opportunity soon to get a good little camera so that I can send you snapshots of the place and the people. The servants around the barracks are Annamites from a French colony (somewhere south of China, I think). One of them entertained us with Oriental songs and dancing yesterday. Some of the boys are teaching him English. His vocabulary is that of a sailor's parrot, and he doesn't understand at all what the words mean, so he comes in the morning and greets us with terrific and insulting expressions in English with the most amiable smile.

THE FOURTH OF JULY IN PARIS

Paris, July 8, 1917

Landing in Bordeaux at about 7 a.m. July 1, we found we had three hours to spare before our Paris train left. Curtis and I, with two Harvard boys, hired a one-horse cab, and drove about the city. The thing that impressed me most was the women. On every street they outnumbered the men, and nearly all were dressed in black. (I think this depressing colour of mourning should be abolished.) Women were driving taxis, carts, and all the street cars. I wanted to take my hat off to every one of them.

Then there were the men. The few in sight were old and gray, or young, on crutches, with arms in slings, legs gone, or heads bandaged. Bordeaux is a city of beautiful parks and buildings, but a city with a broken heart, a city of sadness, yet, as I have noticed everywhere, a city with the nationally unbroken spirit of France.

The long ride from Bordeaux to Paris was lovely. We went on the state railroad through Poitiers and Orléans. Our ride was through beautiful valleys and plains. But everywhere were crops, crops, crops. Except in the woods I cannot remember a square foot of land that was not growing food. The concentration of the farming was tremendous. And in the fields, just as on our train, it was the women who were doing the work.

I came to Paris. I have never been here before. I have spent all my spare time strolling about the streets, watching the people, and going to the few places of interest still open. Paris is a city of women and officers. Every other person is in the blue of the French or the khaki of the other nations—English, Russian, Belgian, American! And that brings me to that epoch-making *fête*, the celebration of the Fourth of July in Paris.

The American troops were to march through Paris! This was heralded by newspapers and posters all over the city for days before. At 8 a.m. about two thousand of the American troops began their parade. I awaited them in the Place de la Concorde. What a sight! I felt like crying! Marching to music they went on up the rue de Rivoli to the Hôtel de Ville. The streets were packed with people. The ranks were broken up by the crowds. I never saw such a demonstration. Everywhere were American flags. Everybody was yelling, jumping, and shouting, all through the three hours' parade. French *poilus* burst into the lines and took our boys by the arms, marching and singing with them. Women did the same, and all the women were weeping.

Then they came to the Hôtel de Ville and the "Star-Spangled Banner" was played. Every Frenchman, Englishman, Belgian, and American bared his head and silently stood at attention. The music stopped and for a few moments there was silence; then the crowds burst again into a tremendous cheer, and the parade went on to the tomb of Lafayette. Paris was wild, frantic. I never saw anything like it. They are crazy over the Americans. "*Vive l'Amerique!*" seems to be still buzzing in my ears. I can't begin to describe the wonderful effect our declaration of war has on the French. It has given them new courage. We came in at the psychological moment. France weeps for happiness; cheers for joy; rekindles her spirit and cries "*Vive l'Amerique!*"

I left the parade at the Hôtel de Ville. I was too weak, too trembling, and too full of emotion to go any farther. My last impression was the picture of General Pershing, riding through the frantic mob, with his hand at a constant salute. I do not think he took his hand down once through the whole three hours' procession except when he spoke and when the flag was dedicated. I was going to enclose a newspaper with the whole talc, but the maid has thrown it away.

And now as to us. We reported to Dr. Gros and had our papers

THE ANNAMITE WRECKING-GANG

sent in to the proper officials. We shall have to wait here in Paris about five more days for these papers to go through. Then we go to Avord, the largest aviation school in the world. There are seventy Americans out there now, about thirty Russians and several hundred Frenchmen. We shall be there approximately five months; then go to Pau for two weeks, and then, if we have proved efficient, we shall go to the Front. I can hardly wait to get there.

Explaining to the Family

Avord, July 12, 1917

I am now in a French aviation school and learning how to imitate the birds. The work is tremendously interesting. The school covers over forty square miles and is, as you can see, a huge affair. There are about 800 or 900 aeroplanes and nearly 2000 student pilots. About seven different nationalities are represented among them, principally French, Russians, and Americans. We spend three months here and then go to a place where we are taught acrobatics, such as looping the loop and the *vrille.*

After two weeks of acrobacy we go to a place near Paris, where we practice with machine guns. The *mitrailleuse* is fastened in front of the pilot and is geared so as to fire through the propeller as it revolves. To aim it you must steer the whole machine, so you need quite a bit of practice before going to the Front. The whole training lasts about five months.

The school here is divided into five classes. The first, which I am in now, is the penguin class. The penguins are Blériot monoplanes with clipped wings and three-cylinder engines. We spend a month on these, trying to drive them up and down the field in a straight line. It looks easy. Everyone laughs at the others, as the penguin will invariably turn in a circle if you are not watching. A sudden gust of wind or a bump on the ground is enough to start it going around. After the penguins we are graduated to the roller class. Here we regular Blériot machines which go over the ground at fifty miles an hour. We have to drive these along the ground (without rising) in a straight line. This is very difficult, because if you get the tail too high, the nose will stick into the ground and you will turn over; if you get the tail down, the machine will rise off the ground and the ending will probably be disastrous, as you have as yet had no practice in landing. It is exciting work and is principally for the purpose of getting one used to the controls and to give confidence and a delicate touch.

A Penguin

The Décollé Class

Learning to imitate the birds

There are 150 Americans here training for the French Army. There is a rumour that next week our army, in the person of General Pershing, to make us an offer to come into the American aviation. I do not think that many will accept, as we all feel that as France has trained us we ought to help the French Army. If we can finish our training here and can then go over to the Americans, I will do it, but not otherwise, as I wish the French training. There is going to be great activity in the air next year. Both the Allies and Germany are building thousands of planes. The future will witness air battles that were not dreamed of two years ago, for I have been at the Front enough to know that the war is going to be won in the air.

Around the school the air is buzzing continually like a giant beehive; there are at least thirty machines in the air at all times. You cannot imagine the speed with which the Nieuports land until you stand and watch them rush by you. It is almost incredible. There are few accidents, considering the number of flights made, although three were killed and one wounded in the last five days. Those killed, however, were themselves to blame, as they were inattentive. Two men in a big observation machine went up in the morning in a fog and ran into a low hill near the camp because they were not watching their altitude. A Russian had his leg broken in landing because he came down too straight.

Five or six of the boys from our section of the Ambulance are coming down next week. Life here is not as pleasant as it was in the Ambulance, as we are under military law and cannot leave the cantonment.

A Fledgling Birdman

Avord, July 15, 1917

You don't get really enthused over aviation until you have been up. You see right away that I have been. It was last night, and it took two weeks to get the chance. The *moniteurs* have many students to take up who are in Nieuport training, and to take up a student outside your class is not according to rules. This *moniteur* is a corker and asked me to go out Monday. So I took my helmet and goggles and went to the Nieuport field to wait until half-past eight. He finally motioned to me and I crawled into the seat behind him, buckled myself in, and called, "Ready." First he skimmed along the ground, then we left it. Gee, but it was fine! We soared over the penguin field and I tried to wave; the wind was so strong that it was like waving under water. He got to the height of 150 metres, then took his hands off" the "broomstick," and all to show me how the machine could run itself. It was very thrilling, though not as scary as looking down from a tall building. You actually feel safe enough to walk out on a wing.

Really you cannot half appreciate the French country until you have flown over it: the woods, the small, different coloured fields, the red-roofed houses, the white roads; it's wonderful, that's all. Once above Farges he did a vertical bank; it was like lying down on your side and watching the ground move slowly beneath your machine. Then he straightened up again; over Savigny he did two spirals, first to the left, then straightened and spiralled to the right. A spiral is like a vertical bank, only you turn round and round toward the ground. At last we got back to the sheds and he cut his motor, and then *piqued* down. When you are in the air you don't seem as if you are going very fast, though when you land you are going 120 kilometres an hour. Now I am more anxious than ever to fly by myself.

Those in my room are Benoit, Shipley, Ash, Sinclair, Bill Rodgers (who was at Culver the summer I was), Bullard, McMillen, Bassett, Holden, Wallie Winters, Herm. Whitmore, Doc Read, George Dock, Boujassy (the French *moniteur* who took me up last night), Lewis, McKerness, Brown, Larry Dowd, Saxon, and Potter: a great bunch!

Barrack Life

Avord, July 22, 1917

We are all sitting out under the pine trees this warm Sunday afternoon. The other fellows sitting here writing are Whitmore and Eldridge from Dartmouth, and Eaton from Harvard. Just asked the latter if he had a brother in my class, and sure enough it was the same, a fellow I knew very well. So we held the customary half-hour conference thinking up mutual acquaintances.

There is a fine crew in this school, men from all colleges and men who don't know the name of a college. For instance, there are about half a dozen from Harvard, as many from Yale, some from Dartmouth, a few from Amherst, Williams, etc. We have a couple of ex-All-American football stars, a coloured boxer, an Australian-American, a Vanderbilt-cup racing driver, men sticky with money in the same barracks with others who worked their way over on ships. This democracy is a fine thing in the army and makes better men of all hands. For instance, the corporal of our room is an American, as black as the ace of spades, but a mighty white fellow at that. The next two bunks to his are oc-

AMERICANS AT AVORD, MARCH, 1917

Standing: Rounds, Doané, Molter, Wilcox, Pollock, Alen, Hager, J. N. Hall, McCall, Turnure, Carter, Doian, Chadwick
Kneeling and sitting: Pelton, Rheno, Wells, Stoddia, G. M'Slee, Baer, Krisonet, P. Wilson, Seanlon, J. R. Adams

cupied by Princeton men of old Southern families. They talk more like a darky than he does and are the best of friends with him. After all it is the "Southerner" from New Jersey and Delaware, who jumps on a chair and shouts when "Dixie" is played, who raises the loudest cry against the negro. This black brother has been in the Foreign Legion, wounded four times, covered with medals for his bravery in the trenches, and now uses his experiences and knowledge of French for the benefit of our room—Result: the inspecting lieutenant said we had the best-looking room in the barrack.

A number of men here have been in the Ambulance Service. Four in fact, Willard, Brown, Collins, and Harrison, came over on the same boat with me. One fellow, Forster, was in my troop of Squadron A. In Parris I met two more from my troop, one in the Ambulance and the other, Henderson, in the French artillery school; he was also in Alsace at the time I was there.

Think I closed my last letter by saying that this camp is the biggest known. Impossible to give a suggestion of its size or of the number of machines contained in the rows of hangars. Each night and morning the air is alive with humming *avions*, a flock of birds circling around the fields. It is also an orderly, spotless, and beautiful place. Concrete is so artistically employed that even the enormous new water-towers and hangars blend into the scheme. The streets of crushed rock, the red-tiled, even rows of houses, the trees, flowers, and hedges, make it a liveable place. There is an outdoor gymnasium and plenty of baseball equipment.

Young soldiers of the class of 1918 do the mechanical work, while the cleaning up and digging is left to Arabs and Indo-Chinese (Annamites). Each of our rooms has an Annamite valet who sweeps the floor and brings our coffee in the morning. We have only to keep our bunks in shape and our clothes neatly folded.

Since I have been advanced a class, the working day is changed a bit, and fortunately we no longer have to walk to the field. An ex-Paris autobus leaves the yard at 4.30 a.m. crammed full of us: Russians, French, and Americans, taking us to the Blériot field. Then the classes start and work until about 8.30. Oh! I almost forgot the breakfast. As there is a role against flying on (or, better, with) an empty stomach, they apportion a slice of bread and a little piece of cheese to each. After class all hands hop the bus back to camp, unless affluent, when they walk back by way of a restaurant where a real breakfast of omelet, jam, and coffee may be had. As it is a continual surprise to a good country

AMERICANS AND RUSSIANS AT AVORD CAUDRON DIVISION

woman to see anyone eat a real breakfast, we usually wait while the good *dame* builds the kitchen fire, robs the hens' nests, accompanying her manoeuvres with the cure-all for impatience: "*Une petite minute, messieurs.*"

Back at camp once more we rest a bit or attempt a bath in the tricky shower, if there is not an army ahead of us. After that there is nothing to do until 10.15 when first mess is served. If a breakfast has been found, the mess ceremony is postponed until the second serving at noon. At 11.15 we line up for roll-call and go through a brief drill of fifteen minutes. We used to remain for the reading of the orders of the day in French, but as there are few who understand, this has been discontinued.

Then we read, write, or sleep until 3 p.m. Appeals for silence are made in the Billingsgate of two languages. They have been fairly successful so that now only one harmonica remains. At a quarter to five evening mess, followed by another bus ride to the field, where the morning process is repeated as long as there is daylight. Upon returning there is a 9.45 supper; bread and jam for those who are hungry. At 10.20 all lights go out, and any candle left burning when the electricity is off calls forth cries of "Shoes! Shoes!"—the articles themselves and darkness.

Experiments

Avord, July 18, 1917

I have had nine *tours de piste* and have flown at 100 metres (300 feet) around the field. Naturally this included *virages*, or turns in the air, which were all new to me, and *atterissages*, or landings, from a height of 100 metres. Never will I forget my first *tour de piste*. On account of its being the first, I was a bit nervous. It was a memorable ride.

Owing to the fact that many machines of different classes are continually rising and flying above the Blériot *piste*, each class has its allotted route and these are supposed to be followed to the letter. Were this not the rule, collisions might easily result.

I started out beautifully, rising gradually in *ligne de vol* and coming to the turning-spot, beyond a line of trees and above two large haystacks, tried my first *virage*. This was started by pushing slightly on my left foot with the *manche à balai* dead centre. The left wing starts down and you begin to turn. But it's a queer sensation as your machine tilts. You are supposed to lean with your *virage*; when you see your wings go down, you ease instinctively to the high side. Then you remember instructions and lean down to the low side—it's really more comfortable that way, but hard to get used to, for at first you feel as though you were about to fall out. I made my turn finally, but in doing so lost considerable height. I had been told to *pique* a bit in the turns, and I *piqued* too much, so that when I came to the edge of the woods I was not very high above the trees. Then I got lost and sailed right over the field of another class; over a line of trees and off toward the village of Avord. In due time I managed another turn, located my *piste* (in the dim distance), and started back, still too low. Another row of trees was skimmed over and the field of another class trespassed upon before I landed at my starting-point.

When I got out the *moniteur* said, "What did you do?"—making a wry face. I responded most truthfully, "God only knows." However, I could see he was amused. I guess he sees many such first trips. He did not blame me at all and after another man had gone around, put me at it again.

It's surprising how much that first *sortie* taught me. My next two were all right. I got good height and did better *virages* and violated the sanctity of no classes. On the last one I struck a bump and received an awful jolt, which to say the least startled me considerably.

A Blériot Pilot

Avord, August 23, 1917

Things are so unsettled here now that no one knows when he is going or what he is going to do. Fifty of the boys have been sent off to other schools in France to finish their training and we are likely to leave at any moment. The American Air Service is very active in France now, and is taking over camp after camp as rapidly as they are filled up with men from the States. There seems to be no doubt now that we shall be commissioned by the American Army as first lieutenants.

I am now a Blériot pilot, as I finished the school this morning, after doing the banks, *virages*, left and right *piques*, spirals, and serpentines. For the last two I had to rise 2700 feet into the air. It was very bumpy and rough, and the light monoplane tipped and jumped in every direction. You become used to it, however, just as you do to a boat rocking. When 2700 feet were reached, I shut off the motor and spiralled down to the field again. You must go up high because every turn of the spiral loses over 600 feet of altitude, and you must come out of the spiral with enough height to head into the wind and pique to your field.

OFF FOR AN ALTITUDE

There were quite a few accidents here this week. The commandant was killed in a collision yesterday. He was flying a Caudron machine when a Nieuport, piloted by one of the pupils, tore into him and knocked a wing off his machine. He fell to the ground and was killed. It was not the pilot's fault. The Nieuport man had his wing loose, but made a wonderful landing with his wing crooked and the Caudron wing hanging on to his machine.

I had a couple of exciting times myself on the Blériot. I was banking around a turn and going up a little when my engine stopped without the slightest warning. I had to point her down at once and straighten out, and finally landed safely in the middle of a field in a forest. When the engine stops, you cannot always find a place to land, and sometimes you come to grief in a forest with no fields.

You feel no fear in an airplane after you become used to it, and are perfectly at home whether you are upside down or standing on your head. Last night we were waiting for calm weather when a motorcycle with a side car drove up with two American soldiers. One wore the aviation wings on his costume, and when he stopped we found him to be Quentin Roosevelt,[1] who is supply officer at an American aviation camp near by. None of the American camps are doing any flying yet, but are getting ready rapidly.

1. *Eagles Rampant Rising* a double edition *The Way of the Eagle* by Charles J. Biddle & *Quentin Roosevelt a Sketch With Letters* by Quentin Roosevelt, (edited by Kermit Roosevelt), is also published by Leonaur.

A Brevet Flight

Vierzon, October 16, 1915

I have time to write only a few lines, for I am having the greatest time of my life. I acted foolishly yesterday, but had more or less luck. I left Camp d'Avord at 2.30 o'clock for Châteauroux. It was cloudy, but the clouds were 800 metres high, so I started out at 600 metres, and had gone for only ten minutes when I ran into clouds at 300 metres, so I went still higher above them all, and flew by my compass and watch. When I thought I was near Châteauroux, I shot down through the clouds, and sure enough, I was there. I landed, and found one of the other fellows who had broken his machine on descending. He wanted me to stay there because it was too foggy to continue, but I said that I had found Châteauroux, and it was still easier to find Romorantin, so I started out again.

I soon ran into a heavy fog and also a little wind, so I was completely lost. For two hours I hunted for Romorantin, but could not see a damned thing. Finally I descended and found that I was within fifteen kilometres of Romorantin. It was nearly night, but I figured I could arrive there in ten minutes, and started out again. I could not see a thing, and passed a little to the right of Romorantin without seeing it, so I was lost again. I flew for a half-hour in the night and fog. I knew I was nearly out of oil and *essence*, so when I saw the lights of this town, I headed for it.

I made three turns above the town, just over the houses, trying to find a place to land, and hoping some one would have sense enough to signal to me or put out a light, but nothing happened, so finally I trusted to luck and shot down. I made a perfect landing without breaking a thing, something that would not happen one time out of a hundred under similar conditions. Well, to end up, every one in the town heard my motor and turned out to see me. Today has been foggy, so I have stayed here, and am to leave tomorrow. I asked a guard for the machine and also oil and *essence*, and a cover for the motor, so now I can rest *tranquille*, and I have the pick of the town for everything I want.

I am followed by two or three hundred people everywhere I go. My machine is covered with flowers, and the names of girls. People meet me in the street with bouquets, and in all I am *bien content*. I have not gotten drunk yet, but it is not the fault of the inhabitants, as they bring out the choicest wines from their *caves*.

A Run of Bad Luck

Château Indre, August 6, 1916

While I was still an *élève* at Buc I started a long letter wherein I undertook to relate, in detail and exact chronological succession, the vicissitudes of my *brevet* voyages, now happily accomplished. I doubt if that letter will ever reach you, for I mislaid it during my visit with *mère* and the kiddies, which followed hard upon the heels of the long-coveted *brevet*. I have not the courage to recommence the spinning of that Homeric yarn of my aerial "misconflips," because the subject is painful.

I know of but one other airman who ever had so much ill fortune; and he threw up the sponge and went back to the infantry in disgust. To begin with, the weather was rotten throughout my trips. On the first, I was caught in clouds and rain, lost my way just as night was falling, and was forced to come to earth and spend the night at a town called Dreux, fifty miles from home. The rest of the time low-hanging clouds obliged me to wing my way at altitudes ranging between 100 and 500 metres, very dangerous work in the neighbourhood of large villages or woods. Besides, the motors I had to deal with were the last word in rottenness. Three times I was brought down in a hurry with motor trouble, and twice out of the three times I had to land on bad ground, and smashed. In the first of these accidents I lit in a wheat-

ENTRANCE TO THE SCHOOL AT TOURS

field; my machine turned over on its back, a head-first somersault, and left me hanging, doubled like an old shirt on a clothes-line, over my belt. The accident was a classic one, known to all French pilots as *le capotage*. It is not dangerous to the pilot, as I was able to observe at first hand.

In my second accident I had just left the airdrome at Chartres when my motor went on strike. I hit the ground crab-fashion, smashed my landing chassis to flinders, stood the machine on its nose, and, my belt having snapped like a thread from the shock, was hurled against the upper plane and received a horrible black eye and an inconsequential cut (which bled like the devil), as souvenirs of a lucky escape.

My third accident deserves a paragraph all to itself. It happened, like the preceding mishap, just as I was leaving Chartres. An intake valve in the motor, after opening, refused to close. At once there commenced a succession of back-fires to the carburettor which at any moment might have spread to the gasoline and sent the whole machine up in smoke. The accompanying explosions sounded like an artillery battery going into action. The motor, of course, all but stopped turning, and my *zinc* began to lose height at once.

Luckily I was able to make an impeccable landing in a ploughed field, a field that was screened by woods from the eyes of a scared crowd, watching my hurried descent from the Chartres *piste*. Having escaped both a fire and a smash-up, I felt pleased with myself, and, climbing down from my perch, I got out of my flying clothes and goggles, and was just lighting a pipe—that old English one you used to smoke before you bequeathed it to me—when I heard a shout, and looked up from the lighted match to behold a gray army ambulance tooting down the road hell-bent-for-election. The ambulance drew up beside my ploughed field and let down the chief pilot from Chartres, the chief surgeon, a couple of stretcher-bearers, and some mechanicians to boot. They had their entire first-aid kit with them and were intent on bearing away my shattered remnants. But my shattered remnants just leaned carelessly against my unharmed Caudron, puffing the old pipe contented-like.

It was a rich situation, but the ambulance crew were too relieved to find me still able to grin to care a hang whether the laugh was on them or not. When the ambulance rolled back to the aerodrome a crowd had gathered to watch the corpse on the stretcher borne away to the morgue. They were flabbergasted when, resurrected from the tomb, I jumped over the tailpiece of the car. One lieutenant in particular, who had spent most of his life in New York, came up and looked me over incredulously from head to foot, then, quite solemnly, shook hands with me and congratulated me in good "American." Next day I received a brand-new motor from Buc and flew home against a head wind that delayed me to such an extent that I had to land by the light of bonfires on the *piste*.

Thanks to the new motor, which my final adventure at Chartres procured me, I was able to complete my last triangle—Buc-Chartres-Evreux-Buc—on good time. As my wheels touched the ground at the end of that trip, I heaved a great sigh, an exclamation of profound thanksgiving, and told myself, "Breveted at last!" That afternoon the camp tailor sewed the red and silver wings on my collar.

A Blériot Brevet
Avord, June 23, 1917

A long time since I have written you, almost three weeks I am afraid. Much has happened since then. I have become a breveted pilot in the French Army, have been promoted to corporal, and retained here as *moniteur* (instructor) of the Americans in the Blériot school. I have been to Paris for two days on *permission*, where I did almost nothing but run errands for the other Americans here.

My *brevet* test came quicker than I had expected. I went through the last class very quickly, though it is the hardest of all. There you are taught to make various curves on descending, in order to be able to land on a chosen field from any height without the aid of your motor. This is a very difficult thing to do, as the field from 3400 feet appears as small as your backyard, and in dropping by means of spirals and curves you can easily get so far away that you will fail to hit it, especially if there is a wind. This might be a dangerous situation if your motor should fail. One might be compelled to land in a wood, in a cornfield, or in a pond, at the last minute.

The last thing to be done in this class is an official spiral from 2800 feet without motor, landing in a 200-foot circle. You take a registering height indicator up with you to prove that you don't put on your motor after you start your *pique* (dive). In my trial spirals I leaned my machine so much that I turned very fast and got dizzy. The earth seemed to rotate under me, as I was pointed down very steeply while spiralling. In my official test, however, I had less trouble, as I knew what to expect and kept the machine from diving too much. I landed perfectly. The next morning I made the two short trips, one after the other; going and coming, thirty-five miles; about forty minutes in the air. You simply go to a neighbouring village and get a paper signed. Nothing difficult except the landing at the other end, where the field is quite small.

That night the weather was stormy, so I didn't start on my triangle till the following morning. Left at 5.30 a.m. and arrived at my first stopping-point at 7.30, a trip of forty-five miles. I travelled at 4000 feet to be safe, as that gives you plenty of time to pick a landing-place if your motor goes bad. At this height I could see for thirty miles, until the slight mist dimmed the horizon. The earth looked like a doll's country. Houses are squat, fields like children's playgrounds, and everything has a cleaned and tidied-up appearance, just like a museum model of a stretch of country. Tiny horses and cows ornament the farms, tiny motors are along the roads, and everything looks flat, as hills and valleys are indistinguishable. This part is very bothersome in case of a forced landing, as you may pick out what looks like an excellent field and on descending find it a swamp, or full of holes, or a steep hill. Then, if you have no motor, you must trust to luck. As I said before, the ground is the aviator's only worry; in the air he is comparatively safe.

Flying along, I steer partly by my compass and partly by my map, which I unfold on its rollers, checking up as towns loom up in front, or as villages, rivers and roads (the latter are difficult to distinguish because there are so many), and forests pass below. Sometimes one is not sure whether a village is this one or that, and you look anxiously for other marks. However, I had no trouble, though many lose themselves completely, especially if there is a side wind, which, if you do not pay attention, will in a few minutes blow you off your course. Some of our Americans have come down many miles from their destination, completely bewildered as to locality.

I enjoyed the scenery to the utmost. The sound of the motor, a never-ending roar, lulls one into a hypnotic repose, until a shift in position warns you that you aren't paying attention, and you look up to see that your nose is pointing down a little, dangerous because your motor at once attains excessive speed. One flies with one's eye continually on the revolution counter and map, with an occasional glance at compass, altimetre, and *essence* or oil gauges. The Blériot carries no speed indicator. It is funny the difference one sees in villages. Some are picturesque, with red roofs among the trees and avenues and buildings spotlessly laid out.

Others belch smoke amid melancholy masses of slate and brick,

The fields of France

and look most forlorn, blots on the countryside. The forests are huge masses of green, of all sorts of irregular shapes, sometimes traversed by a narrow, white strip representing a road, but looking like a whitewashed walk across the green of a golf course. One sees also the aviator's friends, the rivers, best of all landmarks, silvery streaks winding away into infinity, dotted with villages, crossed by bridges, paralleled here in France by canals. Truly one never realises what a garden this earth is until one can rise into the air, where all blends into a mass of green and gold, checker-boarded into little plots or irregularly splotched by forest and village, each field and each town having its own distinctive colour, but each blending into the whole.

About midway of my trip I began to search for the first landing-place, near Romorantin. I found it at last, a little more to the right than I expected, with the field very visible because of a large circle of whitewashed stones. Cutting my motor, I started to drop, and made a *tour* at 600 feet to accustom my eyes and ears to that altitude before landing. I left at 9.30, after my tanks had been filled. The air had now become very warm and was rough, crazily whirling, lifting and dropping, with gusts viciously colliding, a mad mixture of forces. My machine was seized and turned sideways; then, as though tossed by a giant who had instantly changed his mind, it was dropped into a hole, perhaps 100 feet deep. Gusts strike you in front, sideways, behind; up you go over a mountainous wave; then down, falling over the other side. So it goes, gently easing each bump with the controls, sideways, forwards or backwards, with a delicate touch that comes by instinct.

As you climb, however, and get away from the heating effect of the earth, this tumultuous sea gradually calms, until at 3000 feet you can almost let go the "joy stick," and settle back in your seat, giving only an occasional touch with your feet to keep you in your course. I flew at 5100 feet, where the air was calm. My second stop was at another large aviation school, near a city, easily visible from afar. I got some fearful blows on descending, so decided to wait here until evening. Went into town, had a good lunch, slept, and left at 7.30 p.m. The return was perfect in the cool evening, not a jolt anywhere. My home aerodrome was visible fifty miles away, the white buildings of the camp standing out against the dark background.

The next morning was bad, but in the evening I made my height test, mounting to 8200 feet. I went up in a sweater and ordinary clothes, and nearly froze. I was barely able to last out the necessary hour. It was extremely tiresome circling round and round over the country,

Le Camp d'Avord

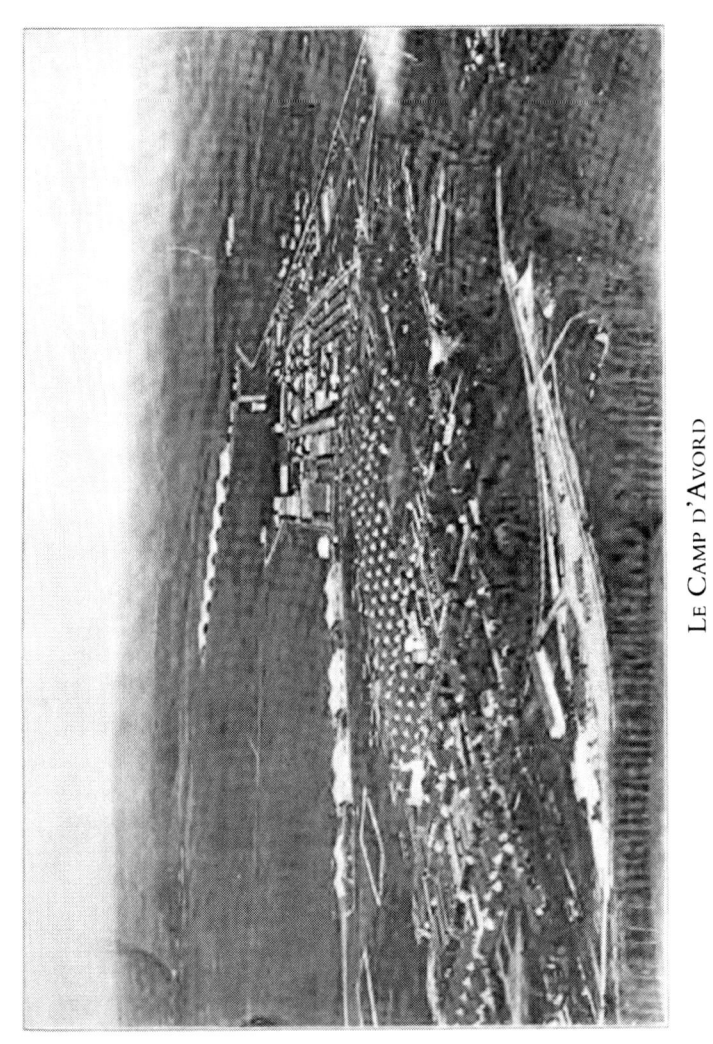

dodging the clouds which loomed up in front of me like enormous white mountains. It was with heartfelt relief that I saw my recording altimetre register an hour above 6800 feet. I went down so fast that I was very deaf and was chilled through for a long time afterward.

The next morning was misty, but at 9.30 I set out at 3100 feet. I could just see the ground below, but ahead it was only a white fog. I flew by compass, checking my position as rivers and villages passed below. At the first landing-place I had the tanks filled and decided to start out again, though the mist had got thicker. The two Frenchmen doing their *brevet* at the same time wouldn't leave me. I was compelled to fly at 2000 feet, as I couldn't see from a higher point, but finally the clouds compelled me to descend to 680 feet. I was following a road which stretched out ahead, a white, thin strip in the fog. But finally it ended in a town and I couldn't see the river that I had to follow from there on. As flying at 200 feet is too dangerous in case of motor trouble, I decided to come down near the town. I circled around, found a field and lost it again in the fog, but finally landed safely. Went into the town to telephone my position and then returned to watch my machine, taking lunch at a farmhouse, a typical one of the French style, plaster house and barns around a large court, in which are grouped the manure pile, pig-pen, and well. One wonders why all French farmers don't die of typhoid; but of course water as a beverage is unknown here. The peasants were of very low intelligence and spoke bad French, hardly understandable.

It was Sunday. On that day in this country the peasants put on their best clothes and go out in the fields. So, naturally, I had the whole town out to see me: girls, boys, women, and old men. All the women in the crowd of several hundred were in black. I was quite the hero, but tried to appear unconscious of the fact; rather difficult, as I was the object of many inviting glances from the French maidens. The weather at 6 p.m. had slightly cleared, but I decided to leave, as it was only a twenty-minute ride from my second stopping-point and I didn't want to pass the night at the village. So off I went, having secured the services of two boys of seventeen to start my motor. I went through all the movements and let them practice first, because the roar and violent wind of the propeller often frighten them into falling and make those who are holding your machine while you try out the engine let go in terror.

On leaving, I flew at 1500 feet and had a good trip except for the last five minutes. At this stage I was obliged to *pique* underneath a large, black cloud which was at 700 feet, and there I struck a violent windstorm just over my landing-field. I thought twice that I should be overturned and was rather frightened, but managed to pull out.

Stayed there overnight and didn't leave until the following evening because of the fog. Had a good bed in the hotel and two good meals, but arrived home with ten cents to my name and had to borrow in order to take advantage of the two days' *permission* allowed me at Paris. Maybe I wasn't relieved when I made my last landing at Avord, which made me an official pilot in the French Army. To think that it was all over and I could at last put the coveted wings on my collar! A *brevet* on a Blériot is something to be proud of, as I have told you. You are far more of an aviator than if you had learned on any other machine.

★★★★★★

I just learned an hour ago that Hall, of whom I have often spoken, who had the bed next to mine for two months, has been brought down by the Boches. He was only at the Front eight days. Ordinarily, the new pilot at the Front is kept back for a month to learn from the others, but Hall was just the kind to dash to the battle line at once. He was a fine fellow, the first American from Avord to lose his life.

Avord, June 30, 1917

As usual this letter is being written in snatches. Have since learned that Hall was not killed, but was badly wounded and may live. He was attacked by five Boches at once and was shot through the foot and through the lung.

I started my Nieuport training this morning. I think that it will go all right.

I arrived in Paris the evening after General Pershing. He had a wonderful ovation; huge crowds lined the route of his automobile, and the Place de la Concorde was crowded in front of his hotel. A crowd stayed there for several days, watching American officers go in and out and cheering. Pershing was rather overwhelmed. You people at home don't realise what your help means to the French, and what a wonderful stimulus our entrance gave toward raising the sinking hopes of the people here. You can't hurry your preparation too much. The need is greater than you can imagine. I wonder if you at home—I don't mean you, but I mean Americans as a mass—realise what you are in for. What do you suppose would happen to you if Russia should back out? Are you really ready, do you think, to back the Allies to your last man and your last dollar?

THE OTHER SIDE OF LIFE AT AVORD

IN THE BUC RESERVOIR

A Crash on Brevet

June 26, 1917

Am in Paris for only forty-eight hours. Have received my *brevet* and am happy to be able to wear wings on my coat. They look pretty sporty. I had a funny experience winning it, though; also a smash-up, the first I have had. I started out on my triangle to three villages, a total of about 150 miles. I got up as high as 3500 metres; that, of course, would not be considered much in a Nieuport or Spad. Well, I got lost, and after flying for over three hours I came down in a quaint little village called Le Châtre. I asked some peasants, who came running from every direction, the way to Châteauroux, my destination.

An aeroplane was quite a novelty to them, I'm sure. As I was anxious to be off, I asked one of them to crank the propeller and another to hold the tail. The old fellow turned the propeller, but it backfired, and dashed into them, breaking the machine all to pieces. The peasants came running toward me, thinking I was killed; but I was only bruised a bit. They were rather surprised to see me smiling. After that they couldn't do enough for me. I then telephoned to Avord and told them what had happened; they told me to wait, that they would send some one to me. I was there for three days, being entertained royally. A large bouquet of flowers was presented to me by a delegation of young girls from the village. The day after my arrival I was surprised by a telephone message from Biddle. He, also, had got lost and had landed just about a mile from me. He had received the information that another American had landed not far away and so had called up. He, however, had only broken a wheel. We were together for the rest of the time until help arrived. He went back in his machine and I in the train. The next day I went out again and finished. They didn't say a word about my break; just said they were glad I was not hurt. I am off for Pau in a few days

"He said my French was very good, but—"

Yesterday I ran out of gasoline when fifty miles south of Tours. I was over the River Loire when it happened, but immediately nosed the machine down, thus getting a lot of speed, and shot for a field on the left-hand bank of the river. It appeared, from four hundred metres up, an admirable place to land, but on coming closer I saw a barbed-wire fence right through the middle of it. I probably could have landed without injury to myself, but the machine would have been wrecked. I saw another field near at hand, which was separated

THE FIRST DEPART ON ROULEUR

from my first choice by a hedge. Having practiced jumping with my machine once or twice before, I thought, "Here is my chance." I made a perfect jump, just skimming over the hedge, and made a landing without breaking even a wire. When the machine stopped rolling after landing, I was within a yard of a big walnut tree.

The people from the town came rushing down, expecting to see me all smashed up. They said I was the first aviator ever to land there, and consequently the machine and I were the victims of much curious inspection. The mayor came up and shook hands and asked me to come to his house. I told him I would first have to telephone the school and report what had happened. To do this I had to go to the city of Saumur, which was about six kilometres from Parnay, the town where I landed, and ask permission from the *sous-préfecture*. He called in the military commandant and I explained to him, in the best French I knew, just what I wanted. Much to my surprise, he answered me in perfect English. He said my French was very good, but thought I would feel more at home speaking English. I then telephoned in and reported. The commandant of the school said since nothing was broken he would send out a *moniteur* to bring back the machine. The military commandant said I need not worry about the machine, as he would send out four soldiers to guard it. He then offered me his machine to go back, but it was only a short distance and I needed the exercise, so I declined the offer.

The soldiers were there when I got back, with a perfect swarm of men, women and children. Some had come from miles away to see what an aeroplane looked like at close range. Soon after the commandant drove up to see if his men were on the job. We went up to the mayor's house and were treated to some of the best wine I ever expect to drink. We talked for half an hour about places the commandant had visited in the States. We also arranged where I should stay that night if the *moniteur* failed to arrive. The commandant had asked me to stay with him, but thinking it would be best to be near the machine, I accepted the mayor's invitation instead. Just as we had it all settled satisfactorily, up drove the chief pilot of the school in his touring car. He said that he had been down to look over the machine, and it did not seem possible to him that I could have landed in so short a field and on such rough ground without breaking anything. He commended me on my good work, and said that an older aviator would have taken a chance on going into the fences instead of trying the jump effect.

Just before I left, the mayor's daughter brought in two of the biggest bouquets I ever expect to see, and presented one to the commandant and one to *l'aviateur américain*. I drove back in the chief pilot's machine and got to the camp just as the boys were going to bed, and you should have heard the hoots and howls that went up when I entered, carrying my bouquet. Of course I had to tell them all my story and I suppose they are planning to duplicate it. I am in Paris on *permission* and leave tonight for five days at Nice and shall probably go to Monte Carlo for a half-day. After that I must report to Camp Avord for *perfection* on a Nieuport. I was very fortunate at the school at Tours. I did not break even a wire. It certainly feels fine to be a breveted aviator with wings on.

A Panne de Château

September 4, 1917

I am sitting in the seat of my untrustworthy machine in the middle of a dense woods on the only clear patch of ground for miles around, waiting for my mechanic to build a new magneto and bring it to me. Where I am I have not the slightest idea. At 7 a.m. yesterday I started for Châteauroux. Kept going all day and at 6 p.m. left there for Romorantin. I kept going and going, but I could not find the place. I flew over rivers, lakes, forests, towns—everything there was to fly over, but no Romorantin. I flew so long that I ran out of *essence*, and when I looked at the ground, behold, I saw nothing but forests, one white patch of ground, and a small village. I went into a tight spiral and came down to within 450 feet over the town. I shall never forget the sight. It looked as if a lot of ants were making a new home—old women, boys, girls, men—everybody was running here and there, dodging into a house to tell a neighbour and rushing out again. I headed for a clear spot and landed, stopping at the very foot of an enormous tree.

I hadn't got out of my machine before people came running from every direction. I got out, and the people stood back from me as if I were a Hun. Finally I collected the wits that had not been jarred out of me by my "bum" landing, and said, "*Je suis un aviateur américain.*" After a little a real count appeared and asked me to stay with him at his *château*, a short distance away.

He had a wonderful *château*, a beautiful brick house, queer in style, with long rows of flowers and a small lake. We went inside and I met the countess. We had dinner and walked through the gardens, and then I went to my room where I'll swear I sank a foot deep in a feather bed.

This morning I went down to my machine and worked on it for an hour, praying it wouldn't start, for I wasn't at all crazy to leave. The thing wouldn't go, so now I'm waiting for my mechanic, and as Avord is at least 150 kilometres (ninety miles) away, and it's now a quarter of six, I can feel that mattress rise up all around me.

This morning my machine was filled with flowers and names were written over its wings and fuselage. My mechanic failed to come and I'm beginning to get anxious. Had a wonderful dinner last night and the count's valet gave me a shave and shined my boots. Feel sorry for the poor man, for the boots are high ones and difficult to shine, but they came back with a rare lustre. Had a man guard my machine last night. It rained and blew very hard and the poor fellow had wild tales to tell me this morning. He has gone now for breakfast and sleeps till noon, then comes back and guards it while I eat. I landed in a pasture, and at present there is a herd of cows grazing there and a little girl sitting near by.

Dropping in on the Baron

Avord, September 13, 1917

Since I last wrote, I have had some interesting experiences; I went on a cross-country flight and got back all right the first trip—no trouble of any sort. The second one I had a lot of motor trouble. Seeing that I could not get to my destination, I picked out a beautiful *château* and dropped gently on the front lawn. The owner, a baron, hurried out, and I stayed for luncheon, while his *mécanicien* rearranged my magneto. Around four o'clock I started out again. I had a most wonderful stay, though. It was a real old castle, wonderful food, and the baron's daughters were most attractive.

After going about ten miles farther, my oil feed-pipe broke, and I had to come down again. This time, I was a mile from any sort of habitation, except an old farm, and I had to go to the nearest telephone station to get Avord. Who should appear but a well-dressed man, who asked me to dinner at his *château* and also to stay as long as I cared to. I had to wait two days for a mechanic from Avord, but even when he came there was nothing he could do, as the motor had run without oil and was grilled.

I spent a most enjoyable two days, and when the mechanic arrived, I returned to Avord by train. The trouble with the motor was not caused through any fault of mine, so I am ready to start out again.

A Petit Voyage on a Blériot

Avord, September 28, 1917

For the last week I have been either flying or out on the field so much of the time that it has been difficult to find the time and energy to write. I believe I told you once that the *brevet* tests, which must be passed before becoming a full-fledged military pilot, consist of an "altitude" which I did some time ago, then two *lignes droites*, and two triangles; the former in my case being cross-country trips to Châteauroux and back, and the latter a three-cornered trip to Châteauroux, Romorantin, and back to Avord, the second being made around the triangle in the opposite direction. They have practically discontinued all cross-country flying here on the Blériots, as they are not getting any new Blériot machines and the old ones are not in very good condition, but as I have been waiting for a long while for room ahead in the Caudron school, they let me make my two *lignes droites* in a Blériot—one last Sunday and one Monday. Sunday was a beautiful day after the early morning mist cleared off, and I got started for Châteauroux about ten o'clock in the morning, equipped with a map, compass, and a barograph—an instrument which keeps a graphic record of the height at which you fly.

The sensation of starting off across country by the map was new to me and has a thrill all its own. It contains the interest, which you know, of travelling in an auto by the map over new country, with the difference of not being able to ask your way of the natives and of having to pick your landing-places from the air in case of motor trouble. I flew most of the way at about 1000 to 1200 metres, got to Châteauroux without trouble, and landed at the aviation school there, the trip taking a little over an hour. After having my spark-plugs cleaned and getting a bite to eat, I started back and made the trip without event, and, as I knew the way from the trip down, I had time to look the country over and enjoy the view of the forests, rivers, and cities passing under me. I went over Issoudun, Charost, Florent, Bourges, and innumerable small villages. Monday was foggy, and I could not start early in the morning, the best time for flying, but it cleared off here at eleven o'clock and I started on my second trip.

When I reached Bourges I was flying at about 800 metres and found that there was a solid floor of clouds or mist below me, extending from Bourges as far as I could see towards Châteauroux, and the ground was quite invisible. It was either turn back or fly low, so I dove down under it to 100 metres and had to make the entire trip at from

S.23   .38.

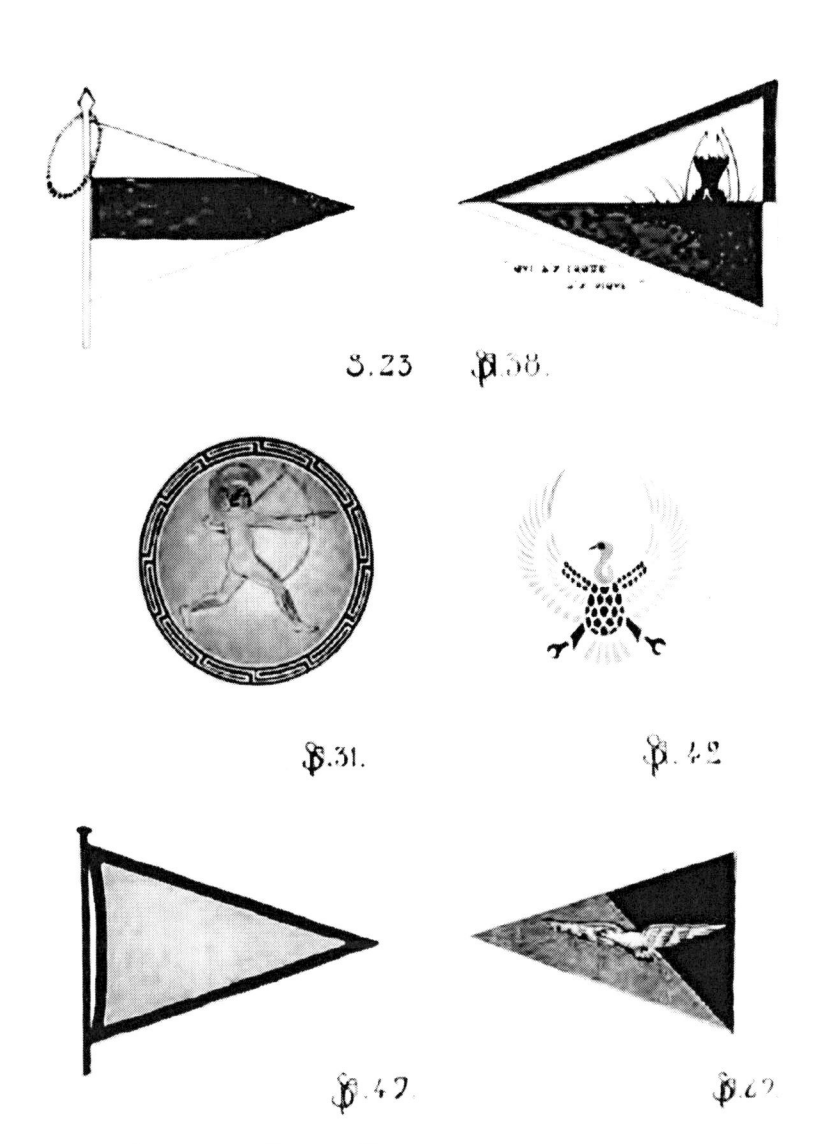

.31.   .42

.42   .

INSIGNIA OF FRENCH ESCADRILLES IN WHICH MEMBERS
OF THE LAFAYETTE FLYING CORPS SERVED
PLATE 1

75 to 300 metres, continuously diving under, around, or through thick clouds of fog, which formed a solid and low roof. It is great fun flying low, but rather nervous work with a motor you are not sure of, as it doesn't give much radius to find a landing-place in case of a forced landing. When about 15 kilometres from Châteauroux, to make things exciting, a stay-wire right in front of my seat snapped and I immediately decided to land and estimate the damage. I was flying at 200 metres over a stubble-field and made a good landing.

Imagine my surprise, on looking around, to see about a dozen American army tents pitched not more than 500 metres away. I strolled over and found that there was a small detachment of American engineers camped there and that dinner would be ready in half an hour. I accepted the invitation, and one of the boys walked with me over to the nearest telephone station in the village nearby. I tried to get Avord to find out whether I should go on or wait for a mechanic, but after waiting half an hour for a connection, with prospects of waiting the rest of the day, I decided to take a chance, as the wire didn't look very important, After a good Irish stew and hot tea with the Americans, a couple of them helped me to start my motor, and after cutting a few capers close to the ground to see that the machine would hold, I went to Châteauroux without trouble, had the mechanic there fix my machine, and started back.

THE BLÉRIOT "BONE-YARD" AT AVORD

Avord, June 1917

The clouds were still low and I was going quite low over some wooded-country near Florent, when my motor suddenly quit dead as I tried to throttle it down to go under a cloud. I was within reach of a pasture clear of trees and made a safe landing, though I had to land with the wind and was very glad when my machine came to a stop just before coming to a ditch beside the road. The danger of landing a Blériot in strange fields and even in woods is not to the pilot, as he is seldom hurt, but to the machine. I found I had plunged down near a large group of farm buildings and a picturesque ruined *château*, and I soon had an audience of about thirty peasants. I dinkied the motor up a bit (as it was only a matter of a small bolt having come out), disconnected a rod controlling the throttle, and got several bystanders to hold the machine while I cranked her up and got started. Nothing more happened and I arrived home at about 4.30, feeling that I had acquired some valuable experience.

Over the Pyrenees

Pau, November 27, 1916

The day before yesterday I had the most beautiful and the most enjoyable flight I have ever experienced since beginning my flying. It was my last flight necessary to complete the actual combat work of the course. I had an hour to do. That morning I had been on a steady flight of two and a half hours with a very excellent machine. The motor went perfectly, so I asked to use it again for the afternoon's flight and the instructor gave it to me readily.

I left the aviation field about twenty minutes of two and mounted directly to 3000 metres, getting to that altitude a little after two o'clock. Small fleecy clouds were forming at about 2400 metres just below the peaks of the Pyrenees, and in the west and northwest thicker, blacker clouds were gathering at various levels. The wind was a gentle one, coming straight from the west. I could scarcely notice it in the machine at all.

By two-thirty the clouds around the mountains were quite thick and were rapidly being blown eastward. Their flaky masses, tumbling and rolling across the peaks and off over the lowlands, were very pretty. I headed south in order to get over them. It was wonderful to look down on these patches of snowy clouds of mist and between them see the earth far, far beneath. The clouds, from 500 to 700 metres below, seemed to intensify and increase the distance to the ground, although I was still at 3000 metres as before. Each way I turned the clouds seemed to be going the opposite direction, as my speed was much greater than the wind, which in reality was driving the clouds eastward.

All this time I hadn't gone much farther south toward the mountains than Pau, but it was so delightful that I decided that I would stay up and do what was strictly *interdit* by the school—go southwest over the twenty-odd kilometres of low foothills and get actually over the first ranges of the Pyrenees. If my motor hadn't acted so splendidly all that morning, I surely would never have attempted or dared to get so far away, as I would very likely have been kicked out had I been forced to land with a bad motor near the mountains. As it was, the kind hand of Providence was with me and I got back without any mishaps and the motor running splendidly all the way. The lowest part of the range in sight from Pau is a bit southwest, so I headed in that direction and covered the distance in less than a half-hour.

As I neared the mountains the clouds began to roll in heavy masses both below and above me—more thickly above than below; but the sun was still shining brilliantly through the frequent rifts, and the colouring of the ground with the little towns and bright fields, the dark green of the trees and the white, fleecy masses of clouds rolling beneath me like splotches of cream, the splendour of the steep slopes ahead which I was rapidly nearing, their tops covered with snow and

AT PAU

rising above the clouds like so many icebergs afloat in a tossing sea, all formed a picture as picturesque and thrilling as I have ever seen. On my right to the northwest and farther ahead, dark, oppressive-looking banks of clouds were rolling up high over the mountainous horizon. I knew there was not much time to spare if I wanted to see my way back at 3000 metres, so I headed over a pretty valley with steep green sides rising to snow-capped summits which extended quite a way up into the main range. I passed the outer rim and then turned east above a lateral valley.

Looking down I beheld far beneath, in the very bed of the valley, a tiny stream winding down in twists and curves from the head, and all along it were little hamlets and farms, and I could see sheep grazing up over the sloping farmlands. Far up the valley was quite a fair-sized village, but I didn't go far enough into the mountains to get over it. Turning eastward, I passed over some of the outer peaks which, snow-capped and bare of all foliage, were scarcely three hundred metres below me. I saw no one moving above the snow-line. It looked bleak, but very splendid in the sunlight, and the higher peaks to the south, which seemed close, but were in reality from five to twenty kilometres away, were a magnificent sight. I drank in the chilling, pure air with delight and fixed the picture so firmly in my mind that I shall never forget it. Then I turned toward Pau.

Pau, July 4, 1917

I have been here a week and am nearly finished. In two or three days I go to a place near the Front called G.D.E., there to await assignment to some *escadrille* at the Front.

In my work here I have done a lot of *vols de groupe*. It is quite a job to follow the machine ahead of you so that you are always about fifty metres above, fifty behind, and fifty to one side. We flew all over the surrounding country, as far as Lourdes, and the other way west almost to the seacoast at Biarritz. In acrobacy I've done a loop, *glissade sur l'aile, vrille, spirale verticale,* and still have one or two other less difficult stunts to do before leaving. I haven't the time to describe each of them now, but you can imagine them from their names. They are all easy to do.

I have had some machine-gun practice here, but think it is chiefly a matter of good pilotage and luck whether you get the Boche or he gets you. The guns used are the Vickers (British make) and Hotchkiss. The Lewis is not used on aeroplanes here because it shoots only ninety rounds without reloading. It is, however, used extensively in the trenches and is really a better gun than the others because it is less complicated and less subject to jam. The U.S. Army was idiotic not to take it when Lewis offered it to them. The Vickers is a good gun and has the advantage of a belt to feed the cartridges. Consequently it can fire an unlimited number, whereas a magazine feeder, such as the Lewis has, can hold only so many. I shall practice shooting every day, so as to be as proficient as possible when I get into my first fight.

THE SCHOOL OF COMBAT

Pau, November, 1917

I am quite tired tonight from my five hours' flying, most of it being between ten and fifteen thousand feet. After 3500 metres one has to breathe through the mouth—at least it is easier. It is quite cold, but we bundle up well; most of the boys have trouble with their ears after a quick descent from high altitudes, but I have found that holding the nose tight and blowing and also frequent swallowing is a tremendous help. *Chasse* patrols at the Front now often fly at an altitude of 6000 metres (20,000 feet); remaining at this height for two hours at a stretch is very fatiguing and in the end affects the heart, lungs, and nerves. The altitude record is 8200 metres, but the pilot had to take oxygen in tanks with him to be able to breathe, and then nearly perished with the cold. I don't believe they'll get much above 30,000 feet for some years. I have never yet been above 15,000 feet in an aeroplane, but probably shall before I leave here.

I have become quite discouraged about the war. Russia is through for good and may even sign a separate peace. Italy's army is permanently crippled probably. The French are scrapping terribly in politics, several serious scandals have become public, and America—good Lord! the amount of rot we read in the papers! Her "latest" airplane specifications were six months out of date seven months ago. From what a French aeronautic expert thinks, the Liberty motor is useless for a Front machine; they took over, as their chief aviation school in France, Issoudun, previously condemned by the French for their own purposes, and they say the most stupid things over here. "How to win the war"—"by an American" is a sort of by-word here. The contingent in the trenches is paying for its swaggering conceit. Well, we all have to learn, I suppose.

Pau, November, 1917

Well, here I am, all my flying tests having been satisfactorily completed; breveted and ordered to Pau on Nieuport, the fastest and most difficult n chine in France. Pau is beautiful, and because of its situation at the foot of the Pyrenees, the climate is almost windless and especially good for flying.

Here is my daily schedule: Up at 5.30, roll-call at 6. Take a truck to the field and get some breakfast, for which I pay good money. Flying starts at 7. I stay at the field till 10.30, making six flights lasting fifteen minutes each. Truck back to camp. Wash for dinner. Roll-call at 1 p.m. Back to field until 5.30. Six more flights. Dinner at 6.30, and bed at 8, dead to the world. Flying is tiring—why, I don't know, as in a Nieuport, after you get height and motor adjustment, you move neither hands nor feet more than an inch at a time, and that only seldom. It is very pleasant here because all the *élèves* are breveted pilots, and therefore each has a certain valuation, is more or less of a proven quality, and is treated accordingly.

Pau, November, 1917

It is the last of November and I have finished my acrobatics. I had to do three, the Immelmann turn, a spinning nose-dive, and a vertical bank. The lieutenant in charge speaks English and wears a monocle; "nuf said," but he is very agreeable and has a high opinion of Americans. Just before I was to fly, a pilot had gone up 1000 metres. He circled around and around trying to get his nerve up. The lieutenant got a crick in his neck looking up and was pretty mad. Finally the man came down and said the clouds were too low. That spurred me on. The lieutenant said, "Start your *vrille*" (spinning nose-dive) "at 1000 metres." I made up my mind the instant the altimetre registered 1000 I would do it. I was scared stiff, but when I hit 1000 I cut my motor, pulled the stick back, jammed my stick and feet way over. The machine hung motionless, then fell with a sickening sensation and started to spin with the fuselage as an axis. To come out you put the controls in the middle. That brings you out in a nose-dive, then you haul back the stick, put on the motor, and are off. Well, I did all those things. When the altimetre reads 900 you come out. The machine drops so fast that it beats the metre. So I really fell 300 metres spinning like a top. When I came out and found I was alive and breathing, I grinned and shouted for joy. The first *vrille* was to the left; then I did one to the right, another to the left, and came down.

I hadn't been very keen for the Nieuport training, but now I am tickled to death. It is absolutely the best in France. The finest part of it all is the feeling of confidence one gains in doing this work. I don't think it makes one reckless, but it does take away fear. I am certainly very grateful for what the French have given me.

Pau, November. 28, 1917

Tomorrow will be Thanksgiving Day and also my last day at any school, if it is halfway decent weather, for tomorrow morning I do the acrobatics and shall then be through. They have cut out the last two classes and we shall get that training during the first two months with the *escadrille*. It is the new system and I think it should be much better. The acrobatics consist of *vrilles*—a spinning nose-dive with the motor cut; *renversements*—a method of turning by pointing the machine up, flipping it over on its back, and then pulling up so that you come out in exactly the same line in which you came; vertical *virages*—another way of turning by snapping the machine around a 180° corner; and wing-slips—a way of losing altitude very quickly (and very hard to follow), by reducing the motor and turning the machine on its side so there is no supporting surface. They say the sensations are rather unpleasant at first. They are hard to do correctly, but easy enough to try and to get out of. When we get our planes at the *escadrille* we have to practice them until we can do them perfectly—here we only learn to go through the motions necessary and get somewhat used to them. So I shall be glad when it is dinner-time tomorrow.

The American colony in Pau is going to give all the American pilots a big Thanksgiving dinner. The flying here has been great fun, but the weather has been very cloudy. Today I finished *vol de groupe* in the 110 horse-power 15-metre Nieuport. Went up the river right over the promenade at 300 metres, as the clouds were low as far as the base of the mountains, then saw a rift and went up through it and saw the peaks of the mountains for the first time since I have been here. At 1500 metres it was a beautiful warm sunny day, with a mass of soft white clouds below, through which now and then I could see the ground, and close by were the mountains sticking' up through the clouds. There was not a movement in the air, so I just sat there and took it all in. I throttled the motor down so it wouldn't climb, let go the stick, and watched the clouds change their formations.

I lost the machines I was flying with in the clouds and mists below, and as I couldn't see any other machine up there, felt absolutely alone in the world. I could judge my approximate position by the mountains, the sun, and an occasional glimpse of the river, so did not worry

THE VRILLE

WATCHING THE ACROBATICS

about getting lost. However, it got lonesome after an hour, so 1 came down and began to dodge the clouds again, as I had to stay up two hours and a quarter to finish.

A couple of days ago we had great sport diving at horses, cows, etc., in the fields down the river. We cut the motors and then *piqued* down at one of them, trying to keep the crossed front strut wires on the animal. This serves instead of the sight which we get later. It was quite hard to do, as it was very windy and bumpy, and I was thrown around and had to keep correcting continually. When we got within ten or fifteen feet we flattened out, put on the motor and went on our way, jumping a hedge, house, or row of trees at the end of the field. When we tired of that we got down about ten feet over the river and tried to follow its winding course. Many times we couldn't do it, as the turns were too sharp, so had to pull up fast to clear the trees on the banks. That was when I realised the speed, as the trees were only a green streak on each side going by well over a hundred miles an hour.

I get forty-eight hours *permission* in Paris; then to Plessis-Belleville to wait to be assigned to the Front—two to three weeks probably.

In 1916

Plessis, December 22, 1916

This is my last stop before going to the Front and, from present prospects, I expect to be going out next week, if not before Christmas. To tell the truth I am hoping it will be after next Monday, as I am very anxious to spend Christmas Day in Paris. After that I want to get to the Front mighty quickly. This place—the reserve camp for all pilots going to the Front—is not very interesting. We can do pretty much as we please, but I don't care to remain for a very long period. We three Americans are staying at the Hôtel de la Bonne Rencontre, a miserable little hole near the camp, and it is rather uncomfortable. Then, too, the weather is poor and there's very little chance to get any flying. Late this afternoon I had my first flight here with an 80-horse-power Nieuport. It felt fine to be up again, for I hadn't flown since quitting Pau on the 10th. From then until last Wednesday, the 20th, I've been vacationing in Paris.

I haven't said anything to any of you yet, but I confess now that I almost decided to take a leave, I could easily have secured, of fifteen days in the U.S., at the end of this very month. I had my plans laid to sail on the Chicago from Bordeaux on the 30th and just walk in and give you all a great surprise. I even bought a suit of "civilians" in Paris

La Bonne Rencontre

"Zut, Alors!"

to wear over there, as we can't sport any uniforms in a neutral country. Finally, after thinking it over a lot, I decided to call it off. My career over here is too precious to risk bringing to a stop by any foolishness, and though I sure do want to see you all, still I'm swallowing my disappointment and am staying here to get to the Front quickly. The suit of "cits" will have to wait unused until the war is over, or a later day, anyway.

We witnessed a very disastrous accident here this p.m. A Voisin biplane, one of the big bombarding machines, crashed to the ground, due to a wire catching in the propeller, and both pilot and observer were crushed to death. The machine was completely wrecked. Very soon I'll be out on the grim Front again and flying out over the lines. Then will commence the real work I've been training for all these months, and I'm looking forward to it with an immense amount of anticipation and pleasure. Why worry?

I hope the New Year will prove a brighter one for us all. For me it doesn't make much difference. For you it does. I'm where individuality doesn't count much—I'm just an atom in this great war, but working for a cause we'll die for.

Paris, Christmas Eve, 1916

It was so beautiful this morning and so vastly different from the windy, rainy days we've had lately that I routed out early and went over to the aviation field for a flight. We fly whenever we wish at the depot. There are very few restrictions—particularly for Americans. I got a good 110-horse-power Baby Nieuport and had three quarters of an hour of real enjoyment in the air. I did more acrobatics in that one flight than I've done yet at any one time. It did feel great to be up in such dandy weather again.

The day before yesterday I wrote to Rivers and told him of my plans. I think it won't be many days now before I and the other two Americans here with me will be sent out to the Front—most probably to join our own *escadrille*, but perhaps to enter some French squadron and later to form the 2nd American Escadrille when a few more of the fellows have completed their training.

I understand that we cannot be called officially the American *Escadrille*. We are now officially the *Escadrille* of Volunteers, although I have heard rumours that we may be termed the Lafayette *Escadrille*. That wouldn't be a bad name at all.

In Summer

Plessis, July 20, 1917

We have all taken rooms with different French families, there being only one hotel in town. If the latter were in the States I can't imagine what name we should give it. Buckley and I live with an English family who have been here for a number of years. They tell some interesting stories about the early days of the war. The Germans held all this part of the country during the Battle of the Marne. Their piano has a hole in it made by a bayonet. Their home was worse than a pig-pen when they returned after the Boches had been driven back. Balsley, an American, who was brought down a short time ago, once lived here, and they are quite proud of him. Rounds, a fine chap from New York, and I flew over Paris the other day. James Norman Hall, who wrote *Kitchener's Mob*, was shot down a short time ago, and is in the American Hospital at Neuilly. We flew low over the hospital and then over Paris, a wonderful sight, but very bumpy. The next day we went in and visited Jimmy at the hospital. He was delighted to see us, and knew that we had flown over the day before.

We fly a good deal here, and shoot on the range twice a day. I have a job during the early morning hours flying observers around while they shoot at a stationary target on the ground. This machine is hard to handle with another person in it, and the empty cartridges come out and hit against my head, for they have no cartridge bag to catch them. There is a French sergeant here who wants me to go to the Front with him. I don't believe I should like a two-place machine.

We are all expecting to go soon to the Front. Somebody leaves almost every day, and we all wish we were with them. On the bulletin board there is a list of casualties at the Front among pilots and observers. We have noticed that almost half of them are caused from accidents, so we have something to think about. The other day we had a hailstorm. A few machines were out, and you should have seen them after they landed: holes through the wings, radiators punctured, pilots and observers bruised; several had to make forced landings.

A few nights ago a Boche night-bombing plane passed over on its way to Paris. We (Buckley and I) were in bed reading when we heard a peculiar sound, different from any we had heard before. It came nearer and nearer, and finally passed overhead. About the same time searchlights and signals began to appear in all directions. This was before the anti-aircraft batteries in the direction of Paris began to bang away. In the meantime we had run to the field hoping to get a machine with a

THE FIRST SORTIE "LÂCHÉ"

gun on it. Rounds also wanted one.

We waited and waited, hoping some one would appear who could give us authority to go ahead. After some little time we heard the Boche returning, going in the direction of Compiègne to his own lines. What we said wouldn't do to repeat. Had we had any authority, some of those machines in the hangars would have gone after him. The next morning we learned that the Boche didn't reach Paris, but dropped his bombs in the fields outside. The searchlights and signals beat any exhibition of fireworks I ever saw. Two nights later another Boche came over and dropped two bombs near our field, only a quarter of a mile from where we lived.

Flights from Plessis

Plessis, August 12, 1917

I am mighty glad to write that I have at last finished my training, and am now a full-fledged aviator. I left Avord July 14. From there went to Pau, in the south of France, at the foot of the Pyrenees—a very beautiful place. I was there fifteen days doing acrobatics.

From Pau I came to Plessis-Belleville, not far from the Front. This is a depot where we wait until called for, usually about twenty days.

Yesterday, for the first time, I flew over Paris; it took me twenty minutes to go, but I came back with the wind in five. I circled around the Eiffel Tower at about 1000 feet; we are not supposed to fly over Paris under 9000. I could see people looking up. It was great. And the other day I, with two other pilots, flew out to the Front. It took us forty minutes. I could see the trenches and also smoke from the big guns. We had not been there long when we saw some other aeroplanes in the distance.

As we had no guns in our machines, we came back. I knew they were Boche machines with the big black crosses on their wings. They would have made short work of our unarmed Nieuports. I was told not to hurry to get to the Front, as there are still thousands of Boche machines to bring down. The fellows out there are not getting them all.

The Germans made trenches round this place when their patrols were so near Paris about three years ago. I have also seen a lot of wire entanglement in the woods. It was very interesting, but I hope they never get so near again.

The U.S. is very careful whom they take into Aviation; one has to be perfect. France takes men who are not strong enough for the trenches, and makes good aviators out of them. Guynemer[2] is the best aviator at the Front. He has brought down more machines than any other pilot in the war—something like fifty to his credit. Wonderful, when one knows anything about aeroplane fighting! France worships him; he can have anything he wants. But really he is not strong at all.

EN ROUTE TO THE G.D.E.

November 9, 1917

Am in Paris for the night on my way from the school of aerial acrobatics at Pau to Plessis-Belleville, where I shall remain a week or two before going to the Front. Plessis is really the Front, as it is in the *Zone des Armées* and but twenty minutes' flying distance from the lines, but while there we have no patrolling to do except in the event of a German aerial attack on Paris. In this case we should be sent up to fight off the invaders. Otherwise the work at Plessis will be in the nature of practice.

Had one rather bad experience at Pau that gave my nerves the worst deal they have ever been subjected to. When I went out to the acrobatic field for my first session there, the *moniteur* told me the first trick would be a *vrille* (pronounced "vree"). This, although decidedly not dangerous, is more dangerous, comparatively speaking, than anything else you can do in an aeroplane. It consists of putting your plane in such a position that it points nose down, falling toward the ground and spinning around like a top at a terrible rate of speed. It is simple to get into this fix, but there is only one possible way the pilot can bring his machine out of it again. If you lose your head and try other ways, you might as well say your prayers. They teach you to "get out" of this because any accident you may have in the air due to mismanagement of controls will end in the *vrille*.

So you may imagine that I was a bit nervous when the *moniteur*, after he had shown me what to do, said: "Now go up 1500 metres and try it." I went outside the hangar, and while putting on my casque and goggles, watched another pilot doing his first *vrilles*. He did one, and then attempted another, but when his machine stopped spinning around he continued to come directly toward the ground, nose first, with his motor running at full speed. Down, down he came, faster on account of his engine than a big boulder could fall. For a second

---

2. *Guynemer: Chevalier of the Air*, a double edition, *Georges Guynemer, Knight of the Air* by Henry Bordeaux and *The Chevalier of Flight: Captain Guynemer* by Mary R. Parkman is also published by Leonaur.

A NIEUPORT CRASH

it seemed as though it would land right on top of me, but I was too struck by the terribleness of it to run, and in an instant the machine had crashed into the earth about a hundred yards off. The grass must have been six inches high, and after the crash we could not see one piece of the debris projecting. There was hardly anything left. The engine of the aeroplane had been buried far in the ground. There was nothing left of the man at all—just some clothes and pieces of flesh.

I thought that after this, acrobacy would be postponed for the day. But the *moniteur* left it optional to the students, and naturally no one wanted to admit he was too scared to go on. So the *moniteur* said:

> Of course you're all ready to continue immediately. Such a thing as this is nothing in the life of an aviator. If the man had done as we'd told him, he wouldn't have been killed.

Somehow, under the circumstances, these words didn't sound cold-blooded. So I got into my plane and the mechanics strapped me tightly to the seat. As a final jolt I saw the body being carried away just as I was leaving the ground. But almost instantly I forgot about the sordidness of the situation because my mind was occupied thoroughly memorizing the instructions on how to get out of a *vrille*.

It took two sessions to finish all the acrobatics. Afterwards the *moniteur* said he would recommend me to go to the Front in a *monoplace* fighting plane. This is the best thing in Aviation, as only the more skilful pilots get there. It is what I've been working for, and so I feel pretty happy about it.

A Bomber at Plessis

Plessis, November, 1917

Our aviation training began at Avord, where there is a huge camp with some 1000 machines. We trained first on a Blériot monoplane, then on a biplane, on which we obtained our brevet, and then I was posted to take Nieuport work and become a *pilote de chasse*. After thinking the matter over, however, I decided to go to the Front on a bombardment machine, and, accordingly, asked the commandant of the camp to shift me, which he did. I was then put on a Schmidt bombing plane, and given two weeks' training on that and told I was finished and ready to go to Plessis-Belleville.

On arriving at Plessis several of us were immediately shipped off to a centre of aviation about ten miles back of the lines and given ten days more training on Paul Schmidt. While here I was almost overtaken with disaster. I went up with a passenger one foggy day, and before I knew it, was lost. We had no compass and steered in the direction of what we supposed was the camp. After fifteen minutes I nosed the machine down until I could see the ground to make reconnaissance, and found we were over the German lines, with the trenches about a mile in the rear. I plunged back into the fog and came about-face in short order. We wasted no time in getting back into French territory, and finally the fog lifted and we found the aerodrome again.

Am now back at Plessis-Belleville, flying the machine we are to fly at the Front, and am only waiting to be assigned to an *escadrille*. We do night flying as well as day flying, and the machine surely is wonderful. It carries two men, four machine guns, and a ton of bombs, and with this load goes 107 miles an hour at a height of 15,000 feet. The engine is 300-horse power, and is a Renault-Mercédés. The machine climbs a mile and one third in eight minutes. The night flying is somewhat difficult, especially the landing. We have a red light on one wing and a green light on the other, to signal, and at the same time show us the inclination of the wings. One has to steer by compass, and on moonlight nights by rivers and canals, which gleam far below as silvery ribbons. In the day bombing we always go in formation of from 10 to 100, with *chasse* machines hovering around as additional protection.

The actual danger in flying is not very great. Avord is a school which maintains 800 pilots, and out of this number there were 40 killed while I was there. Three of the 200 American boys were killed in training. One of these, Hanford, was a special friend of mine, and was killed while we were making a trip together. Part of our *brevet* test was to make two 300-mile trips. Hanford and I started out about the same time one afternoon to make the first leg of the triangle, which was from Avord to the aerodrome at Châteauroux, not far from Orléans. It took us about one hour, passing over a beautiful pastoral country and watching the cattle grazing in the rich pastures and the peasants in the fields. I was ahead, and had just landed when I heard a terrific crash, and, looking up, saw that Hanford had collided with a Farman biplane at a height of 2000 feet. They both fell like stones, and machines and pilots were broken to bits. I did not feel much like continuing the trip, but had to, and finished alone.

The boys used to have imaginary motor trouble and make "forced" landings at beautiful *châteaux*. Here they would be entertained for two days until the mechanic crews from the aerodromes could come out to see what was the trouble. Several had very funny adventures in this way. The captain of the school noticed, however, where all the forced landings were occurring and put a stop to the practice. I had some landings like that and remained a couple of days with a count and his family of beautiful daughters. Of course an American aviator was a novelty to them. I played tennis, drank tea, and forgot the war for forty-eight charming hours.

Homesick

Plessis-Belleville, December 24, 1917

I left Paris the morning of the 22nd for Plessis-Belleville. With all the imagination in the world I could never have pictured this place. I arrived at the centre about eight o'clock, and having made the rounds of all the *bureaux*, I was told to take a certain tractor at three o'clock. We started at 3.30, and a kilometre from the camp the truck broke down. It was freezing cold, but we had to wait half an hour when another tractor came. Whereupon we unloaded all our baggage, about sixty pieces or more, and put it on the other truck. We then continued on our way. About two hours later we arrived at another depot, where we again unloaded our baggage and loaded it on small tractors; some of us coming here, some going to other camps.

Then we were taken to get something to eat. In the mess-hall the temperature is below freezing, and we have not been able to decide just what we think of the food. However, we all ate heartily, and needless to say, rapidly. The place was formerly the loft of a barn, and the gentle breezes waft to and fro all the time. The population is less than forty, not including the camps of about seventy men. We sleep in nearly all our clothes, and I have been here two days and have not been able to find water enough to wash my face.

French village life centres around the *cafés*, and there are two small ones in this place. There we gather to get warm and to write. Bad weather today, so we are not flying.

There are ten Americans here, and I can tell you it is a sad crowd when we think that tomorrow is Christmas. We are all absolutely broke and not even able to buy an imitation Christmas dinner. I don't know when those boxes are going to reach us, but no doubt some time in the not too distant future. Christmas is rather hard to think about under such conditions. One of the fellows remarked that he was just beginning to realise what Christmas really meant. The French don't make much of the season. It takes the English or the Americans to really celebrate it.

We hear rumours lately that all Americans in the French service have been released to be taken by the U.S. Aviation. Rumours are always rife, but this may have some foundation. With all my plans and hopes, I may be transferred against my wishes. But even yet they may be so slow that I can arrange to come home in February. I am still hoping. Well, we are at war, so there is nothing to do but grin and bear it.

I am sending a cablegram today asking for the money I wrote for on the first of December. It is quite important that I have it in a few days. I am leaving for the Front in a very short time, and I shall certainly need money before I go out. There will be many things that will be absolutely necessary to me before leaving, and at present I am "stony." Well, it will all come out in the wash, and whether I come home or not I am thinking of you and hoping to see you all at the finish.

From Plessis-Belleville to the Front

Now that so many Americans are beginning to fly in France, I fancy that the people at home must wonder what sort of a time they are having.

I can speak, of course, only of conditions in the French aviation service; but when our American squadrons take their places at the Front the life is bound to be similar, because experience has taught all the armies that, to get the best results, pilots should be given a maximum of liberty and a minimum of routine, outside of their duty, which consists of but one thing, flying.

Suppose, for instance, that an American boy—I will call him "Zoom"—has passed through the schools, done his acrobatics and combat work, and is waiting at the great depot for his call to the Front. Everyday he scans the list as it is posted, and at last, hurrah! his name is there, followed by mysterious letters and numbers—G.C. 17, or S.P.A. 501, or N. 358. He knows, of course, that he will have a single-seater scout, but the symbols above tell him whether it will be a Spad or a Nieuport and whether he is to be in a *groupe de combat* ("travelling circus," as the British call them) or in a more stationary fighting unit.

Zoom is overjoyed to find he has been given a Spad, and hastens to pack up, in readiness for his train, which leaves at 6 p.m. When his order for transport is given him, he finds that his *escadrille* is stationed at Robinet d'Essence, in a fairly quiet, imaginary sector. Before leaving the depot he has issued to him a fur-lined teddy-bear suit, fur boots, sweater, fur gloves, and a huge cork safety helmet which Wisdom tells him to wear and Common Sense pronounces impossible. Common Sense wins; so he gives the thing to the keeper of the *effets chauds pour pilotes*, and retires.

His flying-things stuffed into a duffle-bag, which he has checked directly through to far-off Robinet, he boards the train with nothing but a light suitcase. He is delirious with joy, for it is long since he has been to Paris, and at the G.D.E. discipline has been severe and luxury scant. Every journey to the Front is via Paris, and the authorities wink a wise and kindly eye at a few hours' stop-over. Outside the station, an hour later, Zoom is conscious of a sudden odd feeling of contentment, which puzzles him until he thinks a bit. Finally he has it—this is what he going to fight for, what all the Allies are fighting for: this pleasant, crowded civilian life; the dainty Frenchwomen going by on the arms of their *permissionnaires*, the fine old buildings, the hum of peaceful pursuits. In the schools and at the aviation depot he had nearly lost sight of real issues; but now it all comes back.

At his hotel he calls up Captain X—— of the American Aviation, an old friend who is in Paris on duty, and is lucky enough to catch him at his apartments. They dine at the *Cercle des Alliés*—the old Rothschild Palace, now made into a great military club, where one can see many interesting men of all the Allied armies lunching and dining together. Dinner over, they drop in at the Olympia, watch the show a bit, and greet a multitude of friends who stroll about among the tables. A great deal of air-gossip goes on: A—— has just bagged another Boche; B——, poor chap, was shot down two days ago; C—— is a prisoner, badly wounded. At the table nearby, Zoom, for the first time, sets eyes on Lufbery, the famous American "ace," his breast a mass of ribbons, his rather worn face lit up by a pleasant smile as he talks to a French officer beside him.

At eleven young Zoom says goodbye to his friend and walks through the darkened streets to his hotel. What a joy to sleep in a real bed again! The train leaves at noon, which will give him time for a late breakfast and a little shopping in the morning. After the first real night's sleep in a month, and a light war-time breakfast of omelet, bacon, broiled kidneys, and coffee, he is on the *boulevards* again, searching for a really good pair of goggles, a fur-lined flying-cap to replace the hopeless helmet, and a pair of heavy mittens.

At length it is train time, and so, hailing a taxi, and picking up his bag on the way, he heads for the Gare de l'Est, getting there just in time to reserve a place and squeeze into the dining-car which is crowded with officers on their way to the Front. These are not the *embusqué* type of officers to which he has been accustomed in the schools—clerkish disciplinarians, insistent upon all the small points of military observance; but real fighting men and leaders; grizzled veterans of the Champagne and the Somme, hawk-nosed, keen-eyed, covered with decorations.

Back in his compartment he dozes through the afternoon, until just as it has become thoroughly dark, the train halts at Robinet. On the platform half a dozen pilots of the *escadrille*, smart in their laced boots and black uniforms, are waiting to welcome the newcomer and escort him promptly to the mess where dinner is ready. Dinner over, he is shown to his room, an officer's billet, with a stove, bathtub, and other unheard-of luxuries.

Next morning one of his new comrades calls for Zoom, presents him to the captain, who proves very *chic* and shows him his machine, which has just been brought out from the depot. The armourer is engaged in fitting a Vickers gun on it, so Zoom spends the rest of the day at the hangar, sighting the gun, adjusting his belt, installing altimetre, tachometre, and clock.

At dinner there is much patrol talk, for the weather has been good.

"A—— had a stiff fight with a two-seater Hun, who escaped miraculously, leaving their machines riddled with holes. M—— had a landing-cable cut by a bullet; J—— had a *panne*, and was forced to land uncomfortably close to the lines."

At eight o'clock an orderly comes in with the next day's schedule:

Patrouille Haute 5000 metres, 8:45-10:45.

Among the list of pilots for the *sortie* he reads, "Caporal Zoom."

This is the typical Going-to-the-Front experience which we Americans in the French service have had. What happened to Caporal-Pilote Zoom, on his first patrol, I will tell you at another time.

5

Adventures in Action

IN HOSPITAL
(The story of the first severely wounded
pilot of the Lafayette Corps)

My first battle in the air was my last. I had fired one shot; my machine gun had jammed. A German was at my left, two were on my right, one was underneath me, and the man I had first attacked was still behind me. From the silence of my gun they would know there was nothing to fear. My fight was over. I was too far behind the German lines to drive straight to earth. I could only manoeuvre back to Bar-le-Duc, where my *escadrille* was stationed.

I swung in every direction; I went into a cloud. Bullets followed. One scratched my machine, and I slipped away from the man who fired it, and threw the belly of my plane upward.

I was then about twelve thousand feet up. It was while I was standing on my head, the belly of my machine skyward, that something struck me. It felt like the kick of a mule. With the sensation of losing a leg, I put my hand down to learn if it was still there. I had the presence of mind to cut the motor. But as my right foot went back with the shock of the bullet, my left foot sprang forward. So, with my commands reversed, my leg knocked out, still standing on my head, I fell into a spinning nose-dive.

Around and down I went. It was all over. Soon I should hit the ground, as I had seen many friends hit it. That would be all. How strange that I, the I who had seemed undying, should hit the ground like all the rest! I remembered a boy I had picked up when I first started training. I should look like that.

Making a supreme effort, I tried to push my bad leg with my hand;

but the controls were so wedged that I could not move them. If I hit here, I should be a German prisoner. Working my right leg desperately with my hands, I felt the kinks come out of the commands at last. Once more the machine was on the level.

Then I heard again the sound of bullets. My gun was still useless, my entire right side was paralysed, and I was bleeding like a pig; but at that sound, I dived again. This time I kept control of my machine. I was low enough now to see through the mist the trench lines and the snaky curve of the river. I put my plane in more than a vertical dive, shooting back under the Germans, so far that the roll of cartridges fell out, and, falling, hit my arm. I thought I had been struck again. Everything was now falling out.

I looked at my altimetre. Eight hundred feet above the ground. I was going to hit in Germany!

I could see the trenches. I must get home! I went so fast that I could hardly recognise the trenches, and so far that I had left my enemies behind.

I was now growing too faint to go on. I saw a green field, and, making a turn to the left, came up to the wind and dived for the field. Too late I saw that it was filled with barbed wire; I was landing between the front-line trenches and the reserve lines. The barbed wire caught my wheels, and very gently my machine turned completely upside down. I knew that it was going over me. I should bleed to death, after all.

In the field next to me I saw a burst of smoke, then a white spot; then another and another, before I realised what it meant. The Germans were shelling me. They had seen me fall; they were trying to destroy my machine.

When the shelling stopped, someone would come for me. I suffered so little pain that I knew I was not badly wounded. I should be sent to Paris. I wondered who my nurse would be. Then I would come back to the squadron and the next time I would get my German. But it was more of the good times in Paris that I thought than of my job.

The shelling stopped. Tired of waiting, I tried to crawl. I could not move. I got up on my hands and knees to try again, but could no more move than if I had been staked to the ground. Finally, catching the grass, I dragged myself like a dog with a broken back. Inch by inch I made about ten yards; then I could go no farther.

It was now about six o'clock in the morning. The sun, which had driven away the mist, flamed down upon me in the unshaded field. I took the shoe off my right foot; it dripped red. Utterly exhausted by this effort, I could feel only a dumb wonder at the sight. Somehow I could not connect that bleeding foot with myself. I was all right. I must let my mother know this at once. Then I would go to Paris for those good times.

After I had waited a few minutes longer, four French soldiers came, stooping low; they, too, had kept quiet till the shelling had ceased. Crawling under the barbed wire, they caught hold of me and asked me what was the matter.

"Bullet—in my—hip," I muttered, choking back with each word a groan at the touch of their hands. The pain of their rough grasp was so severe that now for the first time I wondered, could my wound be worse than I had thought?

Can you walk?" they asked in French.

"*Mais non*" I said, indignantly.

Two took me by the shoulders, two by the feet. Then, like a beast unleashed, my pain broke from its long stupor. Almost crawling to escape the enemy's eye, the four men dragged me, like a sack of grain, through the long grass, over and under and across the web of barbed wire. The pain had now become such torture that I almost fainted.

I do not know how long that journey lasted. All I do know is that at last we came to the dressing-station behind the trenches.

Someone was pulling off my fur combination. As they cut away my shirt and dressed the wound, the anti-toxin that they injected numbed the pain. Now I suffered no more than I had there on the field. It was in this deadened state that, looking around, I saw for the first time the hole in my hip. With a curiosity that was almost grotesque, I stared at that wound.

They carried me face downward through an underground trench, and placed me at last on the floor of the *poste de secours*. As I lay there waiting my turn for the ambulance, I watched three other men go out before me. Again came the intense incredulity. Was it really I waiting so helplessly, or was it one of the men I used to carry when I was an ambulance-driver?

"One moment here!"

A man who had just jumped from a car hurried in breathlessly to the little station and held up his gloved hand for attention.

Is there an aviator here who fell a few hours ago?" I—right here," I said.

"*Oui, oui;* I saw you fall. I am a member of a reconnaissance squadron. My car is at your disposal."

I could have cried out with joy. The fat little Frenchman, with his red point of beard and reddish-brown eyes, took on the glorified aspects of a deliverer. I could not thank him enough.

"*Merci, merci, merci,*" I exclaimed. "*Je suis un Am—ricain y Lafayette Escadrille y Bar-le-Duc. Tout de suite, s'il vous plait.*"

"*Bien, bien,*" said he, calling to his driver to help lift me from the floor.

With the fur coat still thrown over me, my stretcher was placed across the front and back of the opening in the touring-car. Just as we were ready, the superintendent of the station came out to the car.

"To V——," he ordered in a loud tone. "This man is not able to travel so far. To V——!"

There was complete finality in his tone. That long, torturing drive was over one of the roughest roads in France, almost unsupportable in a light car that permitted my stretcher to jerk back and forth. Every time we went down into a shell-hole I could hardly keep from screaming.

At last we reached V——. Here I was carried into a long, narrow shed packed tightly with other men on stretchers like myself. By this time I was half fainting. Perhaps because of this the first sight of the shed had the stagnant horror of a dream. As an ambulance-driver, I was used to such scenes; but then I had been well. Now each mutilated form caught up my own suffering, repeated it, dinned it into my brain, until I thought I had never known health.

My driver was leaving me now. As he put me down, I made a groping movement for his arm.

"Goodbye. Thank you, and, for God's sake," I said—"for God's sake, telephone my captain at Bar-le-Duc to come for me today."

He promised, but as he turned away, a man started to undress me.

"Don't take off my clothes," I commanded. "I am leaving here in a few moments."

He paid no attention.

"I forbid you to take off my clothes!" I screamed. "I am an American; I am going to Bar-le-Duc."

He made no answer. Instead, from the *poilu* next to me came a cry that tore the air. I closed my eyes to shut out the scene. When I opened them again a surgeon was standing over me.

"I'll just look at the wound," said he. " If I can get the bullet out, you can go on to your friends this afternoon."

Reassured, I let them take off my clothes. Then, naked and partly paralyzed, I lay on the dirty canvas stretcher with a blanket thrown over me until I was carried to a table in the little whitewashed shed that served as examination-room. With a radioscope under my body, the doctor marked me six or seven times.

"Only one bullet?" he asked. "Yes," said I.

"I don't believe it hit the bone, but I'll have to take it out. Then you can go to your friends tomorrow."

Tomorrow! I thought I never could wait till tomorrow!

I waited a year.

They carried me to a table in the operating-shed. The last thing I saw before they covered my face with a cloth was the doctor's apron, a solid crimson patch.

I awoke at noon, not in Paris, but on a stretcher. Through my twilight senses I could dimly see my captain.

I dropped asleep. At evening I awoke again. Someone shot some dope into me, and I went back into a hot darkness, which lasted until morning. Again I awoke, begging for water.

Someone brought me a bit of bandage dipped in a cup of water and let me suck it. There was a violent numbness in my hip; weakness and thirst were all I suffered now. With my wounded leg drawn up and my knee doubled tight, I could turn on one side. For the first time I had a chance to survey my surroundings.

Ten miles back from the Verdun front, the great French evacuation hospital in which I lay was near enough for German aeroplanes to bomb us frequently. Indeed, the hospital was intended merely for operation; as soon as a man was able to be moved he was sent on to Paris or elsewhere for treatment. The average patient stayed three days; a few bad cases, five.

As an aviator I had been given the best the hospital afforded. I was in the officers' ward, a long shed containing about thirty cots packed closely side by side. Made of three pine boards covered with a straw mattress, two coarse sheets, a small pillow, and blankets, these beds were very different from those we now give our wounded. Then, at the height of the Verdun siege, every bed was filled. In fact, I never saw an empty one.

As I looked down over the rows of beds I again had the feeling that life was echoing unbearably my own state. There in the receiving-room it had been the torment of pain that had been dinned into my brain by those poor *poilus*. Now in their dumb eyes about me I saw my own drugged and stricken will.

It was toward one person they were all looking. Irresistibly I followed their gaze. *Madame*, the chief of the five women nurses, was just coming in from the dressing-room. Her skirt was like a snowy sail, and on her sleeve I caught the gleaming cross of the *Secours des Blessés*. There was dauntless energy in her profile, which in its bold curve reminded me of the prow of a boat.

Yet it was more than courage that took her to duty under fire. Tenderness was back of it. When she looked at me I knew why they all turned to her so hungrily. Every time she glided into the room she seemed to each man there like some long-waited ship from home.

In the days that followed I don't know what I should have done without her. When she was away I used to long for her to come back into the room. Even her French had a homey sound, and the crooning little way she had of saying "*Mon fils*" made me feel as if I were back with my own mother in Texas. Of course we saw very little of her. For all those fifty portable houses that constituted the hospital there were only five women. The rest of our nurses were young medical students who would have been graduated in 1917. They had intended to go on with their training in the auxiliary army, but, having for various reasons been found unfit for service, had been transferred to the medical ward. This lack of women nurses was not a mere sentimental deprivation. Despite their medical training, the most of these students had none of the sick-room efficiency instinctive in the average untrained woman. True, they would doubtless have done better had they not been overworked; but there were not enough nurses, either men or women, to give us more than the most meagre care.

A few minutes after *madame* entered the room that first day the surgeon who had operated on me came to my bed.

"Ah, ha, my boy," said he, holding up to me a little bag, "I'll show you what I got out of *you*—six pieces of bullet. Want them for a souvenir?"

Strange how lively is the grim humour of the hospital! To the outside world it might seem ghastly, these jokes made by dying men. To us it seemed we were always waiting for a chance to laugh. For instance, a short time after my arrival I heard a young officer saying peevishly to his surgeon: "Why didn't you bring me *all* the bone you got out of my hip? You might have known this wouldn't be enough to make dice."

Now as I looked up at the pieces of bullet he had brought me, I felt myself grinning. My own enjoyment was echoed by a grizzled old major who, brought in yesterday at the same time that I was, lay in the bed next to mine. Painfully wounded as he was, he gave a little crow as I put the souvenirs down on the stand at the head of my bed.

The desire for water was so intense that it absorbed every other sense. I wanted to hear water, to see water, to feel it trickling through my fingers. So violent was this one longing that I was actually blinded. I did not at first see a man standing beside my bed.

Then I saw the heavy, black hair, the great arms, and the sincerest eyes in the world. When I put them all together, I gave a groan of joy. It was Victor Chapman, flown over from Bar-le-Duc.

"Hello, old boy," he was saying. "Here's your toothbrush."

He was holding it out in his great paw, and I think I realised even then how hard he was trying to be matter-of-fact. The toothbrush, the English words, the dear American voice, the aviator whom everyone in our squadron loved deeply!

In a moment the terrible thirst came back to me. "Oh," I thought, with a touch of the craftiness that is part of sickness, "if I can only *look* how thirsty I am, Vic will do something about it. He'll see that I get something better than an old wet bandage to suck."

"Anything I can get for you, old man?" he said.

"You bet," said I. "They won't let me have any water." The way I kept moistening my lips finished the appeal.

"How about oranges?" he said, and turned to my doctor, just at that moment come in.

"*Bien*," answered the surgeon, with a shrug; "but there are not any to be had in the village."

"Guess we'll fix that," said Victor. "I'll get you those oranges if I have to fly to Paris."

I looked from one to the other. Oranges! Why hadn't I thought of those before? There is a certain sublime ignominy in the way a sick man permits himself to gloat over something which he cannot have. I gave myself up to this ignominy completely.

"Don't you worry," said Victor, lingering by my side and giving my arm a pat. "Be out of this in no time."

He was part of my beloved Bar-le-Duc, he was my friend in a world of strangers, yet I looked at him almost impatiently. When would he leave to get the oranges?

The next morning I woke from my hot, drugged sleep to find my captain bending over me.

"Well, my little one," said he, "I have a present for you."

Could it be the oranges at last? I looked up expectantly. Something in the expression of my officer's face drew my attention to the whole room. There was a deep hush, and through it I felt the eye of every man upon me. Then I saw for the first time that my captain was not alone. The major and colonel were with him.

Suddenly the colonel stepped forward.

" In the name of the Republic," began he—he took from his pocket a large box—"I confer upon you le Médaille Militaire and la Croix de Guerre."

"For me?" I asked. "What for?"

The figure in its horizon blue gathered as if about to spring.

"*Pourquoi?*" His light, racing syllables slowed solemnly. "You are the first American aviator to be severely wounded—for France. Suffering greatly as you must have suffered, you flew far, over German ground, to bring your machine back safe—to France. There is sometimes a braver thing than overcoming an enemy. It is overcoming yourself. You, my son, have done this—for a country not your own."

He bent down and kissed me on both cheeks. Then, as I wore no shirt, he laid the medals on the pillow beside me.

My only value to France had been exactly the value of the machine I had brought home. From my decision to stay on the job had sprung my one bit of usefulness; for that decision had come now this honour. It was strange that this cool, efficient colonel should have commended my struggle rather than my performance! No, not strange. That was the spirit of his whole country.

In the solemn hush a cork popped. *Madame*, chief of the women nurses, had produced some champagne, and was pouring a little in the glass of every man in the ward.

"*Vive le petit Américain!*" she proposed, her eyes, as mellow and lively as the wine, smiling at me over the bottle.

"*Vive le petit Américain!*" came back the cheers, some almost a bark of pain, some already feeble with death, as those spectres raised themselves on their pillows.

Now I knew what it all meant—those people grouped about me like the picture of some famous death-bed. Yesterday I had seen two men decorated. Both had died within an hour. So my time had come!

"*Merci*," I responded at last in a scared voice. Then, to my own surprise, I heard myself adding firmly, "But I'm not going to die."

The ceremony was over. The officers had congratulated me and left. Lying back, I looked at my insignia on the pillow beside me. For one moment I thrilled.

As I looked, however, I had a sudden wayward thought. If only those medals were oranges! I thought of oranges I had seen in California groves, of whole boxes of oranges tilted up temptingly in fruit-stands; of sliced oranges dripping with nectar as I had eaten them in Paris *cafés*. If I could only melt those medals and drink them from a glass—melt them into cold, fragrant, golden juice—

"Boy!" I heard the old major who lay next to me addressing me sharply.

I looked up and saw that he had raised himself on his pillow. There was a fierce interrogation in his eyes that made me quail. Had he read my sacrilegious thought?

"Do you understand what it means—that which has just happened to you?" he was saying now.

"*Oui*," I said.

To fight for France, to die for France—it is a privilege given to only a few. You are one of those few. Do you comprehend the honour?" Utterly exhausted, he fell back to his pillow, but his eyes, still fixed upon me, had in them so holy and deathless a joy that I was awed before it.

I stammered that I did appreciate it. I made a giant effort to put away all thought of my thirst, and on some bits of paper I had found began writing to my mother. Then, completely prostrated, I laid the scraps down, and, to keep them from blowing away, held them on the table by my bag of "souvenirs." It took many days of real toil to finish that letter.

The next day the oranges did come, but it was not Victor Chapman who brought them. Instead, Elliot Cowdin, another member of our squadron, thrust a bag of them into my hand.

I did not at first ask why this was. With my eyes fixed on the fruit, I almost trembled to begin. It was only after a few swallows of the cooling juice that I remembered to ask about Victor.

"Couldn't come today; machine's busted," replied Elliot, leaving me somewhat abruptly. "One of the boys will get you some more tomorrow."

The next day a young French officer looked up at me suddenly from his Paris paper. "*Connaissez-vous un Américain*, Victor Chapman" asked he.

"*Oui, oui, oui.*"
"*Il est mort.*"
"*Mais non!*"
"*Mais oui. Voilà!*"

He then showed me the clipping. On his way to the hospital at V—— with a bag of oranges for a wounded friend. I could not keep back a cry. The next orange that I tried choked me. Yet a few hours afterward I was goaded by my thirst into taking another swallow. After that, morning, noon, and night, I held an orange to my lips. It was to me at first a kind of ferocious contradiction. It pressed in more bitterly the real grief over my friend at the same time that it released all the physical longing of my body.

By this time the doctor no longer mentioned my getting to Bar-le-Duc. His present promise was concerned only with the American Hospital at Paris. Tomorrow I should go there; absolutely, yes, I should be moved tomorrow.

But on the fourth day the shifting tomorrow vanished. Then it was that an orderly carried me the length of the ward to the dressing-table. For the first time since my operation my wound was to be dressed.

"*Voilà*," the doctor was saying merrily, "I pack that hole in you like a pony-pack, and strap you up tight like a belly-band. Then you gallop back to bed."

All the time that he was fixing me up I kept my eyes on his face. I had never realised before that my wound was a serious one. I wanted to ask him something. At this moment, however, an orderly seized me, spilled me into bed, and hurried on to another patient. No one person could get much time in the hospital at V——.

It was the day after this—the fifth day at V—— that they gave me water—water with *vichy*. In the meanwhile I had begun to suffer for the food which, because my intestines were pierced in nearly a dozen places, they had not yet permitted me. Now indeed the longest, bitterest hour of the day was at noon. Then the other men were eating. I could smell those savoury French soups, I could see those airy French omelets, but I could never have a taste.

The orderly was a supple, slim-waisted young Frenchman, with tiny black eyes, like a mouse's, which almost met over his long, mouse-like nose; the whitest, the most perfect teeth I have ever seen; and the smile of the hyena. His smile held a shuddering fascination for me.

"I'll bring you a dish, *monsieur*, that is today's specialty," he would say before he hurried off, to return with a long rubber tube twisted over his arm like a rhythmic napkin. He would then jab in his hypodermic needle, pour in a quart of saline solution, and announce with savage obsequiousness, "Luncheon is served."

At the point of the needle my skin would puff out as big as two fists, and my heart would pump the stuff through my veins.

"You have excellent assimilation, *monsieur*," the orderly would comment. "*Voilà*, how quickly you digest your luncheon!"

Then came the day when I banqueted on milk and *vichy*, and finally the day the doctor had set for my release, the day when I first had coffee.

Coffee was salvation. There was the long, hot purgatory of night, when the lights were dimmed, when windows and doors were shut tightly, when the stench of thirty wounded men, unwashed for weeks, was that of a dog-kennel, when every second was a century. Then morning, the wonder how you were to live through the sleepless day, the end of your endurance and—coffee! For days I had watched other men find revival in that steaming cup. Now my turn had come.

The first gulp brought a hopeful sense of vigour I had not known since I was hurt. Excited by the stimulant, exultant over my coming freedom, I lay upon the surgeon's table waiting to have my wound dressed.

Under the feeding of the last few days I had grown less afraid of the ugly hole in my hip. I had indeed almost forgotten that question I wanted to ask the first day the doctor had dressed my wound. This morning, as I drained the hot, steaming coffee, I had actually felt happy. The good times in Paris had begun to simmer pleasantly in my brain.

When I reached the bed my face must have been very white, whiter than ever; for my old major, being prepared for his departure, shot a sharp glance at me from under the deep cliff of eyebrow before he lifted his head and glared about the ward.

"*Il est un brave petit gars, l'aviateur américain*" he announced loudly, with a warlike lift of his gray moustaches. And motioning the stretcher-bearer to bring him closer, he leaned over, and placed a scratchy kiss on each of my cheeks. I was prouder of that salute than I had been of my decoration. It was harder to earn. I have never heard again of my old major, but I cannot forget one who made that bitterest of all fights with such sublime purpose that he did not even know it was a fight.

The events of that day were too much for me. That night I began to bleed violently. I had one haemorrhage after another.

La "Panne de Château"

"Orderly," I called, "I'm bleeding to death."

The orderly's face said, "That's good." The orderly said nothing. He was hurried and tired. Instead of taking time to get a doctor, he wrapped me up so tight that I was in agony, and left me. I knew that he was worn and sleepless. A few hours more or less pain didn't much matter. So I decided not to disturb him again that night.

But about midnight I heard a gasp. To my old major's bed they had just brought a captain with a bullet through his lungs. Finally his head jerked down. I cried out for the orderly. He pulled a sheet over the body, and left it to be taken out in the morning.

On the other side of me that night was a lieutenant who had been shot in the leg. When they had brought him in that morning his skin was green, his face and hands were full of blood. "Don't let them touch me! Don't let them touch me!" he had screamed when first he saw me. All that night, every time that he heard a step, he begged me piteously not to let them hurt him. When I could stir through my own misery I gave him my handkerchief, so that he could wipe his lips. I gave him, too, my piece of muslin to keep away the flies from his face. Before dawn he was breathing heavily. For the third time that night I called the orderly.

I can't do anything for him," said he, irritably.

He's dying," said I.

Then what more could he want?" growled the orderly.

After the last long gasp I reached over, and at the cost of terrific pain held down his eyelids so that they would stay closed. His face grew cold under my hands. The orderly, coming back on his rounds, pulled the sheet up over the body.

A sheeted form on my right, another on my left. The stillness of death made more intense and solemn the stillness of my own brain. All through the long dawn I lay awake with the thought of my future.

I went on living through ten more days of haunted imprisonment—ten more days tortured for sleep that would not come, days when I was too heavy with weariness to brush the flies off my face, too Hot to cover it with the muslin cloth; ten more nights more tortured than the day, nights dingy and endless and noisy with dying. Every night ten or twelve men found the easier way. Every morning the stretcher-boxes came to carry out the dead. Every morning stretcher-bearers came to fill their places with the living. Not for five minutes did I ever see a bed vacant. Was it any wonder that in the hospital at V—— one lost all sense of the dignity of death? It had become a commonplace mechanism.

In a place where men died like flies, where there weren't half enough doctors or orderlies, the filth was of course indescribable. Although the floors were scrubbed every day, this cleansing could not prevail against the constant stream of wounded. As for the patients, they never had a drop of water on their bodies except when they were allowed to wash hands and face every other morning. If it had not been for the huge bottle of *eau de Cologne* with which my friends from Bar-le-Duc saturated me, I think I should have died of nausea.

As I have said, such conditions will never exist again. The Verdun attack had overtaken France without proper hospital equipment. I never blame those who worked here. On the contrary, I have the highest respect for any efforts which were simply titanic. Every man wounded at Verdun passed through that hospital. Doctors, working day and night, often twelve hours at a stretch, operated on one man after another as fast as they could. Give a man the best you can as fast as you can; if he dies, let him die; if he lives, ship him away where he can get better care: this was the purpose of the place. And doctors and orderlies carried it out with superhuman heroism. If at times their treatment of patients seemed appalling, the strain on them was more appalling.

During this time my only comforts were *madame* and the boys from the squadron. Every afternoon some of the fellows came to see me, a sacrifice which I can never have a chance to repay. All but one of the boys who flew with me in that first American *escadrille* are dead now. I am sure that in their life of hard service there was no conflict more exacting than the day-by-day visit to this loathsome hospital.

As for *madame*, I came to long more and more for the sight of that stiff, white skirt, for the separate look, and the crooning "*Mon fils*." I stayed so long that that separate look became just a little more of a gift to me than to others. I was the oldest patient in point of time, the youngest in point of years. She treated me like a son. Every now and then she would snatch a moment to chat with me. It was in one of these moments that I opened up my heart to her on the subject of the fear which lately had begun to stalk me. I repeated to her my talk with the doctor.

"Do you think," I asked, "that I shall lose this leg?"

How it comforted me to see her laugh away my suggestion! That was exactly what I wanted.

You're sure there's no danger?"

Absolutely, no," said she. "He's a clever fellow, that doctor. If you stay with him, he'll bring you through."

After that I was radiantly happy. If I could just go back to my job, to those good times in Paris!

And then came the change which made all my previous sufferings seem as nothing. The skin on my hips broke and festered. July heat, perspiration, solutions that were used, kept my bed perpetually wet. For days I would lie without moving an inch in a reeking mass of blood, pus, and perspiration. Only when my temperature went so many degrees above normal would my dressings be changed. This was usually about every four days. Then as I was lifted up for the trip to the dressing-table, the hole in the bed made by my body would be black with blood and matter. In the hospitals of today, with their marvellous distribution of supplies and nurses, such a condition would be a disgrace. Then it could not be helped.

I was also getting such cramps that I asked the doctor if he couldn't straighten my leg.

"I've been going to tell you, my child," he said hesitatingly, "that I was afraid you'd have to have another operation."

"Hurrah!" I shouted. "Bully for you, Doc! That's the best news I've heard since we licked the crown prince."

"My dear boy, are you"—he felt for the American slang he loved—"are you going to the nuts?"

"No," I answered, with a grin, "but I should go nutty soon if something didn't happen. I need a change, Doc. Anything would be better than this. Let's have that little 'op' right now before you forget it!"

Had I guessed half the pain that change meant, I should have been contented to go on with the bedsores and cramps and reek.

"You're a good subject," he said, getting me on the table. "This time I shan't even have to strap your hands. Now just wait a second till I open up this fellow over here."

He had exactly the air of a grocer saying to a friend, "One moment, till I cut off some cheese for this customer."

From my own table I watched the other operation. When the doctor finally turned back to me, his apron red and dripping, as always, the man was gasping.

"He's gone," said the surgeon cheerfully, with no thought that his casual air might not prove bracing to me. Indeed, it did not trouble me. I was, however, somewhat disturbed by the opulence with which the orderly, listening to talk, was pouring chloroform on my mask.

"Make him give it to me easier, Doc."

Brushing him away, the doctor finished giving me the drug. I thrilled off into a flight more intoxicating than anything I had ever known. I was more joyous than I had been since I was last under chloroform.

The ecstasy was short. My sciatic nerve had been touched by a portion of the bullet and partly severed. Now, when my leg was stretched out for the first time, all the strands of the main nerve, which is as big as a finger, snapped off. A bullet in my hip, that bleeding, bumping journey across the barbed wire the day of my fight, probings, dressings, festerings, thirst—all these were mere discomforts compared with the agony that dragged me from under the sheltering oblivion of chloroform after that operation.

After accepting the worst, the worst passed me by.

Still under the delusion that his peculiar skill alone could save me, the doctor, who was finally ordered to Paris, said he would ship me on to the American Hospital, where he would join me in a few days.

"And remember," said he—"tell the physicians there that I understand your case, and that no one is to touch you till I come and have you transferred to my own hospital."

So, unexpectedly, came the release I had waited for. No more filth, no more loneliness, no more horror.

The morning procession had begun. Stretcher-boxes were carrying out the night's harvest of the dead. In a moment all beds would be filled again, my bed and those in which these sheeted forms had lain. At the doorway the line was halted by the doctor and *madame*, both of whom embraced me in farewell, the doctor for a few days, *madame* for always.

Fortunately for me the doctor did not, after all, come to Paris. I had been the victim of his kindly egotism, of a judgment that had placed his knowledge of my case against lack of care, sanitation, and science. Just in time I reached the American Hospital. I was put into the hands of the head surgeon there, a man with a big heart and a keen brain. He saw immediately what was needed. I was put first into a suspension-box the weights of which prevented my wounded leg from being any shorter than it had already become. Then came the plaster cast in which I lived for many weeks. In the meantime abscesses necessitated half a dozen more operations. Yet the Carrel system of irrigation, which has saved thousands of lives, saved me now. The miracles of science after the forced butchery at V——, the trained and constant and sympathetic care of women after the hurried attention of those poor driven orderlies, radiant cleanliness, the luxury of baths and snowy linen, delicacies that tempted back my appetite, smokes to soothe me in hours of pain—all these made a whole year and a half at the American Hospital pass more quickly than six weeks in the hospital at V——.

It was Christmas of 1917, several months after America had joined the Allies, that the head surgeon gave me the greatest Christmas present a man could ever have. It was the assurance that I would walk again, with only a heavy limp and a cane between me and normal activity.

WITH THE CIGOGNES

Bergues, July 28, 1917

Just arrived at the Front today and am in *Escadrille* N. 73, *Groupe de Combat* 12. The group is otherwise known as *"Le Groupe Brocard"* after its famous commander Brocard, who is one of the great French airmen. One of the *escadrilles* of the group is N. 3, more generally known as *"Les Cigognes,"* or "The Storks" when translated into English. The name comes from their insignia, a stork painted on the sides of the fuselage of each machine, and this squadron is easily the best known in the French Aviation. The whole group carries the stork as its insignia, the bird being placed in different positions to distinguish the several *escadrilles*, and consequently the entire group is often referred to as *"Les Cigognes."* The original *"Cigognes,"* however, which has gained such a wide reputation, is *Escadrille* N. 3.

This group is the most famous fighting one in the army and admittedly the best, so you can see that Chadwick and I were very lucky to get into it. It contains more famous fighting pilots than any of the other French flying units, one in particular, Guynemer, who has to date brought down about forty-eight Boches officially and many more unofficially. To count on a man's record, a victory has to be seen and reported by two French observers *on the ground*, or some such rule as this, so that a Boche shot down far behind the lines, where no one but his comrades see him fall, does not help a pilot's total. Last evening Guynemer got one twenty-five kilometres in the German territory, and as I sit here on the aerodrome he has just got into his machine and started off for the lines in search of another victim.

Chadwick and I and two other Americans who came with us are the first Americans to be sent to this group. An *escadrille* or squadron in the French service numbers about fifteen pilots and machines. We are indeed fortunate to get into this crack group, but as it has suffered rather heavily lately, they had to fill up, and so we got our chance. This morning Captain Auger was killed and our own chief, Lieutenant Deullin, was shot down with three bullets in his back, but will pull through all right. He was shot down last night also, but only his machine was damaged. He went up again this morning, and while attacking one Boche, another got him from behind. He has seventeen Boches to his credit officially, so I guess he is entitled to the rest that his wounds will give him. The captain who was killed had got seven German machines officially, so we are sort of out of luck today, losing two such good men. It seems to come in bunches that way for some reason or other.

It looks as though I shall see lots of service and have a chance to learn a great deal before the time comes to transfer to the U.S. Army, if it does come. We hope to be able to stay where we are for a considerable length of time and that we shall not be forced to leave this French unit before we have learned a lot more about military aviation and have been able to make some return for all the training that we have received. This group is usually, like the Foreign Legion, moved about to the particular locality in which there is going to be an attack, so we shall see plenty of action. It was, for instance, at the battles of Verdun and the Somme, and it seems that it is usually in the thick of it. For this reason it is obvious that I shall not be able to tell you where I am and must be very careful what I write. Since beginning this letter I have been talking to one of the officers about the censorship and have, as you will notice, been doing some censoring on my own account. No details that could possibly be of any military importance, so you will have to be content with much briefer and more general letters than I have been writing heretofore.

You will be glad to know that I got a S.P.A.D. (the letters stand for *Société pour l'Aviation et ses Dérivés*) machine, the kind I hoped to get. Also I shall have a chance to do a good deal more practicing before starting in in earnest. The officers are as usual very nice and willing to help in any way they can. We get a great deal of advice and information here which I have been anxious to get from the beginning. When the time comes to make our first trip in search of a real live Boche, we ought to feel able to give him some sort of a run for his money. Here's hoping that my first adversary is a young pilot like myself. Should hate to bump into a German ace for a starter.

It is quite a sight to see a bunch of the "Storks" starting off at crack of dawn for a flight over the lines, or to see them coming home to roost at dusk. One sees here probably the finest flying in the world, and it will be a great advantage to us young ones, who as yet are not real pilots by a long shot, to be able to watch these men work who really know the game. One is naturally anxious to get started, but I shall take your advice and go easy until I feel able to take care of myself. As you say, rashness only results in throwing yourself away to no purpose and foolhardiness is certainly no essential of bravery. As far as one can discover, the most successful men have been those who have known when not to sail in and take too great chances.

A Raid on Étain

August, 1917

Toward the end of August I had an opportunity to participate in an air raid on a rest camp for German troops, located near Étain, a town between Verdun and Metz. With three comrades I was patrolling between Bézonvaux and Les Éparges, a section of front to the east of Verdun, where the line runs south to the Saint-Mihiel salient. My altimetre registered 15,000 feet. Our patrol took us south to the grass-hidden trenches at Les Éparges. There we turned abruptly, and then, like three great ducks, we swung north to that shell-battered corner where the lines run west to cross the Meuse. Back and forth we beat for more than an hour, nothing interfering with the monotony of the patrol. One enemy two-seater ventured near; was pointed out to us ay the white puffs of the "75's" but beat a hasty retreat to the shelter of is own guns when we threatened to attack.

A Voisin Bomber

Then suddenly fire from the German guns showed us, far below, a giant three-man plane crossing from the French side into enemy territory. On its wings it bore the tricolour *cocarde*. We watched it sail serenely over the lines with white and black shell-clouds all about it. Over the plane and on one side two Spads followed, banking and turning to make up for the difference in speed. The three machines crossed fairly into the enemy's air and flew smoothly along toward Metz. Our group chief made "Russian mountains" *i.e.,* raised and lowered alternately his elevating planes) to attract our attention. Then he swung east in a great arc. We changed our direction to follow him, and it was well we did.

As the bombing plane and its escort passed over Étain the German artillery fire increased in fury, but they continued eastward, not even bothering to manoeuvre, as they flew through the smoke of the incendiary shells. Thousands of feet higher, we remained behind the bomber and its escort, twisting and turning to be always between them and the lines, and climbing as we went.

Suddenly the shell-fire stopped. We did not need the instant balancing of our chief's plane to know that Boche hunters were after the bomber. Then we saw them, two groups of five planes, a little lower than ourselves and less than a mile away. The sun was low in the west and effectively hid us from the Germans.

Our chief balanced the signal, "All ready," as the enemy approached. One group, of four single-seater fighters around a fast biplane of the Roland type, was now very near. They had not seen us. But the second group, farther away and lower, had made us out, showing black above the sun. Coloured rockets were dropped from the two-seater of the farther group to warn their comrades. It was too late, for we dropped among the five German planes just as the first of them, a new and shining Albatross, turned its nose down to attack our bomber's escort.

I dove on the two-seater, intending to pass under its tail and shoot from behind and beneath. As I slid through the air, the enemy machine grew bigger and bigger in my sight. Then the black crosses came into view, sinister against a pure white background, and I saw the gunner frantically shifting his gun to bear on me. The tail hid him from my sight as I passed below. I "stalled" (threw up the nose of my plane) and began firing. The enemy turned sharply to bring his guns against me, and as he did so a hail of machine-gun bullets from his back seat made me turn "at the vertical" after I myself had fired one burst.

But that was the end, for while I was diving and so occupied all of the enemy gunner's attention, one of my comrades placed himself above the Roland. At the moment that I turned to escape the German's bullets, the Spad dropped down in a steep dive, spitting fire as it came. The Roland fell on one wing, then on its nose, and instantly went whirling downward in a twisting dive. Fire and smoke marked its descent.

A hurried glance around showed me that no more German planes of the first group remained. All were down or fleeing. Another glance and I saw that the second group had attacked our bomber and his two escorting planes. Here was a *mêlée* beyond description. A red glare on the ground and columns of heavy, black smoke showed that the rest camp back of Étain was in flames.

The two gunners on the big bombing plane were gallantly defending themselves while the Spads attacked the higher Germans. The enemy machines dove, two by two, on the bomber. The Spads dared not go lower than the highest of the five Boches. But now four of our group fell on the Germans. Two of the enemy machines dropped immediately and crashed in the trees of the forest of Spinicourt. With help at hand the bomber headed for home head down and spitting tracer bullets from both sets of guns. Then suddenly its rear gun stopped.

We circled, dove, fired, and righted our planes. There were two German machines left and they fought together well. One of them, a two-seater, had a crack gunner who protected a "chaser" from attack from behind while the latter dove to fire into the big bomber. At a point about halfway between the forest and Douaumont three of our Spads attacked the two-seater and succeeded in driving it down and out of the fight.

We crossed the lines without difficulty and landed together at V——. The *bombardier* and the rear gunner of the big plane were dead in their seats, and the pilot had been saved only by the armour-plate shield behind him. All the Spads returned safely, although several were damaged. Lieutenant D—— had thirty-odd bullets in his plane; Maréchal de Logis P—— had almost as many, and I counted in the left wing of my Spad a half-dozen shots which had come from my late antagonist in the Roland.

On the other side, four German planes had been destroyed to the best of our knowledge. They had fallen in the forest of Spinicourt, too far to be seen from the trenches and *homologués* (certified as destroyed).

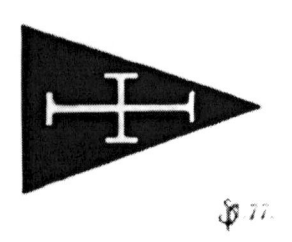

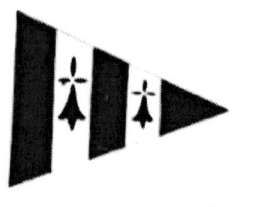

INSIGNIA OF FRENCH ESCADRILLES IN WHICH MEMBERS
OF THE LAFAYETTE FLYING CORPS SERVED.
PLATE 2

The official report of the fight said:

> Patrol of 5000 metres. Bezonvaux to Les Éparges. 17 hours 30 to 19.30. Protection of bombing plane. Combats with German patrol. Four German planes shot down.

OLIVER CHADWICK

August 14, 1917

The King and Queen of Belgium received us here yesterday. I was introduced to them both and said a few words to the king. Will write you all about it soon, but not now. My friend Oliver Chadwick has evidently just been killed. We are not absolutely sure yet, but there is practically no hope. He was the best of them all, and we have been together all the time for months. I had come to know him better than I have ever known any other man, and he was as fine and fearless a Christian gentleman as ever lived. He was apparently shot down from 2000 metres in a combat and fell inside the German lines over the little destroyed town I have described. I am glad he died with his boots on, as he wanted to, but my heart is sick and I cannot write you about it till later.

Saint-Pol-sur-Mer, August 21, 1917

Just a line to tell you that I am well, but I have so many letters to write that you will have to wait until next week before I shall be able to write you fully. My friend, Oliver Chadwick, was killed by the Boches on Tuesday. He sailed in to help out another machine that was being attacked and was in turn attacked from the rear by two other machines. At least this is what happened as far as we can learn. We are not even sure that the machine that was brought down in this manner was Oliver's, and as it fell in the Boche lines there is no way of verifying it, but the evidence is very bad, and I am afraid there is little hope. There is the barest chance that he may be a prisoner, but it is very slim.

Then on the 18th Julian (Biddle) was killed; so it was a very bad week for the Americans here. I am terribly sorry about Julian, and I naturally feel his loss very keenly, for we were always very good friends and had had a lot of fun together since coming to France. He was an excellent pilot in the schools and extremely conscientious and hard-working. He got his military license in a remarkably short time and sailed through all the tests without the slightest mishap. Once he had had time to gain a little experience here at the Front I felt sure that he would have done very well. Julian and Oliver and I might have had some great Boche hunting expeditions together if luck had not broken so against them. I am glad to say that M—— arrived here the day after Oliver was lost, so I am not left the only American in the *escadrille*.

Hobnobbing with Royalty

Saint-Pol-sur-Mer, August 24, 1917

Got a rainy day today, and as I have pretty well caught upon the writing I told you I had to do, I can now drop you a line about what has been going on recently.

On August 13 we were inspected by the King and Queen of Belgium. We all got dressed up in our best and stood at attention while the King conferred some Belgian decorations on some of the men for bravery and the work they had done. I have some pictures of Oliver, Julian, and myself standing in the line of pilots with the king and queen in front, and shall send the photos along as soon as I have an opportunity. The commandant stopped in front of us and introduced us all three to the king and queen. You see we are the first American pilots in the *escadrille* and therefore somewhat of a curiosity, so we sometimes receive attention to which our rank would not ordinarily entitle us. Shook hands with them and called them "Sire" and "*Madame*" as per the commandant's previous instructions. Had a few words with King Albert, who said he is hoping for great things when America gets her forces over here. Glad to say he spoke English, as I was scared to death lest I might have to talk French to them. Kings and telephones get my goat when it comes to talking French. I guess little Willie is some pumpkins hobnobbing with royalty and such, eh, what!! The king is a very fine-looking man and the queen is most attractive.

German Revenge

August, 1917

The night following the attack was set apart by the Boches for revenge. At ten o'clock, while we were at dinner, the lights went out—a signal that enemy planes were overhead. We had set up half a dozen machine guns in trenches and holes about our barracks, and we hurried out to man them at the first notice of a visit. To the north the sky was marked by hundreds of *éclatements*. Powerful searchlights combed the heavens and searched a few scattered clouds. "Caterpillars," as we called the string of incendiary balls shot from the trenches, rose over the lines, and soon the droning hum of motors was heard directly overhead. Our camp was as dark as the grave. Not a light shone in the town, less than a mile away, where army headquarters was stationed. The large base hospital at V——, some eight hundred yards north of us, was indistinguishable in the darkness.

We strained our eyes and ears to locate the Boches. There were two of them; by the sound, bimotor Gothas. Then, amid the crash of the artillery and the whistle and shriek of falling shrapnel, we heard the stutter of a machine gun. Following the luminous trail of its tracer bullets, shot from the corner of a wood near the field, we saw a giant black form outlined against the blue-gray of the summer night. It was directly overhead, flying placidly through a storm of bullets and shrapnel. The noise of its motor suddenly ceased, permitting us to hear that of its mate, off to the right. Then the whistle of the wind passing through the machine's wings came to us as he dove. A series of eight tremendous explosions followed, throwing us face down in our shallow trench and casting dirt and stones in every direction. We rose immediately to peer up at the Boche. There he was: only a few yards above us; as we fired at him, he turned on his motor and dashed off over our hangars. There must have been twenty guns blazing at the enemy machine as it came across the field. The rattle of the guns, pierced by the screams of some poor devil near us who had been wounded by bombs, was deafening. Then, as the first Boche disappeared to the east, a voice in our trench cried: "*Mon Dieu, l'autre est sur l'hopital!*"

We turned to the west as one man, to be greeted by the crash of the first bomb. It exploded fair in the centre of the largest hospital building. A quick flash of flames showed the entire group of buildings with the huge red crosses on their roofs, and, plain as day, we saw the great bird of ill omen circling above. Five times he turned, dove, dropped two bombs from less than three hundred feet high, and disappeared into the night. The sixth time we saw the two gunners lean far out of their cockpits, while they poured machinegun bullets into the burning hospital buildings. Curses and cries of rage rose from all sides. At last the Boche disappeared, followed all the way to the lines by a trail of shells and bullets from the ground.

"*Ah, les cochons!*" cried Tir-Tir. We leaped out of the trench to see the results. Eight bombs had fallen among the buildings of our camp. Three men were wounded, and a soldier of a battalion of *Chasseurs d'Afrique* lay with his skull crushed beside the path to the road. Not

A DIRECT HIT

one bomb had struck a building, but almost every *barraque* and tent was pierced through by the bits of *éclat*.

"*Ils reviennent!*" The cry drove us back to our trench. This time again there were two of them. They flew over the field at a greater height than before, still pursued by the searchlights and shells of the *Défense contre Avions*. "It's not for us this time!" cried a voice as they passed over.

Then the motors stopped—and crash after crash rent the air, as the great bombs fell into the village. We counted twelve. The town was in flames in four different places before silence fell. Then we heard the noise of a motor in the town. It was plainly an automobile, and, while the Boches circled overhead, we saw in the glow of the burning houses three ambulances of the Norton-Harjes Section, then stationed at the evacuation hospital of S——, gathering up the wounded along the main street of the village. The American volunteers were living up to their precedent and reputation.

All night long the Huns came, and in the morning we learned that every hospital behind the sector in which we had attacked had been bombed and set afire.

At V——, near us, seventy Frenchmen, recent *amputés*, had been burned alive because they could not be quickly moved. Two heroic nurses, who had refused to leave their charges, died at their posts, and a score of wounded German prisoners were killed by their own steel.

A Collision at 3500 metres

August, 1917

Went out yesterday evening about six o'clock on a voluntary patrol with C——; we manoeuvred around over the lines for more than an hour, hoping to catch some Boches napping. Toward seven o'clock 1 attacked an enemy patrol, but was unable to get close enough to shoot, as they *piqued* desperately into their lines at sight of us. I took altitude again waiting patiently for a better chance, with C—— keeping close behind as is his custom. At 7.10 I made out a group of three Germans well below us and approaching our lines. I manoeuvred to get into the sun and drop on them. We were at 3500 metres above the German trenches in the region of Avocourt.

Suddenly I heard a crash and felt a formidable shock. My companion had seen the Boches and, diving directly on them with full motor and eyes dazzled by the sun, had crashed into me as I turned. The sound was terrible; his machine carried away the whole right side of my elevators and lateral stabilizer. Next moment my machine was hurtling down in a *vrille*—a mad descent varied with breathless side-slips.

At 2500 metres I perceived the trenches exactly beneath me. Would I fall into the hands of the enemy or would my remains be picked up by Frenchmen? My compass marked north; German territory. I made efforts to change the course of my fall toward the south. Suddenly I remembered the sun, which showed that I was sliding to the south and would fall in friendly territory. I used every means in my power to slacken the speed of my fall, but my efforts seemed only to accelerate it. I resigned myself to the thought that this was the end; my only hope was that a crash among the trees of the forest of Hesse might break the final shock. Suddenly I heard the stammer of a machine gun. It was one of the Germans I had been about to attack. He had seen the collision of our machines and thought that by shooting a few bullets in my direction he would be able to confirm the destruction of a French machine without danger to himself.

The trees of the forest of Hesse appeared. They seemed to approach at a. dizzy speed. I shut off the spark to avoid fire, and as the tree-tops rushed at me, I pulled back the stick in a last desperate effort to redress.

A tremendous crash! A tree higher than the others tore off my right wings and whirled the machine around on a pivot. I closed my eyes—a second shock less violent; the machine had crashed down on

A bad crash

Incredible Luck

its nose at the foot of the tree which had broken its fall.

I unfastened my belt, which luckily had held, to let myself slip to the earth, astounded to feel no pain. My head felt heavy and a little blood trickled down my cheeks. I drew a long breath, I coughed, I moved my arms and legs, more and more astonished to find that nothing was broken. At that moment a number of artillerymen arrived and took me to the dugout of their captain.

A hasty examination showed that I had escaped with only the slightest of wounds. My head had struck the windshield and my goggles, which I had failed to take off completely, were broken to splinters, which had cut my right eye and upper lip. Prodigious, incredible luck! To fall from 3500 metres in a machine from which half of the tail had been cut away! To escape with nothing but a few scratches! What had I done to deserve such good fortune!

As for C——, his machine was so slightly injured in the collision that he was able to come down almost normally. He landed near by, but had the bad luck to strike a high tension line which made him do a couple of loops before arriving at the ground. He was unconscious when taken from his machine and his face was badly bruised, although no bones were broken. Unfortunately he has internal pains which may mean serious trouble. Until he saw me he refused to believe that I was not dead or grievously wounded.

Here I am living the life of a country gentleman. They all think that I bear a charmed life.

Over a Battle at Verdun

August, 1917

As the month of August wore on, the long trains of artillery passing toward the Front, and the frequent convoys of ammunition wagons, told us that either we or the Germans were going to attack. One afternoon our commander called all of us into his office and announced gravely that on the following morning at dawn an attack would be made by the French, along a front of twenty miles in our sector. He familiarised us with the signals which were to be used from the trenches to show the progress of the infantry, and mapped out our work. My squadron was chosen to begin the attack.

There were two patrols, one to fly far behind the German lines to give battle to enemy planes, and the other to fly close to the ground, protect the aeroplanes which were designated to observe and report on the infantry progress, and attack German troops, roads, artillery, and placements with our guns and with bombs issued for the purpose.

At dinner that night all topics of conversation other than the attack were abandoned. Those of the squadron who had been through former attacks explained to the newer men what the work would be, and we went to bed early to prepare for the morrow.

At 3.30 a.m., while it was still dark, we were routed out. After our usual breakfast of black coffee and bread we went to the hangars. The stars were shining brightly, promising a clear day. We found our commander and captain, and the two officers in high command of the French aviation, waiting for us. At a quarter to four my motor was ready. A faint band of light in the east told us that day was not far off. The first man to take the air was Lieutenant de R———. I followed him after a few seconds, but immediately we lost sight of each other in the darkness. A few minutes later I was alone at 2400 feet over the line of fire which marked the trenches. I circled around and around, waiting for the dawn to give me my bearings. Suddenly, as the gray light came, a crash beside me brought the news that the Germans were shelling. It was too dark to see my compass, and I was confused, so I circled to and fro for a short time, until the light showed me the dial of my instrument. I found I was several miles behind the German lines at a height of about 2000 feet.

The firing on the ground increased with daylight and the German and French front lines were marked by continuous streaks of smoke and flame. Then, as the light grew stronger, I saw three Spads so far beneath me that they seemed on the ground. I took a long breath, dove through the barrage and joined them. The marks on the wings showed them to be the three French commanders. For several minutes we circled over the lines, until we were joined by two more Spads and, with our commander at the head, set forth into the German lines to *strafe* the Boches. Suddenly we saw the French barrage fire move north, and I realised with a thrill that the attack was on. We were too low to offer a target to the anti-aircraft guns, and the German infantry was evidently too busy with its own affairs to shoot at us. At any rate, during the two hours following, in which we shot up roads, infantry, and German guns, I did not perceive once that I was being fired upon. However, in crossing the lines, we all saw distinctly shells passing us, going in the same direction as ourselves.

The rockets, which showed the progress of the infantry, were proceeding steadily northward, indicating that our troops were not meeting with great opposition. After two hours of work we returned to the

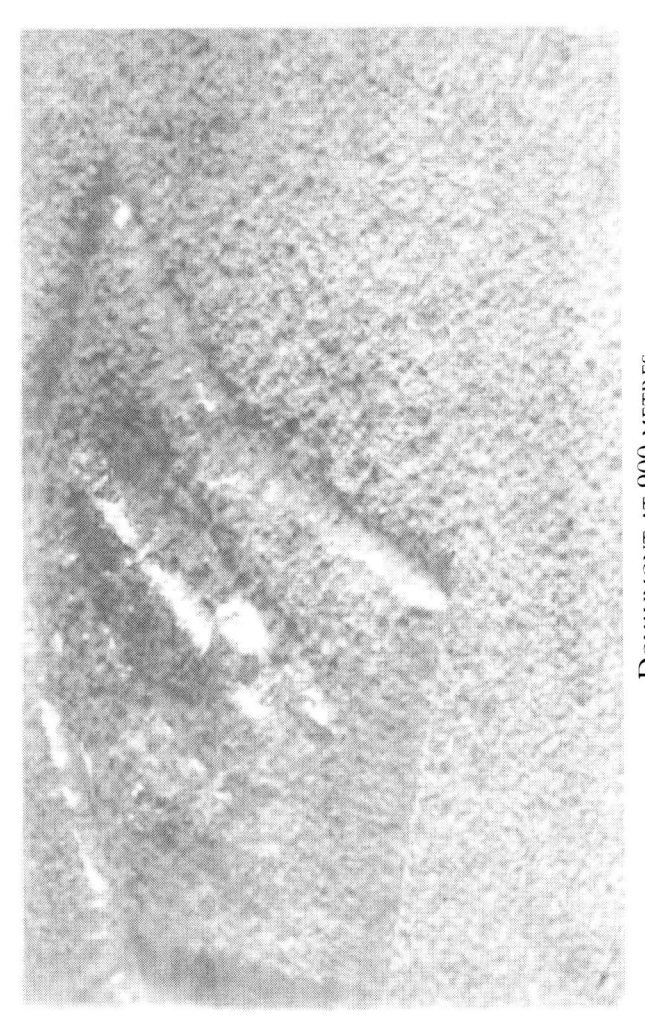

Douaumont at 900 metres

field and rushed immediately to the office to watch the progress of the advance on the large map made ready for the purpose.

During the day I flew three times for periods of two hours each. We met with little opposition in the early part of the day. In the afternoon, however, the Germans reinforced their aviation, and the task became more difficult. We were each attacked once, but the superior speed of our planes, and our *élan*, due to knowledge of the success of our troops, carried most of us through safely.

The next morning we found to our satisfaction that the infantry had gained all objectives and was consolidating its gains. The losses on the ground had been remarkably low, slightly over four *per cent*, and the aviation had been complimented for the service rendered in the attack.

THE GERMAN GUN FOR DUNKIRK

Bergues, October 3, 1917

The sector of the Front where we do practically all our flying runs from Dixmude[1] to Ypres. The Belgians are on our left and the English on our right here. As you are seeing by the papers, the British have been giving the Huns "what for" around Ypres, and I hope we can keep it up and make substantial progress before the bad weather sets in. It has been much improved lately. When we fly really high Ostend is plainly visible, and I often think of the days that you and Mother and I spent there, swimming, going to the races, etc. Times sure have changed! Not long ago several of us were protecting an artillery regulating machine when our big guns were trying to blow up the huge Hun gun that bombards Dunkirk. This work was nearer the sea than usual, and at 16,000 feet Ostend looked almost as though you could drop a stone on it.

It is interesting when this big Boche gun bombards at night. When she goes off our men signal it in from near the lines; they blow a whistle in Dunkirk and all the people take cover. Between one and two minutes later, I should think, the shell arrives and there is an explosion which, with one exception, beats any other I have ever heard. After that you can hear the crash of falling bricks and broken houses.

The one exception I mentioned was when our camp was bombed again about ten days ago. For the second time in ten days our cook shack was wiped out and my room wrecked along with the others. It took a lot of time to fix things up again, not to mention being a great

---

1. *Dixmude* by Charles Le Goffic is also published by Leonaur.

nuisance. This time, I was in a trench with the other pilots just in front of the barracks. The trench had been prepared for such occasions and it certainly came in handy. Three bombs fell close to us, of which one was about thirty yards away and the other fifteen feet from the corner of the trench, where M—— and I were. It bulged in the side of the trench, blew our hats off, and threw dirt all over us. The hole in the ground was about four feet deep by about ten or twelve across, and needless to say this was the fellow that broke all my records for noise. I was not quite sure for a few seconds whether I was all there or not. As we were below the ground, however, it never troubled us, though for a while I thought it had about caved in one of my eardrums, but that is all right now.

A night bombardment is a fine sight to watch from a safe distance, but when you are yourself the target it is the most unpleasant thing I have yet struck, especially when the novelty has worn off and you know what to expect. You always know when the Huns are coming by the anti-aircraft guns and the peculiar sound of their motors humming up among the stars. When these motors tell you they are almost overhead it is time to lie low in a trench.

A Comrade's Grave

Plessis-Belleville, November 18, 1917

Here I am again at Plessis-Belleville, and it seems a long time since Oliver and I left here together for the Front in July. I flew an old machine down this morning and now have a little while before my train leaves for Paris. You see when a plane is considered no longer fit for service at the Front, it is sent here to be used for instruction purposes. The fact that a machine can no longer be used at the Front does not necessarily mean that it is not strong, but simply that it has lost some of its efficiency and cannot climb as well or fly as fast as it once could. I had to come to Paris anyhow to get my own new machine and fly it back, and as we had at the *escadrille* an old machine to be taken to the rear the captain told me to fly it down instead of going by train. As you may guess I vastly prefer the former method, for the trip is an interesting one and the time required to go by air is about one hour and a half as compared with fourteen or fifteen by train.

It was quite misty this morning so that I flew all the way at about six or eight hundred metres. Not being able to fly high and the visibility being very poor, I came by way of the sea, keeping it always in sight until I struck the mouth of the Somme, then followed the river to

Ypres, April 23, 1916

Amiens and from there on down the railroad. The country is still new to me and I did not wish to get myself lost in the mist. Going back, if the weather permits, I shall take the direct route behind the Front, for I am anxious to get to know this section of the country. It may be very useful when we are in the U.S. Army. The return trip should also be very interesting, as it will take me over the country evacuated by the Germans last spring, the famous battlefield of the Somme and also that of Arras.

All this explains why I am now at Plessis-Belleville writing to you in the little Café de la Place, where I lived while I was here in training, and of which I think I have sent you a picture. Tomorrow morning I shall go to the great distributing station for aeroplanes near Paris, see that my machine is all right, take it up and try it out, and then next day (weather permitting) fly it back to the Front.

Being here again reminds me very much of Oliver, for it was here that I really came to know, and I hope appreciate him, and we did have lots of fun, flying together, and in off times taking long walks through a beautiful country and talking in frightful French to the people we met by the way. He knew more words than I did, but I think I could beat him sometimes on accent—New England and French inflections are a trifle different.

I have been thinking a good deal about Oliver lately, and I am sorry that I shall have to be again the sender of bad tidings to his father, for last Thursday I found his grave. I told you in one of my letters not long ago about a couple of the Frenchmen in our *escadrille* having been brought down; one was named Jolivet and the other Dron; you have pictures of them both, and I remember I sent you one of Dron, with a cigarette in his mouth and a little puppy in his arms. Captain Deullin went up to the lines some time ago to see if he could find where they had fallen, and when he came back reported that he had found the graves of both. He had not told me that he was going, for I should certainly have asked to go with him; he reported, to my surprise, that he had found the grave of Jolivet in almost exactly the same spot where I thought Oliver had fallen. Thursday the whole *escadrille* went up behind the lines to arrange the graves of the two Frenchmen. I was glad to go and also glad of the opportunity at last to look personally for some trace of Oliver.

When we arrived at what the captain thought was the grave of Jolivet, lying scattered about it were the fragments of a shattered plane. I at once searched for a number, and soon found what I was looking

CHAUVONCOURT

for, 1429, almost obliterated by the rains of the past three months. That was the number of Oliver's machine, and in the midst of the wreckage was a rough grave; at its head a wooden cross that some one had made by nailing two pieces of board together, and on the cross written with an indelible pencil, "*Ici repose un aviateur inconnu*" ("Here lies an unknown aviator."). All around the grave were a mass of shell-holes filled with water and the other decorations of a modern battlefield. I tried to describe to you before what it is like, and this was but a repetition of the rest, that is, at least in this sector. A flat, low country torn almost beyond recognition by the shells; here and there the dead shattered trees sticking up from the mud and water; occasionally a dead horse, and everywhere quantities of tangled barbed wire and cast-off material. Just beyond the grave was the German first line before the attack on August 16. It is marked by a row of half-wrecked concrete shelters, "pill-boxes" the English call them.

Just beyond this is a village, but I stood on what had been the main street and did not know that there had been a village there until the captain showed it to me on the map. This little town has been so completely blown to pieces and churned into the mud that there is literally nothing left to distinguish it from the surrounding country. Not even a foundation stone is left standing.

The grave is only about 1500 yards from our first lines and not far in front of the heavy artillery. I have marked it exactly on a map, and there can be no doubt whatever that this is where Oliver is buried. Although scattered and still further broken by the weather, the wreck of the machine is recognisable as the same as that shown in the picture taken by the priest; the same broken roof of a house in the foreground, and in the distance the same sticks and splintered trees.

I am having a plate engraved by one of our mechanics who was an engraver before the war; on it will be:

Oliver Moulton Chadwick, of Lowell, Massachusetts, U.S., a Pilot in the French Aviation, born September 23rd, 1888; enlisted January 22nd, 1917; killed in action August 14th, 1917.

This will show that he was an American pilot in the French service, enlisted as a volunteer before America entered the war. I think the simpler such things are, the better. Around the grave now is a little black wooden railing, which we put there, and a neat oaken cross; on the cross a bronze palm, with the inscription, "*Mort pour la patrie*." The captain and I are going back soon to put the plate on the cross and I have bought a little French flag and an American one, for I think he would like this. Also I thought I would try and get a few flowers. The spot should be a peaceful one after the war, for it will take years to make anything out of that country again. Just at present there is a great deal of artillery close behind; the roar of the guns was almost incessant when we were there and a stream of shells went whining overhead on the way to the German lines.

A Winter Raid

January 9, 1918

The day before yesterday was beautiful; dawn broke clear for the first time in a week. We all knew that work was ahead and at 8 o'clock every one had assembled at the *popote* for *café au lait* and toast. There is no such institution as breakfast in France; the first heavy meal comes at noon.

The orders of the day arrived by messenger, and we learned that we were to leave at 10 o'clock for a long bombardment trip into Germany. We were to bomb a town about a hundred miles from the lines. From 8 to 10, we passed the time feverishly getting into fur suits, helmets, and shoes, studying our maps so we should not get lost, testing the motors, putting the bombs into position, and so forth. Each of us carried eight large bombs, and as there were thirty machines starting, you can picture the hail of destruction to be let loose.

Do not imagine that our friends the Boches have a monopoly on

A Voisin

works of destruction; on the contrary, they have not enough machines to do day bombing. All of their bombing work is now done at night.

At 15 minutes of 10, thirty engines were roaring in unison, while the anxious ears of pilots and mechanics listened for false notes in the harmony. Every motor ran well, and at 10 sharp Lieutenant Castelli, with Adjutant Cambrai for his observer, sped off with all the noise that a 300 horse-power Renault can make. I was third in the formation.

It was a wonderful day, clear and cold, with a slight haze and clouds hanging feathery and white in the far horizon. Our field is on a high plateau, and as I rose I could see the river, winding like a silvery ribbon through the valley below, where groups of American soldiers, drilling in the fields, craned their necks as they watched us disappear.

We followed the leading machine until we arrived at the rendezvous, a height of 10,000 feet. I slowed my motor and waited for those behind. Below us were the trenches, barely discernible, as there was a half foot of snow on the ground, and far in the distance Bar-le-Duc and Commercy. When everyone had fallen in, we started to get more altitude, at the same time falling into the defensive formation in which it is absolutely necessary to cross the lines.

At 15,000 feet Castelli made a quick turn and headed for the lines; the whole formation swept around and we were off. Soon, black puffs bursting around told us we were in Germany, but the aim was bad and only a few broke near enough to cause us uneasiness. We went on for half an hour without incident, not a Boche plane in sight, and the formation began to straggle a little, as every one thought there was nothing to fear.

I had trouble in going slowly enough, as my machine wanted to run away from the others, and if I throttled the engine she lost height and sank below them. I was puttering with the mixture of air when I saw two specks in the distance, rapidly drawing nearer. They proved to be two dark-gray Boche fighting machines, but after taking a look at our thirty Bréguets, they prudently withdrew to about 600 yards and proceeded to follow along behind, in the hopes of intercepting some straggler. No one straggled, however, and the Boches left us when we arrived over the town we were to bomb, as the anti-aircraft guns began to give us a barrage. I never saw such accurate shooting. The shells were breaking exactly at our level—17,000 feet. I saw Castelli plunge into the mess, and soon I was in it. Between the instinct to dodge the shells and the duty of getting directly over the munition factory, we

THE SPY, OR THE SUSPICIOUS GENDARME.

were ordered to bomb, I had a lively time.

Finally a shell burst, with a magnificent "*woof*," right under my tail, I felt the controls become loose and thought, "Here is where I spend the rest of my days in Germany or some other place"; but it was only the violent air displacement and I soon got her under control again. Kinsolving, another American, was flying beside me, and he waved and grinned broadly at my discomfiture, but no sooner had the grin fairly commenced than he received a terrific one, between the wings and the nose, that sent him skyward for fifty feet. We go so fast, however, that these jars are only momentary; it is all over in half a second, and a moment later we are a hundred yards away, I saw the buildings break into flames and think we got direct hits, but am not certain. We had the advantage of a thirty-mile wind to help us home and soon passed the trenches and were again in France. Here we all began to separate and choose our own route back to the aerodrome.

My troubles now began. We had started with only one map between us, and the observer had taken that. While we were gone, a heavy pall of clouds had come up below and we could barely see the ground. I saw the other Bréguets go diving into the clouds, so I came

"Mais il est fou, celui-là!"

down in a hurry to find them, but when I emerged all had disappeared in the distance. I had no map, was now completely lost, and had a fearful headache. We had been for over three hours at a height of 17,000 feet; I had broken my goggles and could scarcely see with my left eye, as the rush of the air for so long had put a film over it. Therefore I turned around and yelled at the observer, "*Quelle direction?*" Hearing no response, I looked back and saw that he had fainted; the altitude and long voyage had been too much for him. Later on he told me that he had left with no breakfast at all; very foolish, as it is absolutely necessary to have something to eat before flying. I went on in a southerly direction and finally saw an aerodrome. It was not ours, but I decided to land.

There was a strong wind, and I was so tired that I did not pay enough attention to the ground, which was covered with snow. I straightened out from the glide a little too soon, and fell about four feet. Ordinarily nothing would have happened, but by bad luck the wheels struck a ridge, hidden by the snow, and caved in. The speed of the machine made it turn a beautiful somersault and it wrecked itself completely. The poor observer was just reviving, and this jolt brought him around in short order. I was strapped in and pinned under the machine until they loosened the belt. We were about fifty miles from our place and landed (or rather smashed) at an English night-bombardment squadron.

They treated me wonderfully and I remained there for supper. Then I was taken about ten miles to where a squadron of American flying officers were building an aerodrome. They were flying officers, but only two of them, the major and the captain, could fly, and they had never been over the lines. They were very nice, however, and I remained with them overnight. Next morning they took me back to the aerodrome by automobile. There I found that out of eleven who had started on the morning before, only four had returned. All had arrived in France—safe, but out of gasoline which forced them to land all over the country. Every one is back now excepting Lehr, an American, who smashed his wheels about sixty miles away. Thus goes our life when the weather is good.

Cheering up the Infantry

Friday, January 25, 1918

After that terrific cold spell, we now have weather almost resembling summer. With the warmth has come fair weather these last two days, and I do hope it will continue a while, to give us a chance to break the monotony by flying.

Three or four days ago we pulled off a nice little stunt. Four of us were sent out to machine-gun the Boche trenches in a rather troublesome sector. These *mitraillage* expeditions do little, if any, actual harm to the enemy, but are supposed to be a fine stimulant to the *poilus*. It is a very dangerous game. The anti-aircrafts shoot at you, the soldiers shoot at you, the trench *mitrailleuses*, and now and then the trench artillery. It isn't a very friendly reception they hand out. We cruised over to the lines at 3000 feet, *piquing* just before we reached them to about 2400 feet. Then we got in Indian file. The leader crossed No Man's Land, and when directly over the Hun first line, turned, dove, and shot across No Man's Land to our side, and started climbing to repeat the stunt. Each of us followed exactly the same process, and by the time the last had finished, the first had regained his position, and dove again, followed in regular order by the rest of us. In all, we turned about 1500 shots on the trenches. It was pretty good sport, though a bit too risky to be very comfortable, and I don't believe it hurt the enemy in the least. It seemed to tickle the *poilus*, though, for I could see them waving their arms and their casques in the second and third lines.

We had to make a patrol afterwards, so had to save about a hundred balls apiece in case of a possible party with Fritz. After two dives each, therefore, we climbed to 2400 feet (very low, as flying goes) and gave a little stunt exhibition in formation. The soldiers must have opened their eyes. Barrel turns, *renversements*, *vrilles*, vertical *virages*, loops; we ran the whole gamut several times each. It was great. The "Archies" had got our range well by now, and were crashing around us pretty regularly. It got a bit hot, so the leader hauled clear, and we climbed to make our patrol.

The clouds were low, 9000 feet, and we were in them practically all the time. I climbed up through several times, to see if Fritz was lurking in the ceiling, but seeing no one anywhere, stayed on the bottom edge or in the vapour the rest of the time—R.A.S. (*rien à signaler*). I'm not crazy about clouds *chez nous*, but they're good friends *chez eux*. They're wet and cold; it's impossible to see anything in them; the wind-shield, mirror, and goggles get covered with a thick mist which generally freezes in this weather, and the cold is penetrating. Incidentally, they are very rough, and we are tossed about like a feather in a squall.

Had quite a *panne* yesterday. Started out on a patrol with the captain and another chap. My engine began to growl a bit, and all of a sudden there was a crash, the grinding of metal being torn; grating, and rattling, so that I didn't know whether my plane was falling apart, or what had happened. A valve rod and cylinder head had broken, had cut the metal engine covering, and stopped, snapping off short when it hit the *mitrailleuse*. For a few seconds I thought my last hour had come. Instantaneously I cut the contact (shut the switch), then to stop the propeller and engine turning, pulled the machine up as far as possible without tumbling, and by thus decreasing the air resistance, managed to kill the engine. Then I turned and started *piquing* for home. I was at 6500 feet, and didn't know what damage had been done, so couldn't be sure whether my machine would hold together or not, which made the volplaning more or less unenjoyable.

I was too far away from home to make the *piste*, so *piqued* for the aviation field where I knew the Lafayette Escadrille was stationed. It's a bit of a knack landing exactly where you want, after planing far with no motor, but luck was with me and I brought up right in front of the hangars. Telephoned to No. 94, and they sent an automobile to fetch me. Today the mechanics brought a new motor to the field, put it on, and this evening I was told my machine was ready. I motor over and fly it back tomorrow morning.

THE HAZARDS OF DAY-BOMBING

February 1, 1918

A great time this week. We had four days of good weather and made six long bombardments in that time. For the first three trips we had no trouble whatsoever. The last three times we got some real excitement, furnished by the flying circus commanded by Baron von Richtofen.[2] He seems a good sort, for when you fight him and both miss, he waves and we wave back. We had been at it consistently for four days, and so they sent these birds down opposite to make life more interesting for us. On the next raid we reached our objective and bombed it before the Tangos appeared. There was a heavy fog below, so I took a couple of turns to make sure we could see our objective; dropped the bombs and then turned to the right to see the damage. I had to make a large turn, for the "Archies" were shooting pretty close. I looked for my *escadrille* and saw three machines way off in the distance. Started for them and soon caught up.

---

2. *Richthofen & Böelcke in Their Own Words*, a double edition, *The Red battle Flyer* Manfred von Richtohofen and *An Aviator's Field Book* by Oswald Boelcke is also published by Leonaur.

Then I swerved and tipped up to them, for I thought them a little strange. I got up closer, and *wow!* all three dove at me, shooting. Bullets flew by—cutting my plane—so I pulled up at them, fired, swerved so my gunner could let them have it also, and then saw the Iron Crosses flash by. I started climbing and was getting high when the Boches got the sun between them and my plane and came again, but I expected this and *piqued*. They went under me and that left me in position to shoot, so I gave them about 120 bullets, and one went for home. The other two came by again and I went into a tight spiral so my gunner could pump at them—but nothing doing. They beat it home and so did I, for it had been three to one. When I landed I had five holes in my machine.

February 10, 1918

We have been pretty busy and have had some exciting times. I almost got mine day before yesterday and feel pretty lucky to be here. Started out on a long trip into Germany and all the way over we had no trouble at all. After we had dropped our bombs, my observer and I dove down on some villages and used our own guns on them. We got so low that the anti-aircraft guns were popping too close, so we beat it. Soon saw a bunch of hangars below us and dove down on them and shot them up. In a few minutes a bunch of Huns came up from the hangars, so we beat it to catch up with the others. Caught up with them and looked behind us and there were a number of Germans sneaking down. Then the battle commenced and for forty minutes we had a hot fight. We picked off a couple of them and they went plunging down in flames. After that the others went home, and we all returned safely, but I noticed that my machine worked queerly, and when I landed I barely got to the ground without smashing.

I looked the machine over, and you should have seen it! From top to bottom it was one mass of holes. One bullet passed through my combination and hit a can of tobacco. Another cut a main spar in one of the wings; and another hit my stabilizer, tearing it nearly in two. One hit my gas-tank and put a hole clear through it. Luckily my gas was low and it did not explode; but, believe me, I was lucky.

April 20, 1918

The orderly has just tapped on my window to put down my shade, which means the Gothas are on their way. The guns are starting. This attack has been frightful—day after day long lines of ambulances roll by our camp, carrying wounded. Tomorrow we shall continue our work of knocking down their batteries and bombing their railroads. Tonight they are trying to get us.

I started on a *permission* about three weeks ago and had beautiful visions of peace and content for a week, but was called back immediately at the beginning of this attack. Things look bad. Our work here has been hard and exciting and done in any kind of weather. While our losses have been heavy, we have accomplished wonders. Going over on stormy days, when black clouds hang down to within fifty metres of the ground—spotting a group of trucks, a line of cars, or a concentration of troops; bombing them, shooting them up with your machine guns and zooming back into the clouds through a rain of luminous machine-gun bullets: it is interesting work. Out of twenty-four trips we lost eight machines. Chuck Kerwood was among them, an American boy from Philadelphia, who has been with us for five months.

I had a chance to go back to the States as instructor and almost took it, but when the time came to leave this band of men who have been in it for almost four years, I couldn't do it. They are men, and have pulled me out of tight holes when I was green at this game, and they did it at the risk of their lives. Now I've seen them drop off one at a time, fine young Frenchmen, and I guess the least I can do is to stay by them. I feel that my work is here.

In Hospital, May 3, 1918

Well, here I am at last, but I fooled them for six months. Finally one slipped up behind me. Didn't see him, but I felt him all right. Only got it in the leg, so it isn't very serious, except that the bullet was incendiary. They have sulphur on them and I'm afraid of complications. This is a good hospital in a nice location; the only thing I hate about it is that I may not be able to get back to my *escadrille* for fifteen or twenty days.

In Hospital, May 16, 1918

Going to have another operation tomorrow and then I think I'll be well. And, believe me, I am going back and get somebody for this. We are now on the Somme; I suppose you know Baron von Richtofen has been brought down. I'm sorry; he was a game, clean scrapper—I know, for I had several brushes with him. The Huns came over last night and dropped sixty bombs, killing 125 people and wounding I don't know how many more. Several of the bombs hit within 300 metres of me and our beds shook like the dickens.

Dark Days

March 25, 1918

Today (to be explicit, at 10.40 this morning) I brought down my second official Boche in flames. This one fell near the banks of the Oise River, during the third day of the terrible offensive. Oh, it was a wonderful sight! I watched him fall all the way to his last resting-place, in the middle of a railroad track, amidst a cloud and explosion of smoke and flame, just as if a shell had hit the ground, instead of an aeroplane—a machine which two minutes before contained two living human beings. I can think of nothing more like the whole spectacle than tissue paper burning as it falls from the hand, the pieces of the wings—black, charred remains—trailing down slowly, listlessly in the air, like the burned paper they resemble. Then the beautiful big body of the graceful Albatross, spinning, nose first, with the two left wings gone, the whole mass making one final plunge to disappear in black smoke, which for several minutes trailed upward like the funeral pyre it was.

Then I sailed away, exulting, beating first one hand, then the other against my knees in the happiness of having conquered another enemy; all the time, however, keeping a weather eye out for possible Boches who might at any moment come driving down on me, the avengers of their fallen comrade.

It was a wild, barbaric exultation, far, far removed from the Christian ideals upon which our world and lives are founded. But again comes the only comforting thought: they tried to destroy me. They were the eyes of the advancing armies.

The lines are bending backward, Parisward, all the time. One does not know where the true line rests. We see the shells exploding one place today. Tomorrow, they are farther to the rear. A German balloon rests over a certain wood. Tomorrow, it rests at the beginning, instead of at the end of that wood. A pilot comes in and announces great masses of German troops moving toward a certain town. Another brings in the report that he saw a train of German artillery five kilometres in length advancing toward that same spot from another direction. Still another pilot says he fired from a few hundred metres with his machine gun, upon a convoy of automobile *camions* several kilometres in length. On the map in the headquarters is the newest marking showing where the Germans have advanced beyond the Somme.

Now comes the news that day after tomorrow we must move, with all our belongings, to a position where we shall be closer to the centre of operations, in the heart of the English positions. And so it goes, for the day. A million things out of the ordinary happen. The most wonderful tales of deeds and happenings come in. Here is one which I think worthy of repetition. It happened this morning.

One of the best pilots in the group, a young lieutenant, went out for some deep reconnaissance over the Boche lines accompanied by two others, who, by the way, did not long remain with him. He was deeply engaged with affairs on the ground when he was set upon by five Albatross. He tried his best to get away by outmanoeuvring them. Failing in this, he did a *vrille* with full motor. Only a Spad will stand this terrific strain. He *vrilled* to within twenty metres of the ground, jumping the trees and houses and fields, with two on either side of him, and the other three over and behind. In trying to get out of this pocket by a sudden vertical jump, his motor stopped, just as he started. Of course, his plane came tumbling to the ground, turning over and smashing it to bits.

He got out. And then, those Boches proceeded to use him as a target, each taking turns at shooting at him. And what do you suppose he did? Played dead, lying there stretched out on the ground, with bullets spattering all around him, expecting any moment to have one finish him. Then and only then did they go away, believing they had killed another Frenchman. He was only cut around the head.

While waiting for aid to come, after having telephoned his safety to the *escadrille*, what did those Boches do but come back an hour later and take photos of his wrecked Spad, lying there upside down. Now that is a story, I think. How my Albatross falling in a flaming *vrille* pales alongside an adventure like that!

And still the Boches are advancing. It seems to me that even the attack on Verdun will take second place to this, the final German effort of the war. If we can only weather this storm, it will be the beginning of the end! We *must* weather it!

Why are the British giving in in this unlooked-for manner? If the French, who saved Verdun and Paris, would only come—*soon, soon, soon!* What makes it so terrible is that the British retreat is not like an ordinary retreat. It resembles that of the Italians, a precipitous flight, with the loss of goods, ammunition, guns, almost everything. No one understands it. The newspapers talk optimistically, to hearten the reading public, naturally But anyone can see that the papers are "stringing" a lot of gullible people.

By the time you receive this letter, the results will cither be good or bad, for us. At any rate, you will know then, what I cannot as I write. I am not afraid of the final result. Not a bit of it. We shall surely win in the end. But things are serious at present. And what I do fear is a weakening of the will of the people, should we lose in a single month all the results of three years of effort, bloody and long. Of course, if the Boches can hold their gains, there will be a cloud-burst of propaganda for peace—from the Germans. And in this moment of temporary depression, I am afraid of the masses of uneducated and unthinking and unreasoning people losing their "grip" for a fatal moment.

There is just one thing, I think, which will bear the French Nation up enough to go on in the face of another reverse. And that is the faith in and the aid of the United States. It is perfectly marvellous what childish faith each and every French man and woman, high and low, has in the power and ability of the U.S. We are everything from Saints to mighty dragons of destruction. We have, indeed, a tremendous responsibility to be worthy of. I wish that we were ready to shoulder that responsibility in a manner befitting us! America has procrastinated, while France has bled! I am proud of my citizenship, but I am still prouder that I answered the call of France, and that now, in the moment of its greatest peril, I am standing at an advanced post.

Nerve-Strain

Au Front, March 28, 1918

Well, all's well that ends well! But I feel queer and weak and happy after my experiences of the past few days and more especially because of this morning's happenings. For three quarters of an hour I flew about some thirty kilometres back of the German lines, lost in a fog. And all the time I was no higher than 500 metres. I sure thought I was a goner. It was some experience, especially as I found an aviation field and when I started to land discovered it was full of Boche planes. Then, a little later, I met a Gotha in full flight and found another aviation field with a German "sausage" tied to the ground. When I saw the "sausage" I knew I was getting close to the lines. And before long I saw the smoke of burning Noyon and was soon in the midst of bursting shrapnel. However, I mounted up in the mists again where they would have difficulty in finding me.

Oh, Mother, if you could only know what agony I passed through all the time I was lost! And then what thankfulness at getting safely back!

My compass? Yes. But it doesn't work half the time, due to the

AT THE SCHOOL OF ACROBACY

magnetos and the metal *manche à balai*. When I move about much in the air it refuses to work, remaining pointed in one direction. And to cap the climax, I thought I had been the cause of the loss of two new pilots—just arrived. And that caused me more anguish almost than I could bear. But happily they both are safe. One landed in our lines, having been struck by an anti-aircraft shell. And the other landed at another aviation camp. So it was I, after all, who came nearest to not returning.

This offensive is certainly proving to be the most thrilling, most exhausting, most instructive, and most terrifying experience I ever expect to have. To go back to where I left off in my letter of the 25th: I brought down my second Boche as you now know, and it was made official. The next day things began to happen. The Boches pushed right through Guiscard, Ham, Roye, and Noyon. Well, it was up to us. This was serious. The Boches had demoralized all the French and English communications. Also they were in a fair way to split the two armies apart before help could arrive. All the French observation balloons were brought down. Because of the rapid advance of the Boches, all aviation fields had to be abandoned in that region. This left practically no one to carry on aerial operations. Every one was moving or seeking safety in flight. The advance was so rapid that not even the French knew where the lines were. There were no wires operating, no balloons, no *Corps d'Armée* aeroplanes. The British were running away without making a stand. (Just why is something neither the public nor I will ever understand, I suppose.)

The Boches were all the time advancing, and something had to be done. Well, the way our *groupe* has stepped in has been a wonderful thing. Two *escadrilles* of Bréguet machines and our *groupe* were the only French planes available those first two or three days. We ourselves were scheduled to move up to Montdidier, but when all our belongings had left in the *camions*, the Boches were reported within seven kilometres of that place, so we were ordered to remain here. It is a good location for our work.

Yesterday the other groups and *Escadrilles des Corps d'Armée* began operating in earnest. It was not all plain sailing at first. I begin to feel a bit tuckered, though the work has only just commenced. And this is what we—a *groupe de combat*, accustomed to fly only at the highest altitudes—have been doing: We have done all the reconnaissance; shooting up troops on the ground, and convoys on the roads; and establishing the lines of communication, at altitudes ranging from twenty to five hundred metres, operating at times eight and ten kilometres in the enemy lines at that altitude. I am enclosing a French *communiqué* from today's paper which relates the work we have done. It is absolutely accurate in statement.

All day yesterday I flew at not more than three hundred metres over the Boche lines locating their positions and those of the French, viewing the destruction of the towns, hunting for columns of troops and convoys on the roads. This morning it was the same thing, only there was a heavy fog and it was impossible to see. I got lost in consequence. Certainly things have gone a-humming these past few days. It is all too vast for me to describe, the burning towns sending up great columns of smoke; the exploding of ammunition dumps abandoned by the French; the dead horses and men scattered along the roadsides; the exploding shells and shrapnel over the enemy's positions; the nerve-strain of flying so close to the ground that the bursting shrapnel makes you jump; the hammer-like blows of a *mitrailleuse* below, which you know is peppering away at you from the ground and which sends up streams of luminous bullets like so much fiery water from a fountain.

And today the Boches are established at Noyon, Lassigny, Montdidier, Albert, and so on. They have got a long way, but I think they are about due for a halt. The French and English were to pull off an attack this afternoon which should put such a crimp in that Montdidier salient that it will never appear again—provided the attack succeeds. I pray God it may. Undoubtedly the Boches are aiming to cut the French-British communications at Amiens and then to drive the latter into the sea.

Word has just come that Pétain has been made *maréchal* in command of all the armies on the French lines and that Foch has been given command of the French-English troops operating at the point of attack. This news is most satisfactory. We all feel sure that these men are capable of redeeming the situation. The French are truly wonderful. The way they have held all along the line is stirring. And now they are taking up the burden of the English as well—and ours. Where are we, the Americans? Still discussing the shipment of troops, while France holds the line! . . .

It does my heart good to see the continuous flash of French guns all along the Front, to hear them explode just beneath me, though my plane is made to bounce like a little boat in a high sea. The continuous firing is a mighty roar all day and all night long. And the Boches do not answer it as we give it. The French Front is holding, and the British must be doing likewise.

A terrible scene meets the eye as one flies over the devastated regions, larger towns like Noyon, Ham, Roye, Lassigny, and Montdidier all flaming and smoking. Smaller towns are mere jumbles of stone and ruin, entirely burned or shelled out. The trenches are easily discernible, bunches of men dressed in the reassuring blue revealing the French lines.

A little ahead is a hill over which bursts French shrapnel. Through the smoke can be seen the dull grayish-green of the Germans snuggling in newly made or captured trenches. The national roads are empty at this point, but on a side road entering Lassigny we see two automobiles. We dive down to one hundred metres and recognise the red crosses painted on the white coverings. We rise again amid the bursting of German shells, all within a radius of fifty metres, while a machine gun spouts up red and white fire. On the other side of the town we see open shell-holes filled with blue-clad soldiers. They border a road strewn with the motionless forms of horses and men. In a trench we see thick groups of men. At fifty metres we recognise them as French. On another road a group of madly galloping cavalry. They are not blue. Are they Germans? Again we dive close enough to distinguish the details of their equipment. They are English cavalry in flat helmets. Farther on a group of many horses dashing along a road minus their riders. This time we discern the grayish uniforms of Boche soldiers beside the road. We let go with *mitrailleuses* as they dive for cover. Then comes the pop-pop-pop-pop of rifles taking a fling at us. And thus we have established the German lines as running over the crest of that hill.

As we turn and pass over Noyon at three hundred metres, shrapnel bursts around us. Down below the streets are empty, houses are burning in all directions. I can even see the bare rafters and a statue in a square. All roads radiating from the city are empty. But along the canal, standing idly on their tracks, are long lines of railroad cars with their locomotives unmanned. The bridges at various points along the Oise and the canal are either entirely destroyed or still smouldering slowly. On the bank of the river in French territory lies a wrecked plane bearing the cockade of the French service. Close to the town lies a dark plane, well within the German lines, marking the fate of two unfortunate British pilots. Not a Boche plane has appeared. There are numerous French planes and now and then a slow-moving English bus. I notice with pride that there are no other French planes as low down and as far within the Boche lines as my patrol.

I lost my patrol in the mist some kilometres within the enemy lines.

Upon returning to camp I found that the others had come in—all except one new pilot. I felt horribly anxious. And then after dinner word was received that he had landed safely within our lines without gasoline or oil. Oh, how relieved I was!

This morning was like yesterday, only worse. I had with me two new pilots and one old one. One of the former failed to follow after a while, so we numbered three. When we reached the lines the haze was at five hundred metres. I flew over the lines and trenches for about twenty minutes. Suddenly a fierce cannonading commenced with shrapnel bursting about us in all directions and great showers of incendiary bullets coming from the *mitrailleuses* below. And all this happening when I thought I was entering our own lines! I realised that I was lost. I saw the two other planes heading in one direction and on the other side of me still another French plane which I tried to follow. But I lost it in the fog at three hundred metres. My compass didn't work. It registered north whichever way I went.

Below me a troop train of wagons passed in the opposite direction. I thought I was heading for home. In an open field I saw a dozen cannon firing rapidly. I felt sure they were French, and I wondered why I did not come to the Oise River. Then I thought of climbing through the fog and getting my bearings by the sun. Soon the earth vanished completely and above was the bright spot which I knew was the sun. My motor began to race, so I pulled back on the *manche à balai* thinking to climb. The bright spot became clearer, then began to fade. The controls didn't work correctly. I knew I was not right side up. I couldn't tell what I was doing. I decided I would have to get within sight of the earth, although I had no idea where I was.

Suddenly I shot down out of the mist on one wing. Off to the right was an aviation field full of planes. "English," I said to myself. I descended to a couple of hundred metres. Imagine my consternation when I saw every plane marked with huge black crosses on the wing tips. They were of the Rumper and Albatross type. When the *mitrailleuses* began spouting I thought of nothing but leaving; and soon was in the mists again. I determined to use the compass if it was possible. I settled down after leaving that Boche field and headed for the south. I saw a canal. What canal was it? I did not know. Then I saw a French *biplace* in front of me. Lost also, I thought, poor devil! The mist was rotten, but I held steadily to my course, sometimes east, sometimes south. Off to the left was another aviation camp, but no machines. When I thought of going back to inspect it I remembered my scant gasoline supply. I could not waste it in useless flying. I had already been out an hour.

Then a machine hove in sight off to my right, a huge yellow bus with black crosses on wings and body. I recognised it as a Gotha. You may be sure I let him alone, passing directly over him with only fifty metres separating us. And he never fired a shot at me, strange to say.

A little later I saw the gleam of water off to the left and ahead it was getting clearer. Perhaps I could find the sun! Perhaps the water was La Fère and Saint-Gobain! I saw a "sausage" close to the ground. It was like the olive branch to Noah. I knew I was getting near the lines, glory be! Then I saw a straight national road—perhaps the road from Roye to Noyon—and a few minutes later the burning houses of Noyon came into view dead ahead, with the Oise and the canal off to the left.

My joy was soon lessened by the bursting of German shells and I entered the mists again, barely keeping sight of the ground below. And so, happily, I journeyed home.

SHOT DOWN IN FLANDERS

May 25, 1918

On the morning of May 15, at about 9.30, Hobe Baker, Lieutenant Baer, and myself sallied forth in response to a telephone call saying that there were a great many Huns on the lines and more of our machines were needed. We three were on the *alerte* patrol for the morning and it is the duty of such a patrol to send out machines in response to special calls, etc. I was leading the party, and when we got to the lines the Huns had evidently gone in, for there were none in sight except very far within their own lines. We cruised about for a while, quite high up, and Baer had to go in owing to motor trouble, leaving Baker and myself. I noticed a lone Boche two-seater sailing about in his own lines, but he was very low down and not in a good position to attack, and I did not want to go down and lose all that altitude until we were sure the activity up above had quieted down. I mean the activity which brought the telephone call, for we had certainly seen none ourselves to speak of. To go down from 4500 to 1000 metres, and then have the Huns come along at the altitude you have just left, means that it will take you about fifteen minutes to get up to them again; and then, nine times out of ten, it is too late. Accordingly, we took another turn about, and seeing nothing, I went back to see if the low two-seater was still there and saw him still sailing around in wide circles, evidently regulating artillery fire. Also I noticed a large white cloud just over the lines opposite and above the Hun, so I thought we might try to spring a little surprise. We dove down on our side of the cloud where he could not see us, flew along just above it until the Hun made a turn near the lines, when I ducked down through a hole and went for him.

Unfortunately, he saw us coming, and when I was within 150 yards of him, up went his tail, and he started diving full motor into his own country. I dove after him as fast as my bus would go and overhauled him a little, but could not get to good close range; started shooting at about 100 yards range and the Boche commenced zigzagging as he dove. I got in about seventy-five shots, I suppose, and suddenly I saw the machine-gunner apparently almost fall overboard, then throw up his arms and disappear in the fuselage.

THE STING OF THE BIPLACE

Evidently he had got it, even though the pilot had not. Just at this moment, when I think with a few more shots I might have finished the whole outfit, my gun stuck, due to a defective cartridge, and I had to give it up. I thought for a few minutes that the Hun might crash anyhow, but he pulled up just over some houses and very low down, for I could see his shadow on the ground close beside him as he dashed off out of sight into his own back areas. The scrap ended three or four miles in Hunland and we got rather heavily "Archied" coming out, but nothing close enough to be dangerous.

When we got back to our lines a few minutes' work sufficed to get my gun running again, and we started up the lines in the direction of home, as our gasoline was getting low. Ten minutes after the first fight, we were flying along inside our own lines, when I noticed a peculiar two-seater circling very low down between the trenches; he could not have been more than 600 metres up. I took him for an English infantry *liaison* machine, which he very much resembled; but then noticed that he seemed to circle into the Boche lines with remarkable impunity, considering his very low altitude, so decided to investigate. Sure enough, there were the old black crosses showing plainly, as he swung almost under me in making a turn over our lines.

I said that this Hun was flying between the trenches, as he was; but in this most terrible of all the battle-fields that I have seen, it is almost impossible to distinguish the trenches from above, and in many places they consist simply of shell-holes joined together. The particular spot where we encountered this Hun is less than two miles from Oliver Chadwick's grave, so that from the pictures and descriptions I have already sent you, you know pretty much what the country is like: very low and flat, and the ground nothing but a conglomerate mass of shell-holes filled with water and barbed wire; here and there a wrecked concrete shelter or "pill-box" and the shattered stumps of trees.

The only way that I knew that my friend was really a Hun was by his crosses, for it was the first Boche machine of the kind that I had ever seen, and indeed I have never heard of any one that I know running into one like it. He had a rounded body like some French machines; the tail was square, and the lower wing much shorter than the upper like many of the English two-seater observation planes. All the Hun two-seaters that I have ever seen or heard of before have both the upper and lower wings approximately the same length. In addition to this it was the slowest bus you ever saw, and I think I could go two

In Flanders Fields

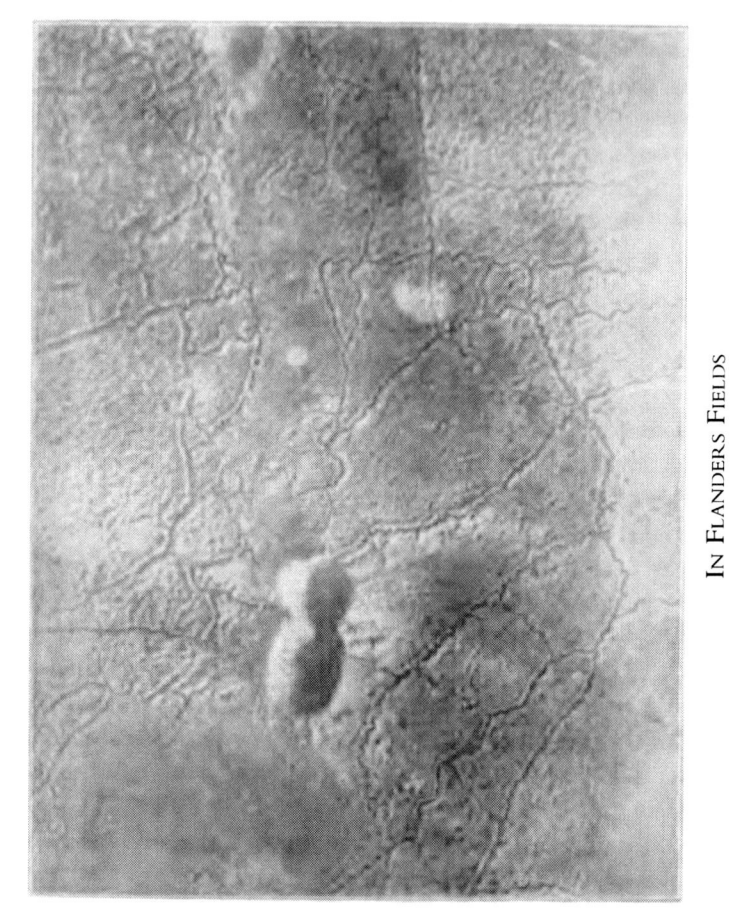

miles to his one. All this leads me to believe that it was a new type of German armoured plane which they call "Junkers" and which I have read about in the aviation reports. They are built especially for this low infantry *liaison* work and are heavily armoured about the fuselage to protect them from fire from the ground. In consequence of their great weight, they cannot go very high and are extremely slow. This fellow must have been a squadron leader or something, for he had four big streamers attached to his wings, one on the top and another on the lower plane on each side. Perhaps, however, these may have been merely means of identification for the benefit of his own infantry, although it is very common for patrol leaders to carry such streamers, so that their pilots may easily distinguish them from the other machines in the patrol.

Personally, I have a big blue band around the fuselage of my machine and also a blue nose, which serves the same purpose. Whether or not this fellow was what I think he was, I hope that when I am flying again I may see him or at least another like him, and have another go at him. He certainly got the best of me, and I don't feel at all vindictive about it, as it was a perfectly fair fight; but just the same it would give me more satisfaction to bring that boy down than any five others. It would also be interesting to see whether his hide is thick enough to stand a good dose of armour-piercing bullets at short range. An incendiary bullet in his gas-tank might also make his old boiler factory a warm place to fly in.

As soon as I was sure that the machine was really a Hun, I dove down after him and made up my mind this time to get to good close range. I did. and ended up fifty yards directly behind his tail and slightly below; but I made one bad mistake, a real beginner's trick, which was the cause of all my troubles. Evidently I was not quite far enough below him, and I had not fired more than four or five shots when I got caught in the back draught from his propeller, which joggled my machine about so that anything approaching accurate shooting became an impossibility. I saw one bullet go three feet to one side of him and another several feet on the other side, so stopped shooting for a second to get in better position. Anyone with a little experience should know better than to get himself caught like this, especially myself, for I had the same thing happen with the first Hun I ever brought down. That time I dove a little before shooting at all, and then fired from a good position a little lower down.

Hence, when I found myself in the same trouble this time I tried to remedy the situation in the same way; but in doing so, I entirely failed for the instant to appreciate the very slow speed of the Hun. I was already close to him, and when I dove down and then pulled up to shoot I found to my astonishment that I had overshot the mark and was almost directly under him, so much so that it was impossible to get my gun on him.

He started swerving from side to side to get me out from under him, so that the machine-gunner could shoot, and I tried to stay under him, swerving as he did, and at the same time slowing down my motor to the limit, so as to let him get ahead of me enough to allow me to start shooting again. The Boche and I were at this time about twenty yards apart, and if he had only had a trapdoor in his bottom he might have brought me down by dropping a brick on my head. However, he did not need it. The Hun gave a twist which took me for an instant beyond the protection of his fuselage. It was only for a second or two, but that was sufficient for the observer, who proceeded to do the quickest and most accurate bit of shooting that I have yet run up against. As a rule, in such a situation, you see the observer look over the side of his machine at you and then swing his gun around on its pivot and point it in your direction. While he is doing this, you have time to duck.

In this case, however, I saw a black-helmeted head appear over the edge of the Hun machine and almost at the same instant he fired, as quickly as you could snap-shoot with a pistol, or with a shotgun at a quail in the bush, for instance. In trying to slow down as much as possible I had almost got into a loss of speed, so that my machine did not perhaps answer to the controls as quickly as it would otherwise have done. This, however, made no difference, for although I tried my best to swerve back under the Boche's body to get out of his line of fire, and in spite of the great quickness with which he shot, he was as accurate as he was quick, and his very first shot came smashing through the front of my machine above the motor and caught me just on top of the left knee. It felt more like a crack on the leg from a fast-pitched baseball than anything else I know of, except that there is also a sort of penetrating feeling one gets from a bullet.

How many more hit the machine I don't know and never had a chance to find out. My motor went dead at once, so that knocked out all chance of any further shots at the Boche. I dove under him out of his line of fire, and then twisted around and planed back for our own lines, trying to make the most of the little height I had. A glance at my gauges showed no pressure in the gas-tank, and that, together with the way in which the motor stopped, made it quite obvious that the trouble was a severed pressure or main gasoline pipe. Now we carry a special little emergency tank which is operated by gravity and is for just such occasions. It will run you ten or fifteen minutes—plenty of time to find a good landing-place. I tried to turn it on, but the little stop-cock would not budge, so I dropped my controls and, letting the machine take care of itself for an instant, tried with both hands to move it. Still no effect; it had evidently also been put out of business by a bullet, probably the same which cut the main connections. It only took a few seconds to cover the distance to the ground which, after I had got turned in the right direction, could not have been more than three hundred yards. I kept working away until the last minute, trying to get the motor going, for every one who knows this country also knows that it is utterly impossible to land any machine in it without crashing, let alone a Spad, which requires at least as great speed for landing as any other type.

ll my efforts were useless, however, and I saw that there was nothing for it but to smash up as gracefully as possible. The thing that bothered me most, however, was not the smash, for that would probably only result in a little shaking-up, but I thought I was farther in the Hun lines than I really was and had most unpleasant visions of spending the rest of the war in Germany, which is not at all my idea of a good time. If, however, it was No Man's Land where I was going down, I thought the Huns would probably turn their guns loose on my plane as soon as it crashed, and that the best thing to do would be to get out and away from it as quickly as possible. I held my machine off the ground as long as I could with the double purpose of getting as far toward our own lines as possible, and also so as to reduce my speed to a minimum before I touched the ground and the crash came. I braced myself inside my cockpit and tucked in my head like a blooming turtle in his shell.

Just at the last moment I veered the machine a little to one side to avoid landing in the middle of a barbed-wire entanglement, and then the instant my wheels touched the ground, over my machine went on the middle of its back with a loud crash. As soon as it was over, I unbuckled my belt and scrambled out, and lost no time in rolling into a near-by shell-hole. I looked around rather expecting to see a bunch of Huns running up to grab me, but there was not a living soul in sight and the place seemed remarkably quiet. Fifty yards away was a German advanced post, but luckily for me it was not occupied that day. It turned out afterwards that I had come down in No Man's Land about one hundred yards from the Hun front lines and three hundred from the English.

Twenty yards to one side was an old artillery observation post made of sandbags, which looked as though it might make a fairly secure hiding-place, so I decided to get there while the going was good, for I felt sure that it could not be long before things started to happen. I crawled toward this shelter as fast as I could go, trying always to keep out of sight in the shell-holes, rolling over the edges of the craters and half swimming, half wading, through the water and muck with which they are filled. On the way I passed a dilapidated lot of barbed wire. I suppose I reached the shelter in less than a minute after hitting the ground and just as I got there machine guns seemed to open up all around. The Hun whom I had so unsuccessfully tried to bring down was flying overhead and I think shooting at the wreck of my machine, although I did not look to be sure.

Then the Boche gunners in the trenches turned loose with a machine gun or two on my plane and the English infantry began firing at the Hun plane to drive him off. The English also seemed to be firing at me, and I learned later that this was true, for they at first mistook me for a Hun. Altogether, there was quite a rumpus, so I just lay low in my shelter, and as the bullets went singing by was mighty glad I had a shelter to lie low in. The Boche plane was still flying around, and I did not dare come out until he had gone, for he would have seen me and potted me like a rat.

While I waited I tore open my pants and had a look at my knee. It did not seem to amount to much—two or three holes as big as the end of your little finger and about a dozen little ones. It looked as though I had stopped a load of bird-shot more than anything else. It bled very little, but I tied it up with my handkerchief anyhow to keep the mud and water out. In less than five minutes after I had come down I heard the sound which I had been expecting and dreading—the whine of a Boche shell coming. The first one landed about a hundred yards over my plane, but the line seemed to be perfect. I waited to see where the next one would go, and the next five or six all landed in about the same place, perhaps seventy-five yards in front of me, but rather effectively cutting me off from the English trenches. They were all big ones (5.9 inch calibre) and came at perhaps thirty-second intervals to start with; later they speeded up a bit, and sent sometimes three or four over at the same time. They used high explosives, luckily for me, instead of shrapnel, but the H.E. makes a terrific commotion when it goes off and throws a column of mud and debris nearly a hundred yards in the air; seems to have rather more bark than bite, however.

Pretty soon they began to come closer, and though I hated to leave my cosy shelter I decided to get moving again, for if one of those boys had landed in my immediate vicinity, there is no doubt at all but that my shelter and I would have gone for a ride. It seemed just a question of time until this happened, so I took to crawling and swimming in the shell-holes again. Stopped for a minute to rest in another little shelter and a couple of 5.9 shells went off just behind it, rocking it from side to side and throwing dirt all around me, which made crawling seem a very slow method of getting away, so decided to try running. Before my leg stiffened up, it did not hurt much; but even so, with these big shells coming that close I think I could have given a pretty good imitation of running without any legs at all.

While in the first shelter I had taken a good look at the sun and at the German and English lines of "sausage" balloons, so that I was fairly sure of my direction. Hence, I waited until a shell had just burst and then got up and made a dash for it along the edge of a little old narrow-gauge railway, where the going was smoother. Had not gone far when a sniper's bullet cracked into a rail alongside of me and I heard the whiz of some more big shells coming. Down goes little Willie flat on his face in the ditch; and boom, boom, boom, went three of them just to one side.

After their first long shots, the Hun artillery evidently got a couple of practically direct hits on my overturned machine, for they blew the wheels off, tore the wings from one side, and generally finished it, thereby making me exceedingly glad that I was no longer in it: all this within ten minutes, which speaks well for their accuracy. After this they seemed to change their range again and began putting them back where the first ones had fallen, and as I had by this time reached this spot they came much too close for comfort. I suppose when they saw me running they thought they would make sure of me. There was nothing for it but to get on as fast as possible, for crawling won't help you if one of these big fellows decides he wants to share your shell-hole.

I kept on running and crawling as opportunity offered, and each time I heard a shell coming I dove head first into the nearest shell-hole. As they are all full of water I made a great splash each time. You can't imagine how the sound of a big one coming close makes you want to hug the mud in the bottom of any old hole that comes along. I guess I had the "wind up" all right (English for being scared); but then I am not used to this kind of war, and I hope I shall never have to be. I struck two more lines of barbed-wire entanglements which were in good condition and very thick. I was afraid to stand up in full view of the Huns and try to climb over them, which would probably have only resulted in my getting completely tangled up, especially as I still had on my heavy fur-lined flying combination.

Therefore, in both cases I went under, rolling in each case into a big shell-hole, submerging up to my chin and swimming under, pushing the wire up with my hands as I went. Funny, what one will think of in such a situation, but I had to laugh at myself as I remembered Bairnsfather's comic drawings "The Better 'Ole" and "When do they feed the Walrus?" If you don't remember them, look them up in the collection of Bairnsfather drawings that I sent you by X——— and you will see what I mean. I don't think I ever really appreciated all there is in those drawings until then. Finally I sat down in a shell-hole to take off my combination, for being soaking wet it weighed a ton and had me so "all in" I felt as though I could lug it no farther.

Just then I looked up and have never been so delighted in my life as when I saw half a dozen Tommies beckoning to me over a low parapet about fifty yards away. I was pretty well fed up with crawling and swimming by this time, so decided to cover that last fifty yards quickly—bullets or no bullets. Forgot all about how tired I was and made a run for it, and it is too bad some one did not have a stopwatch to take the time, for I think I was about two seconds flat. I fairly threw myself into that trench, and the first question asked was, "Sure and who are you?" They were much surprised to find an American. Someone yelled over from another trench near by to know if they had captured a Boche, and one of the Tommies said, "Ay say, Maitie, when you furst come down we was after thinkin' you was a bloody 'Un." They had been led astray by the different arrangement of the colours in the American *cocarde*, red, blue, and white reading from the outer circle in, instead of red, white, and blue, as in the French; and blue, white, and red, as in the English.

This trench where I ended up was an advanced post at the extreme end of a corner salient, so that my choice of direction was very lucky, as it took me to the nearest possible friendly point. It was, however, completely isolated, so that no one could go or come during the hours of daylight, and there was nothing to do but to wait until dark. I reached the trench about noon, having been only about thirty minutes in No Man's Land, but it seemed as many years. The trench was manned by a platoon of the Royal Irish Rifles, most of them from Ulster, and, of course, all volunteers, and a mighty good lot they were. One of the stretcher-bearers put some iodine and a bandage on my wound and another fellow produced bread and butter with good hot Oxo soup made on a little hard-alcohol stove. Cigarettes were plentiful and we settled down to an infantryman's day in the trenches for a change. The weather was beautiful with a warm sun and just a few fleecy clouds floating about.

The Huns kept on for a while dropping 5.9's around the wreck of my poor machine, of which we could see from the trench a portion of a shattered wing, and then things subsided into what the men considered a rather quiet day. There were no officers in the trench, the platoon being in charge of a couple of very intelligent and capable sergeants. We sat and chatted about the war and the affairs of the nations in general, and every now and then some one would produce a cup of hot tea, cocoa, or coffee with hard-tack, bread and butter, and such knick-knacks. These men get their breakfast at 3.30 a.m., and then nothing comes near them again until 9.30 p.m., when it is dark enough to bring up supper, so naturally they take a lot of little odds and ends to spell them in between times.

The trench was an open affair with no head protection except in one or two places where a piece of light sheet metal was thrown across, but this would of course stop nothing worse than a spent piece of shrapnel. The Huns shelled our immediate vicinity very little except for four shells, the first of which fell a hundred yards away, the next fifty, and then two at about twenty-five yards on each side straddling us. No one paid much attention to them; one or two of the men would look up, laugh, and say, "Hey, there, Jerry's wakin' up again." Several times we saw some Hun two-seaters in the distance and twice a patrol of *monoplaces* passed over well up. Our "Archies" got after one patrol of four and split it all up so that I prayed that one of our own patrols might come along, for those four solitary Huns would have made fine picking. The English artillery was much more active, and our own shells kept shrieking just above our heads all day long, for an hour or two in the afternoon becoming very lively indeed. We could watch the shells landing on the Hun trenches four or five hundred yards away and throwing up great clouds of dirt and wreckage, and a most interesting and comforting sight it was.

Toward sundown the men began to get restless from the long hours of sitting in cramped positions and commenced moving about in the trench and showing their heads above the parapet in a way that seemed to me foolish. You may be sure that I did not show even the end of my nose, for having got that far I was taking no more chances than I had to. The sergeant cautioned them, but they did not pay much heed until suddenly "crack" and the dirt flew from the end of the parapet where a sniper's bullet had landed. If it had been six inches higher a Tommy who was standing directly in line with it would have now been in Kingdom Come; but then this war is all "ifs" of that sort. This warning was luckily sufficient, for pretty soon another bullet jostled a sandbag directly in front of where I was sitting.

After one more ineffectual try the sniper called it off, but the episode called forth an anecdote from one of the men. He said that a year or so before he had been sitting in a trench when one of the men had carelessly shown his head. A sniper took a shot at him and missed by a couple of inches, to which the intended victim replied, "Hey, there, Jerry; missed me, didn't ye; 'ave another go at it"; and stuck his head above the parapet again. Quick as a flash—crack, and the man next to him caught the foolhardy soldier as he fell with a ball squarely in the middle of his forehead. " Now," added the teller of this story, "that guy was just arskin' for it and he got it. You guys there will get it too if you keeps on arskin', so help yourselves, but not me!" This was the wisdom of an old-timer, and I think it was wisdom which many soldiers would do well to take to heart.

I had an interesting day with these fellows; they had seen a lot of service. Several of them had come over in 1914 and been at it ever since, many of them wounded—all the old-timers seemed to have been. Finally, as darkness began to fall, an officer came on his rounds inquiring for "the missing airman," and I hobbled off across the duck boards after him, using an old pick handle as a cane, for my knee had grown very sore and stiff during the day. Our path was in plain view of the enemy trenches; but it was by this time too dark for them to make us out, so we were not disturbed. A walk of four hundred yards brought us to company headquarters, and there I had supper with three officers in their bomb-proof shelter. It reminded me more of a large dog kennel than anything else, and to negotiate the door it was necessary to crawl on all fours. The colonel had sent up word from battalion headquarters that he hoped that I would dine with him; but as the officers at company headquarters had also invited me I was glad to take the first meal available.

The dugout where we ate served as a general dining-room for the officers and also as living quarters for two of them. It was perhaps three and a half feet high and certainly not more than eight by six feet in extent, but of course a vast improvement on what the men have. While on duty in the front lines they just flop down anywhere they can when it is not their turn on guard. My day as an infantryman made me very glad to be in the aviation, but the peculiar part about it is that you will rarely, if ever, find a Tommy who envies us. I can't imagine anything much worse than the existence of these fellows with whom I spent the day in the frontline trench. With nothing but an open trench to protect them, they have to stick it there for stretches of a week at a time, and sometimes, when there is an attack on and the reliefs are scarce, the sessions are much longer.

The bottom of the trench is always full of water; the duck boards keep you out of it in dry weather, but when it is wet, they are submerged. All day and night the shells fall around them, sometimes very thick and again only at long intervals. If one lands in the trench or on the parapet, it of course means heavy casualties. The incautious showing of a head may bring a sniper's bullet or a burst of machine-gun fire at any minute. The sergeant told me that he thought what made the men more "windy" than anything else in such an advanced post was the thought of being severely wounded and having to lie there all day before being able to get to a doctor.

In a very serious case where it meant life or death to get a man operated on at once, the stretcher-bearers would of course chance it and take a patient in, in full view of the Huns; but the sniping of stretcher-bearers has become so common that this is done only when absolutely necessary. What a contrast with our cosy billets far in the rear, where we have nothing to fear when not flying other than an occasional bombing at night. Bad weather brings the hardest times of all to the infantry, while to the flying corps it means idleness in comfortable quarters. Nevertheless, the infantrymen will tell you every time that you earn your comforts and that you only fall once in an aeroplane, or words to like effect.

After supper with the company officers I crawled out of the dugout and started on a walk of perhaps a half-mile or more to the battalion headquarters, the nearest point to which an ambulance would come up. As we passed along the trench I noticed a couple of large fresh shell-holes that had blown in the edge of it, and my guide informed me that one of them had blown the company sergeant-major to pieces the night before. By the time we were started across the duck boards once more the last light had faded from the west and a brilliant moon in its first quarter lit up the whole scene. This country, as I have tried to describe it to you, is fantastic enough during the day, but by moonlight it becomes more so; behind the trenches on both sides the sky is constantly lit up by the flashes of the guns and their shells go winging overhead in weird fashion. It would not take much imagination to hear in them the shrieks of the thousands of departed spirits, whose earthly carcasses are rotting in this same ground.

The trenches themselves are lit every few seconds by star-shells and there is a constant procession of Very lights and chains of luminous balls which look like those which come from the burst of a rocket. I do not know what they all mean except for certain kinds of chains of fiery balls which we call "flaming onions," and which I believe the Huns send up to guide their night flying machines. Every now and then there comes a burst of machine-gun fire, from first one point and then another, as some gunner gets jumpy or thinks he sees something suspicious in the gloom of No Man's Land, or the trenches beyond. The tracer bullets from the machine guns make their contribution to the greatest display of fireworks imaginable.

Above it all comes the throbbing of the motors of the night-bombing planes of both sides as they cross the lines in search of their various objectives. Speaking of this, you may have noticed in the papers that the Huns have been again at their old tricks of bombing hospitals and been very successful at it, as they usually are at such work. As we trudged slowly along we passed reliefs coming up to take their turn in the trenches, stretchers loaded with hot suppers for the men, etc., etc., for those front lines in this flat country must be fed and supplied in the dark. I could not help but think of Andalusia with the same moon sparkling on the river, shining on the great white pillars of the house and throwing the shadows of the stately trees across the lawn on a peaceful spring evening. Quite a contrast with this wreck of Flanders.

Battalion headquarters reached at last. The doctor dressed my knee again and I went into the mess-room where I found the colonel. Headquarters proved to be a veritable mine, an intricate arrangement of corridors and rooms all sunk at least thirty feet below the ground so as to be proof against the heaviest shells or bombs. Pumps were constantly working, drawing off the water, for otherwise such a place would be nothing but a well. The colonel produced a bottle of Scotch for which I was very thankful, for I felt like a bracer, and thought I was justified in breaking my usual regulations. While I waited for the ambulance I told him what had happened, and he seemed to think I had done well and been mighty lucky to get out of it, for it so happened that he had been in the front lines at the time I came down and had seen the whole show. He was most agreeable and we had a long talk, as the ambulance was a couple of hours in getting there. He had sent up one of his engineer officers to save anything he could from my machine and blow up the rest.

I discouraged this plan, for I recalled the sad experience of a French patrol which tried to reach a Hun machine that I brought down last month between the lines on the Chemin des Dames. I had had some eighty hours of flight out of my machine already, so it was about done anyway and not much of a loss, and the Hun artillery had pretty thoroughly finished what was left of it after the crash. We take great care not to mark on our maps anything on our side of the lines, so there was nothing the Huns could learn even if they did reach the wreck. Perhaps a few instruments, such as the compass and altimetre, or even the machine gun might have been saved; but to my mind the mere chance of this is not worth risking lives for. Needless to say, I had stopped for nothing once I hit the ground, but only lost an extra flying helmet and pair of goggles so far as my personal effects went.

I would like to emphasise again the kindness and cordiality which I have always met with at the hands of the English. This is the third time that I have been thrown upon their hospitality, and always with the same result. It has not been merely the officers, but all ranks that have shown this spirit of fellowship. There was nothing that the men in the front trenches did not try to do for me. They were continually producing hot drinks and insisted on sharing with me all the little comforts they had and would hear of no refusal on my part. At first I did not like to accept, as I would soon be out while they had to remain, but I soon saw that by refusing I would only hurt their feelings, so ended by being forced to eat almost more than I wanted. I learned that several of the men and two of the officers had volunteered to go out and bring me in out of No Man's Land in broad daylight.

When I came in they were preparing to start. This meant leaving the comparative safety of their trenches and taking a long chance of being killed on the possibility of being able to reach me and bring me

THE ARRIVAL AT LE PLESSIS-BELLEVILLE

in, and would have required a large amount of nerve and self-sacrifice. For me it was a case of being "*between the devil and the deep sea,*" and running one danger to escape a worse; but for them there was no such alternative. As I have already told you, by the time I got to company headquarters I had two invitations to dinner and there was nothing for my comfort and assistance that these fellows did not think of.

At last the ambulance arrived and proved to be one of Henry Ford's vintage. I was never so glad to see a "tin Lizzie" in my life, for I had had enough walking for the time being. Just as I piled in, a poor fellow who had been gassed came staggering along, supported by two comrades. They propped him up in a corner of the ambulance, and as we drove along in the darkness, for of course no lights can be shown, he sat there gurgling and gasping for breath, evidently in the greatest pain. Every now and then a spasm would strike him and it seemed as though he must choke to death. In spite of the modern masks, every time there is a bombardment with gas-shells there are always a few men who get caught by it. The rotten stuff seems to lie for days in shell-holes and such places, and men will suddenly be affected when no gas has been sent over for a day or so. This is one form of war which the infantry has to face that, thank Heaven, we are not troubled with.

We finally reached the ambulance headquarters about 3.30 a.m., and after getting an anti-tetanus injection I turned in on a cot, just as day was breaking, for the rest of the night, for there was no ambulance going to the hospital until morning. My knee hurt too much to permit of sleep and there was a big British gun concealed in a wood near by which kept pegging away, shaking the whole place at each discharge. This, together with a lively bombardment going on farther away, but which nevertheless sounded pretty close, would have made sleep an uncertain quantity for one accustomed to only more distant bombardments.

Among the officers at this place were four American medical lieutenants who seemed like a very nice lot. I breakfasted with them and the English officers, among the latter a colonel, and felt rather ashamed of my sorry appearance. I certainly looked more like a second-class soldier than an officer. Since I have been armament officer of the squadron, I have taken to wearing a pair of enlisted men's breeches cut down to fit, for my work requires a certain amount of tinkering with machine guns, which plays havoc with one's uniform. Then the American tunic, with its high tight collar, is almost impossible to fly in if one is to do any looking to the rear. Hence, I wore simply a sweater over my army shirt and have also stuck to my French *poilu* boots, the most comfortable and serviceable footwear I know. On the morning before, we had gone out unexpectedly so that I had not had a chance to shave, and altogether, in my torn breeches held together with a couple of safety pins and the whole outfit caked with mud, I was indeed a pretty spectacle of an officer.

After sending off a cable to you I got an ambulance about 9 a.m., and started for a British casualty clearing station. I was sitting in front with the driver, when, about halfway there, what should I see coming but one of the squadron light cars with Bill Thaw, Hobe Baker, and Maury Jones in it. I leaned out and yelled at them as we passed, and when they saw who it was they all looked as though they had seen a ghost and nearly fell out of the car.

The day before Hobe had been unable to do much in the fight owing to his having been out a little longer than I had and his gasoline being nearly all gone. He had seen me start down when the Hun shot me, and then smash up in No Man's Land. That afternoon they had got a report from the English that I had been seen to get out of the wreck and jump into a shell-hole and that a patrol would be sent out that night to try and find me. I had sent them a wireless, but it had not reached them and when I tried to telephone I had been unable to get them. Not hearing from the English any report as to the result of the promised patrol, they had naturally concluded that I had been killed or was at best a prisoner, more probably the former, and the major had sent in a report to headquarters that I was missing. I most sincerely hope that my cable reached you before this rumour got out.

When I met them they were on their way to the Front to see what news they could get of me, and as you may imagine they were a bit surprised when I yelled at them. We had a grand reunion, and I think the people of the small village where we happened to meet thought that the American officers had gone crazy. It was a bit dramatic; Jones and Baker did not say much, but both looked as though they were going to cry, and if I do say so myself, I think they were all glad to see me. Bill offered to send me to any hospital I wanted, to Paris even; but as I knew this one to be so excellent and near at hand, I asked to come here. I, therefore, left the English ambulance and went back to the squadron in the light car with the others and then came directly here. At the squadron they were no less surprised to see me than Bill, Maury, and Hobe had been.

Château-Thierry

June 7, 1918

Just at dusk last night, another chap and I took our old ships (they aged and decrepit and I sometimes think arc like "The One-Hoss Shay") an flying very low—about fifty metres—we slipped up to the lines. We aiming for a town on the river which is held partly by the French and partly by the Germans, the stream being No Man's Land. By flying very low we figured we should be safe from enemy planes, as we should be too low for them to see, but, if attacked, would dive for French territory and land. There are no organised trenches as yet. We kept flying lower and lower, so that when we approached the river we were jumping trees. What we hoped for was a convoy to shoot at. Swinging toward the river, I saw an American sentry who looked very business-like. He was a kilometre from the town. From there on I saw absolutely not a soul. It was uncanny: as if a blight had been put upon the land. Wagons were standing by the river, a farmhouse burning. I half expected to see men standing by the farm, rigid as if suddenly petrified while at work.

But, no, I swept over the river into German territory. A train stood on the siding by the station with flames licking up the sides of the coaches. Over the town I flew with full motor, looking for German troops or German motor lorries. I whizzed down the main street, across the village square, and what do you suppose I saw? One dead horse and that was all. But the place was getting on my nerves; I almost expected something supernatural. In every house I thought there was a sniper. I was inclined to turn back, but swung on over two more towns held by the Germans. Absolutely not a living thing in sight. It was ghastly. I got home all right. My companion had been shot at by a machine gun, but thought it was I shooting and paid no attention to it You would suppose that there would have been at least a few persons visible in one of those four villages—but no, not one.

Today we patrolled over the lines rather low—5000 feet—but saw nothing. The French batteries were flashing; the French balloons on one side of us and the German ones on the other, but we were not shelled, nor did we see enemy planes. There was a town down below blazing merrily, but that was all. I saw what I thought was fog, but our French lieutenant said it was a gas attack. I have a new motor in the old ship now and it is doing rather well. If a new motor lasts four or five hours it is good for forty or fifty in all probability.

A French village in late afternoon

Infantry Liaison at Montdidier

June 10, 1918

Since I last wrote you we have been having a rather rough time of it. Of a patrol of six, the first we sent out from here, only two got back. They had the misfortune of being very low and of being far in the Boche lines when the "Tango Circus" found them. Of course they just cleaned them up; of the two who did get home, one was wounded and died a few hours after landing. I have probably written before that he was my room-mate, and a good comrade. We were all mighty sorry to lose him. The day after this clean-up, we went out on a patrol of ten to drop down to a hundred or so metres over the fields where the French were advancing to machine-gun whatever troops we found. The sights we saw there I don't believe any of us will ever forget. You may have read in the papers at that time of the counter-offensive the French started east of Montdidier to relieve the pressure farther down the line, toward Compiègne and Paris.

It was in that we were engaged. Up to the present the only trouble I have had over the lines came from the "Archies" of anti-aircraft, but here it began five kilometres back. The machines were tossed about every few moments by passing shells. These were the big ones fired on objectives far distant. Just over our lines it was much worse, for there we got into the trajectories of the smaller shells; the French 75's and the Austrian 88's. These went by with the same sound as rifle bullets make on the ground. At first I thought they were machine-gun bullets, but they, I believe, can't be heard in a plane. Besides the shell trajectories, there are the machine guns which are very dangerous at an altitude of 200 metres.

Below us we saw scores of tanks. They were ambling along, through or under anything in their way, while shells were digging up the ground all around them. Some distance behind followed the infantry, all in beautiful formation in spite of heavy shell-fire. Passing the tanks we found the first German positions pretty well dug in, but behind the trenches columns of troops were moving up, evidently as reinforcements. These we machine-gunned mercilessly. That is another thing I never shall forget. I trained my guns on a small column of about 150 men and let fly with both at the same time from 200 metres to 50 metres off the ground, and though there were many that fell right and left leaving gaps in the column, they kept right on marching in formation. I was thunderstruck to see discipline carried to such a point. It seemed cowardly to keep on firing, but German machine guns reminded me that ours was not a one-sided game. Later we found a battery of small-calibre guns, and again we started to fire, but here we found that the Boches were more sensible and took cover under their guns, wagons, and anything else they found.

Shortly after this, while shooting up trenches we were surprised by twelve Germans who dropped on us from out of a cloud. At the time a lieutenant (Cramoisie) and myself were bringing up the tail of the patrol, so of course we were the first to get attacked. I saw poor Cramoisie, who was a new pilot, make a feeble turn instead of a brisk one to evade the attack, and a moment later go down in a spinning nose-dive evidently, but I think they found his body in our lines. At the same time Cramoisie was attacked, I found two Boches on my tail, but thanks to my good machine I was soon able to get away from them. That was the closest shave I have had yet with the enemy. Upon getting home I found I had only five bullet holes in my machine, and they were all in the tail. They came most probably from ground machines.

Between the Lines

June 11, 1918

I have some news which you may be proud of; in this second attack I have won the *Croix de Guerre* with two citations for bringing down two enemy airplanes (officially) and one which was not official. This latter one was about fifteen kilometres behind the German lines, too far back for an observer to see. In addition, I have been proposed (and will get it as soon as the general of the army comes around to decorate) for the *Médaille Militaire*, which is the highest medal given by the French to a non-commissioned officer. It has not been awarded to more than ten Americans out of about two hundred who volunteered in the French Army, and out of those ten there are only three left—the others have been killed or captured. When the general decorates me and gives me the citation, I will send it to you.

This is the first time during this attack that I have had a chance to write you. We have been working all the time and there has not been a single time that I have flown that I did not get into a fight.

I am going to try to tell you the story of one of the causes of my being awarded the *Médaille Militaire*. It is, perhaps, the main reason, and also one of the worst experiences I ever had.

We had been sent out to patrol behind the German lines to attack anything we saw. Having incendiary balls in my gun, I was preparing to attack a German "sausage" (observation balloon). Just as I was beginning to descend, I saw a Boche *biplace* machine going in the direction of our lines to do photo work. I put on full motor and signalled to the others to follow. They evidently did not see me signal, for they did not go down with me. (I found out afterwards that only one saw me and that I was diving down so fast he could not catch up.) At one hundred metres from the German, I started shooting. The observer started his two guns at me. I must have gotten him immediately, for as I pulled up to make another dive he did not answer with his gun. Then something happened which would make any man "cuss"—my motor stopped absolutely dead. There was only one thing to do; to dive and lose the Boche plane and try to volplane to the French lines.

As I went past the German machine, it came diving down and put some bullets very close. I then did all the acrobacy I ever learned. When I finished I had come down from 10,000 feet to 1000 feet, and there was no Boche in sight. I looked for a place to land and saw a fairly good place off to my right. I made a fine landing; stepped out of my machine right on the face of a dead German. It took me a minute to realise what was happening. I awoke to the sound of bullets whizzing past my head. That did not disturb me much, because I was wondering why some one had not buried that German. I took off my combination, which is a very heavy affair to keep you warm in the air, and took a look around at my surroundings. All I could see was dead Germans. It suddenly dawned on me that I was in No Man's Land.

Of all the landing-places in France and Germany, I had to choose the worst! Realising what a predicament I was in, I began to devise some way to get out of it. The thought came to me that if I were nearer the German lines than the French, I had better get rid of the incendiary balls in my machine. If you are captured with incendiaries they shoot you without trial. I got back into the machine (to the tune of bullets) and took out a band of three hundred cartridges, threw it on the ground by the machine, and removed my compass and altimetre. I put the two instruments with my fur combination on one wing of the machine. I then looked for a place to hide the cartridges. The first thing I struck was an unfinished grave with two Germans in it. I eased myself into it, lifted up one of the Germans, and put the cartridges underneath him, feeling like apologizing for the disturbance. I started walking back to my machine, and as I got near it, the Boches opened up on it with machine guns and rifles.

The French started firing, too, but at that time I did not know

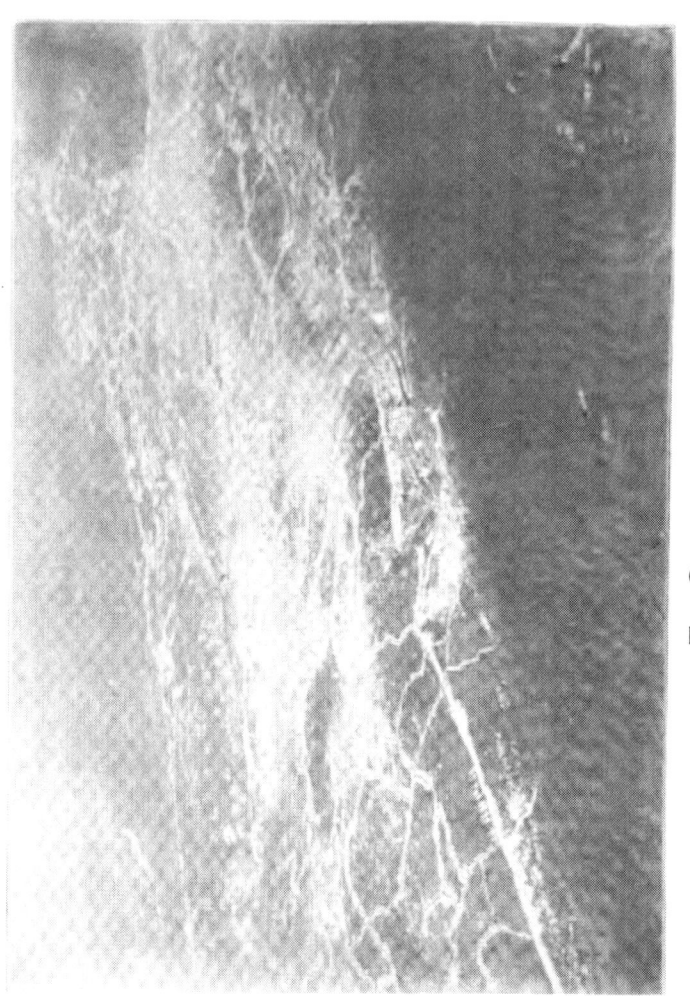

THE CHAMPAGNE FRONT

which line was which. I walked for about five hundred yards right between the two lines, with a steady stream of bullets around me all the time. One ball passed my face, missing me about three inches. I then decided to go to one line or the other, as there was no way of finding out which was the French. Hearing a plane just over my head, I looked up and saw white puffs breaking all around it. That decided me. The French anti-aircraft shells burst white, and they were coming from the lines to my right.

I turned and went straight for our lines. Something hot passed my face, and I threw myself flat on the ground and did not move for five minutes. When I did turn over and prop myself on my elbows, it was to see a young German officer who had been killed a day or two before. I crawled to him and turned him over, looking for a revolver, for I was sure that it was my finish and I intended to make it a good one. He had no revolver, so I was left without a fighting chance. Imagine how I felt when suddenly I saw a French officer beckoning me to come in. If there has ever been a faster fifty-yard sprint, I never heard of it. I ran right into him and nearly knocked the pistol out of his hand. I showed him my identification card, and then started cursing him out for shooting at me. He apologized, stating that they could only see my head. They were in a sort of valley and mistook me for a German. I found out later that the Germans had made a strong attack three days before and that I was the first live man that had been on the hill since.

They took me up to the general of the division. I reported that I had seen over three hundred Germans dead and only two Frenchmen. It made him so happy that he gave me dinner and complimented me, saying that he was very glad I was alive without a wound. He called the chances a thousand to one against me.

Convalescing

Hôpital de l'Océan, Vinckem, Belgium
June 11, 1918

At last it is definitely decided that I am to leave this hospital tomorrow—just four weeks since I came here. When I came in I expected, as you know, to be laid up for only a short time; but knees seem to be very slow and contrary things with regard to getting well. Have been taking walks each day of a couple of miles, so you see I am all put together again. Major Thaw is coming for me tomorrow to take me back to the squadron, stopping on the way at a French review, where a general is to confer decorations. Among the recipients of the *Croix de Guerre* will be several men from the squadron, of whom your angel child gets a cross with palm. This for making a darn fool of himself and letting a Hun shoot him, when, if he had done as he should have, he ought to have plugged the Hun. It seems rather funny, when one stops to think of it, to get more credit for being shot down than you would for shooting down the other fellow.

Soon after writing my last letter to father, the whole hospital was evacuated from where we were on the sea, and we were moved some fifteen miles down the line. We are still about the same distance from the Front and our sausage balloons are very plainly visible. As I was taking the air outside the hospital after supper a few evenings ago, a lone German came across the lines and shot down two of our balloons in flames. The evening before another one tried the same thing, at the same time, but missed the balloon, although he forced the observers to jump in their parachutes. The Boches were heavily "archied," but got away safely both times, and I met Lieutenant Coppens, a Belgian pilot, the other day who has brought down seven Hun balloons in flames in the past three weeks. You see, therefore, that ballooning is not such sure death as father seemed to think; true, they are more dangerous than attacking enemy machines, but, on the other hand, they are a great deal easier to get.

Another evening, a few days ago, I was taking a walk and saw something happen which I think must have occurred but a very few times during the war. The Boches were intermittently shelling one of our balloons with a big gun. They were coming fairly close, but the balloon kept changing its altitude to throw them off their range, and it is not often that a balloon is brought down by shell-fire. They are too far behind the lines and the range is too elusive to make it pay. Both sides have rather given up shelling them, although they still occasionally indulge in the pastime. The evening in question I saw a shell burst a considerable distance above the balloon, and then, as I watched, another burst several minutes later and perhaps a hundred yards directly below. The balloon swung around and started skyward, at the same time drifting toward us in the light breeze. The shell had cut the cable, a most remarkable piece of luck for the Huns when you consider that the range must have been at least eight miles. She had not gone far when two black dots dropped from the basket and then slowed up as their parachutes opened up.

The observers came sailing down as their balloon went sailing

Ñ.3.   Ñ.67.

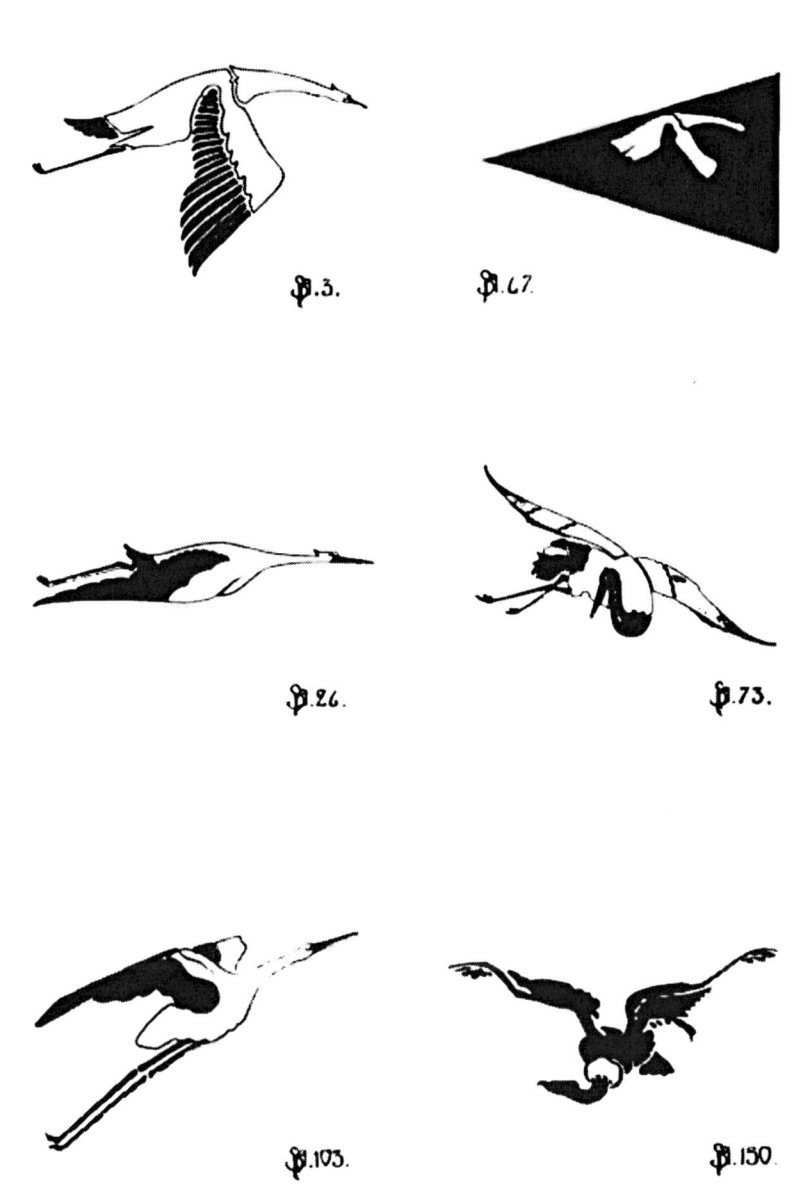

Ñ.26.   Ñ.73.

Ñ.103.   Ñ.150.

INSIGNIA OF FRENCH ESCADRILLES IN WHICH MEMBERS
OF THE LAFAYETTE FLYING CORPS SERVED
PLATE 3

away, getting higher and higher each minute. These captive balloons are equipped like free balloons with a safety valve, etc., so that they can be brought quietly down by the observers in case they break away. These fellows evidently got frightened, however, and jumped as quickly as they could, without even stopping to open the safety valve. Naturally we don't want to lose a balloon with all the equipment in the basket, if it can be helped. A *chasse* machine was sent up from a nearby field and shot enough non-incendiary bullets into the gas bag to let it quietly down in our lines.

Perhaps a minute after the observers jumped, and as they were coming down side by side in their parachutes, the Huns took another pot at them, and the shell seemed to burst just between them, and very close; but, apparently, did no damage.

The other day I met the colonel who is in charge of this hospital walking in one of the corridors with Queen Elizabeth. I saluted as I passed them and then the colonel called me back and introduced me. The queen had evidently been surprised to see an American there and wanted to know what was the matter. She is most attractive and was very kind and considerate.

HAULING DOWN THE DRACHEN

Next day I was standing in front of the hospital with a couple of British officers I know, when who should come up but the Prince of Teck, the brother of Queen Mary of England. He is a brigadier-general in the English Army He stopped and chatted for about five minutes and wanted to know what had happened to me. Now, of course, I do not mean to boast by telling you all this; but I just want you to realise the kind of a fellow I am, and appreciate the society in which I move. When I come home I don't know whether I shall be able to bring myself to associate with you ordinary folks or not!!

But *sans blague*, I did stop and talk with the queen for about five minutes, or rather she stopped and talked with me. She started right off in English, so I did not have a chance to air my French on her. For future reference I might say that it is technique or etiquette or whatever you call it, when one is passing the time of day with royalty, to allow them to start the conversation. I spoke of having seen her last summer when she came with the king to *Groupe* 12, to confer decorations; but I don't think she understood me very well, for she looked at me in a blank sort of way, as if she thought my wound had affected my brain. I did not see the king this time. Both he and the queen seem to keep very busy, and do a great deal of good; they tell me the latter sometimes assists as a nurse in the operating-room, and I know she goes very frequently to the hospitals.

THE MOTOR'S LAST KICK

June 17, 1918

We moved again a few days ago, and from the look of things I think we shall probably stay here for some time, as we can work on two fronts equally well and they will be the busy ones when things start up again.

We were out on a low patrol and I saw a Hun observation plane coming up the lines, so I went down to have a whack at him. I was just getting around into position when my motor stopped. Was not very high at the time, but I had some wind at my back, so *"piqued"* for an open spot in the woods, the only one in sight, but well within the lines, I thought. It happened the Huns had advanced a couple of kilometres on that sector since we had left, so the lines on my map were wrong—and when I was only one hundred metres up, I saw their front-line trenches in front of me. I had been fooling with the *manettes* on the way down, and just then, as luck would have it, the motor gave a few extra coughs, which enabled me to lengthen my *pique* and get into our lines.

Just in front were nothing but large shell-holes and trees, neither of which looked inviting. A few more kicks carried me over them, with little to spare, and I finally landed on the side of a hill between some trees, just in front of the second-line trenches. It didn't take me long to climb out, taking such instruments as I could grab off quickly, and beat it for cover. I finally wandered back to division headquarters and was sent back to rail-head by auto.

That night the Huns advanced farther, taking the ground where the machine remained, but they did not get it, for I left orders to burn it up in case of a further retreat.

A Crash in the Tree-Tops

August 13, 1918

We were five on the patrol; crossed the lines late in the afternoon at a height of 14,000 feet, and were still climbing. Had gone about eight miles into the Hun lines when I saw a black-crossed two-seater making for our lines. He was all alone, strange to say, for whenever you see a *biplace* alone, you can bet that there are some Hun single-seaters around. I had a good look around, under and above, but there was not another German in the sky. Then I pulled my throttle open and signalled the others.

All this was done in about two seconds. Then I dove, full motor. It was a drop of 7000 feet. I got within 500 yards of the Boche and began to fire, both guns at once. I could see the German observer standing up in the back seat, turning his guns on me, and his incendiary bullets were getting uncomfortably close, each bullet leaving a thin line of smoke. He was getting too good, so I changed my tactics, and banked around to come at him from the other side, at a blind angle if I could. I attacked again, both guns working perfectly. Suddenly I saw the Boche machine-gunner throw up his arms and disappear from sight in the fuselage of the plane. The pilot turned and started for home, but I cut him off, by circling in front. He made "S's" trying to get away. When I got him where I wanted him, another "party" began.

I heard a rattle of machine guns behind me and found myself surrounded by Fokker triplanes. I admit I thought it was all over with me. I did every piece of acrobatic flying I knew, and some things I had never done before. Reached the lines at about 2000 feet, with seven Fokkers still on my tail, their tracer and incendiary bullets clipping my wings now and then. Suddenly my motor stopped dead. "*What goes up, must come down"*—I came down! I was in a bad fix now, with no motor and the Boches still trying to get me.

I went into a nose-dive and they either lost me or let me go. Then I looked around for a soft place to land: shell-holes, in fields of barbed wire; trenches everywhere; and a bit to one side a small field with trees about ten feet apart. I knew I was going to have a beautiful smash, and so I pulled my goggles off and chose the woods. I saw the trees coming nearer and nearer and then I went to sleep.

When I came to, I was lying on the edge of a shell-hole, with four French infantrymen standing over me. Believe me, I gave a sigh of relief that they were not Boches. I got up and found that I was a bit lame and with a cut on my face, where I had been thrown against the wind-shield; my right knee was bumped pretty hard against the magneto of the machine.

NO ONE HURT

OUTNUMBERED BY SIEMENS-SCHUCKERTS

September 12, 1918

I must have written you that we have given up *biplace* work and all the *escadrille* is doing *chasse*. This meant that all my old observer friends had to leave; for consolation I was the proud possessor of a brand-new 220 horsepower Spad, picked out to my own taste. Supervised the placing of the two machine guns, tried them on the target to line up my beautiful English telescope sights; then had the wolf's head painted on each side of the cuckoo. Instead of numbers we now use coloured bands, so I chose white and red, and the captain let me paint two blue pennants on top with white stars, making it a Yankee machine.

Well, I had a week's flying; most interesting. Going low over the attack, hearing the shells break on the ground, waving to our soldiers, enjoying it immensely after the high, cold flying I had become accustomed to. Last Saturday I had to say goodbye to my new machine. Went out on a 6.30 a.m. patrol with four others. We flew over the lines without seeing anything interesting, and suddenly my motor began to say unusual things and refused to turn over faster than 1800 to 1900 revolutions. That is speedy enough except in emergency, when you want it to roar along at better than 2000. So I left my Wolves and started for our lines.

Shortly after I lost them from sight, four strange insects loomed up behind and slightly above me (the ceiling was at 1000 metres). Of course I tried everything to make my *moulin* grind faster, but it was no use, and the four pursuers (they were Siemens-Schuckerts, latest and fastest of enemy single-seaters) walked right up to me. The first baby Fritz dove on my tail and opened up with incendiary bullets. I waited (diving) until he had lots of speed and was quite close, then turned sharply, let him pass and dove on him giving him a shower bath in turn. Followed quite a way and saw him do some funny stuff; hope he did the last of it head first into the earth, but I had to turn to fight a couple of others that were making it hot from the rear. I met one face to face and we fired point-blank until each had to dodge to miss ramming the other. Then I went around in a merry-go-round with another, each getting a few shots at the other's tail.

But they wouldn't let me alone for a second, so I started dodging and shooting at anything that came by—not hard to find a target wherever I turned. All this was a downhill fight, the motor slowing so that a dive was necessary for speed; also the odds in numbers drive you down, for they can always have a couple of machines overhead. Finally I jumped a row of trees, banked behind some more, skimmed the ground, cut the contact, and rolled into a low fence, smashing the running-gear and lower planes. As the Huns saw I was unhurt, they continued to shoot. You can imagine my speed in hopping out and running for cover. With the luck that followed me through the show, I came to a road and slid into the ditch with the four most advanced of our attacking soldiers!

Oh! how good the blue uniform looked! Seeing that I had run

across the open without drawing enemy fire, it was concluded that the Boches had retreated. So two non-coms and I walked back to my poor crippled bird to save the instruments. We found ten bullet holes. Hope the Germans had some too. Back of the lines they gave me a horse to ride and a man to carry my stuff. All the officers insisted on feeding me bread, jam, coffee, rum, anything they had. Then a colonel gave me a car and sent me to the general. The latter insisted that I have lunch with him and his staff, although I looked like a bum (only a torn sweater and breeches and no hat). Then another car to bring me here where I got a rousing welcome.

SAINT-MIHIEL

September 16, 1918

I was with the 103rd Aero-Pursuit Squadron, the old Lafayette Escadrille, one of the four squadrons forming the Third Pursuit Group, under command of Major William Thaw.

On the 11th of September, 1918, at twenty-one hours, Major Thaw called a meeting of the Squadron Commanders. Captain Rockwell, my C.O., was away at the time, and upon the major's orders I represented the 103rd. Major Huffer of the 93rd, Lieutenant Hamilton of the 213th, and Lieutenant Jones of the 28th were the other squadron commanders present.

Major Thaw then proceeded to explain to us the details of the American attack scheduled to commence the following morning at five o'clock. It was an unforgettable meeting. The attack was to be under the personal command of General Pershing, extending over a front of some seventy-five kilometres from Verdun to the east of Pont-à-Mousson. American troops and American aviation, aided by French troops and French aviation, were to be under American leadership and direction. It was an inspiring thought.

Major Thaw, who had returned that afternoon from a conference with the wing commander, detailed to us the part the Pursuit Aviation and our *groupe* in particular, was to play in the attack. The shooting-up of troop trains, convoys, and the like with our machine guns, the bringing-down of enemy observation balloons and the harassing of towns by dropping bombs, was the main work assigned to us. The dropping of bombs was an entirely new operation for pilots of American pursuit squadrons. We were also expected to bring in reports of all activity observed upon the ground, and when necessary to carry out special reconnaissance missions behind the enemy's lines.

I returned about 10.30 and explained to the fellows the seriousness of the approaching operation and the part each man would be expected to play. Everything conducive to rest, sleep, and well-being was strictly adhered to, that each man might be able to give the best that was in him on the following day. My announcement of the approaching attack caused a great stir. Many of the fellows were new to the Front. I myself felt a thrill and found it difficult to keep still. After bidding them goodnight and recommending early retiring I returned to my barracks and advised the two other flight commanders (Tobin and Dolan) of what I had learned. I had no difficulty in falling off to sleep for all my inner excitement. Outwardly I tried to give the impression of perfect self-control and calm. I think I succeeded. Just what our particular work was to be on the following day I did not know, because the orders had not come from Wing Headquarters and were not expected until later that night.

When I awakened at six, the guns were hammering faintly away off to the north. The sky was dark and overcast, with rain beating against the roof of the barracks, rain driven by a strong west wind. As I lay in bed wondering about the flying orders and the weather, I could hear the roar of the motors being tested at the hangars. I wondered if the day would prove as bad as the day before when I had made a special reconnaissance trip at low altitude some twelve kilometres back of the German lines, dodging below the clouds at 400 metres.

While I was eating lunch a telephone order came from the Group Operator's office that I was wanted at fourteen hours for a special mission. I presented myself, with curious little thrills agitating my spine; the future looked uncertain and exciting. I received orders to follow the route Mont Sec, Pannes, Beney, Thiaucourt, and return, reporting on all enemy activity on roads and railways. I decided to cross the lines at 1000 metres and then dive, to gain speed. Just before leaving, the clouds broke a little, allowing me to go to 1500 metres. I was thankful for this, as I did not relish the idea of crossing the lines at 400 metres.

As soon as I had passed them I put the nose of my plane down and went to 500 metres, striking first Pannes and then Beney and coming out along the road leading from Thiaucourt to Regiénville. A high wind was blowing from the west. The trenches and roads were practically deserted. Between Pannes and Beney I saw a *camion* train of some twenty-five trucks, and a few cars on the railroad going north from Thiaucourt. Coming out I was shot up a bit by "Archies" and machine guns from the ground. When I landed—rather pleasantly surprised because my work had proved less difficult than I anticipated—I found my propeller had been broken and a hole put in the wing by machine-gun bullets. I had the pleasure of meeting General Patrick, Chief of the Air Service in France, and Mr. Ryan, Chief of Aircraft Production. They, together with General Foulois, asked me several questions about my trip and then allowed me leave to 'phone my report in to Wing Headquarters.

The next morning at two o'clock the Americans started their preliminary bombardment. At five they went over the top and the great attack was on.

At seven o'clock flying orders for the squadron came in. We were to be on *alerte* all day, commencing at eight o'clock. At the hour designated fifteen pilots were at the Operations tent, their planes on the line ready for anything that might turn up. At 8.40 a call came in for a special reconnaissance mission around Thiaucourt and Lachaussée to observe enemy movements on the ground. Three pilots left immediately, covering the mission at 400 metres altitude. All reported the roads greatly congested, with traffic moving in a northerly direction. One pilot got lost, but found his way out again by means of his compass. At eleven o'clock we were all called out to machine-gun and bomb the road from Pannes to Beney. Fifteen of us started. We discovered the road full of artillery, all pointing to the north, but standing still beneath the trees. I let go with my two guns.

The others followed suit. I let go my two bombs on Beney and saw two houses go up in smoke and dust. The two dull booms from the exploding bombs sounded very real. I then returned to the lines and started back for the road once more. I saw American cavalry drawn up in the fields before Pannes, waiting to advance. On the other side of the town the German artillery was retreating. I gave them a long burst and saw the men scatter and break. As I turned away from the road a machine gun had a good chance at me and hit my plane in several places. At that moment my motor went bad, so I came back as rapidly as possible, with a broken tachometre and coughing motor. In the afternoon we went out again on the same sort of work.

Excitement was very great everywhere at the field. At one time three squadrons went off at the same time, sixty planes leaving together. It was a wonderful sight. At another time a formation of fifty Bréguets passed over our field, heading for Saint-Mihiel and intent upon bombing. The clouds were never more than 600 metres high, generally lower. Every half-hour squalls of wind and rain swept down from the west. Yet we kept on making our patrols and accomplishing our work. It was a rip-snorting day! In the afternoon the Americans had captured Mont Sec, the strongest position between Saint-Mihiel and the Moselle River. It was splendid news. By evening the line ran thus: Saint-Mihiel, Mont Sec, Nonsard, Beney, Jaulny, Pont-à-Mousson. The French were to attack in the region of Dommartin-la-Montagne at ten o'clock to meet the Americans at Vigneulles. No word came from them until the following day.

Friday the 13th was a worse day than the preceding—if such a thing is possible. The clouds were at not more than 400 metres and it was very misty. Again we were on *alerte* for the day. About 9 o'clock word was received that the Germans had evacuated the salient of Saint-Mihiel, making their line Fresnes, Vigneulles, Saint-Benoit, Xammes, Jaulny, Norrey. This was thrilling news. About 9.30 the order came to *mitrailler* and bomb the road between Chambley and Arnaville. My motor was running badly over the field, but I determined to stick it out if possible. Upon reaching Chambley, it was going from bad to worse. I did not dare go close enough to the ground to use my machine guns. I dropped my bombs at a cross-roads filled with troops, then started back for the lines, fear and trembling in my heart on account of my bad motor. The five fellows with me shot up the road and then followed me out. I just did manage to make the field, with a couple more bullets in my wings. The roads were filled with retreating Germans, wagons, artillery, etc. I could see them distinctly, walking and riding, on my way out.

After lunch we returned to the Operations tent, ready for action. At 5.30 we were ordered to shoot up and bomb the road running south from Mars-la-Tour to les Baraques, reported choked with German artillery. We started in two formations of seven each, I leading the first, Jones leading the second. As we left the field a rainstorm blew up from the west. The day before I had flown in rain so thick it was impossible to see the ground, so the present drenching did not worry me. We went by Lake La Chaussée, then headed for Mars-la-Tour, going as much with the wind as possible. Jones's formation was about a kilometre behind mine, following the same route. The roads around the lake were generally deserted except the few leading into Chambley. By this time a heavy rain had settled in from the west, covering Mars-le-Tour and all the adjacent region.

I headed off for Chambley, intending to drop my bombs on the railroad yards and shoot up the roads to the south. We were flying at

500 metres. Suddenly the sharp bursting of shrapnel just behind us drew my attention. As I glanced back I saw Jones's formation gyrating around in a crazy fashion, evidently shooting up troops on the ground—so I thought.

At that instant I saw a Spad burst into flames and drop straight down. I continued on dropping my bombs on the yards at Chambley. Directly they were released I looked up to see coming straight toward us above a rainstorm a formation of six Pfalz and one Albatross *biplace*. They had surprised me while I was intent upon the ground. By this time they were shooting at us from the ground with machine guns. I gave a hurried glance above and behind, figuring how best to meet the situation. My motor was running very badly all the while, causing me to feel anything but secure. My first thought was to get into the rainstorm to cut off pursuit. Accordingly I headed for it, the two planes close to me following. It was curious to feel and see these seven Huns just overhead coming for us. I knew we were in for it good and plenty. They seemed very black and imminent with their dark camouflaging and black and white tails. I thought to myself: "Now we are in for it; we are going to get it this time all right." I really didn't see how we could escape. All day I had been thinking someone would get it and asking myself who it would be. Now I wondered who the two were manoeuvring around behind me.

I kept "S"-ing, to keep myself from being a steady target. No Boches appeared to be specially near me. Instinctively I kept climbing (the others told me this later) to get into the thick of the clouds and rain. In a few minutes I could discern very little of what was going on behind me. I kept wondering about my motor, whether she would continue or quit dead. I wanted to go back and help those behind, but could not do so with a motor which threatened to stop any second. To go on seemed almost a cowardly course, yet the only reasonable thing to do was to retreat under cover of the rain and clouds.

We were at a tremendous disadvantage, only 500 metres from the ground and surprised by a formation that outnumbered us by at least three planes. Momentarily I expected to be attacked. As I glanced back I could see a few Huns following, taking it out on the end men of my formation. I wondered if they would be able to get away. It was horrible to be running ignominiously in that fashion. But I did not dare get into a tight scrap with my motor on the point of failing altogether.

In a few minutes I saw a Spad dive steeply, zigzagging from left to right and followed closely by three Boches, all firing at the Spad. I expected the latter to land any minute, he appeared to be going so slowly. "The poor devil," I thought. "Another one done for!" I was then about 900 metres high: two other Spads following me and several Boches following us. I looked for Pont-à-Mousson. It seemed miles away. I watched the lone Spad below, skimming the low land that borders the west bank of the Moselle River. Behind him was one Hun, not gaining, but still following. The Boche did not appear to be firing, so I thought the Spad had a chance. We were still eight kilometres from our own lines and I did not dare go down to his aid.

It was here that I felt the worst, for neither of the two Spads following me could go to the aid of the poor luckless fellow below—he was by this time jumping the trees in the river-bed—on account of two more Huns joining in the pursuit. Finally the single Boche following the Spad turned back and the Spad made his lines. Then two more Boches left us, leaving only one. He kept coming on. Directly I was within gliding distance of the lines, I turned about sharply to meet this following Hun. Head on I gave him about fifty shots and he went over on his back in a half-turn, going down in a *vrille*. I thought I had him. Then he seemed to right himself and fall away toward his own lines, but one of the other two Spads followed him down close to the ground, driving him into a wood.

At last we got home, three of our number missing. Later that night, however, the fellow who had been chased by the river showed up in a side car and another 'phoned in, leaving only Jones, who had gone down in flames. The one who had had such a narrow escape by the river had forty bullet holes in his fuselage alone, all passing within a foot—and at places less than that—of his body. His propeller was broken in four places by bullets, and a spark-plug had blown out, giving him only one half his power. But he had got the *biplace* in flames and was as tickled as could be, apologising to me (he was in my flight) because his plane had been hurt so much. Imagine thinking of his plane before himself! Some nerve! We were lucky to get out of that place with the loss of only one. That night the *groupe* had brought down seven Huns.

The next day there was a little less activity, the weather clearing up and the attack stopping before the Hindenburg line, our *groupe*, however, asked for confirmation on four more enemy planes brought down. In the official reports of the First Army, the *groupe* was mentioned three times as often as anybody else. Besides, General Pershing sent a personal congratulation to the wing for the work the pursuit planes had done in shooting up the ground. *And that was sent to us, because we did that work alone.* Pretty good, eh?

GOOD NEWS FOR MOTHER

October 12, 1918

Last night while reading the Paris edition of the *New York Herald* I chanced upon a most exciting surprise. I saw a heading—"American troops deeds of valour gain them D.S.C."—And the first one named happened to be no other than myself. I shall enclose the clipping which explains better than I can.

You can imagine my surprise! Not a word did I know about any proposition for this medal of medals. As soon as the news passed around the camp, the boys came to my bunk and for hours all I did was shake hands. Nothing was too good for me. One of my friends appointed himself my adjutant and every one came to me through him. Of course this was a little comedy on their part, all the boys laughing and joking all the while. How glad I am today that I am an American! What more can one say?

Now your son with whom you so loathed to part, in December, 1916, has brought high distinction to the family. This regret at parting soon turned to pride I know. You soon realised what my going meant, what joy it caused you after the unimportant natural grief had died away. Nothing has aided me more than to know I have a good mother who sympathises with my conduct and who, should a telegram from official offices be handed her announcing the death of her son on the Field of Honour, would say, *"A sacrifice of which I am proud. Were it possible I would gladly give more."*

Now, dear Mother, just take care of yourself and our family, and as God has so guided me safely against the dangers of battle, may He safely guide you.

A BIT OF PROPAGANDA

1918

We didn't go in for much of that sort of work in our *escadrille*. Most of the men were quite satisfied to make their two gun-spotting flights a day, one in the morning and one in the afternoon, and call it a day's work. There was no jealousy or over-competition, for each took his turn as it came and no one was allowed to go up without his orders. So everything was lovely until the G.Q.G. opened their Bureau of Enemy Psychology. Then they started to swamp us with clever ideas. Pamphlets began to arrive, bundles at a time; paper ammunition, intended to be rained down upon the heads of the benighted Boche until he broke beneath the weight. And they were weighty, too. I could read a bit of German once, and I appreciated their appeal more than did my French comrades. There was, for example, a fake newssheet purporting to emanate from Berne. This gave all the latest news of the Allied victories, coupled with most pessimistic statements of certain German Socialists. There was a similar page from Holland, the country that furnished the sand and cement for so many Boche forts in Flanders. The Holland news, as set forth in the Something *Tageblatt*, showed clearly that Wilhelm and his associates had been operating the business at a loss and were about to be sold up.

Then there was a dainty little card printed in tricolours that touched the heart by its human appeal. It was for the common soldier of Hun extraction unused to involved arguments and economic theories. This was brief and clear. *Soi-disant*, it was a friendly little letter written by one common soldier-of-Hun-extraction to all the rest of his comrades at present under arms. He was a prisoner in France, brave fellow, and so kindly was he treated by his captors, so generously was he considered, that he wanted to pass on the good word to all his fellow Boches. If there were any among them that felt slightly ground-down under the heel of the oppressor (meaning Germany), they could easily come over to a land of liberty, of victorious democracy (meaning France).

And the way was clear. They had only to steal out of their trenches at night, crawl to within hearing distance of the French trenches, lift their two hands to heaven and give the international password. "*Kamerad, ne tirez pas!*" This was pronounced, "*Nuh tiray pah.*" The simplest could understand it. The charming picture of the deserter's reception in France made me feel like deserting to France myself, but I was already there. As I said before, we did not use much of this ammunition. It came in firing charges of five pounds and took up so much room in the observer's seat that he couldn't do his regular work. No one wanted to make a special trip over the lines, so the bundles slowly built themselves up into a small monument in the rear of the hangar, unconsidered by all men except the cook, who started his matutinal fire with them.

In February, 1918, the *escadrille* arrived at Fismes, where the Front was still tranquil. A few artillery *réglages* and a photographic review of the whole sector was the first week's routine. There were very few Boche machines to be seen, and we looked forward to a quiet month which would give us plenty of time to install ourselves comfortably. Our last camp in Flanders had lasted six months, so we expected at least as long a stay at Fismes. Every morning the camp woke up to a sound of hammers. Pilots and machine-gunners spent their idle hours in putting together haphazard furniture and shelves for their quarters. Each evening was the opportunity for the needy to fare abroad in search of planks and window frames from the ruined houses in the valley. These necessary odds and ends we could not acquire in the daytime, but once they were in our possession they were irredeemable. Our quarters became ornate with all the flotsam and jetsam of a bombarded and deserted village.

The beginning of our sorrows was the finding, in a ruined paint-shop, of three quarters of a roll of wall-paper. The lucky finder wove with it a gorgeous background of purple poppies upon two walls of his room. Envy and emulation seized us all. Bare boards for walls were no longer *de rigueur* and every sort of material appeared to cover the honest pine planks. Barault had sheets of printed calico which he bought in the town, but this was paid for and was not considered either clever or fitting. Rehan tacked up several yards of fairly clean straw matting, which kept out the winter breezes effectively. Another pilot used the painted burlap concealment envelope of a hangar. This was so inflammable that we insisted on keeping it soaked with water, and so, of course, he had to take it down. For my roommate and myself there was nothing left except the white canvas landing "T," which was large and clean.

But although the "T" was never put out on the landing ground, we had not the courage to requisition it. It was too much like stealing the *ligne de vol* itself from the Headquarters Office, where it was reported to be kept in a silver case. We complained that the "crawlers"—the *caporals* in the bureaux and the other non-flying entities—were always the first served when it came to a question of house furnishings. Being groundlings, they were evidently entitled to all that was found on the ground, such as roofing paper, pine planks, and barrack lamps. We, the flyers, the youth and beauty of the outfit, were entitled only to what we could find in the air. But Article 22 of the Military Code, *Chacun se débrouille comme il peut*, was now cited. This unhappy reflection was responsible for my papering our room with several pounds of the literature intended for German uplift.

HIS FIRST SPAD

It stuck well, thanks to a flour paste made by our cook. Before the war he was the head cook in the Maritime Restaurant at Marseilles. His paste was delicious to the nose and the entire barrack partook of it for twenty-four hours. But the work was well done. Along the north wall were twenty copies of Ludendorff's character in black and white, mostly black. The rest of the space was taken up with Allied victories in Switzerland, trimmed with a neat row of the red-white-and-blue appeals from one deserter to his distant comrades still under the yoke. My comrades declared it exquisite; the officer observers said it was very practical, indeed; and the captain thought it a bit exaggerated. Then the commandant of the *groupe* of *escadrilles* happened in to see how his pilots were lodged, and he was the only one genuinely interested. He said:

> Yes, that reminds me. This morning we received another bundle of propaganda to be dropped in the enemy lines as you dropped the others. I have sent it to your *escadrille*, for I suppose this work will be of interest to you personally. The service is intensely practical and comprises little risk. You will take up the pamphlets with you the first day there is a strong west wind and drop them in such fashion that the winds will distribute them in the five kilometres immediately behind the German trenches. You haven't much work these days and this will keep your planes in working order.

Before I could reply he was gone.

I wanted to tell him that I would do my part in getting rid of his important pamphlets, "in the same way we got rid of the others." As for our being idle, we had our mess-room to furnish with our own hands and five stoves to put up. But the pamphlets came that evening. They were "of interest to me personally" because they comprised about twenty pounds of Wilson's Speech!

I had too often used my lucky nationality to gain favours that gave me advantages over the others. For two years I was allowed to celebrate our sacred national holidays, such as the Fourth of July and Thanksgiving, with a short furlough to Paris, where all good Americans go when they die. I had impressed my ignorance of French language and regulations to allow me to pass where passing was forbidden. I had taken liberties, as an American volunteer, which would have put a French conscript in prison. True, my comrades bore me no grudge because of my racial superiority, and my Turkish cigarettes—from Connecticut and Virginia—were much in favour in a tobaccoless land. But for once I tried to make them forget these distinctions.

It was quite evident to the entire mess that I was fatally indicated for the chore: a two hours' flight in a heavy wind; a most uninteresting flight which meant the loss of my turn for a really exciting discussion of targets with the heavy guns around Corbeny Wood. My argument was that such very special work was fit only for a much older pilot; that I had never done such a job; that it was a useless stunt and should be performed by the latest arrived pilot at the mess; that my plane was out of order and had been useless for three days; and last, that I did not want to lose my turn at the regular work. But I was crushed under the combined protests of the others. I was American and so was Wilson's Speech, and the two of us must go together. I conceded the point gracefully, so strong was their logic. For Washington's Birthday was approaching, which I hoped to present as a sort of American *Quatorze Juillet*, to be spent in Paris.

The following afternoon the weather was favourable for the expedition. One of the younger lieutenant observers went with me. He carried with him, in the rear seat, forty pounds of eloquence printed in German. The pages were done up in half-pound rolls fastened with an elastic. Our other weapons were two Lewis guns on a revolving turret. The west wind was behind us, driving us *chez eux*. Opposite we could see the Plateau de Californie stretching long and raw to the east. The plateau was riven with galleries, of which we could see the entrances and the smoke that wreathed up from the internal fires. Troglodytes lived in those caves, a race of men whose manner of living was that of their forbears who fought the cave bear and the sabre-toothed tiger.

Where the engineers were digging their mines and countermines, they disturbed the bones of these earlier tunnellers of the clay, and mused on the circumstance which even in that day had forced men to hide themselves underground from their enemies. And many of these fighters with gunpowder and steel left their own remains within the hill. Some five hundred years hence, when another world war is disputed, some soldier of the Nth Engineers, piercing the plateau in his subterranean tank, will find the relics of the men who first captured the heights from the Boches. And he will smile as he recognises the relics of primitive war, the puny guns and the digging tools that depended upon the strength of a man's arm. He will think, "We are progressing."

As I sailed overhead in my plane I also thought, "We are progressing." It was warfare in the ultimate degree. Instead of killing our enemy by sudden dismemberment, we rained down upon him the power of the printed word, to unjoint his moral strength and dislocate his will to resist. It was a triumph of reason over matter. But the idea was not entirely new. Several centuries before Christ an Assyrian king laid siege to the Egyptian city of Bubastes, of which the patron divinity was the Sacred Cat, and in which all other cats were worshiped for his sake. But the men of Bubastes were content to rest behind their solid walls and refused to try the issue of a doubtful battle. Whereat the Assyrians gathered together all the cats in the surrounding country and with them made propaganda in front of the Egyptian walls. men rode up and down, each with a mewing and struggling feline tied by the tail to his saddle-bow. Thus the Egyptian! were compelled to come out and fight the desecrators, and fell victims to their rashness.

Behind me the observer was slipping the elastics from the rolls. Each roll, as he loosened its fastening, he threw downward so that it would not burst into a cloud of flying sheets before it was well clear of the control wires. We marched the airplanes up and down, three miles behind our own first lines. The steady wind caught the message and floated it eastward to the enemy. It was a slow job, and we untidied the clean sky for two miles north and south. Five hundred metres beneath, we saw the fluttering leaflets we had dropped on each previous trip.

A SALMSON

At first I thought I was looking at flocks of swallows, whose darting wings twinkled in the sunlight, but it was only our own work going on beneath us.

We were quite alone. There were no Huns in the air to disturb us and our own machines were not yet up. Even the "Archies" let us pass unannounced. Generally the Boche battery in Corbeny Wood spoke to us as we went by. If they saw us today they must have thought us game unworthy of their powder. If, on returning, I could only say, "They shot well today over Corbeny," or, "Another hole to patch in the left wing!" I should have been happy. But there was nothing to justify our carrying weapons on the aerial highway.

A cloud-bank formed in front of us, and I dropped a quarter of a mile to avoid it. The paper ammunition had all been shot off and we turned downward and homeward. I had my eyes on the oil gauge when my motor began to give snorts of uneasiness and to buck. I worked the throttles to feel its heart, but I could not coax it back into its accustomed stride. It snorted louder and pulled more feebly. I had two more wooded valleys to cross ere I could afford to slide down the long gravity road that ended on the home landing-ground. To land in the woods meant a broken machine and no dinner for the passengers—and we were dropping fast. I did everything that the inventor of the motor had provided for me to do. I opened the auxiliary gasoline tank; I pumped the auxiliary gasoline pump; I turned the auxiliary ignition switch, and I wished ardently for an auxiliary motor.

When still half a mile high and home not yet in sight, I decided to give up and come down before I had to come down like Davy Crockett's coon. There was no place to land with any hope of saving the plane, but I was angry with the cranky machine and wanted to save my own precious neck. Below was a dark green patch that I recognised for a little wood of dwarf pines, closely planted and only ten feet high. With a dead motor I could reach the pines, skim over their tops as over the daisies on a flying field, and come to rest there when the plane lost its speed. This meant an insignificant ten-foot fall to earth, the fall broken by the tree-tops. And so I planned my descent. I made my last turn while still four hundred yards high and sped the length of the wood to be sure to touch near the middle of it. My observer was now showing unusual interest in the piloting of the plane; a thing rare in observers.

At last the sharp pine-tops were skimming beneath my wheels. The plane was levelled out and losing speed slowly. I saw clearly how the smash was going to wreck the poor old bus completely and leave us without a scratch or a bruise. The swift moment of waiting was sublime. Curtius about to leap into the gulf; Joan of Arc mounting to the stake; Arnold Winkelried facing the Austrian spears; I had all the sensations of these. And then happenstance spoiled the climax; the gulf closed before the horseman leaped; the fire refused to burn; the spears missed the heroic breast; and my undeserving plane dropped heavily and unharmed in a clearing in the wood, a clearing so small that I had not seen it!

We dismounted, my passenger and I. His was the mood of a man escaped from imminent death, and I took my cue at once. I became the experienced old pilot, accustomed to making forced landings in woodland clearing sixty yards square! "*Bon Dieu de Mille Bons Dieux,*" I panted; "I was afraid for a moment that I'd miss it"—this with the accents of recent mental stress.

The cause of the motor trouble was the cause of the expedition itself, a bit of propaganda, a bit of Wilson's Speech that had flown into the internal workin' of my motor when I ducked under a cloud and into a shower of my own paper. The motor had caught a couple of sheets between the cylinders and the mouth of an exhaust valve had chewed up an oily wad of it and ruined its digestion therewith. This bizarre accident was kept secret. The eight *escadrilles* on our field knew of it, and my friends in Paris, but no one else. We feared that if the Huns heard of it they might use the idea and make the sky untenable with a continual paper barrage. I write this account during the Armistice.

We reached home that night two hours late for dinner, but not too late to find sympathetic ears for my wonderful tale of pilot-craft. I told it in full, and even added that I had long had my eye on that sixty-yard clearing as an emergency landing-ground. They had to believe me, for the field was there and the plane posed in the middle of it. Rehan was doubtful. He wanted me to explain how I had planned to get the plane out again from the clearing. There was a runway of sixty yards and a ten-foot obstacle at the end of it. A dirigible could clear it, but not an aeroplane. I proved to them mathematically and aerodynamically that a plane could get out of any place it could get into—provided, of course, that the pilot knew his business. Rehan promised to come out with me on the morrow and watch me do it. He had been driving planes only three years and he wanted to learn from me, he said!

That same night the wind rose and the gale howled and the trees of the forest bent beneath the storm. My plane was overturned and torn into detached pieces by the tempest, so Rehan was disappointed. I felt the loss less keenly myself, for the result would have been the same in either case. Besides, it's not every pilot that sees his plane a mangled wreck, himself not in it!

So ended the launching of propaganda in our *escadrille*. It was put down as dangerous and unprofitable and to be done only by volunteers. No one volunteered. We often calculated the probable results of this one attempt at it. Whenever the big guns made unusual noise at night we got into the habit of saying, "That's the propaganda, you've got the Boches aroused to their danger," and when the nights were quiet, one remarked, "They scarcely resist at all these days, since Wilson's Speech got among them."

The Big Show is over now, and perhaps this bit of propaganda did as much to bring about the happy ending as I myself did to bring down my plane safely in the middle of the woods. In any case, it's a good story for a man's grandchildren.

6

Life on the Front

A FLIGHT ACROSS THE TOUL SECTOR

Malzéville, Friday, August 20, 1915

I was overjoyed and entranced to receive your delightful letter with the interesting enclosures. A day or so after I received my change of corps and was sent to Nancy, I found myself in the escadrille of Prince and Cowdin, as *mitrailleur* or *bombardier*. Both are away. Prince is said to be in the north, and Cowdin is in Paris presumably getting a new machine. It has been very dull here. I did not kick at once to be sent to a school to learn to pilot, as I had understood from Cowdin that one could learn at the Front, without being side-tracked for a considerable time in the rear; and a little practical experience, I thought, would help in any case.

Well, neither of them has returned, and since a young Lieutenant turned up I was assigned to him and have made three or four trial flights. I have written to Prince and Cowdin; but evidently I've not their address. So I have written to Paris to find out the state of affairs. This morning, having put the letter in the box, I leisurely came over from the tent where we slept, to the aeroplanes. There was to have been, at six o'clock, bomb-practice. My arrival was heralded by shouts, "*Dépêche-toi! Le Capitaine t'appelle.*" The latter called me over and said that since I made such a face about not being allowed to go with the Russian lieutenant the other day, would I like to take Parran's mechanic's place and go on the big raid on the Imperial Palace at Treves.

"*Je ne demande pas mieux.*"

"You know how to load the 155 and the use of the sighting machine?"

"Yes."

So they bundled me up in overshoes and fur coats, rammed a *passe-montagne* and *casque* on my head, and led me over to the spot where the machines were already lined up. I cranked up the motor and watched the machines before us depart at intervals of fifteen seconds. Sixty left in all, so I am told. But I forget to explain to you that this corps is for nothing but bombardments, and they are all Voisins here except two or three Nieuports to chase *Aviatiks* if they come to Nancy. The *appareil* before us left, and we bounced over the ground and glided off the plateau. The weather was clear, few clouds, only near the ground were bits of mist looking like the wool which sticks to a dark suit after one has been lying on a bed. Our route was not to go straight across the lines at Pont-à-Mousson, but, passing by way of Toul, Commercy, and Saint-Mihiel, to cross the *ligne de feu* north of Verdun, and thence a direct course to Trèves.

You don't know what it looks like to be in an aeroplane with the land of France below; its woods cut with straight edges and the patch quilt of cultivated land in tiny rectangles. The French like to make everything in straight lines and this well-populated region shows the effects. We gained a good altitude over the forest of Nancy and Toul—1200 to 1800 metres; but I began to find more and more fuzzy clouds in the low lands and river valleys. West of Toul, where we crossed the Meuse, and followed it, the north wind became very strong; but below us the bank of mist became thicker and thicker. North of Commercy we lost sight of the earth altogether under two layers of clouds, one sticking like a blanket to the earth, and another flowing under us.

It was like *Alice in Wonderland,* where one had to run very fast to stay in the same place. The view ahead and on the east side was like snow-fields of soft wet snow, with here and there hillocks rising in it with blue shadows. The sun shone full upon us, and looking down I could see our faint shadow on the filmy veil of moving clouds surrounded by sometimes one, often two rainbows, which formed a complete circle. Before us ever bobbed and dipped other *appareils*. Sometimes one saw only three or four, sometimes fifteen or more. Oddly we appeared always to fly steadily in a straight line, yet the other planes flitted from side to side and dipped below one another. Now and then in the crevices between the clouds, we saw bits of trenches, for inadvertently we had crossed the salient. Trenches from above, with their *boyaux*, look like worn furrows one sees on dead tree-trunks when the bark is removed.

Then we began to notice that all the aeroplanes before us veered off to the west, and I suddenly saw a ball of white smoke, which I afterwards learned was the signal to return because of unfavourable weather. There was a rift in the clouds just where we wheeled and the German gunners must have noticed us, for they sent several shrapnel shells up. One gets such an enormous feeling of space, having nothing definitely near one, that those little puffs of smoke looked pitiably inadequate and ill-placed. Twenty-odd planes I counted distinctly before me at the turning-point. We fled south, always with the other machines flitting before, and got our bearings again by seeing ground and the big double curve that the Meuse makes by Saint-Mihiel, with a canal like a bow-string across it. We passed over Void and were flying lower as we neared Toul. Toul itself looks like an ancient walled town. At any rate it has a fringe of trees all around it which slopes down to the river's edge on two sides, narrow, intricate streets and red roofs with a big twin-towered cathedral emerging from the place, like a picture of similar edifices on bad maps of Paris.

Again the forest with its edges as though cut by a pair of scissors, and straight lines of roads traced across it. Odd, the roads in the open wind all over creation, but on entering the woods they go straight as an arrow, as though to form prearranged geometrical patterns. Nancy, a great, irregular cluster of houses, is easily recognised by the two great cones of iron ore debris south of the town near the river. They must be very large, for they look as large as a city block—one is black, the other white. Then, taking a dip, we sailed down to the aviation field with its white tents and numerous aeroplanes looking like so many white moths pinned on a green background. As we drew near, and I saw the trees and suburban gardens on a large scale, it came upon me how very much greener they were getting. The little willows and the tall grass by the very crooked little stream just sparkled in emeralds and sapphires when seen from 2000 metres (that's a mile and a quarter).

I started this to Uncle Willy, but suddenly remembered that everything was opened on entering Switzerland, and the names here given are perhaps of military importance. I hope to go on another raid tomorrow if the weather is fine. I have done not a little *mitrailleuse* practice lately, otherwise it is very dull here.

From Saint-Mihiel to the Argonne

Verdun, Esc. N 124, S.P. 24, May 23, 1916

Many, many thanks for the books. All but one of them are new to me and I shall enjoy re-reading the *Ordeal by Battle*.

We are really settling down to work and I begin to feel I am actively saving France and no longer toying with her expensive utensils.

I got twenty-seven hours' flying over the Boche lines the week before leaving, but had no luck in running on a Boche. Two of my companions, however, finished off two Germans.

Now we are at—shucks! I forget the censor. Anyway, I think I may say, morning and evening, when the weather permits we fly high and low over the smouldering inferno which has been raging since February: yesterday morning from Saint-Mihiel to the Argonne and back again well inside their lines, over two and a half miles high (4300 metres); yesterday afternoon low, to protect a slow machine from Douaumont to Côte 304; back and forth an hour and a half.

The landscape—one wasted surface of brown powdered earth, where hills, valleys, forest, and villages all emerged in phantoms—was boiling with puffs of dark smoke. Even above my engine's roar I could catch reports now and then.

To the rear, on either side, tiny sparks like flashes of a mirror, hither and yon, in the woods and dales, denoted the heavy guns which were raising the dust.

One of my fellows who was flying high to protect us, fell upon a Boche and brought him down.

I think it must be my turn soon. Even from above, one had the sense of great activity and force in the country to the rear. From every wood and hedge peeped out *parcs* of autos, wagons, tents and shelters—while all the roadsides showed white and dusty with the ceaseless travel.

I have since heard we retook the fort of Douaumont, but lost Le Mort Homme while I was flying overhead; smoke completely hid the infantry, I suppose; besides I was busy keeping beside, the *réglage* machine.

Clouds

June 5, 1916

From now on you must not believe too much what the papers say; we made the mistake of letting —— do a little publicity, and he has very bad taste. The reporters in town see their chance for news; and they will soon have us bringing down a German a day apiece, and dying gloriously weekly. I am reported killed twice already, and more than one of us has been severely wounded several times. Nothing much has happened; intermittent rainy weather. Oliver Wolcott,

Above the Clouds

Carlton Burr, and a couple of other Harvard men whom I knew at college are with the Ambulance here. They all behave well and picked up the dead and wounded off the streets at the time of raid.

We had another *alerte* yesterday; but the Boches did not come here. Hall surprised one farther north and thinks he got him; but the German plane fell through the clouds, and Hall could not see if he hit the earth or not. I ran afoul of two with Prince yesterday morning, but we did not have unity or concentration of attack enough to get them. I enclose a few awful photos which may interest you.

Everyone says he gets tired of flying: "It's monotonous"; I don't see it. On the contrary there is infinite variety when there is a slight sprinkling of clouds. Clouds are not thin pieces of blotting-paper; but liquid, ceaselessly changing steam. I played hide-and-seek in and out of them yesterday; sometimes flat blankets like melting snow on either side below me, or again, like great ice floes with distant bergs looming up, and "open water" near at hand, blue as a moonstone cloud, floating full, for all the world like a gigantic jelly-fish (those that have red trailers and a sting). In the nearer pools the mottled earth, piebald with sun and shadow, showed through; and it was thanks to these I knew my whereabouts.

I was going from below the clouds to above them, circling in some hole; thus I realised the size and thickness of the walls—300 metres sheer from top to base, of dazzling whiteness. Some have many feathery, filmy points and angles, others are rounded and voluminous, with cracks and caverns in them. These are all the fair-weather, fleecy clouds; for there are the lower, flatter, misty ones, and the speckled, or mare's-tail clouds, above which one never reaches. There are a lot of trumpet-shaped and wind-blown clouds this evening and I should like to go out and examine them; but it's a bore for my mechanic, and I doubt if I could go high enough to warrant crossing the lines.

Escadrille Lafayette—1916

Luxeuil, September 25, 1916

I have been here for a week, and it is a fine place: natural hot-water baths, a general health resort all the year round, though cold in winter. You had better look the place up, as I have no doubt you will know more about it than if I wrote a thousand pages. Besides, I have other stuff to write about. We are all in one hotel and everything is fine, as to grub, service, loafing, etc. It looks as if we were here for the winter (but who can tell?), and I am content with the prospect: hunting, fishing, skating, skiing, etc. We are here to protect bombardments, but as no machines have shown up with tanks sufficient for oil and gas for long flights, and as the six squadrons here have made only two bombardments all summer, I think there is little chance of our going out again this winter.

As yet eight of us have no machines. We expect them in about a month, and will use them as we please. That is we shall go hunting for Germans when the spirit moves. And believe me I shall use my nut, but am out for blood when my machine shows up. As you know by now I have lost one friend who was a man in every sense of the word. No papers can write and do justice to this boy or to his brother. If France were made up of Rockwells this war would have been over the day it started. We put Kiffin away today. As nearly as I can find out, his fight took place over a small town near where he brought down his first German. He came down on the German (a *biplace* machine) and received an explosive bullet in his chest, which made a hole about the size of the bottom of a large glass. It was a quick death. The fall broke him up, and I am glad that I did not see him, as I shall always remember him as I knew him in life.

We have a bunch of English pilots here and they seem to be a fine lot of boys. They would all like to get on or near a real front and see some action. So would I, but what is the use of kicking? It is a fine town, beautiful country and a chance for many sports out in the open.

Dodging Shells and Monos

July 27, 1917

Yesterday was an eventful day for me. I went out in the morning for two hours on a low patrol: with Coatsworth and a French pilot. We were flying behind the Boche lines, but did not meet any enemy planes. That should have finished my day's work, but in the afternoon so many reports came of Boches over the French lines, that our captain sent out an extra patrol. I happened to be sitting in the office at the time, so naturally I was the first one picked. Three of us got away at 5 p.m., joined up at 4000 metres above the *piste*, and started to hunt for Boches. About 6 p.m., while I was flying at 5200 metres, the patrol leader dove on a *triplace* Boche machine. I followed him down and shot about 25 shots, but the German dove and got away. When I came out of my dive I looked for my friends and thought I saw them above me. When I flew over to join them, I saw a third machine which I thought was the Boche coming back.

When we got close enough to see each other, I found I had picked up three Boche *monoplace* machines and that my friends were not in sight. We manoeuvred around shooting at each other until they chased me from 4500 to 2000 metres. I had been unable to get them, and every time I got one on the run, the other two dropped on me and I had to do a *vrille* to get away. My face and glasses were full of oil, so I had to take the glasses off to see at all. Finally I decided it was time to come home. I held my plane steady long enough to get a reading on the compass and then flew as fast as I could. My Spad was a little faster than the Boches and as soon as I began to leave them they let me go and their anti-aircraft batteries took me up. They kept me on the jump until I got across the lines over French territory. Two of the shots came very close to me, but none of them hit.

When I got home I looked over my Spad and found three bullet holes in one wing, one in the stabilizer, two in the elevating planes, and two in the cowl near the radiator.

August 20, 1917

The French started their attack north of Verdun this morning and it was some battle. My *escadrille* was on the *piste* ready to go up at 5.30, but our first patrol did not leave until 7. We had three patrols out, one at 1000 metres, another at 2500 metres, and one at 4500 metres. I was one of the five pilots in the middle patrol, and it was the longest two hours I ever spent, as well as the busiest. I thought a Spad was fast, but

AN ANTI-AIRCRAFT GUN

twice as much speed would not have been enough this morning.

We had been on the lines only a few minutes when a group of six Boche *monoplaces* appeared. We flew back and forth, parallel to each other, for some time and finally their group broke up. Two of them managed to slip through our guard, and dove for the top man in the low patrol, who happened to be Coatsworth. He was above and behind the others in his group and the Boches were faster than he. They put one ball through his wind-shield a few inches from his head. The bullet exploded upon striking the exhaust pipe at the side of the fuselage, and tore it to pieces. Another hit his gun and ploughed through the top of the radiator. The commandant of *Groupe* 14 came to the rescue just in time, and the Boches flew back into their lines. Coatsworth has a slight cut on the leg and another in the left hand, but will be flying again in a few days.

As for myself, I was not in any combat, but between keeping with my patrol, watching for Boches, and dodging anti-aircraft shells, which were breaking about and below us, I had no time for pleasant thoughts. It is some sensation when you hear a big explosion and see a cloud of black smoke a few metres away and your machine is thrown out of balance by the concussion. You open the motor wide, wonder why the damned thing won't go 250 miles an hour instead of 125, throw the control over to make a *virage*, and then wonder whether you are running into or away from the next shell, which will come along in about twenty seconds unless they are shooting several guns at once.

AFTER THE RAID

DECORATED BY KING ALBERT

Escadrille C 74, September 2, 1917

Full moon tonight and a clear sky. The damned Fritzies have been peregrinating around overhead all the evening, dropping bombs hither and yon with a right good will. When I hear those sinister motors churning along under the stars, I get a combination of the jim-jams and Saint Vitus's dance. I settle my steel *casque* on my head and get ready to flop on my belly when I hear the bomb begin to spin down. I never shall get used to these darned bombing parties. They've got my goat all the way down to the chin roots.

It's funny, too, because when I'm flying over the lines I don't mind being shelled a darned bit.

Things have quieted down a bit at last. Our own bombers are going out to give Fritz a taste of his own medicine. Good luck to 'em. I'm going to turn in now. Gosh, what a relief!

The moon continues going strong and so does Fritz. But the worst of all are the anti-aircrafts. They shower us with spent shell fragments every blessed night and there's no safety in our tents until the wee sma' hours. Still, even this life has its compensations. The other day King Albert came around, passed our squadron in review, and decorated the five senior non-commissioned pilots, of whose number I am one, with the "*Ordre de Léopold II.*" To be precise, he "created" us "*Chevaliers de l'Ordre de Léopold II.*" Get that word: "*Chevalier*" Some class! Only, as one of our waggish mechanics remarked to me after the ceremony, "*C'est bien, mais où est votre cheval?*"

The king pinned a shiny silver cross on my jacket, shook hands and congratulated me. We spoke the few words there were to be spoken in French, as he was not aware I was an American. He merely asked me what machine I flew and how I liked it. I replied that I flew a twin-engine Caudron and was satisfied with its performance. He started to say something else, but changed his mind and walked off. There is no doubt that he is personally a very brave man. I know for a fact that he has made flights as a passenger over the lines. If it takes nerve for an ordinary mortal, whose life is of no particular importance, to do this stunt, how much more nerve must it take in a king who knows, or ought to know, that he is the present idol of a large portion of the civilized world, and will go down to history as one of its greatest and noblest figures? Not because he is King of the Belgians, but because he's a real white man. I feel greatly honoured to have gotten that silver cross from Albert.

Prospects over here, just now, are brightening up. There seems to be a strong probability that all Americans in the French Army who wish it will be transferred before November. Major Gros, of the Signal Corps, Aviation Section, has written to us all asking if we desire the change, and intimating that as soon as all our replies are in his hands the deed will be done very rapidly.

NUNGESSER

Escadrille Lafayette, November 27, 1917

Last night we had Nungesser here for dinner. You know he has nineteen Boche machines to his credit; stands next to Guynemer (who has twenty-three), and is therefore the second greatest pilot in the world—a wonderful chap, blond and handsome, blue eyes, and rather square, clean-cut face; slight sandy moustache; a striking feature is his smile which reveals two solid rows of gold teeth. He lost all his own teeth and wears a silver jaw; also walks with a limp—his left leg a little out of kilter.

We had also a Scots machine-gun officer to dine. He thought Nungesser with all his medals, about the greatest thing on earth and didn't hesitate to so express himself. He was funny as could be; he has been wounded once the infantry, and now thinks the machine-gun

THAW AND NUNGESSER

corps quite the safest billet. He said the "Blighters" (the Huns) could counter-attack every hour of every day; he shouldn't mind, lie "felt as safe as a judge" behind his guns.

This evening we have as guests four Scots Guardsmen, a major and three captains of the old Regular Army—splendid chaps and funny, my word! The meal will be one long laugh, I know. Then on Thanksgiving Day we shall be hosts to four English transport officers. I think I have mentioned them before. We have been their guests twice. Have a big fat turkey—bought in Amiens yesterday. I hope you will also have a good turkey dinner.

Day after day we sit around in the mud; the weather is so bad that I have not been up since Friday. Three went up yesterday afternoon, but had to come down in a few minutes.

The pictures have been taken at last with Bob's big camera. In one I am holding the lion. Do you know that we have four mascots? "Whiskey" comes first, of course; he is getting bigger every day, a black knob forming on his tail and traces of a mane. Then we have the captain's big police dog "Fram," good-looking, but pretty much of a coward, we think. Next comes "Miss," a bright, intelligent little brown dog; Lieutenant de Laage found her in a ruined Belgian village in the early days of the war. Last but not least, "Carranza the Comedian," a very young and clumsy black-and-white dog, without an ounce of

LAFAYETTE PILOTS

brains. From his ears and other points, would say his grandsire was a cocker spaniel. He belongs to Masson, who used to be a captain in the Mexican Army.

The other day we went in the tractor to call on some English officers as the weather prevented flying. We bought some foodstuffs, bacon, ham, tea, and cigarettes, out of their stores—much cheaper than in Amiens, as they are supplied direct from England—and at cost—very decent of them, don't you think? We took the lion and two dogs along. Everyone enjoyed the lion hugely. "Anzacs" along the route were loud in their praises; even the Hun prisoners working on the roads stopped to look and point at him. Am now proposed for "Sergeant," but it does not go into Headquarters until the 10th. Everything official leaves on the 10th of each month.

Winter Weather

December 19, 1917

At last we have a stove installed in our barracks, and I have my fingers sufficiently thawed out to write a letter. Since I wrote Father the other day we have moved our *escadrille* about fifteen kilometres, and have been busy getting settled in our barracks and doing all the necessary things to get the new *escadrille* started, for the unit of fifteen pilots that I am in is brand-new. As pilots there are six Americans—Tyson, Parker, Nichols, Ovington, Johnson, and I, and nine Frenchmen, with the flock of mechanics, servants, cooks, clerks, etc., that go to make up the family. I have a little room with Johnson, fitted up with two board bunks, a washbowl and table, and am not uncomfortable, except for the all-prevailing cold. We pilots have our mess or *popote* which is supported by a few francs a day subscribed by each of us, and it is very fair. There are several *escadrilles* stationed here, forming a *groupe*. We are on one of the main military roads in the sector, so there is a great deal to watch, for a newcomer to the Front like myself.

December 20

Our little camp is a desolate-looking place especially in the windy, snowy weather we are having now. On one side of the road, on a bare, rolling field, are the barracks, several hundred feet apart, belonging to the different *escadrilles*—about eight buildings in all. They are long and narrow, built of boards. On the other side is the landing-field, about half a kilometre long, and too narrow for comfort when there is a strong wind blowing across it and it is necessary to land crosswise of the field. There is a small village ten minutes' walk down the road,

Winter Quarters

which has been pretty thoroughly bombed, as have all the towns in the vicinity, and a large proportion of the buildings are in ruins. A few miles in the other direction is Verdun. The vicinity as a whole is not unlike the rolling, partly wooded districts around Minneapolis. All the traffic on the roads is strictly military—supply trucks in long trains going back and forth from the trenches, and officers' autos. All the little towns are full of soldiers *en repos*.

A German aeroplane comes over once in a while taking pictures and they say that on clear moonlight nights we are bombed quite regularly.

December 22

Yesterday afternoon I went to a supply depot about thirty miles from here, and flew back a new machine for our *escadrille*. Nothing exciting happened. This morning I had my machine assigned me and my *mécano*, Sylvestre. I find that I shall have to wait several days for a machine gun before I can start work over the lines. Meanwhile I shall get some flying, I hope, to get thoroughly acquainted with the geography of the sector. We had notice this morning that the Americans who wanted to transfer to the United States Army should go into Paris to arrange for the transfer and get commissions. All but Tyson and myself have already done so. We are going to stay with the French for a while anyway, as it is very uncertain what will be done with the American aviators, and I don't want to take any chances of being sent to a school as a monitor, or put on a bombing-plane. I am perfectly happy where I am. I was sorry to hear a couple of days ago that Stuart Walcott[1] was brought down inside the German lines. He attacked a Boche *biplace* from above and got it, but three one-place Boches came down on him while he was attacking and got him.

I would like to send a Merry Christmas by cable, but find it is a hard thing to do from here. I am going to write the Credit Lyonnais in Paris to do it for me, but it probably won't get to you in time. My Christmas will be spent here and we are going to get up a feast for the occasion and try to be as gay as possible.

CHRISTMAS EVE

December 26, 1917

Before going farther I will answer the questions in your letter of November 30. I always carry an official identification card, and as soon as I get an opportunity intend to get a little metal identification tag to wear on my wrist. In case of accident my *escadrille* would immediately be notified, and an official cable sent to father. Also the other Americans in my *escadrille* would see that you were kept fully informed by cable or letter. In the case of M. and P. the bodies were buried in metal coffins, as the families wanted to bring them home after the war.

Of the packages of which you sent a list only one has arrived, with the three little books in it. It got here the day before Christmas, and was very welcome indeed. Did you notice the article by Norman Hall in the *Atlantic* called "High Adventure"? It would interest you, as it is about Avord and flying, and it is well written. Shortly after he got to the Front he mistook three German machines for a French patrol and did not discover his mistake until he got a bullet in his arm. He fainted and his machine came down over the French lines. While unconscious he instinctively "redressed," or pulled his machine back into a position for landing, at the right time, and landed right in a French third-line trench without hurting himself. He was laid up for quite a while and is now back in his *escadrille*.

Christmas Eve after dinner we all sat around the stove in our *popote*, or dining-room, and were as gay as we could be under the circumstances. We managed to get together enough wood to keep a fire for a couple of hours, and the *chef-de-popote* brewed a bowl of hot *pinard*

---

1. *Angels Defiant*, two accounts of pilots on the Western Front during the First World War 1914-1918, *Above the French Lines* by Stuart Walcott and *The American Spirit* by Briggs Kilburn Adams is also published by Leonaur.

punch and brought in a cold supper, and a very sociable time was had. We had a big Christmas dinner last night, of which I am enclosing the menu. It wasn't a regular Christmas dinner, as we couldn't get any chickens or turkey, and there was an entire absence of cranberry sauce, mince pie, and other essentials, but it was good—for the Front. I, for one, was thinking more about what was going on at home than what we were eating. I am sorry the things you sent to eat couldn't have arrived, and I am afraid they will be slow in coming, as there must have been a congestion of traffic on account of all the things sent over to Americans in France.

This is a fiendish climate in winter, and there are many days when flying is impossible.

Day before yesterday I had a wonderful view of an air battle which occurred near our field at about 3000 metres altitude. A Boche *biplace* came over alone, about eleven in the morning, probably photographing. We knew it was a Boche before we could see him, on account of the little puffs of smoke popping out around him, which were French anti-aircraft shrapnel bursting. Suddenly four French *monoplaces* appeared out of the distance at a great height and made for the Boche. He saw them and headed for home, but he had a strong wind against him, and the smaller, faster French *chasse* machines were soon around him. We could see the tracer bullets drawing lines of smoke between the Boche and the French planes, as first one and then the other would close in on him and exchange a few shots. A one-man machine can only shoot straight ahead, so in attacking, one has to close in straight toward the Boche, get in a few shots, and then manoeuvre for another chance, while all the time the two-place machine can shoot at you from his rear, side, or straight ahead.

You can imagine what a fascinating and terribly thrilling sight it was, to see the big plane sailing along, constantly changing direction, with the four little planes around it, doing *renversements*, vertical turns, and every conceivable kind of manoeuvre to get in a position for a close shot. The Boche stopped firing pretty soon, showing that the passenger was hit. One of the French planes dived close in, got in the lucky shot, and probably killed the pilot, for the Boche plane keeled over and started nose down for the ground. When it got about a third of the way down, it burst into flames with an explosion of the gasoline tank, and fell to the ground trailing a sheet of flame probably fifty feet long. The passenger's body was found over a mile from where the plane fell.

I took a long walk this afternoon with Tyson and Nichols down the "road that saved France" at the Battle of Verdun. They say that during that attack, night and day for weeks, there was a line of trucks, absolutely unbroken, running on the road, which is the main one feeding the Verdun Sector. It is always an active sector and there is a great deal going over the road even now, guns, ammunitions, and supply trucks, officers' autos and motorcycle dispatch riders, in an almost constant stream.

One rather humorous thing passed us today, a wagon containing a huge cask of *pinard*,—the *poilu's* red wine, camouflaged—painted with protective colouring in dull brown and green splotches, so that it will not be seen by enemy planes.

"UN MOINS QUI MANGE LA SOUPE CE SOIR"

You may think it sounds foolish or as if one was blowing a bit to talk about attacking five when we were only two, but an attack does not necessarily mean that you charge into the middle of them and mix it up. On the contrary you can, by diving at high speed from above, get in some shots, and then by using your great speed climb up above them again out of reach before they can get in a shot. If you remember to leave your motor on as you are diving, and in this way to come down as fast as possible, without at the same time going so fast as to interfere with your shooting, the great speed gained in this way will enable you to make a short steep climb and thus regain a position perhaps two hundred metres above the heads of the enemy, where they cannot effectively shoot at you. I am now, of course, speaking only of an attack on a group of single-seater machines. If the engagement ends here the chances of bringing one down are not great, but you can sometimes, by such methods, and by, for instance, hitting some part of one of the machines, so worry them that one will in the general confusion get separated from his comrades so that you can get a fair crack at him.

This was about the first time I had had a chance to try it, however, and I made a botch of it. I saw I was getting in too close, but did, I think, hit one of them, though not seriously. In my haste to get out, I made a false manoeuvre, and fell on my nose instead of climbing up, as I should have done. The result was, that the one I had been shooting at and who had turned, got behind me on my tail in a most unpleasant position, where he could shoot and I could not. Naturally I did not let him stay there long, but had to dodge and beat a retreat. He did manage to hit my machine a couple of times, one bullet through a wing and another through the body of the machine about six inches behind me, but never touched me, and did my plane no harm whatever. It did not take much thinking to see that my little manoeuvre had been very badly executed.

My companion and I started off again to see what else we could find, and fifteen minutes later I spotted six more in almost the same place, this time four two-seaters with two single-seaters above and behind them acting as protection. The two-seaters were far enough below not to have to bother about, so I tried the same plan again and came down on the rear of one of the single-seaters. I blazed away at him, and he made the same manoeuvre as had the first one, but this time I kept shooting until very close, then sailed up over his head, did a quick turn, and dropped on his tail again. Before following him, I looked to see what the other single-seater was up to, and saw him bravely making tracks for home, leaving his friend to shift for himself. I therefore kept after the first, and poured in all about two hundred shots into him, many of which I am sure hit the machine, for I could see the tracer bullets apparently go almost into the pilot. I think my first burst of bullets put his engine out of business, for he did not seem able to dive very fast and I could catch him with ease.

Several times when he would do a *renversement* he would turn up and slide off on one wing, as though he were going to fall, and I thought I had him sure. Three times I was so close—only about thirty feet—that I had to pull up to avoid running into him. I could see the pilot sitting there staring up at me through his goggles, the colour of his bonnet, and all the details of the show. This kept up from 4000 to 1800 metres, and he never got in a shot, I am glad to say. Why he did not fall, I do not know. There is, however, always a very good reason why they get away, I think, and that is because you do not hold quite close enough. I know the experience taught me a lesson about being too hasty in my shooting. I finally had to let him go because I caught sight of nine of his brethren coming to his rescue, and when they started after me and began to shoot, I thought discretion the better part of valour and got out. At this time the Boche was flopping about in the air and letting out a considerable quantity of smoke.

Being busy in the getting out, I could no longer watch my would-be victim, but the American who was with me, and who had stayed above as a sort of rear guard, was able to watch him, and said that the last he saw of him he was still going down in a spiral, with black smoke coming out of his tail. The latter means a fire on board, and if this was the case I think that German's flying days are over, unless he gets a pair of wings in some Boche heaven. Be that as it may, I am sorry to say I could not get any confirmation, by someone on the ground, of the Boche having been seen to fall, so he does not count officially for me; if he fell, as I think he did, he came down considerably in his own lines. I wish I could have got him at the start, for he then would have fallen in our lines, and the machine was one of the new type. *Mais si le Boche est mort, c'est la première chose.* As the Frenchmen say when they bag one, "*Un moins qui mange la soupe ce soir*" If that Boche ever did get down alive, I am sure in my own mind that he is at least at present sojourning in the hospital. My manoeuvring worked out all right this time, and if I can catch another like that and do not get him beyond question, I shall promptly admit that I am a punk aviator.

First Patrol

Escadrille N 98, January 7, 1918

My machine isn't quite ready yet, but yesterday I borrowed one and made a flight over the lines, flying in formation with two other pilots. Practically all the chasse machines go out in patrols of from two to six, and at times as many as ten or fifteen. We are situated in a very active sector in the centre of a large salient, with the lines swinging around on three sides of us. Yesterday we made the circle of the lines to get familiar with the ground. We stayed up about an hour and a quarter. Of course it was exciting being over the lines and under fire for the first time, especially as it was a very clear day and there were machines in the air in all directions, to be watched and classified. The proverbial three-ring circus is a complete rest for the attention compared with it. I wish I could give you a mental image of the thing, but it is hopeless, I know, as I have never been able to imagine correctly in advance the various sensations in this game, even talking and thinking it constantly as I do. We went over to the hangars about ten minutes before we had agreed to start, dressed in fur-lined combinations over our uniforms, fur-lined boots, fur-lined *casques*, fur gloves, and goggles, leaving only the eyes, nose, and mouth exposed. The mechanics had the machines out in front of the hangars, so we climbed in and they started the motors.

The Frenchman who was leading the patrol got his machine started first, ran out into the field, turned around so as to start up into the wind, opened up his throttle, and was off and up with a roar. I got

EVENING PATROL

started next and was up to 500 metres in about the time it takes to tell it, got behind the leader and a little over him; then we flew around at that level, keeping over the field and waiting or the third man who was having trouble getting his motor started. Pretty soon we saw him taxi across the field and take the air, and when he got our level we manoeuvred into position. I was about 150 metres to the left of, behind, and above the leader. Johnson was in a similar position to the right, but a little higher, so we would not interfere with each other on the turns. We then started toward the lines, climbing, and were at about 2000 metres when we got over them, and flew at about that altitude for the rest of the trip.

When we got near the lines we each started flying in the form of an "S," making the banks very nearly vertical, so as to see under, over, and behind, as constantly seeing everything in the air is the essential thing. Now you can picture me comfortably seated in my *coucou*, coasting along at well over one hundred miles an hour, constantly over on one side or the other, with one eye on the leader. This keeps one eye fairly active, as he is leaving me at the rate of over two hundred miles an hour when our "S's" cross. The other eye is comparing my map with the ground, taking in flash impressions of the lines, watching my altimetre and compass, without at any time neglecting any portion of the sky for more than a few seconds, and all the time doing automatically plain and fancy flying that would have required my undivided attention a few weeks ago. Now, just to add a tinge of excitement to the pastoral scene, imagine a few little black round clouds popping out in the blue sky, a little to the right of me at my level. They are Boche anti-aircraft shrapnel bursting, and aimed at me; also there are occasional machines, probably Boche, in a beautiful position to drop on me if I get separated from my patrol.

It sounds scary—as a matter of fact, it wasn't at all. It was very interesting and I thoroughly enjoyed it. I felt no thrilling sensations as I expected. The captain of our *escadrille*, who was up near the lines and saw us, said the Boches had our range pretty well and were giving us a heavy dose of shrapnel, but to my inexperienced eyes it looked as if they were away off. Another thing is that the first few patrols one doesn't see a quarter of the machines and shells that are there. As for the anti-aircraft guns, they always shoot at you, but very seldom bring down a plane. They say it is exciting, though, when the shells burst close under you, as the concussion makes your plane do some involuntary acrobatics.

As I have said before, the sensations in an aeroplane are not in proportion to the danger, which you realise only intellectually. It doesn't come to you with a noise; the roar of your motor drowns everything, and that becomes like silence after a few minutes. You don't see the danger until it is on you. Of course the real excitement will come when I mix up with a Boche some day, and the machine guns start popping. At present our job is to keep the Boche photo, artillery, *réglage*, and observation planes on their own side of the fence.

As we learn the game, there are all kinds of things to do if a man wants to, especially during attacks. One can drop bombs, attack sausage balloons, shoot up the trenches, or organise small expeditions into Germany looking for trouble. I am expecting to have the time of my life, and am happy as a lark to be in it. I hope the feeling lasts.

The French have a very expressive way of saying that a man has lost his nerve—they say that he is *dégonflé*—deflated like a flat tire. Many men have become *dégonflés* after they have flown for a certain time, and it is a recognised phenomenon. That is why Guynemer was such a national hero. After bringing down about seventy Boches dead, and being brought down seven times himself, wounded, or with his plane badly crippled, he was as full of fight as ever. Yesterday I was told that I was to take a ten-days' *permission*. I was much surprised, as I hadn't asked for it, and was not keen to go before I had done some work. We

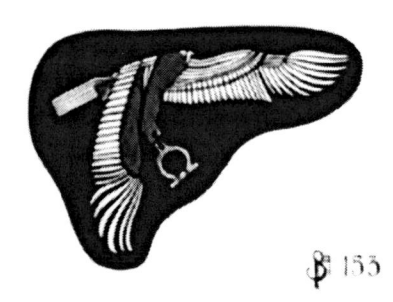

INSIGNIA OF FRENCH ESCADRILLES IN WHICH MEMBERS
OF THE LAFAYETTE FLYING CORPS SERVED.
PLATE 4

get ten days every three months. I have never taken one, and a three months' period ends January 31, so I have to take it now or miss it entirely. I have some important shopping to do in Paris, in the light of what I have learned about necessities at the Front, so I shall probably leave for Paris tomorrow.

One thing that reconciles me is that with the present weather I shall miss very little flying. It is just about a month since I have had all my clothes off or taken a bath. We have had to melt the water to wash with most of the time. That is a temporary condition, however, as we haven't had supplies to fix our rooms. We have them now, and Johnson and I are papering our room, including ceiling and floor, with two thicknesses of paper, and I shall get some kind of gasoline stove that will keep it warm when I get to Paris; also curtains and other things to make us comfortable. Life is really delightful here, or will be when we get fixed up. We have a room about 10 by 12 feet, a washstand, two beds, and a table, all home-made. There is nothing in the barracks but dining-rooms, small office, and the rooms of the fifteen pilots, including the captain and two lieutenants.

We have absolutely no duties but flying, and no discipline except to be here when we are wanted to fly. An orderly brings around a list of the patrols every evening for the next day. A boy brings in very good coffee at 8.15, or earlier if you have an early patrol. Johnson and I keep condensed milk for coffee, also bread and butter and a little gasoline stove, so we lie in bed and make toast and keep the coffee hot. If we want eggs we can order them brought in with the coffee. If it is very cold, we stay under the covers and read and talk to our neighbours, Ovington and Parker, through the partition, until ten or so, unless there is flying. We then get up, heat water enough to wash, probably go out to our hangars to see what our mechanics are doing, and look over our machines. *Déjeuner* at 12 o'clock.

In the afternoon, when not flying, we walk in to Souilly, or up the road, or visit the hangars or some other *escadrille*. J. and I usually make chocolate and toast at four o'clock. Dinner at 6.30. The food is good plain food. We have whatever we want and can buy, as we run the mess ourselves. We have an excellent cook and I am gaining all the weight I lost last summer. About five hours every day I am talking aviation with some one or other. It is a subject I never tire of. I feel that my training is just starting. Being a good flyer and a good *chasse* pilot are two different things.

One good thing about our *escadrille* is that our captain is a very *chic*

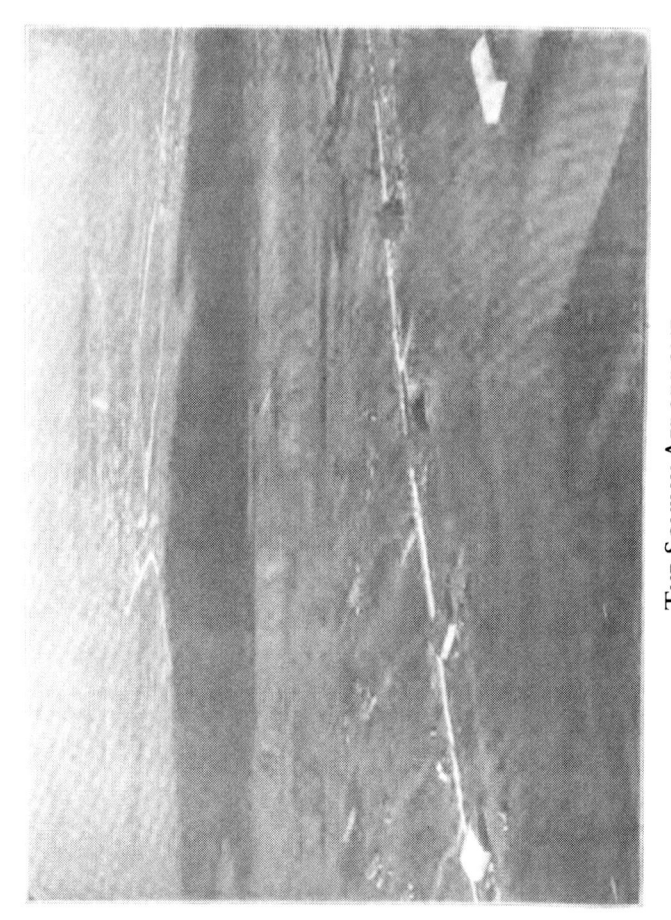

THE SOUILLY AERODROME

type indeed, full of ideas, an old pilot, and a very pleasant, accommodating man. Up to the present he has been subject to the orders of the *escadrille* under whose auspices we were forming, but from now on we shall be separate, and I am sure he is going to let us fly when we like and work out all our own ideas.

Another good thing is that starting in the winter when work is light and the Boches are not *méchants*, I shall get a lot of good experience before things get lively, and we shall all get used to flying together and work out our own flying combinations. Later on we shall doubtless be in on an attack, flying four to six hours a day.

I just read a letter from Edgar, in the same *escadrille* with Rufus Rand, saying Rufus has just had his first brush with a Boche. Both his *escadrille* and mine have Nieuport machines, but we shall have Spads before spring.

Tyson had an amusing thing happen yesterday which was almost serious. He was on patrol and several kilometres the other side of the lines, when his motor stopped dead. Luckily he was quite high, so he headed for the lines and started coasting down, making such distance as he could, first firing his machine gun to attract the attention of the patrol leader, who followed him down far enough to see him land. When he got nearly down, the ground below was a network of old and new trenches and was pockmarked with shell-holes, and he could not tell where the front-line trenches were, nor whether he was landing in French or German territory, but he thought it was German, as there were a lot of trenches still ahead of him. He landed, just missing two shell-holes, and ran into a bunch of barbed wire, taking off both lower wings, and completely smashing his *coucou*, but didn't hurt himself.

Then out of the apparently deserted fields emerged several hundred people, from shell-holes, dugouts, and trenches, and started for him on the run. He felt very lonely and discouraged, but thought up a greeting in his best German, looked up and waved goodbye to the patrol leader, who had come down to 150 metres, and when he looked around saw the most beautiful sight of his life—some sky-blue *poilu* uniforms. They took him to a large dugout where two generals were lunching: they invited him to lunch with them and he went from *hors-d'oeuvres* through roast chicken to *liqueurs*. After they had had a long visit one of the Generals sent him back here in his limousine, everybody along the road *salaaming* at the sight of the general's insignia on the car.

Flying Partners

February 25, 1918

The officers in our *escadrille* are five; the captain, two lieutenants, and two *sous-lieutenants*, all pilots. The other pilots, five of them now, are young Frenchmen, all very likable chaps, always gay, and easy to get along with. It is rather difficult for me to distinguish them for you. I can't even spell their names correctly, and know very little about them outside of the *escadrille*. Knowing so little of French life, it is impossible for me to classify Frenchmen the way we unconsciously do Americans, by their language, education, dress, families, etc., especially without seeing them against any social background excepting the *escadrille*. I know that we have lived together for three months in the closest intimacy without an unpleasant word or feeling, a pretty hard test of temperaments. Nearly all the Frenchmen here have been in the war for two or more years and have been cited for bravery. The majority have been wounded, and they have no illusions about war. Like the French nation as a whole, they know how to make the best of a horrible situation, and get all the fun out of life the circumstances will permit.

We learned yesterday that we are to move in a few days to another part of the Front, to be formed, with some other *escadrilles*, into a new *groupe de combat*. That means we shall get our new machines soon and the work will be more interesting, so we are in high spirits. It has been raining for the past two days—no flying—but it has cleared up tonight, and I shall probably do high patrol from eleven to one tomorrow; good sport on a clear day, but pretty cold in this weather. My roommate, Jacquelin, is trying to go to sleep so I will say goodnight and turn the light out. He would stay awake all night rather than intimate that I was disturbing him.

"I'm not going to take my permission"

March 5, 1918

This has been a great day, and though it's about finished, I'm going to use the remaining half-hour telling you about it, because it interests and concerns me personally. I made my first flight today—that is, the first flight since I joined the *escadrille*. The lieutenant told me to take a machine and do everything I could, but to pull no acrobatics below 500 metres. As the machine was a 200 horse-power Spad, I didn't. You see in the 200 horse-power the propeller turns to the right instead of to the left, as in all the other machines, and this reverses everything one does. I had never done acrobatics in a 200 horse-power Spad before, though I had tried a few in the 180. Needless to say I made a holy mess of things—at one time getting hung up on my back in a *renversement*, but the lieutenant said I did very well, on the whole, so I am satisfied. I shall work hard each day so as to be able to go on patrol with the others as soon as possible.

Now I'm *with* the *escadrille*, but not *of* it. All the chaps treat me wonderfully well, but I'm still an *élève*, not having received my "baptism of fire." This fault I hope to remedy soon. At present I am the only American in the *escadrille*. There is another, but he is now on a *permission*. The Frenchmen are a fine bunch of boys. The *escadrille* increased its score today by two *biplace* Boche machines. They were both brought down in this morning's patrol. Four of our busses did the trick—hunting in twos. We had quite a celebration tonight. Over the wine, bought by the victors, they told how they did it.

This afternoon one of the chaps went over to see the wreck of his victim and told us all about it upon his return. He also had the machine guns, magneto, and what-not from the machine for souvenirs. This particular Boche—the first one of the two—was brought down in flames, and the adjutant told us with great gusto how the pilot fell forward on his controls—thus causing the machine to plunge straight down with full motor. It then turned slightly on its back, and as it did so it burst into flames. The jolt of the machine turning on its back threw the observer out and he fell sprawling for a mere trifle of 3000 metres. Then the machine began to disintegrate and came to earth in chunks. You should have seen the adjutant's black eyes snap as he told it. The other plane was brought down far behind the Boche lines and so will probably not become official.

It seemed strange to me—sitting here tonight—to listen to the story in all its details; to see the little adjutant, his arms waving and his eyes all puckered in smiles, tell how the observer fell with legs and arms outflung like a stuffed straw man, and to see the smiles and chuckles of the crowd. War plays queer tricks. The adjutant is a very friendly little man—he left his supper tonight to go and open the door for the dog whining to get in, and he goes out of his way to do one a service. But he is a dead shot and brought down his seventh *official* Boche today. That means innumerable combats and perhaps a dozen or more Boches actually shot down. It's not that the boys are hard-hearted—they know from bitter experience it's shoot or be shot at; so they shoot their best, and when successful laugh and brag about

IN OUR LINES

PRISONERS

it. They have beaten the other man to it—that's all. The little adjutant had looked at his victims this afternoon—described them and their costumes to us; but it did not spoil his appetite for supper—improved it rather. We jest about the taking of life—Boches; of course, but men anyway. How different from civil life! And I, who have never yet killed a man am green with envy and nearly ready to cry because I can't go tomorrow and attempt the same thing.

Our *escadrille* is the possessor of an unusual record—twenty-seven official Boches shot down in eight months with never a man or machine lost. We have five "aces" in the bunch—men who have got five or more Boche machines, and all the others but three have one or more. The *escadrille* has received an army citation for its good work. I am most fortunate to be a member and shall try hard to be worthy of my place here. It will be some little time before I'll be permitted a place on regular patrol, but I'll work hard and make it as short as possible.

The Spad I drove today was a beauty—but I didn't understand it, naturally, it being my first and maiden effort on a plane of its type. As I said, it has 200 horse-power (really 220) and also two machine guns—a distinct advantage for a green man, as one throws twice as much lead. They are fast—mount like rockets. They give Fritz something to think of—sometimes they put a stop to his thinking for all time. Well, it's late—all are in bed excepting myself, and I think I'll make it unanimous. Hope to fly again tomorrow.

I am more than happy and contented here. I'm not even going to take my *permission* of ten days—haven't the money and would rather stay here. Want to do some work. Speaking of work, I'm redesigning our emblem, a running greyhound painted on each plane.

CHANGING SECTORS

Bar-le-Duc, March 7, 1918

I think the last time I wrote you that we had just received orders to move to another sector. We were delayed three or four days on account of bad weather (snow and rain), and after packing all our belongings in trucks ready to move, we had to stay on at S—— eating our meals at other *escadrilles*. We finally got off the day before yesterday morning, the pilots in aeroplanes, and the other hundred or so non-flyers in trucks and automobiles. We all made the voyage safely, but our captain, who had motor trouble just after leaving the ground, smashed, and is now thinking it over in the hospital. He will be all right in a couple of days. We were supposed to fly down in two groups, but we all had different ideas of the best way to go, so Parker and I headed off alone and had a pleasant hour's flight. I was ahead and didn't know exactly where our new field was, so when we got to the vicinity I landed at the first aviation field I saw. Parker was after me, and we found we were only a couple of kilometres from our destination. We smoked a cigarette, then took the air and hopped over to our new home. As the trucks with our bedding, etc., would not arrive till the next day, we all (the pilots) ran into C—— and spent the night and most of the next day there—hot bath, big dinner, regular bed. Ran back to camp yesterday afternoon in the auto, and started fixing up my room. In our new barracks each pilot has a little room to himself. We are much more comfortable and in a far more pleasant location than at S——. Will describe it later, as I am writing this on the run.

This morning Ovington, myself, and a couple of lieutenants in the *escadrille* started back by auto to S——, to get the machines of the pilots who are sick and on leave. I am seeing quite a bit of France from the roads and the air, *n'est ce pas?*—and under exceptionally pleasant circumstances in spite of the war.

LOST IN A SNOWSTORM

March 22, 1917

I got up early this morning and tried my Spad. As with all new types of machines I have tried, I did not care for it very much. We had an early lunch, and went out *en patrouille* at 11.30. The captain and I were in Spads, and I followed him. It was strange weather. The clouds were at all altitudes, and formed into mountains and valleys of cottonwool, through which I had to follow "his Nibs," as Ted calls the captain. To add to the worry of playing hide-and-seek on a machine with which I had only a bowing acquaintance, I found the wind-shield much too low, and received most of the icy blast on my head and face. And it was cold! We could see the ground only through drifting clouds, and before we had reached the lines, the captain turned west. I suppose he meant to go home again and was lost.

Heaven knows I could not have helped him find the way. He did some clever diving into cloud-holes, and I finally dove after him through a snow flurry, to find myself over our old hunting-ground at Cachy—'way north. The air crawled with big English machines, but I saw no sign of the captain. Circled a little, and then set out for home.

I passed Montdidier all right, but the bad weather was forcing me nearer the ground.

Over the end of our home wood I swung to the right and saw a black wall of cloud almost close enough to touch. I dove to 300 feet and there saw the edges of the snowstorm sweep below me and envelop the tops of the trees. Lower I went, but the storm was lashing the very ground, and there was no escape that way; landing was out of the question. There remained one thing—to climb. But now the storm was all about me, and the tiny snowflakes dashing by and into my face. My glasses began to freeze over. I was shut into my machine as by a gray curtain, let down from the edges of the planes. I could not tell at what angle I flew. All I could do was to put all my controls in the centre, and watch my altimetre go up. I'd have liked to go north into the wind, but felt I dared not move my controls; I must hold a straight course. Then I threw up my elbow to look at my compass, it was slowly revolving: I was turning! I sat and endured something of hell, and prayed very earnestly that I might weather the storm. How my brain flew, as a dog's must, when he is on the operating table—tied down; no outward movement, but raging activity within. Once I caught a glimpse of the sun, but it was hidden again immediately in a swelter of flying gray. For almost ten minutes I flew in the gray light you would find in a broken tomb. At 8000 feet I saw the blessed sun and the blue sky.

I was in much the same place as when I had entered the storm (12.35, by the way) and I was able to drop down through a hole, on to the field at Mesnil-Saint-Georges—where I waited better weather to come borne. Saw Grillot there, who was very agreeable and sent you both his regards. On returning I found both Ted and the captain had landed elsewhere, and two others of the patrol had to land elsewhere for *essence*. Another machine was out in the storm, turning right above our field and unable to land. They could hear the sound of his motor.

I conceived a sort of affection for the new Spad; we pulled it off together.

UNE PRISE D'ARMES

Escadrille Spad 79, April 3, 1918

The socks were fine and came at just the right time. But spring is almost here, so our feet will soon warm up, and everyone at home can stop knit. Many signs of spring with us; the crows, magpies, quail, partridges, pheasants, and many birds that I do not know, are here—

UNE *PANNE DE MOTEUR* IN PYJAMAS AT A STRANGE AERODROME

A TWO-SEATER SPAD

the dandelions, wild pansies, and pussy-willows are coming out, and I even saw two stupid toads in a pond, trying to decide where to take up their summer residence.

Walked over to look at the swamp today, as it was raining and unfortunately no flying. Could only visit it on a rainy day anyway; for all good days we fly, and when we start out we practice with our machine guns on target in the middle of the peat-bog—so it's a bad locality to visit on those days. Today there were some boys fishing there—catching perch. I must try my luck the next time it rains and see if I can catch enough for our mess.

By the way—do you know how our machine guns work? They are fixed on the hood and timed to shoot between the propeller blades. So we point the nose of our bird on the object, get it in the sights, and pull the trigger—*tac*—*tac*—*tac*.

Within the week our *escadrille* has brought down three Germans—two of them official. The boy that got one of them has also brought down others. He has been wounded twice in the air and had just returned from the hospital this time. So he received the *Croix de Guerre*—and he well deserves it. We were all lined up for the ceremony—our mechanics all dressed up, for once. The commander of the *groupe* read the citation, then pinned the medal on the boy, and kissed him—according to the old custom—on either cheek. It was the first decoration I've seen—very impressive. Another unforgettable incident of the week was the return of one of our officers after a combat in the air. A fine, tall, red-haired chap, he managed to climb down from his machine and stand up giving his report of observations, with his hand pressed against his back, where two bullets had wounded him; then men rushed up with a stretcher—he calmly lay down on it and they carried him away. I believe he is recovering all right.

We lost one of our other comrades—and that is especially sad in an *escadrille* where we are only a dozen, the best of friends. A vacant place at mess means so much. He was a nice boy too—a later arrival at the *escadrille* than I. Full of ambition—carefully marked all the bullet holes that he had acquired in his machine. Told me that he wrote to his mother once a day and that she wrote to him twice every day. And her two letters came regularly until today, for they have had to wait a few days, to see whether he was lost in France, before reporting him missing. Of course there is a chance that he may have been taken prisoner.

That is my one big horror—to be taken prisoner—I would a hundred times rather be killed in an air fight. So you can guess how carefully we make our mechanics look after the motor and try it each time before starting out—for once in the air we are at its mercy, and if it ever stops in Hunland, there is nothing to do but come down.

Don't know why I should write so much about the unpleasant things when there is so much that is pleasant. Our work is extremely interesting, and lots of it just now, as you know. The news every day is more encouraging—the Germans pushed the British back, but the latter, with the ever-ready French, turned the tide, which, you know, is the greatest feat of all. Perhaps I told you about a detachment of French soldiers that I saw in the beginning of the affair, on their way to help their English comrades. Have never seen such wonderful morale. Far from being discouraged, they were singing—after all they had been through—and looking eagerly, cheerfully toward the grim future.

We have a real bird's-eye view of the fighting on the ground—see the twinkle of the shells, and the puffs of smoke, and the red glare of burning towns.

Our main task so far has been to report all we see of the movements of the enemy and to dive, shooting at them, if they follow open roads or gather together. Of course they shoot back, but although the wings need patching almost every time, it is hard for them to strike the heart of a mechanical bird travelling at such a terrific speed.

Un Prise d'Armes, Chaudun, (Aisnes Sector)

We have the best of treatment with the French. Each *escadrille* is like a small club or family, and every one's worth is measured in what he does—not in rank.

NERVES

April 4, 1918

It's raining today, so our valiant *aviateurs* are idle. I had expected to go out to grab a Dutch "sausage" this morning and wrote Dad to that effect last night. The rain spoiled it for the time, but I'll probably be sent as soon as the weather becomes better. So now, while I have the leisure, I'm going to try and tell you a bit about our work and its impressions on yours truly—though my impressions are so vague and so changeable that it's hard to put them into words.

Our end of this business is a funny one—it's like seeing a war film in the movies. I have been flying over one of the greatest battles in history and I have heard scarcely a sound but the droning of my own motor. At times, when diving upon Boche soldiers, batteries, etc., I have heard the "typewriters" clacking away at me, and sometimes an "Archie" puts one close enough so one can hear the cough of the explosion and feel the lift of the air, but that's not very frequent, thank the Lord. With all kinds of firearms and cannon banging away, the aviator works in silence. I say in silence; of course the motor makes a fearful roar, the wind shrieks through the struts and rigging, and we can hear our own guns when we shoot, but these become so much a matter of course that we don't hear them consciously.

When the motor misses or the machine gun jams, we become aware for the first time that there has been any noise. When the shells hit beneath us—the flash of the guns and the puffs of smoke from the shrapnel shells—we see spurts of dirt and rubbish. Sometimes we see little gray or blue or khaki-coloured masses crawling along with the smoke puffs blossoming over and amongst them, but they don't seem like men, nor as a part of our own game. It's a bit uncanny, I think. The only real and tangible things to us are the "sausages"—big black bags suspended either under or over us—usually far beneath as we fly regular patrols at about 4000 metres or more, while they are usually at about 1000.

At the high levels we see absolutely nothing of the battle-field. It's just a peaceful, quiet map to us, with crooked, crazy lines of brown or white zigzagging through the greens and plum colours of the grass and ploughed fields. All that exists for us is the air—above, under, and around us. We watch for those black spots which so quickly become other machines—either friend or enemy—make sure every other member of the patrol is in his place and that none are missing; also that we have no new member with us. Sometimes it is possible for a Boche to sneak up from behind at our own level (of course, one sees nothing but the edge of the wings and the radiator). He trails along, and should one of the end machines of the patrol lag behind a bit, he pounces on it during that fraction of time in which the pilot realises that the machine behind looks strange and has no business there. This happens very rarely, as it is a risky thing for friend Boche, but when one slip is usually all one has a chance to make, one pays attention to details.

We now have against us, among others, an *escadrille* of which you may have heard—the "Tangos"—so called because of the colour of their machines—tango orange. They are one of the crack *escadrilles* of the Boches. I have not yet seen one, but suppose I shall soon—they don't hide to amount to anything. We fly now in larger bunches, as Herr Boche likes to hunt in packs—nine or a dozen machines in one patrol. I have no more right to an opinion than either of you, but my guess is that this is only the first act of this little play the Boches are giving. I think we shall see a hell of a lot more before it's over. Going to be a big scrap, but we are all confident, though we realise the seriousness of things. Damn the Russians—what? When they quit they gave Fritz a wonderful lift—all the Eastern Front troops over here now. There are going to be some dead Germans before they get through— and also some Allies, though the Boche is losing more heavily.

So much for a picture—a very rough sketch, I'm afraid—of our view of this offensive. As for how it impresses me or affects me, I'm darned if I know exactly. I've tried to analyse my emotions several times, but don't get anywhere at all. I do know that I get most awfully scared at times, and yet I enjoy it and should hate to leave while it's still going on. Mostly, I'm nervous on the ground—in the air one is fairly busy and has no time to spend in imagining things. Have to keep on the job.

When a patrol is announced, I'm always afraid I shan't be one to go—when I find I am, I'm nervous and imaginative until we get away. Over the lines it's the same. When we don't find Boches I'm sore; when we do I'm in a fever of excitement for fear I'll not be able to make good in the mix. It's tiresome. I've always had an idea I had a yellow streak—thought I'd find out for sure over here, but I don't know any more than I did. I'd like to know how the other boys feel who are with me when we point our busses down and begin plugging away at a trench or battery. For me, it's fine going down—both machine guns popping away and the wires howling, from the rush of air, but when I pull her up and begin climbing again I can't help hunching my back a bit and waiting for a shot to come along and plug something personal belonging to my anatomy or machine.

It's just the first few seconds—then it passes; but I shan't be satisfied until I have a real scrap with another bus and find out just how I'll behave. I know I'll stick, but that's not a matter of "guts"—it's pride, I think. For instance—the first time we went out "trench raiding" they told me to *pique* at about 600 metres and shoot until I got to 100 or 200 metres, but not to go lower, as the machine made too big a mark that low. To show them (and myself) that I wasn't frightened, I kept on shooting down to 50 metres or less. I could see their faces plainly as they looked up at me. And the joke of it was when I did get down there and wished I hadn't come so far. Of course, when I got up high again I was quite tickled with myself. That's the way it goes—when I'm busy I'm all right, but given a chance to think a bit I'm a blame coward. Don't know why I write all this junk to you, unless it's to try and straighten it out a bit for myself.

We are all very nonchalant and care-free with each other here—never are frightened—a mere trifle, you know, to fly, and all that sort of thing—"don't know whether I'll kill a Boche today or read the paper" sort of business. But I notice when we are in our flying clothes and waiting the signal to leave, every one who is going gets very happy—whistle and sing and slap their machines on the back—all impatient to be off. But I know how *I feel* when I'm waiting and I wonder sometimes. . . . I used to whistle and sing happily when I passed a cop with my blouse full of apples I had swiped. But it's a mistake to try and analyze emotions (or the coffee) here and I must stop.

It doesn't matter how we feel as long as we do our work. The results are the same, whatever our own secret feelings may happen to be from time to time. *Vive la guerre*—I don't think!

YOUTH

Secteur Postal 185, April 10, 1918

I hope that you are all well. I am all right.

It has been raining for several days and we have not done much flying. We all hope that it will soon be fine again.

I have a new machine, and it goes very well. Yesterday the captain said, "See how soon you can climb to 1000 metres, then make a *vrille*, and a few *renversements* to each side." I stopped my motor in the *vrille* (a spinning nose-dive in America), and did not have enough height to catch it again. I could not make the *piste*, and had to land on a little strip of narrow ground between two muddy ploughed fields. I had great luck. Did not break a thing.

My first mechanic is the best in the *escadrille*. He works very hard, and the machine is always in good trim. He always wants to know just how everything went; and if anything is wrong, he does not stop working until he has fixed it. When I can get some films for my camera, I shall have both our pictures taken with the machine.

The guns fire much more now than when I was first out here. When flying, you can see the holes where the shells have fallen.

The mails are slowed up a bit by the big battle. I have not received very much for quite a while.

I meet Americans once in a while, but not very many just now.

I went out shooting with a French comrade several days ago. We both had shot-guns. He shot one partridge and I shot two. I got one on the way home in the dark. Heard him start up, and shot in direction of the noise. Was very lucky. We had a great feed several days later.

My captain is an "ace," and gives us much good advice. He has brought down eight Boches. He isn't one of the kind that stays on the ground and tells the boys what to do. He goes up and does the hardest work himself. He is more strict than our old captain; but I like him just as well. They are both great fellows.

April 13, 1918

I didn't finish the other day, but will try to now.

Went up this morning (four of us), and were up so high that it was hard to breathe. Stayed there too long. One of my comrades fell and was killed on the way down. I was near him and saw him go by in a *vrille*. He had started to come out of it when he hit the ground. I landed right away, and a bunch of us ran over to where he fell. It was a bad sight. I liked this fellow very much.

He was always pleasant and full of fun. His name was ———. This kind of puts a gloom on the bunch.

The two fellows, whose room is next mine, shot down a "sausage" yesterday. They had *some* time.

I must go to bed now, because it is 10.30 p.m. Have nothing to keep you up late out here. You can't chase Boches at night.

April 19, 1918

Good news: Tommy Hitchcock was not killed. He is a prisoner and slightly wounded.

Bad news: "Herm" Whitmore has disappeared. He was in the big battle. No word from him. I hope that they didn't get him. Tom Buffum and he were together.

Saw Lufbery the other day and talked with him. He is a major in the American Army now. Has brought down eighteen Boches. You ought to see him fly! I guess that you have read about him.

April 20, 1918

I did not finish last night. Went on a patrol this morning, but it was very cloudy. Did not see any Boches.

I have a white-winged horse painted on each side of the body of my machine. A winged horse is the insigne of the *escadrille*.

Things are going badly just now; but the Boches are going to get licked. The French Army is "there" today just as much as ever. I hope that U.S. keeps working.

Sugar is very scarce over here; but I did not think it would be so in America.

I have never received the box from home. It is hard luck. I may get it later.

I fly a good deal now that the weather is getting better. I learn something every day. I never thought I should be doing this when I left America a year ago.

Shonny (Clarence B. Shoninger), an American who rooms with me, is having a hard time making landings. He smashed up a machine today and has partly smashed them before. I am afraid that the captain will not let him stay. It will be very lonesome here for me if he goes. He treats me very nicely and we get along well together. He is a very funny fellow, and he makes the Frenchmen here laugh quite often. He was in the Ambulance for a long time before I came over here.

I think that we shall probably be moving again before a long time. You never know where you are going to be from one time to another.

The middle of next June I shall be going on another *permission*. These *permissions* are great things to look forward to. They have been suppressed for the time being because of the big offensive.

I suppose that there is a lot of this "Somewhere in France" stuff going around at home. The fellows here don't think much of that expression. Better not use it.

I must go to bed now. Take good care of yourselves and don't get any more colds.

April 25, 1918

I received letter (3), and was very glad to hear from you. I hope that all are well. I am in good health.

I have not received the package yet.

I haven't much of anything in the way of harmonicas now and I have taken to a *mandolin*. I bought one for thirty francs and I am making good progress. Nordy is sitting on my bed now playing. Shonny is going to get one also, and he can then make as much noise as I do.

I am going to Paris soon to get another new machine.

I was in Paris the first day they began shooting the long-range gun. It did not worry people as much as you would think.

My *mécano* continues to be as good as ever. He will go to Paris when I do.

Shonny and myself are going to make a voluntary patrol tomorrow morning at 7 a.m. and I must get some sleep now. Will finish tomorrow.

April 26, 1918

I have just arrived back at the camp. We didn't see any Boches. Were shot at a little. There were a good many clouds. It was Shonny's first patrol, and he thought it was exciting.

Tomorrow morning I am going for another new machine. It will be much better than the kind I have now.

May 22, 1918

I never finished this letter.

Today I received a notice that there was a commission as 2nd Lieutenant waiting for me at Paris. This is in the American Air Service. I am trying to decide what to do. I hate to leave my *mécanicien*, machine, captain, etc. I suppose that I shall change; but I am going to try to stay with my French *escadrille* for a while if possible.

"Herm" Whitmore is prisoner in Germany. Chapman, who was in postcard picture with "Whit" and myself at Nice, was shot down in flames; as was poor Tom Buffum. Tom was one of the best fellows I ever knew. He did a good deal for me.

I received the two bundles with everything O.K. The sweater was fine, and the candy was excellent. Thank Mrs. N—— ever so much for the orange-peel candy. It was fine.

I am sending you a picture of my *mécanicien*. He gave it to me to send to you.

Lufbery, the best flyer and fighter of the Americans in French Aviation, was brought down not far from where I am. I knew him. He was a major in the American Army.

June 15, 1918

I hope that all are well at home. I suppose that you will be at the lake when this letter reaches you.

I am all right and in good health.

No news from Shonny as yet. I looked over his things and found his will. He was a very rich fellow. His parents are dead. I hope that he is a prisoner.

It was exciting the other day. Five of us went out in a group and shot up the Germans on the roads and in the woods. We flew low. When I arrived at our *piste* found a hole through the tail of my machine, in back of the seat.

The first day I went on patrol in this new *secteur*, I got lost. I saw that I had very little *essence* left, and that I had better come down somewhere before all was gone. I saw a good-looking field near a *château*, and landed in good shape. There was no *essence* and no one to turn my propeller; but about 300 people from all the countryside came to see the machine. At last the old fellow who owned the place came in his machine and invited me to eat with him and stay overnight. I said, "Fine," and he put me up in the best way possible. He had a guard placed around my machine all the time I was there. The next day he gave me some *essence* and we found a *mécano*. I soon started the motor and was off. I gave them a little exhibition, and then went back to my *piste*. My *escadrille* hadn't received my telephone message and they all thought that I was a "goner." They were glad to see me back.

My *mécano* has been in the hospital ever since I was at Château-Thierry, *en panne*. He came back last night, and I was glad to see him.

My machine is very good, and I hope that it will keep that way. It is "some" fast.

Nordy is still here.

I hope that our army does some good work before long. I think that they are going to be good.

I suppose that things in America are very different now.

I have received several cards from you. Thank you very much.

It is very fine weather today. I am going to fly in a minute.

I just met General Duval, who is Chief of French Aviation. He asked if I spoke French. I told him, "a little." He asked if I was contented with the French, etc., etc. You can't beat these French officers. Most of them are wonderful fellows.

Well, I must stop now. Write me all the news.

June 29, 1918

No news from Shonny as yet.

The day before yesterday I had an exciting time. Four of us were up three miles over Germany when we ran into eleven Boches who were a little above us. We played around for a while trying to get into position; but they got on our tails after a while. My motor wasn't in the best of trim, and I did some stunts to keep out of range, as I couldn't get above. All of a sudden two of them began shooting at two of my French comrades. One German was very near one of our new pilots shooting a rain of fire; but he could not seem to hit him. The other was farther away; but he made a wonderful shot, and my comrade's machine was all flames. He went diving down, and I thought he was a "goner," but all of a sudden the flames went out. I couldn't get above and I went down with him for about a mile, full motor and straight like a stone. He kept on going and landed all right. I dodged a few Boche patrols and got back. That was some stunt for my comrade—to be brought down in flames and get out of it without a scratch.

Yesterday I was up over the lines when my pressure gave out. I had to land in a wheatfield and I did some loop the loop! Not a scratch, but the machine (the one in the picture) was wrecked. I am without a machine today.

I hope that you will have a good time this summer if you go to the lake.

I do not see very many Americans because I am always with the French.

The French commander of my *groupe* is a fine fellow. He eats with us now, and I make him laugh once in a while. You can't beat a Frenchman when he really wants to be nice; neither can you beat the kind that want to be mean. I find many fine fellows out here.

The Americans have done some good work; but I think they will do a lot more before the war is finished.

I suppose that America is very different now than before. I hope that everybody is working hard.

I still have my "mec," "Mas," as you will see by the snapshot I am enclosing. I don't know what I shall do when he leaves me, or when I go to an American *escadrille*. He is a very good mechanic, and he works very hard. They are not all like that.

Do you receive all of the "snaps" that I send you? I hope so.

What do you think of my American uniform?

Well, take good care of yourselves.

August 28, 1918

I received 13, 14, and 15. Was very glad to hear from you all, and hope that all goes well. I don't believe that 12 has reached me yet.

I have *repos* this p.m. Attack tomorrow. You will read about these attacks in the paper. The war is going well now. I think that we have the Boches on the run.

You speak of my captain in letter 14. I guess that I forgot to tell you that he was shot down a few days after Shonny was taken prisoner. It was too bad. The commanding officer now is Lieutenant Rougevin. He is very funny, and I like him very much. The other morning at 6 o'clock he came to my room with his shot-gun and a few cartridges. He told me that there were some partridges out back. We took the gun and went about two kilometres in our pyjamas. We did not find one. I have killed several, and we have had good feeds with them.

There are only two of the fellows left in the *escadrille* of fifteen who were at Lunéville when I first went to the Front. We had some hard luck, but things are going better now. I am the third oldest in the *escadrille*.

We have been at all of the big attacks this year. They have been exciting sometimes. When we fly low over a battle we can hear the guns very plainly in spite of the noise of our motors.

I was leading a patrol of five several days ago when I saw a Boche *biplace*. The gunner was in the back with his two machine guns, and the pilot had one or two in front. I dove on him, and let him have about two hundred cartridges; but he didn't go down. You should have heard them shooting at me! I have been out looking for another *biplace* several times since then, with the best French lieutenant here, but we haven't found one yet. When you start shooting your two machine guns, an awful shower of steel goes through the air.

The U.S. Army came around to visit Americans in the French Army the other day. They gave me a large 45-*calibre* Colt revolver. It is pretty good. I am going to carry it in my machine. It may come in handy some time.

I am leaving for a *permission* of ten days plus travelling time in two or three days. I expect to go to Urcay, France, and take it easy.

My "mec" is still on the job. He will go on "perm" about the same time as myself. My machine has never been driven by another. I ran the first motor sixty hours, which is very good; and now I have a new one. It seems to be more powerful than the other. I shall probably get a new machine when I return from "perm." I guess that I shall miss my "mec" when I change to an American squadron. I hope that there will be some good American "mecs."

Some American officers were here the other day. They want to take the few fellows who are with the French and put them in the new American formations. I asked to remain here for a while longer. The captain of the *groupe* and my lieutenant also asked to keep me. The French officers are generally very nice. I shall soon have some pictures of all the officers in the *groupe* together, but I don't believe that I shall be able to send them home.

In one of the photos "Mas" (my *mécano*) is lying on the machine, working at something. You have to be an acrobat to work on one of these machines. He did not know that I took the picture.

I have a second "mec" who is very good also. I took a picture of the two of them working on my machine; but I don't believe that the sun was strong enough.

It is too bad that Aunt Emmie is sick. Send her my best wishes and tell her that I hope she will soon be better.

I know about Shonny. He is a prisoner. I guess the prisoners will have a hard time before the war is over.

I slept in the same room at Avord with "Stew" Walcott. He was a very nice fellow. I also know the fellow "Wright," who writes for the *Saturday Evening Post*. He certainly is putting up some bluff over there. I suppose that you have read some of his articles. Somebody is going to call him before long.

I should like to get back to U.S. now and see how things have changed. It must be very different.

I must close now. I have many letters to write *comme toujours*, but I never write them. I hope to catch up some time.

September 24, 1918

I hope that all are well and enjoying life.

Several days ago I came back from my *permission* at Urcay. I found that the bunch had left; but it did not take me long to go after them.

I lost my bag on the train. It had my little camera, which I thought a good deal of, and several other things. I shall miss the camera.

Captain Bailly (French), a good friend of mine, disappeared while I was away on permission.

Captain Rougevin is the same old boy. He is the best of them all. We have a good time once in a while.

I shall know all the Front in great shape if we keep on changing places. We are living in a tent now, four of us.

I have not received mail from you for a long while, most a month.

I had a fine time at Urcay. The family of a girl friend of mine invited me to spend my *permission* at their summer place in the country. They fed me in great shape, and made many cookies, cakes, and chocolate creams. I went hunting and shot some *perdrin* and another bird—I don't know its name. I had a fine rest down there.

De Slade, the French "ace," had dinner with us last night. We have some very interesting fellows eat with us sometimes. They can tell some great stories.

I bought a trunk several days ago for seventy-five *francs*. I hope that it holds together.

Things over here are very dear. I think that we may miss out on potatoes this winter. There do not seem to be very many. I like potatoes very much, and this will be a loss to me.

The war is going well for us now. I hope that these attacks will help to bring the end sooner. The Boches are going to be good and sick of it before they get through. I did not know what was going to happen when they crossed the Marne last July; but now I am sure.

I rode up through Château-Thierry, etc., on the train, and it was very interesting. I had flown over very much, but it is more interesting on the ground. You can't imagine how these towns look.

I have flown over Montdidier a good deal. It is just like an ashheap. I never saw such a sight. It will take some time to replace these towns.

I hope that I do not have to leave my *escadrille*. I would like to stay with it until the war is finished.

I can understand most anything in French, and I can say most anything I want to. I speak French most of the time. I am forgetting the English, because when I write letters I want to put in the French forms. When I meet an American, I mix the two languages.

I must go to dinner. Take good care of yourselves and write.

SOUVENIR-HUNTER'S PARADISE

August, 1918

One of our pilots "crashed" yesterday and we heard that he had been wounded. So the C.O., I, and others chased out to the field hospital and found that he had already been evacuated to a base hospital. We took the instruments off his machine and learned from a doughboy there that the flyer had probably fainted near the ground. He was badly bruised. As I was the only one around today who knew where the crash was, I was sent out to get it. The sergeant in charge of the men asked me if we could not go a round-about way and see some sights. I, being an agreeable soul, said we would get the crash first and then go sightseeing. While the men worked, I stood around and looked wise and answered questions—"Did I fly the Liberty motor?" "How can we transfer to Aviation?" "Was I ever scared?" "How could I shoot through the fan without hitting it?" All of these questions I answered painstakingly. While I wanted to laugh, of course I didn't, and so the questions went on.

When the bus was loaded on the trailer, the sergeant came up again and asked if we could do a bit of sight-seeing. I agreed, and off we started. The road was jammed in one place with French *camions* piloted by Annamites. They are stupid-looking Chinamen, who refuse to stay on their side of the road. The horizontal stabilizer, which is like the tail of a fish, extended about a foot on either side of the trailer, and, as we were making our way through the *camions*, it hit an Annamite who was leaning out the side of his car. Well, the whole cavalcade stopped, the Chinks piled out, and you never heard such a hubbub. It was entirely his fault, and after ascertaining that he was not hurt we went on, as I had no desire to be caught in a Chinese uprising. As soon as we had turned from the main highway into a territory that the Germans had occupied a few days before, we came into a souvenir-hunter's paradise. There had been a hasty retreat on the part of the Huns and a hurried advance on the part of the "Alleys."

Between the stuff left by the Germans and that left by the Americans, the piles were heroic in size. The first French salvage party had been through burying the dead and collecting most of the junk. In one pile I noted a Pullman towel, a Boche helmet, a French helmet, an American knitted muffler, a pair of German boots, mess-kits of the three nationalities, ammunition and grenades of all descriptions—

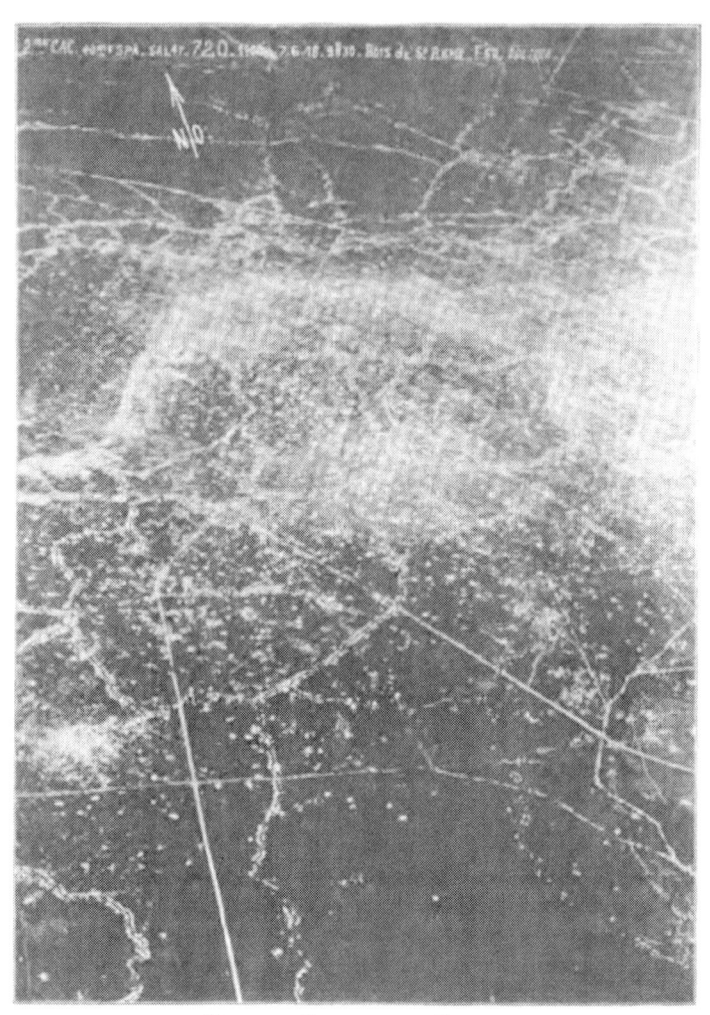

ON THE CHAMPAGNE FRONT

all mixed together in a conglomerate mass. Then we stopped and walked through the woods. It beggars all description. It is a wood made famous by a branch of the U.S. Army. The place reeked with the dreadful odour of decaying things. The flotsam and jetsam there was awe-inspiring. Packages of food and ammunition on all sides. Letters, French and English, all about, and the graves—grave after grave all well taken care of and numbered. We came away with 2000 rounds of Boche ammunition to use in a Boche gun we have, and the men had every bit of armament they wanted—and were no end pleased. As for me—well, it made me realise that the infantry are the ones who do the work and have but little fun, while aviation seems almost a slacker's job. My hat's off to the doughboy.

I went up toward the Front the other day to bring back a machine, and while waiting for the men to get the bus ready, noon came around. The men had nothing but canned goods and had eaten that, so I told them to get into the truck and we'd go down the road until we ran into an army encampment, and there get a meal. I was ready to eat with the men, but another pilot there wanted me to dine with the officers; so I did. I am very glad of it, as I dined with what is left of a very famous regiment. They were *en repos* after having seen some terrific action. I sat there enthralled at their tales. One of the lieutenants was very proud of his men. They were tough and hard-boiled; in short, to use his own words, "Rough cookies." "I'd give an order to stop advancing," he told me, "but on they would go, paying no attention to me at all. So all I could do was to stay ahead of them until they stopped."

We walked down the street after lunch and the men certainly showed that lieutenant lots of courtesy. There was a Y.M.C.A. man with the regiment who, just before the attack, got excited, grabbed a tin hat and a rifle, stuffed cookies into his pockets, and went over with the doughboys. He was over fifty years old. After the first attack he threw away the rifle and for four days and nights did nothing but minister to the wounded. A Catholic priest went over the top with them without even a helmet.

We had a patrol yesterday and saw but one Hun bus, but he had the sun and a thousand metres altitude over us, so we could not attack. Some of the towns we fly over look pretty well razed and the country is fairly pockmarked with shell-holes. The best fun of a patrol is the home-coming. Your formation well intact flies over the lines, gets well into French territory, and then slowly disintegrates. You relax, throttle

La Chandelle

down, and fly steadily. Everything takes on a pleasant tone. You land. Your "mecs" help you out of your flying clothes and you are through. Your work has been well done, which is sweetest of all rewards.

A.M., Patrol—P.M., Golf

1918

We had an early patrol the other day and saw neither Huns nor that worst bugbear—"Archie." "Archie," as you probably know, is German anti-aircraft shrapnel, or sometimes H.E. It was very peaceful up in the sky, and on the ground so far as we could see. The land was dotted with shell-holes, and, with spots of light khaki in the green of the fields, looked beautiful even from our height. There was nothing to tell us that a great battle was raging below. After an hour of patrolling we came back and the C.O. said we could take the Packard and play tennis or golf. Just imagine—well inside German territory in the morning and in the afternoon—one hundred and fifty kilometres away—golf. The course is a very tricky one, hilly and rough, with basaltic rock jutting out on every side. After the game I took a hot bath and had dinner, which was ended with a wonderful chocolate *soufflé*. Then we came back over the most wonderful roads in the world. You see, France has a finely organised system of automobile truckage with which they move their troops and supplies behind each big drive. To do this successfully the roads have to be kept in good condition and the auxiliaries or men unfit for military service are kept working as road-makers.

Yesterday we went out "on protection," hovering over an American photo bus. We were some ten kilometres inside the German lines when down below us appeared twelve dirty gray "Dutchmen." We couldn't dive, as we had to stay with the *biplace*. They looked like evil fish skulking to trap an unwary pilot. Every now and then they would pull up on their tails and let drive at us—then float away. The other day I lost my patrol and seeing six machines in formation joined them, only to find that they were French. My "wind" was surely up, as they might easily have been Boche. I streaked for home, and when I crossed the lines you may be sure I heaved a sigh of relief.

We have a 5.45 patrol tonight. The clouds are high and white, auguring well for friend "Archie." As someone has rather well said, "'Archie's' bark is worse than his bite, but he can always get your wind up." He's an ugly customer, and should be treated with respect and not derisively. One young man in the R.F.C. was being "archied" recently and to show his scorn placed his thumb on a prominent part of his face, extended his fingers and wriggled them in a manner accepted the world over as registering contempt. "Archie" took notice, and a piece of shell whanged off the fingers. The moral is obvious; don't underrate "Archie."

1918

    I have the grand job of being officer of the day. The chief duties thereof consist solely of the censoring of the mail. I censored about one hundred letters and to me they were rather interesting. One was written by my rigger, giving all the news of his new pilot—which is myself. I have two mechanics, a rigger and a fitter, the former taking care of the plane and the latter of the motor. When I arrived at the squadron I had my choice of three machines. Knowing nothing about the machines, as it was a type I had never flown, I took the bus that had, in my estimation, the best rigger and fitter. I want my mechanics to like me and to take an interest in my work, but I think all the mechanics do that. I go out and ask a fairly intelligent question, or as nearly so as my motor knowledge will permit, and then the fitter goes off in an ecstasy, draws a deep breath, and starts in. Much of it is Greek to me, but it seems to give him no end of pleasure. Then the fitter, rigger, and I have long discussions about the plane every now and then. The point of the whole thing is that they seem to think I take an interest. You may rest assured I do.

    Yesterday my rigger said, "Say, lieutenant, how would youse like a steel plate to sit on?" If shrapnel and bullets are coming from beneath, the advantages of a steel plate are obvious, so I manifested my rapture at the prospect, and, lo, the next day I had a steel seat. I noticed two lovely round holes in the plate and mildly inquired what put them there, and he answered, rather naively, "Oh, I took her out on the range and fired two shots at a hundred yards, but say, sir, that ain't nothing; that's a swell seat." Every time I leave the ground it's always "Good luck, sir, and be careful." When I come down and happen to make a good landing—"Gee, that was a peach of a landing. You never bounced a bit, sir."

    A bit ago one of our pilots didn't return. Five or six times a day his mechanics used to come to the tent asking for news. Then they started taking turns. One day when all the rest of the men were out playing ball and these two were sitting under the hangar, the major came along, "Well, boys, your boss is safe on this side of the lines."

Those men jumped up and down, threw their hats, and certainly registered joy.

Two days ago one of our machines failed to return, and the mechanic, who had been with the pilot six months, went to the major and said he wanted a job in the kitchen; he never wanted to work on a machine again. The loyalty of these men is marvellous. Just show a little interest and they will work their heads off for you. And if you get a Hun for them—well, that's the best way you can repay them. Well, to get back to my man. He said in the letter that he had a new boss and that he was the best fighter and pilot for a new man that had ever come to the squadron, and added, "He treats me fine and sure is a swell guy." Over Hunland this morning and friend "Archie" was so wild that I smiled to myself. Just then one went off under my wing, boosted the plane way up and scared your dutiful son no end. My respect for "Archie" has increased, and if you had seen me dashing all over the sky you would have laughed. We saw some Huns, but as they have a *penchant* for picking on inferior numbers they did not bother us today.

Off the Map

We are about to move to another front, and as I am one of the advance party I start to morrow at 6.30 a.m. My roommate and special "buddy"—an All-American from University of Pennsylvania, Irish, and as happy-go-lucky as myself—in short, a whale of a boy—goes with me. We go only provided the weather isn't "dud." Our mechanics are splendid, and my guns are going well, due to the good work of the gunnery department.

Went on patrol day before yesterday and was "Archied" in a rather desultory fashion as if the gunners weren't a bit interested in their work. We saw one bus which looked like a Hun two-seater, but he had the sun and altitude, and when we started after him he nosed over and dived for Germany. We drifted off our maps, and when we started home I only knew about where I was.

Finally we got well into France, I saw the right river, and then "What a grand and glorious feeling." Motor throttled down, all the cylinders hitting, well inside our own lines about two thousand metres up, all relaxed, no Huns, no worry. You can sing or hum, slouch down in the seat and enjoy life. I make a good landing, my two "mecs" run out to meet me, all agrin that I am back. It is really a marvellous life. The other side? Well, we don't think of that or we couldn't go on.

Indisponible

October, 1918

I have been hoping the attack would soon be over and the two sides settle in for the winter, but on they go—push—push—push. Oh, well, the harder the Allies push, the sooner it will be over—the Huns are pretty near their finish.

We are having a hard time to get machines. At present I have a machine, but not a motor for it, and in the meantime have to fly a borrowed bus. I don't like that, but it's only fair to go in one's turn, regardless of the plane, as two hours over the lines are equal to about twenty in the S.O.S.

Just made a patrol and home again. The push goes on and we continue to fly in atrocious weather. It certainly will be a relief to do high patrol again. I've had all I want of this six hundred metre business. The blamed old Huns know it and are always just above, ready to dive down if they get a chance. They are wily, never going out alone or taking great chances. They have just sent over some toy balloons with propaganda. The big argument was that the German people are ready for peace and that we, the cats-paw for England and France, were keeping the war going on. Pretty good line if it were not so humorous, but you don't expect a German to have any sense of the latter.

We have two Englishmen with us, belonging to a day bombing gang. Their particular stunt is to bomb the home of the Hun—far off in Germany. The pilot is a cherubic youngster of perhaps eighteen, while the observer is a hard and toughened veteran of the infantry—aged twenty. They flew two hours and a half into Hunland, dropped down to two hundred metres, released their "eggs," and started home. They lost their formation, had to fly entirely by compass, as a very heavy fog had set in, and fought off three Huns who pursued them sixty kilometres. They flew three hours and a half in the direction of home, saw an aerodrome and started to land, but a terrific burst of "Archie" and machine-gun fire warned them they were not at home. The pilot kept on and was again greeted by friend "Archie."

It was too misty to see the ground clearly and he had no idea where he was. Just at that moment the gas gave out. He planed down, landed, and was waiting, matchbox in hand, to set fire to his plane if German soldiers came up. He had landed a mile from our aerodrome, and, telling us about it, said it was all in the day's work. Imagine staying in the air six hours and a half.

October, 1918

Coming home from a patrol today, I saw an American bus come tearing out of Germany with three Huns on its tail. The Huns, who were above, apparently saw us, and hastened back. There was no artillery fire to speak of and all our balloons were down. After wasting an hour over the lines, we came home. Then a bus had to be tested and I was elected. I got just over the hangars when the motor stopped. Now when a motor drops from 2100 revolutions to zero there is quite a jar. Simultaneously with the stopping of the motor was the ceasing of my heart, as I had visions of another crash. Then the motor picked up again, then quit, then full tilt. I just managed to squeeze onto the field. For a moment my "wind" was up higher than a kite, but directly after landing, I got into another bus and made a patrol.

The fog rolls in so thick that often one cannot see a foot ahead. Tonight I got lost in a two-hundred-yard walk from headquarters. It's getting no end disgusting. The Huns run us out of the sky because we have only four machines. We have only four machines because that is all that are serviceable. Why not more than four? Because we can't—but if I go on I might get court-martialled for *lèse majesté*. Oh, for plenty of good machines! The Huns are using parachutes, a fine idea which I hope we shall adopt. There are certain contingencies which might arise when a parachute would be useful.

FLYING AT FOUR HUNDRED METRES

October, 1918

I have never flown so much, so long, or so often. The French squadrons go *en repos* now and then, but not we. From one attack we go to another, and during an attack it's no fun, especially this one, as we are not allowed to go above six hundred metres, which height exposes one to machine-gun fire from the ground. The guns, of course, are hidden; you sail over unsuspecting, and then, *tac—tac—tac—tac—tac—*. You begin to zigzag, dive, and climb all at the same time, but it seems an eternity until you get out of range. Two days ago two of us went out alone. It was very "dud" weather, with the clouds at about four hundred metres. We were well inside the enemy's lines and saw nothing. Not a Hun plane, "Archie," or machine. Suddenly I saw a German tank; in fact seven of them. I dove on the first. Well, those Boches never did a thing. Just let me come as low as I wanted, which was about one hundred metres. I had them nicely in my sights when every gun, revolver, rifle, and machine gun the Huns have on this

A GERMAN AERODROME

sector opened up. I straightway lost all interest in tanks. The machine guns sounded like so many twigs cracking.

If ever you run into one of those "intrepid heroes of the air" like De—— W——, etc., and he tries to tell you that "Archie" is most effective at two thousand metres, you tell him that he knows not whereof he speaks. They surely did open up on me. Now "Archie" as a general rule is a fearsome thing so far as getting "one's wind up," but as a menace not so much to be dreaded, as but one out of two hundred thousand shots connect. But that day it was no end annoying. Every time one broke I jumped. Now an aeroplane is not conducive to jumping about in, so every time I jumped the old bus jumped. I was so low I could not recognise where I was, the sun nonexistent, and my compass going round in circles. I had no time to lose. I took what I thought was south and made for that. No, I did not sail back into Germany, but right down the lines neither to one side nor the other. The shooting continued, because as one battery would stop, another would start, or, as I thought, two pick up when one quit. I sailed along the lines for about two miles when I picked up a landmark and turned for home. I had a piece of shrapnel and nine nice bullet holes in my plane, some too close for comfort.

One gets awfully fed up with flying in the American Army, as there is nothing to look forward to. The British have six months in France, then six months at home. But with us it's different. If a man ever stops to think, he's gone. If one can live from day to day, all's well. My one hope is that I shall continue to do my work and not break. Flying is not so bad, because the longer one flies the more careful and skilful one becomes, but the thing that is wearing is the keyed-up state of one's nerves while over the lines. The other night I volunteered for a night patrol, but did not have to go. I had my first crash the other day when I landed in our advanced field and hit a shell-hole. I stood the old bus on its nose, but after a bit we pulled it down, put in a new prop, and away I flew.

BRINGING HOME THE BUS

November, 1918

I went out on a very comfortable patrol this morning. The sky was full of our busses. 'Way off in Hunland was an enemy two-seater, working up and down the lines. Their scouts, which have bothered us so much of late, were nowhere in evidence. I looked above and to all sides and saw nothing but our own scouts. I settled down to enjoy

OVER DIXMUDE

myself, when suddenly an oil lead broke. My compass was off, or I thought it was, and I couldn't see the sun. I headed south and came lower to look at the troops. Of course they were in khaki. It surely looks good. I have always thought of khaki as rather ugly, but now it's pretty fine-looking.

Yesterday was "dud," so I took a car and went up to the Front to look for one of our busses which had crashed there. In the good old days we had trenches, the Huns had trenches, and between was No Man's Land. But these days, during and since the big push, there is a space some five or six kilometres wide between the two armies. There is nothing to mark it, only an outpost here and there. We were getting close and ran through a town totally deserted; not a soul there and only German signs. According to my map we were at least two kilometres back of the lines. We went almost to the top of a hill when we ran into a barbed wire across the road. We stopped and a Frenchman ran out. He was greatly excited; waved his hands and acted like a Jack-in-the-box—the point of it all being that if we had gone over the crest of the hill we should have run into a German sentry.

The French sentry made us push our car to the side of the road, saying the Germans were shelling it and might hit the machine. We had our gas-masks around our necks, but it would have taken me a few minutes to adjust mine. We got into the machine and started back. Just then many guns went off. Of course I thought they were our guns, but I wasn't sure. I don't know yet. We got out as fast as we could, but it was slow, as we got lost every five minute). There was a heavy fog. I always did think the doughboy had the hard row to hoe, but now I know it. We have an early patrol in the morning, so I bid you goodnight.

November, 1918

The C.O., Pat, and I, and Connelly, an armourer, all went to the Front yesterday, after the same plane I went for the other day. We were to go some five or six kilometres behind the lines. We got on a different road, near the lines, and were about to go down into the selfsame deserted village, when, *Whang*, and a huge cloud of dust arose in the middle of the metropolis. The driver stopped the car, echoing the sentiments of all the pilots, the armourer included. A doughboy "Loot" rushed out breathless. He had a gas-mask at the *alerte*, a tin hat, and a *worried* look. We had a Packard Twin Six, rather a dumb look on all our faces, no tin hats, and were a bit superior (we appeared so, as we were too startled to be otherwise). We were camouflaged in leather and fur coats (issue stuff). He thought we were staff officers, generals. perhaps. He was pretty sure Mr. Pershing wasn't with us, but thought maybe we were Blackjack's "buddies." Plenty of majors and colonels flitting about in Fords and Dodges, but here we were in a Packard. His reasoning was obvious.

He came smartly to attention, and though very much agitated, allowed as how we mustn't go into the town as it was being shelled every five minutes and was full of gas. We thanked him and did *not* go into the town. We approached the place where the machine was, very slowly, and gingerly walked up the hill. They were shelling the woods where the machine was—about a thousand yards away, but it sounded rather near! We had on our tin hats and were standing by the road. It was that eerie hour of dusk when everything takes on an unnatural look. Suddenly a group of grayish figures appeared, ran around a thicket, and approached us with their guns all ready. It was a ticklish moment. They ought to be French, *but were they?* They were, my dear, they were! It was a grand and glorious feeling! We were nothing in their lives. They rushed by us. We piled into the Packard and rolled on. The airplane may or may not be there—I know not and care less. We got stuck for two hours in a shell-hole and when we got home we were dead.

I am in the process of changing my fourth gas-tank in two days. In the meantime I am flying someone else's bus.

BRINGING HOME THE BUS

Last night the rumour was rife that peace was about to be declared, that Hun generals were to be sent over to confer with French generals, and the next minute we got orders to strafe a road. Road-strafing is about the worst job that the pilots have to do. The fire from the ground is no end annoying, and then one is five or six kilometres from the lines—if any Hun planes are above, you've not much chance to get away.

November, 1918

I have been in Metz for a few days and found many prisoners coming through. Of course now that the war is over the world will shrug its shoulders and forget. But, oh, how can one who has heard the experience of those who have been in the prison camps of the Huns! The cruelties practiced and the sufferings inflicted are beyond words. One of the pilots of the group who has been missing for a long time turned up the other day with some terrible tales. He is a first lieutenant and when wounded landed in the German lines. Not until he got to Karlsruhe did he have anything but a bit of paper on his wounds. An Alsatian in the bed next to him received a postcard with a picture on it of Quentin Roosevelt's mangled body beside his crashed machine! Now wasn't that a rotten thing to do?—a part of German propaganda.

High Patrol

November, 1918

Perhaps you would like to go on a patrol with us? The mechanics have already started the busses that are to go, and the propellers are turning over lazily. We all go to the office and take a last look at the lines and the towns we are to patrol over. The altitude settled, there is much grumbling, as it is too low for comfort. Five hundred metres is good range from the ground for Hun machine guns. The patrol leader assigns us to our places. You will fly last on the left and I last on the right. You and I will be the end of a V which tiers up from the leader, each man being fifty yards to the side and above. It will be your duty and mine to keep constant watch that Hun scouts don't tumble down on us and catch the leader napping. We climb in, secure the straps and look at our gauges, oil at five—low, but enough. Pressure on the gas-tank? The needle hovers just between the red and the blue—just right. Temperature? Fifty; the motor is warm enough. With your rigger at the left wing and your fitter at the right, you slowly open the throttle. You watch the revolution counter anxiously. The needle creeps up,

1600, 1700, 1900. You frown a little, as it is not enough. Suddenly the quivering needle jumps and settles at 2050. You slowly throttle down and nod to the men. They pull the chicks away and you taxi out in position.

The patrol lines up on the ground in exactly the same positions it will have in the air. Suddenly the leader's tail goes up and he races across the field. Before the leader has left the ground the others are rolling across the field. It's your turn now—you wave to your men, one on either wing. The fitter salutes and off you go. You hit a bump. Not having attained flying speed, down you come. Another bump and up you go for good. Once around the field and all fall into position. Number one on the left suddenly waggles his wings and dives for the aerodrome. Motor trouble. On we go in a diamond now. You are high and behind. Suddenly another turns and streaks for home. But three are left. It reminds me of the old song of ninety-nine bottles. We have fallen into position behind the leader in a small triangle. The old trenches come into view.

As you look down, you think of a forced landing which means a crash. A hasty glance at the gauges is reassuring and you settle back. The roads, which have been filled with trucks and troops, commence to thin out and soon a veritable waste country comes into view. It's the modern No Man's Land with patrols of both armies wandering about. We turn and head west. The end of our sector is a huge forest. Again we turn and come back. You are continually scanning the sky. 'Way over in Germany you see a formation of ten little black spots which you recognise as Hun scouts by the fact that they are not being "Archied." They have the sun and altitude and outnumber your pitiful little three. You keep them in view, as they may pounce down any minute. Suddenly you see a whitish bus away below. Your mission is to keep low-flying busses away from our lines. Down you go and swing in from the unprotected side. You see the American *cocardes* and disgustedly climb back into your formation. Then down toward the river where "Archie" batteries lie in wait for the unwary. "*Woof*," "*Woof*," and ugly black balls of smoke break out right in front. You pull round to the left, and then to the right, down and up, but the "Archies" still "*woof*" at you. Your "wind is up" a good bit.

Soon "Archie" is left behind. It's almost time to return and you've been watching the clock. The leader makes a sharp "S" and dives. You turn, dive, and look back. About five hundred metres behind you are eighteen Hun scouts, all tumbling down on top of you. You jerk the throttle wide open and push the stick forward. You keep looking back and see the Huns shooting, but it's too far away. They turn back, as the Huns don't like to come down and jump trees. Your leader turns back and climbs along the lines, hoping that perhaps one or two Huns will come down, but, no, they turn back into Germany. Time is up, so we fly homeward. You look for a field hospital, dive down, and throw them your bunch of yesterday's papers. They run after the bundle, pick it up, and then wave at you. Now for home. You look at your gauge and throttle down until the engine starts to ring to you. You settle back to ride and enjoy the scenery.

The airdrome comes into view. You plane down, make a good landing, and taxi up. The two men are there. They look a bit anxious. "How did she run?" You grin, "Oh, fine." Out you climb, sign the book, and go to mess. Not a very glorious day's work. Run out of the air by the Germans because you've not the machines, but, oh, well! there are lots of things wrong, but life is too short to kick, so we carry on the same. To be sure, if we keep the Huns away from our infantry, it's worthwhile, but just the same it's too bad to have an American patrol run out by a bunch of Boches.

We are fixed fairly well these days so far as living conditions are concerned, though not so well as at our last field. There we had billets and they were pretty nice, but here we have barracks and cots. I have a good bedding-roll, and the other day when my motor quit near the Front, I got a nice big French quilt. I was there for the night, so they sent my roll with the men who came to rescue me. They brought their blankets and we hustled around and found a dugout which had been inhabited by a French general. It was a nice young mansion. Then for breakfast we traded in some of our tanned stuff for hot food from the mess of some enlisted men. In this army one seldom lacks for food.

The longer I fly the more I pity the "doughboys." I feel sorry for them and their "Loots." After listening to their tales you wonder how they stand it, but they just carry on and not complainingly either.

Getting Confirmation

I remember the case of a man in my squadron who had attacked and shot down a German at seventeen hours and twenty minutes. The infantry had seen the Boche fall, but the report that was made was rather indefinite. "A German plane was shot down by a Spad in the German front line, where the Hun smashed beautifully," the report said in effect, but it failed to mention the time of day. To verify the

HOMEWARD BOUND

SAFELY HOME

report, several of us jumped into an automobile and set out for the front line.

Our journey took us through shell-scarred Verdun and out through Faubourg Pavé, where I had driven an ambulance the year before. Then up the well-remembered Belleville Hill and along the Froide Terre Plateau, where the Boches had tried so bitterly and so ineffectively to break the French defences in 1915. We passed through the Bras, and then at a point a short distance beyond we left the car and descended into a narrow communicating trench. We continued our journey on foot through a labyrinth of trenches, walking for several miles to the post of the commanding officer of the ——th Regiment of Infantry. From him we obtained permission to see the soldier who was on guard at the time the enemy plane fell. Another walk forward through twisting trenches, while shells burst and the "75's" replied with their rapid, whip-line crack, and we found the soldier.

"Well, old man," said the claimant for the scalp of the Boche, "were you on guard on the 27th?"

"The 27th? What day are we now?"

"That was day before yesterday."

"Wait a minute. Let me see. Was I on guard day before yesterday? Hey, Jules!" he cried to a comrade.

Jules came forward and regarded us with the politely tolerant disdain that the exclusive *poilu* has for all other branches of the service.

"Yes, old post (a term of endearment), you were at the firing step in the —— trench. I worked on your *briquet* (meaning he had filed a cigarette lighter belonging to the man who had been on guard)," the second man replied.

"Did you see any combats in the air?" we asked of the first.

"Yes, we see them every day. But the Boches still come to machine-gun us at dawn and—"

"But never mind that," interjected his captain.

The infantryman cannot be made to understand that the Aviation cannot wholly prevent air attacks on the trenches, because of the feeble altitudes at which they are made and the brief time required to shoot up a trench and return under the shelter of machine-gun fire.

"Did you see a Boche fall over there?" the claimant pressed.

"Well, I saw one fall. Yes, it was day before yesterday. What time was it? Let me think. Oh, yes, it was just before the soup."

"Which soup, old man? The morning soup (11 a.m.) or the evening soup (6 p.m. to any time when they can get it)?"

INSIGNIA OF FRENCH ESCADRILLES IN WHICH MEMBERS
OF THE LAFAYETTE FLYING CORPS SERVED.
PLATE 5

"I couldn't say. I don't remember. It was before the soup."

And that is an illustration of what the pilot has to contend with. It would be humorous if it were not so pathetic. The poor *poilu* loses all count of time. Days and nights do not count. The hour is measured by a meal, a shell in a trench, or an attack.

GUYNEMER

"My plane is nothing for me but a flying machine gun—" so said Guynemer. His work began every day with a careful and minute examination of his weapons and his motor. He killed Germans, to use his own words, "by firing at them more bullets, more skilfully aimed, than they fire at me. But," he continued, "it's not enough to hit the Boche and hit him first; you must be able to ruin him."

A year thereafter Guynemer had shot down nine enemy planes. Two months later he shot down two in one day, his seventeenth and eighteenth. On the 25th of May, 1917, less than two years after his first appearance on the Front, he shot down four enemy planes, bringing his total to forty-two. On July 7 he brought down his forty-seventh and forty-eighth in our lines, shooting both in the same minute with eight to ten shots for them both.

I was on the field with him during this period. No one who saw him then could have believed that two years before he narrowly escaped being sent to the rear for lack of ability to fly. He always wore the black uniform with the three stripes of captain. His eyes were dark and bold and belied the deathlike pallor of his face. He was a strict disciplinarian—a natural soldier—and he unbent to none but his few intimates. We respected him almost to the point of worship. We knew him to be very ill—a sick man—and rumour had it that he was dying on his feet. We had heard that he had already fainted in the air, that he knew death was waiting for him, and wished to account for as many of the invaders as God would permit him to kill before going himself. Whether or not a tenth of the stories we heard were true, we never knew. At least, the hypothesis of a fainting spell would account for his disappearance much more readily than the idea that any German could get near enough to him to kill him.

Guynemer's tactics when he began were simple. They were the same which caused the loss of so many young pilots. He saw an enemy and he dove at him from a superior altitude, with all the speed at his command. He dove, knowing that if he failed to kill the pilot of a plane superior to his own in armament, or failed to set the plane on fire, its gunners would easily kill him after he had passed it. His success where many others failed was due to his wonderful skill in marksmanship. His last victory, the fifty-third enemy proved destroyed, fell in our lines in Belgium on the 20th of August. On September 11, 1917, he disappeared.

FRENCH COMRADES

On the morning of July 6 we went back to our old camp on the Aisne. The next day at dawn the squadron migrated to V———. We flew in groups of four or five in order to hide from the enemy the movement of such a body of flyers. The same night our worldly possessions arrived by motor and we set about installing ourselves in our new home. Here, as before, we lived in portable wooden houses 150 feet long by 24 feet wide with windows of oiled muslin. There were two squadrons, about thirty men, in each barrack. In the north end of our building we had a mess-room for fifteen men. The farther end was taken up by a real American bar. The remainder of our half of the building was divided off into rooms, ten by eighteen feet, in each of which two men lived. The interiors were often surprising. The Frenchman is always artistic and can do a great deal with a very little. Give him a few planks, several yards of cheap but carefully chosen material for hangings, a coloured print or two from *L'Illustration* or *La Vie Parisienne*, and, behold, a house beautiful.

Some of the rooms were strikingly well fitted up. In one the beds were in alcoves at each end. The walls were papered with a sort of buff wrapping paper. A stencilled design in vivid yellow and black, running around the tops of doors and windows, showed a procession of ducks pursuing each other. The curtains and ceilings were of bright-coloured muslin. The toilet stand, covered with white oilcloth, was built against the one large window and under it was kept the water supply. The only suggestion of the Front in this cosy little nest was a black cross painted on a square of canvas, which had formerly been part of the wing of a German scout plane.

It was a matter of personal pride to have one's room as well decorated and equipped as possible. We spent many hours of work on improvements, and the rivalry as to apartments ran almost as high as the spirit of competition in the air.

The "bar" was a most important bit of equipment, so important that several times a delegate was sent to Paris to return with boxes of supplies marked "ammunition" or "machine guns." (May I state

SUMMER "POPOTE"

in defence of the "bar" system that never during my sojourn at the *escadrille* did I see one man who abused the privilege?) Day after day we did our patrols over the Front, attacked the Germans, killed a few and missed a great many. After dinner all the members of the squadron would gather at the "bar" to exchange opinions on the day's work, relate reminiscences, sing soldier songs or play bridge. Visitors from neighbouring squadrons would often drop in to discuss, over a cordial, the details of air combat in the intensely technical language of the Aviation. Someone always had a new story and there was the latest gossip from Paris—the civilians there had nothing to eat; it was ten times worse than at the Front; meatless days, no coffee, etc. Ah, yes, the poor civilian had much more to endure than the soldier.

The latest arrival from *permission* would recount his exploits while on save, and tell us of the new fighting plane he had seen tested at the factory. "Old man, it is a marvel!" a pilot exclaimed on one such occasion. "It flies at 250 kilometres an hour. It has 300 horse-power, and is only 12 feet across. Day before yesterday I saw them try it out. The pilot climbed and until he was out of sight."

"How high did he go?" I asked.

"One doesn't know," was the reply; "when I left Paris this morning he hadn't come down yet."

There were several under-officers who frequented our rendezvous, Adjutant Jailler, an "ace," with a record of seventeen Boches, was a frequent visitor. Our old pilots had formerly been his squadron mates, and he had a warm place in his heart for their friends. Jailler was one of the most original characters in that very eccentric organisation, the French Aviation. He was never in uniform: an old tunic minus most of the buttons and a disgracefully faded *képi* (cap) over one ear were his apology to military convention. His decorations he never wore. In their place was a faded strip of ribbon, also disgracefully dirty. He was known by all the 1200 men on the field, and he greeted them all, from the major to the mechanic's helper, with the same cheerful grin and absolute lack of military etiquette.

A visit from Jailler meant roars of laughter, for his vocabulary knew only such words as were current in army circles and the low quarters of Paris. It was a delight to have him tell how he got his last German, including what he said to the enemy when he first sighted him a half-mile away and three miles high, what the enemy replied, how the Boche fell, and the victor's remarks to the defeated as the latter crashed to his death far below.

The Maréchal de Logis Soulier, an "ace" with seven Germans to his credit, was the direct opposite of Jailler. The former looked like a boy of sixteen, was about five feet tall and weighed perhaps one hundred pounds. He was absolutely beardless and always dressed to the last minute in the creations of the most fashionable military tailor in Paris. Surely in no other army in the world would one see such strikingly opposite types.

The first time I saw Soulier come into our bar, I thought he was a mascot. When he took off a brilliant blue trench coat and displayed the flashing array of decorations which he had won by killing Germans, I was amazed. And I never did understand how such a wee bit of a chap could be such a demon of destruction in the air. On the ground he was overdressed and overscented and seemed more like a window dummy for schoolboys' suits than a fighting man. In the air he was afraid of nothing. He was not physically strong and had more than one attack of vertigo in the air, yet he was always postponing his departure to the hospital until he had another German.

"It is fine to be an ace," he remarked elegantly when he had five German planes to his credit, "but it is rather regrettable to be the last ace on the list. I shall bring down another." In December, 1917, he had seven enemy planes to his credit and I fancy he is still looking for another.

When someone in the squadron shot down a German or received

a promotion, it meant a round of champagne. In fact, in the early days every pilot had a few bottles hidden somewhere, with instructions to the barman that the wine was to be drunk in the event of the owner's disappearance or death. I shall not forget one such incident. Lieutenant L——, then sergeant, was shot down near the Chemin des Dames. His plane was seen by his comrades to fall and crash, late in the afternoon. After dinner the entire squadron adjourned to the bar to drink Lieutenant L——'s wine and bid him Godspeed on his longest flight. Imagine our surprised delight when half an hour later we heard his own voice announce gayly:

"A bit premature, *mes copains* (comrades). Drink with me to my health."

He had escaped unscathed from the terrible crash of his plane, had hidden in a shell-hole near the French front lines until rescued, and now, a bit muddy, but happy and quite unshaken, was back among his friends.

Rainy days were our delight because there was no work to be done. Everyone who could get leave—and that meant almost every pilot—dressed in his smartest uniform to "raid" one of the nearby large towns—Épernay, Bar-le-Duc, Châlons, or Château-Thierry. We visited them all in turn. We left early in the morning, piling into a motor truck, or, if lucky, into a powerful touring car. An hour of riding is little when there is a holiday at the end of it, and when one sings the songs the army has sung for a hundred years. Then several hours of shopping and strutting about before the towny *belles*—the flyers in the French army are very young—followed by tea and dinner with a white tablecloth, flowers, and real china.

The day that our squadron arrived at Verdun the captain gave us a dinner in Bar. We went there late in the afternoon and strolled about in pairs. On the corner of two main streets, where the town's most popular drugstore would be located in an American city, stood a group of American "doughboys" lounging against the immaculate front of a bank. They were airing their American opinion of all things foreign in a deliciously independent way. We came in for our share, thanks to our red breeches and other parts of the aviator's uniform.

"Where do these fellows think they are going?" asked one.

"Fishing for frogs, I reckon," was the reply.

Imagine their surprise when the frog fishermen stopped to inquire what in the name of the infernal regions they meant by criticizing their superiors, and imagine, too, their delight when, diplomatic relations having been established, the French bought beer for the Americans.

On another day in Bar—it was the 16th of July—I met a delegation of infantrymen returning from leave in Paris, where they had marched on the national holiday to show the civilians that all is well at the Front. About a score of them were returning to the trenches to show something to the Germans. That something was "Old Glory." They were in front of the station, and supported on a rack of guns alongside of them was the American flag. In one minute I had their lieutenant's permission and led them into the nearest *cantine*.

"We shall hoist the flag, with the tricolour, over our trenches," said a corporal of nineteen years who had been decorated three times and wounded twice.

"Did you see the Americans?" I asked.

"Yes. They are rich, they are great, these 'cowboys' (kooboys). The Boches will not have it in the belly when those savages go out."

Every American is a cowboy with two revolvers and a lariat in rural France.

Chef de Popote

I have just been made *popotier*—I don't know what you call it in English, but it means the individual who attends to the mess: buys provisions, wine, and so forth, makes out menus, keeps accounts, and bosses the cook. A doubtful honour, but one of which I am rather proud when I think that a crowd of French officers have entrusted to me the sacred rites of the table. I was never much of a *gourmet*, but what little I know stands me in good stead. Today was the occasion of the first considerable feast under my *régime*—a lunch given by the officers of our squadron to some distinguished French visitors. The cook and I held long and anxious consultations, and finally turned out a meal on which every one complimented us: excellent *hors d'œuvres*, grilled salmon steaks, roast veal, asparagus, and salad. A dry Chablis with the fish and some really good Burgundy with the roast. Not bad for the Front, really.

I give the cook each night enough money for the next day's marketing. The following evening he tells me the amount of the day's expenses, which sum I divide by the number present, giving each man's share for the day. Very simple.

Nearly every day one or two or three "big guns" (*grosses huiles*, the French call them) of Aviation drop in to lunch or dinner. Down from a patrol at 10.30, and scarcely out of the machine, when up dashes our cook, knife in one hand and ladle in the other, fairly boiling over with anxiety. "Commandant X—— and his staff are coming to lunch—I can't leave the stove—what on earth shall we do?"

An hour and a half. Just time for the cyclist to buzz down to the nearest town for some extra *hors d'œuvres,* salad, and half a dozen old bottles. In the end everything runs off smoothly, and when the white wine succeeds the red, the usual explication *des coups* begins—highly entertaining inside stuff, from which one could cull a whole backstairs history of French Aviation. It has been my privilege to meet many famous men in this way—great "aces" and great administrators of the flying arm; men whose names are known wherever European aviators gather. I wish I could tell you half the drolleries they recount, or reproduce one quarter of the precise, ironical, story-telling manner of a cultivated Frenchman.

A captain who lunched with us today, bearer of an historic name, was recently decorated (somewhat against his will) for forcing a Boche to land in our lines. The truth is that in the single combat high above the lines, the captain's motor failed and he coasted for home, manoeuvring wildly to escape the pursuing Hun's bullets. A few kilometres within our lines the German motor failed also, and down they came together—the Boche a prisoner, the Frenchman covered with not particularly welcome glory. Not all our guests knew the story, and one high officer asked the captain how he manoeuvred to drive down the Boche. "Oh, like this," erratically said the captain, illustrating with frantic motions of an imaginary stick and rudder.

"But the Boche—?" inquired the other, puzzled, "how did you get him down—where was he?"

"Ah, the Boche; he was *behind* me," answered the captain.

Another officer, recently promoted to a very high position in the Aviation, is a genuine character, a *numéro* as they say here. He recently spent many hours in perfecting a trick optical sight, guaranteed to down a Boche at any range, angle, or speed. He adored his invention, which, he admitted, would probably end the war when fully perfected, and grew quite testy when his friends told him the thing was far too complicated for anything but laboratory use. At last, though he had reached a non-flying rank and had not flown for months, he installed the optical wonder on a single-seater and went out over the lines to try it out.

As luck would have it, he fell in with a patrol of eight Albatrosses, and the fight that followed has become legendary. Boche after Boche dove on him, riddling his plane with bullets, while the inventor, in a scientific ecstasy, peered this way and that through his sight, adjusting set-screws and making hasty mental notes. By a miracle he was not brought down, and in the end a French patrol came to his rescue. He had not fired a shot! At lunch the other day some one asked what sort of a chap this inventor was, and the answer was so exceedingly French that I will reproduce it word for word: "He detests women and dogs; he has a wife he adores, and a dog he can't let out of his sight." A priceless characterisation, I think, of a testy yet amiable old martinet.

One of my friends here had the luck, several months ago, to force a Zeppelin to land. A strange and wonderful experience, he says, circling for an hour and a half about the huge air-monster, which seemed to be having trouble with its gas. He poured bullets into it until his supply was exhausted, and headed it off every time it tried to make for the German lines. All the while it was settling, almost insensibly, and finally the Hun crew began to throw things out—machine guns, long belts of cartridges, provisions, furniture, a motley collection. In the end it landed intact in our lines—a great catch. The size of the thing is simply incredible. This one was at least ninety feet through, and I hesitate to say how many hundred feet long.

Three more of our boys gone, one of them my most particular pal. Strange as it seems, I am one of the oldest members of the Squadron left. We buried Harry yesterday. He was the finest type of young French officer—an aviator since 1913; volunteer at the outbreak of war; taken prisoner, badly wounded; fourteen months in a German fortress; escaped, killing three guards, across Germany in the dead of winter, sick and with an unhealed wound; back on the Front, after *ten days* with his family, although he need never have been a combatant again. A charming, cultivated, witty companion, one of the most finished pilots in France, and a soldier whose only thought was of duty, his loss is a heavy one for his friends, his family, and his country. For a day and a night he lay in state in the church of a nearby village, buried in flowers sent by half the squadrons of France; at his feet his tunic ablaze with crosses and orders.

It was my turn to stand guard the morning his family arrived, and I was touched by the charming simple piety of the country-folk, who came in an unending stream to kneel and say a prayer for the soul of the departed soldier. Old women with baskets of bread and cheese on their arms brought pathetic little bouquets; tiny girls of seven or eight

THE FIRST "FRITZ"

came in solemnly alone, dropped a flower on Harry's coffin, and knelt to pray on their little bare knees. The French peasants get something from their church that most of us at home seem to miss.

At last the family came—worn out with the long sad journey from their *château* in middle France. Harry's mother, slender, aristocratic, and courageous, had lost her other son a short time before, and I was nearer tears at her magnificent self-control than if she had surrendered to her grief. Her bearing throughout the long mass and at the graveside was one of the finest and saddest things I have ever seen in my life. Poor old Harry—I hope he is in a paradise reserved for heroes, for he was one in the truest sense of the word.

A Hater of War

On the train *en rou*te Front to Paris
June 6, 1917

Our *escadrille* has moved from south of Saint-Quentin down south of Soissons, in order to be closer in touch with the sector around Laon. The battlefields of this region appear, from the air, almost as terrible in devastation as those of the Somme offensive of last summer. Last evening we had a splendid patrol. The whole air above the battle was so filled with French aeroplanes that the German pilots were obliged to stay away, and only watch the German anti-aircraft shells bursting around us all. It was very exciting. My motor failed me, however, and I was obliged to return to our field before the others. The days are so long now that sometimes our *escadrille* goes out at 3.30 a.m., and the last patrol does not return till 9 p.m. Of course the work is divided, and we have only two patrols each day, of two hours each. That is plenty, since the hours in the air are very exhausting. Just at present a great German raid on Paris is expected, and we have special *alertes*. The nights are of surpassing splendour and we sit out and watch the wild and tragic display of war fireworks to the north of us.

As my aeroplane is not in running condition, the captain has given me a day in Paris, of which I am very glad. I need many things and the holiday will be intensely refreshing. It is tremendously impressive and inspiring to feel the full tide and fire of life about one, after isolation on the Front, and the sheer glory of it all is intoxicating. As I write, I am riding through a wonderland of spring. I am alone in my compartment, except for your presence and for the wondrous flood of fragrance pouring in through the open windows.

The joy and thrill of the spring enhances the poignancy of the plight of Europe. How long must the slaughter continue! Grim and unutterable loss fills all the human atmosphere, though the flowers nod as gayly and the songs of the birds are as sweet as though the world were singing through the Infinite, as it might, instead of being a chaos of mud and death.

I am going to Paris! Hurrah! Let's be glad for a day at least, and revel in freedom and dreams and Life!

July 27, 1917

We are now in a *secteur* where we can see England from the air. All is as well as can be. We are in tents and enjoy the sea-bathing. Our American flag floating above the *escadrille* serves as a good target for German airships and we are shot at by long-distance guns, from both land and sea.

August 29, 1917

A royal sunset crowned the beauty of this summer day. Now, in the night, a great clean wind is sweeping up across France, Spain, Italy, the Mediterranean. One is glad to breathe deep of its power. Northward it sweeps across the graves of unnumbered thousands of Europe's youth. Their spirits do not rouse me to hatred. They are from both sides and all are youth—and they believed.

It is strange to live in the atmosphere of death. I used to imagine what I should say and do if ever I knew that I was to die immediately or soon. In this tragic drama one never knows, and the agony of the failure to express something cuts very deep. A man longs to be the torchbearer—for whatever light he feels is in him to give to the world. A selfish desire, some say.

Others will bear the torch just as well, they say. They are fools. An individual has some light, feeble or bright, that others can never bear. So, I loathe death. I loathe this slaughter, where nations enlist on the side of humanity's worst enemy—death.

August 27, 1917

You are wrong if you believe that I have regretted enlisting. One may doubt and question and yet be loyal. From my point of view, the man most loyal to a cause is the one who refuses to just blindly follow. I would not be elsewhere than where I am in this war. I have been and am convinced that my decision was not mistaken. My loathing for war will continue to be a consuming hatred, however.

The attack at Verdun has been a splendid success. The artillery activity was terrific.

October 19, 1917

I am sorry Mother received the idea somehow that we are to be teachers in the rear after our transfer to the U.S. Air Service. I would loathe that most sincerely.

Our place is out here at the Front. For my part I do not want to spend any time in the rear until this deviltry is over. The abyss of misunderstanding between the two sides was never wider and deeper than now. The bluffing and boasting and *"last man and last dollar"* speeches of the diplomats and statesmen are widening the breach. I guess the only way to close it now—is to fill it up with dead. Anyhow, René Viviani quotes the saying: *"Les morts tiennent plus de place que les vivants."* The ambitious man should, then, aspire to death. It is evident now that there are no men, in this generation of leaders, great enough to lay the foundations for the future, without further slaughter. Let us slay, then, and pray that they will be at least great enough to make the most of their revenge. The trouble with vengeance is that it is so endless, and there is such a thing as the collapse of civilization.

Germany's awful guilt is obvious. But the object of this war is not revenge upon Germany—a small thing compared with the building of foundations for a limitless future. *Allons!* Almost the whole world is now engaged in making this a real Armageddon! Slay the Hun! Even though you slay the hopes of the whole world in the doing of it. If he is really Hun and devil, we can best please him, and best give him his victory, by going on with the murdering. A British captain told me on the way to London that the best way to end the war would be to put all the editors and prime ministers and diplomats in the front-line trenches for a day. A British Tommy's solution was, to make every one in the armies a private. I only hope that future generations have some greater men to lead them.

Well, my pencil ran away with me, but I'll send all this along, since I have written it. To America, France, England, and the new Russia, I give all my loyalty, in whatever they wish to do; but some higher loyalty commands me to question their acts and words, and not just to follow blindly. Again I say, it is the highest loyalty to the Allied nations to oppose the doctrine of the suppression of thinking and speaking until the enemy is crushed.

Waiting for his U.S. Commission

I hope to know very soon whether or not we are to be transferred to the American Army. The long delay has worked hardships on a good many of us, as of course no pilot could begin to live on the pay we get. The Franco-American Flying-Corps Fund (for which, I believe, we must thank the splendid generosity of Mr. Vanderbilt) has helped immensely in the past, but some of the boys are in hard straits now. I hope we shall be transferred, because the pay will make us self-supporting, and any American would rather be in United States uniform nowadays, in spite of the bully way the French treat us, and our liking for our French comrades, with whom it will be a wrench to part.

The point regarding our present pay is this: all French aviators are volunteers, knowing conditions in the air service beforehand. Before volunteering, therefore, they arrange for the necessary private funds; if not available, they keep out of flying. We get two and a half *francs* a day (as against five *sous* in the infantry), but, on the other hand, we are lodged, and forced by tradition to live, like officers. It is fine for the chap who has a little something coming in privately, but tough for the one who is temporarily or permanently "broke."

Our boys are going to do splendid things over here. Everywhere one sees discipline, efficiency, and organisation that make an American's chest go out. The first slackness (unavoidable at the start of a huge and unfamiliar job) has completely disappeared. People at home should know of all this as quickly and as much in detail as expedient: they are giving their money and their flesh and blood, and prompt and racy news helps wonderfully to hearten and stimulate those whose duty is at home.

For myself, there is nowhere and nobody I would rather be at present than here and a pilot. No man in his senses could say he enjoyed the war; but as it must be fought out, I would rather be in Aviation than in any other branch. A pleasant life, good food, good sleep, and two to four hours a day in the air. After four hours (in two spells) over the lines, constantly alert and craning to dodge scandalously accurate shells and suddenly appearing Boches, panting in the thin air at 20,000 feet, the boys are, I think, justified in calling it a day. I have noticed that the coolest men are a good bit let down after a dogged machine-gun fight far up in the rarefied air. It may seem soft to an infantryman—twenty hours of sleep, eating, and loafing; but in reality the airman should be given an easy time outside of flying.

I was unfortunate enough to smash a beautiful new machine yesterday. Not my fault; but it makes one feel rotten to see a bright splendid thing one has begun to love strewn about the landscape. Some wretched little wire, or bit of dirt where it was not wanted, made my engine stop dead, and a forced landing in rough country full of woods and ditches is no joke. I came whizzing down to the only available field, turned into the wind, only to see dead ahead a series of hopeless ditches which would have made a frightful end-over-end crash. Nothing to do but pull her up a few feet and sail over, risking a loss of speed. I did this, and "pancaked" fairly gently, but had to hit ploughed ground across the furrow. The poor *coucou*—my joy and pride—was wrecked, and I climbed, or rather dropped, out, with nothing worse than a sore head, where the old bean hit the *carlingue*. Now all the world looks gray, though our captain behaved like the splendid chap he is about it: not a word of the annoyance he must have felt.

The very finest motors, of course, do stop on occasions. Better luck, I hope, from now on.

As the days go by, I find much that is novel and interesting about the aerial war, which in reality is quite different from any idea of it that I had had. I will try to give a rough idea of how the upper war is carried on.

The trenches, sometimes visible, often quite invisible from the heights at which one flies, form the dividing line between us and the Boche. Behind them, at distances of from seven to fifteen miles, are the aerodromes—a few acres of tolerably flat land, three or four or half a dozen hangars (often cleverly camouflaged), barracks, and sheds for automobiles. Each side, of course, knows pretty well the locations of the enemy aerodromes. This gives rise to a certain amount of give and take in the bombing line, which, in the end, accomplishes very little.

It is a curious fact that in certain sectors the aviator's life is made miserable by this ceaseless bombing, while in other places a species of unwritten understanding permits him to sleep, at least, in peace. I have a friend in a far-off *escadrille* who has to jump out of bed and dive for the dugouts nearly every clear night, when the sentry hears the unmistakable Mercedes hum close overhead, the shutting off of the motor, and the ominous rush of air as the Huns descend on their mark. He knows that the Germans get as good as or better than they give—but the knowledge does not make up for lost sleep. In my sector, on the other hand, we could blow the Boche aerodromes to atoms and they could probably do as much for us, but neither side has started this useless "strafing." Just before an attack, such bombing might be of military value; otherwise it only harasses vainly men who need what sleep they get, and destroys wealth on both sides, like exchanging men in checkers without profiting in position. I have heard parlour warriors at home say, "By all means make war as unpleasant as possible—then it won't happen again." But there is a limit to this when nothing of tactical value is accomplished.

THE HARDSHIPS AT THE FRONT

On a raw foggy day, in the cosy living-room of our apartment, with a delicious fire glowing in the stove, and four of the fellows having a lively game of bridge, one is certainly comfortable—absurdly so. Talk about the hardships of life on the Front!

The mess is the best I have seen, and very reasonable for these times—a dollar and a half per day each, including half a bottle of wine, beer, or mineral water at each meal. A typical dinner might be: excellent soup, *entrée*, beefsteak, mashed potatoes, dessert, nuts, figs, salad. While no man would appreciate an old-fashioned home-type American meal more than I, one is forced to admit that the French have made a deep study of cookery and rations designed to keep people in the best shape. There is a certain balance to their meals—never too much concentrated, starchy, or bulky food. The variety, considering the times, is really wonderful. Breakfasts my pal and I cook ourselves, occasionally breaking out some delicacy such as kidneys *en brochette*.

We have an amusing system of fines for various offenses: half a *franc* if late for a meal; a *franc* if over fifteen minutes late; half a *franc* for throwing bread at the table; half a *franc* for breaking a tailskid (on a "cuckoo"); a *franc* for a complete smash; a *franc* and a half if you hurt yourself to boot; and so on. A fellow hit a tree awhile ago, had a frightful crash, and broke both his legs. When he leaves the hospital, the court will decide this precedent and probably impose on him a ruinous fine.

Of course no one ever pays a fine without passionate protests; so our meals are enlivened by much debate. As we have a very clever lawyer and a law student almost his equal, accuser and accused immediately engage counsel, and it is intensely entertaining to hear their impassioned arraignments and appeals to justice and humanity: deathless Gallic oratory, enriched with quotations, classical allusions, noble gestures; such stuff as brings the Chamber to its feet, roaring itself hoarse; and all for a ten-penny fine!

A good bit of excitement lately, over uniforms. In Aviation, one knows, there is no regulation uniform: each man is supposed to wear the colour and cut of his previous arm. The result is that each airman designs for himself a creation which he fondly believes is suited to his style of soldierly beauty—and many of these haven't the slightest connection with any known French or Allied uniform. One may see dark-blue, light-blue, horizon-blue, black, and khaki; trousers turned up at the bottom; open-front tunics (like the British officers), and every variety of hat, footwear, and overcoat.

I, for instance (being in the Foreign Legion), wear khaki, open-fronted tunic, a very unmilitary khaki stock necktie, Fox's *puttees*, and United States Army boots. Naturally, I have to duck for cover whenever I see the General loom up in the offing; for he is a rather particular, testy old gentleman, very military, and can't abide the *fantaisies* of the aviator tribe. Lately he has caught and severely reprimanded several of the boys; so I guess that I shall have to have the tailor make certain unfortunate changes in my garments.

The weather of late has been wretched for flying. A low, frosty mist hangs over the countryside; the trees, especially the pines, are exquisite in their lacy finery of frost. The few days we have of decent weather are usually interesting, as the Hun ventures over *chez nous* to take a few photographs, and with a little luck we are able to surprise him into a running fight.

At night, when the tired war-birds buzz home to roost, a crowd of pilots and mechanics gathers before the hangars. All gaze anxiously into the north-eastern sky. The captain paces up and down—though he has flown four hours, he will not eat or drink till he has news of his pilots.

Suddenly a man shouts and points, and high up in the darkening east we see three specks—the missing combat patrol. Next moment the hoarse drone of their motors reaches our ears; the sound ceases; in great curving glides they descend on the aerodrome. We hear the hollow whistling of their planes, see them, one after another, clear the trees at ninety miles an hour, dip, straighten, and rush toward us, a yard above the grass. A slight bumping jar, a half-stop, and each motor gives tongue again in short bursts, as the pilots taxi across to the hangars, snapping the spark on and off.

Then a grand scamper to crowd around our half-frozen comrades, who descend stiffly from their *zincs*, and tell of their adventures, while mechanics pull off their fur boots and combinations. Other *mécanos* are examining the machines for bullet- and shrapnel-holes—often a new wing is needed, or a new propeller; sometimes a cable is cut half through. Snatches of talk (unintelligible to outsiders) reach one; we, of course, know only the French, but the R.F.C. stuff is equally cryptic.

The German Monos

Now that the Armistice is signed and the censor is beginning to relax, I can see no harm in telling you something of the enemy machines and their qualities as compared with the French planes. You will be surprised to hear that, in my opinion at least, the Germans ended the war with better machines than ours.

Perhaps you remember, in the early days of the war, the German announcement that they were about to produce in quantity a type of aeroplane which would guarantee an overwhelming supremacy in the air. This was the Fokker monoplane of 1915, designed on the general scheme of the Morane, and equipped with a rotary *monosoupape* motor of 100 horse-power, called the Oberursel, almost an exact copy of the Gnome. It mounted a single Spandau gun, timed, by means of a cam arrangement, to shoot through the arc of the propeller. Although a French pilot, some time before the appearance of the Fokker, had arranged a gun to shoot through the course of the propeller, in which were placed countersunk plates of steel to ward off ill-timed bullets, the Germans must be given credit for the invention of the timing mechanism. The Fokker marked the beginning of true *chasse* aviation. It was fast, climbed rapidly, manoeuvred well, and in its day was master of the air.

The French answer to the Fokker was the Nieuport—the 13-metre type, equipped with the 80 horse-power Le Rhône (later the 110 horse-power), and armed with a Lewis gun, mounted on the top plane and shooting over the propeller. The machine was superior to the Fokker—all the old-timers agree on that point—but the Lewis was subject to constant jams, and its drums contained only forty-seven rounds of ammunition. On account of its position, the gun was difficult to clear when jammed, and a change of drums in the air was a feat for a contortionist. The Nieuports did not appear in numbers on the Front until the last of 1915, and were still somewhat of a novelty when the Escadrille Lafayette was equipped with them in April, 1916. During the summer of that year, many months after the appearance of the Fokker, the French produced the 15-metre Nieuport, armed with a Vickers gun with a timing mechanism like that in use by the enemy, and far superior to the 13-metre type, owing to its much higher ceiling. Many of these machines carried, in addition to the Vickers, a Lewis gun, mounted on the upper wing.

The German designers, meanwhile, had not been idle. They re-

FOKKER D 7

ALBATROSS D 5

PFALZ C 1

HANOVRANNER GERMAN TWO-SEATER FIGHTER

HALBERSTADT GERMAN TWO-SEATER FIGHTER

FOKKER TRIPLANE

alised that the Fokker had many weaknesses, chief of which was low factor of safety; had examined captured Nieuports, and heard tales of the superior qualities of the French machine. Several new types of single-seaters were produced—one of them marked a really notable advance in design: the Albatross D 2. This was a small biplane, very strong, beautifully stream-lined, equipped with the 170 horse-power Mercedes motor, and armed, like the Fokker, with a Spandau gun. It was easily recognisable by its shovel-shaped tail, single bay, and pointed, shark-like body. The Albatross was very fast, climbed well, and dove like a stone, but the weight of its motor, coupled with its enormous *empennage*, made it a little awkward in manoeuvre. It was less manoeuvrable than the 15-metre Nieuport, probably a shade faster, and certainly much faster in a dive.

While the first Albatross were appearing on the Front, the 140 horsepower Hispano-Suiza motor was being perfected in France—destined to make the Spad a possibility. In September, 1916, Guynemer took the first single-seater Spad over the lines, and his report on its performance caused a great stir in the French Aviation. This was the 140 horse-power single-gun machine. On the day of the Armistice the entire French *chasse* was provided with Spads, practically unchanged from the original model (though mounting two guns) and with the same motor, unchanged in bore or stroke, but raised, by supercompression and gearing, to 220 horse-power. During the twenty-six months which elapsed between the appearance of the Spad and the signing of the Armistice, the French designed and tried out a great variety of single-seaters (notably the small Morane monoplane, which was *réceptionné* and ordered in quantity before its failings were discovered), but none were found fit to supplant the Spad—a fact illustrative of the extraordinary complexity and difficulty of progress in military aviation.

The Germans, on the other hand, though for a long period unable to produce a machine superior to the Spad, seemed to have discovered the secret of improving and changing their types of single-seaters with amazing rapidity. The Albatross D 2 was soon superseded by the D 3—very fast and strong, and armed with two Spandau guns, shooting forward: probably the first machine to be so armed. This model, with its graceful wings, V strut, and really exquisite stream-lining, was considered by many pilots the most beautiful *monoplace* developed by either side during the war. It was followed by the D 5—practically the same machine—which in turn gave way to the Pfalz, a slightly improved type on similar lines. I remember hearing of the Pfalz in

December, 1917—it probably made its appearance in the late autumn of that year.

During the early months of 1918 we heard frequent reports of a small and very fast German triplane, which was seen at great altitudes over the lines, but had the air of being on trial flights, rather than looking for trouble. It was the Fokker triplane, which the enemy had manufactured in quantities and was holding in reserve for the great attack of March 21. Herr Fokker made a personal gift of one, equipped with a 120 horse-power Le Rhône motor, taken from a captured Nieuport, to Baron von Richtofen. When the attack came, the sky was thick with Fokker "Tripes," manned by the crack pilots of the Jasta II and similar fighting units. They seemed peculiarly *mordant*, these triplanes: they burned balloons; they came far inside our lines to shoot up troops; and long strings of them, in formation as elastic and easy as that of migrating wild-fowl, trailed across the sky. In combat they were wicked things to handle, for they manoeuvred like swallows, and seemed to care nothing for the advantage of altitude, relying on a trick of standing on their tails beneath one, while their guns spit streams of evil-looking smoking bullets. And climb! They seemed to dart up or down at the same angle and at equal speed! When Richtofen fell at last, in the British lines, he fell in his special triplane.

Herr Fokker, meanwhile, was not wholly content with his triplane, which had a disconcerting way of losing its wings in a steep dive. This folding feature was different from that of the French Sopwith and other celebrated folding machines, in that the wings tended to fold straight back, giving way to head resistance—an eccentricity common to all triplanes. The solution was a biplane embodying the good features of the triplane—internally braced wings, making wires unnecessary, great ability to manoeuvre, speed, climbing power, and exchangeability of parts. With these points in mind, Fokker designed the Fokker D 7, and in the task he proved himself a master designer, for the result was probably the most formidable *chasse* plane produced during the war. Equipped with the 170 horse-power Mercedes, its performance in speed and climb was equal to that of the 220 horse-power Spad, which it far excelled in manoeuvre. Added to this was an astonishing simplicity in knock-down and assemblage, and a reliability of motor which made the Spad pilots who tested captured Fokkers shake their heads in melancholy envy. " If we had had *ces taxis-là* . . . *qu'est ce quails auraient pris, les Boches!*"

The D 7 made its first appearance in numbers on the Marne, during the attack which began on May 27, 1918. Pilot after pilot reported encounters with bands of awkward-looking *monos*, short in the lower wing and with a curious N-shaped strut. When the attack began, the enemy far outnumbered us in the air, and many of these early Fokker biplanes were seen in a series of apprehensive glances to the rear. They were manned by "aces," too—certainly the German *chasse* never seemed more formidable than during June and July on the Marne. But before long one came down intact in our lines and the mystery was explained, though there seemed little chance of profit to our designers, who announced that without the motor and the welding process used in building up the metallic fuselage, the machine's good features were not available to the Allies.

The German Aviation seemed tireless in its efforts to improve and perfect—they were not content to consider the D 7 the last word. The Siemens-Schuckert Werke had long experimented with, and brought to perfection in the summer of 1918, an eleven-cylinder rotary motor of 180 horsepower. This was installed in a very fast and handy biplane, a few of which were seen on the Front before the close of hostilities. Another manufacturer, using the Siemens-Schuckert motor, produced the tiny Junker monoplane (not to be confused with the Junker all-steel biplane for *liaison* work) which was said, by the few who saw it, to be a machine of extraordinary performance. It was certainly a novel and interesting type—a tiny parasol, with a single internally braced wing, without an external wire or brace of any kind, except the *chandelles* attaching it to the fuselage.

The end of the war was a blessing to every pilot, but it is interesting to speculate on the machines which might have been developed had hostilities continued. The Spad was doomed, and the French had several new single-seater types under test at Villecoublay. The beautiful Nieuport monoplane, with the 180 horse-power Le Rhone, had been tried out at the Front and found wanting by Madon. The Spad 300 horse-power, with its curious strut, was being tried by De Slade, who pronounced it excellent, though a little slow in manoeuvre. There was also a brand-new monoplane (I do not recollect its name) which was rumoured to climb 5000 metres in twelve minutes, and to attain a horizontal speed of 250 kilometres per hour. In any case it is certain that France, the Mother of Aviation, had something up her sleeve.

French Mechanics

Each pilot has his own mechanic, who does nothing but look after his bus, and is usually a finished comedian in addition to being a crack mechanic. In truth, I never ran across a more comical, likable, hard-working crew than the French Aviation mechanics. They are mostly pure Parisian "*gamins*"—speaking the most extraordinary jargon, in which everything but the verbs (and half of them) is slang of the most picturesque sort. Quick-witted, enormously interested in their work, intelligent and good-natured, they are the aristocrats of their trade, and know it. You should see them when they go on leave. Jean or Charlot, ordinarily the most oily and undignified of men, steps out of the squadron office arrayed in a superb blue uniform, orange tabs on his collar, a mirror-like tan belt about his waist—shaven, shorn, shining with cleanliness, puffing an expensive-looking, gilt-banded cigar.

Is it fancy or is there a slight condescension in his greeting? Well, it is natural—you can never hope to look so superbly like a field-marshal. A little crowd of pals gathers around, for it is just after lunch; and presently the motor bus draws up with a scream of brakes and a cloud of dust. The motor has "AV" in big letters on the side, and its driver (not to be confounded with any mere ambulance or lorry chauffeur) would feel it a disgrace to travel under forty miles an hour, or to make anything but the most spectacular of turns and stops. The driver produces a silver cigarette case, passes it round, takes a weed, taps it on his wrist, and chaffs the *permissionnaire* about a new godmother on whom he is planning to call in Paris.

Presently the captain steps out of his office; the departing one spins about, head back and chest out, cigar hidden in his left hand; "click!" his heels come together magnificently, and up goes his right hand in a rigid salute. Smiling behind his moustache, our extremely attractive captain salutes in return, and shakes Charlot's hand warmly, wishing him a pleasant leave. He is off, and you can picture him tomorrow strolling with princely nonchalance along the *boulevards*. What if he earns but five cents a day!—he saves most of that, and his pilot presents him with a substantial sum every Saturday night, all of which is put away for the grand splurge, three times a year.

In Paris, you will recognise the type, well dressed in neat dark blue, orange collar with the group number on it, finger-nails alone showing the unmistakable traces of his trade; face, eyes, and manner registering alert attention and intelligence. As likely as not you see him on the terrace of some great *café*, a wonderfully smart little *midinette* (his feminine counterpart) beside him, with shining eyes of pride, and at the next table a famous general of division, ablaze with the ribbons of

FRENCH MÉCANICIENS

half a dozen orders.

The *mécanos* dress as nearly like the pilots as they dare, and after flying is over in the evening are apt to appear about the hangars in the teddy-bear suits and fur boots of the *patron*. Some funny things happen at such times. There is a class of officers, called "officers of administration," attached to squadrons and groups of aviation, who do not fly, but look after the office and business end of the *équipe*. They are worthy men and do absolutely necessary work, but are not very swank.

One day it became known that the revered Guynemer was to visit a certain *escadrille*, and naturally all the officers were on fire to shake the hero's hand—a reminiscence to hand down to their grandchildren. The administration officer, a first lieutenant, was late getting away from the *bureau* and when he got to the field, Guynemer had landed, left his machine, and gone to have his sacred *apéritif* of five o'clock. Meanwhile the chief comedian of all the mechanics, dressed by chance in his pilot's combination and boots, and proud to tinker (with reverent fingers) the famous Spad, had run out to where it stood, filled it with gas and oil, touched up the magneto and cleaned a couple of plugs. The officer, as he came to the hangars, perceived the well-known "taxi" with the stork on its side, and a furry figure strolling toward him. A snap of heels, the position of attention, and he was saluting (as he thought) one of the most glorious figures of France. The comedy mechanic, taking in the situation at a glance, strolled by magnificently, with a careless salute and a nod. The officer never inquired who it was he had saluted—but what a tale to pass around the barrack stove on winter evenings! Mistaken for Guynemer! Saluted by a two-striper!

In clothes and get-up the mechanics follow the pilot's lead, but in language the situation is reversed—we take pride in memorizing, chuckling over, and using at every opportunity the latest words or phrases invented by these gifted slangsters.

During the war French Aviation has developed a quaint and racy slang, almost a language of its own—the argot of these master jesters, the *mécanos*. Rich in curious figures of speech, it is sometimes obscure, even vulgar, but always picturesque. The following might have been heard at any French aerodrome; the returning pilot who hastens to the bar to tell of his adventures:

J'ai un gros coup à expliquer! J'étais à cinq mille deux, attendant le

Fritz d'onze heures. À onze heures quinze, coups de canon au nord. Je mets pleine sauce et dans dix secondes je l'aperçois—un beau Fokker au lieu du Rumpler habituel. Je fiche un renversement; je coupe; je pique à mort . . . a cinquante metres je lui séringue une giclet—je vois mes lumineuses qui rentrent dans sa carlingue. Je trouve que je le possède, mais il envoie une chandelle fantastique, ce cochon-là! On tourne en ronde, et tout à coup il est derrière moi—zut alors! C'est un As, qui me possède à son tour . . . des incendiaires qui passent partout—fichtre! il va fort! Clac—une balle dans mon moulin; ça bafouille, raffut formidable. Il exaggère, mon Boche—il cherre un peu! Il faut bien le plaquer. Mon moulin tourne toujours un peu; je pousse sur le manche—je pique à la verticale—je le laisse tomber carrément avec un bruit métallique. Je le sème dans la crasse. . . . Oui, je prendrai un Porto blanc.

7
Combats

FIRST VICTORY FOR THE ESCADRILLE LAFAYETTE

May 18, 1916

Well, I at last have a little something to tell you. This morning I went out over the lines to make a tour. I was somewhat the other side of our lines, when my motor began to miss a bit. I turned around to go to a camp near the lines. Just as I started to head back, I saw a Boche machine about 700 metres under me and a little inside our lines. I immediately reduced my motor and dove on him. He saw me at the same time, and began to dive toward home. It was a machine with a pilot and a gunner, carrying two rapid-fire guns, one facing the front, and one in the rear that turned on a pivot so it could be fired in any direction.

A CAPTURED RUMPLER TWO-SEATER

The gunner immediately opened fire on me, and my machine was hit; but I didn't pay any attention to that, and kept going straight for him until got to within twenty-five or thirty metres of his machine. Then, just as I was afraid of running into him, I fired four or five shots, and swerved my machine to the right to keep from having a collision. As I did that I saw the gunner fall back dead on the pilot; his machine gun fell from its position and pointed straight up in the air, and the pilot fell to one side of the machine as if he too were done for. The machine itself veered off to one side; then dove vertically toward the ground with a lot of smoke coming out of the rear. I circled around, and three or four minutes later saw smoke coming up from the ground just beyond the German trenches.

The captain said he would propose me for the *Médaille Militaire*.

WITH THE ESCADRILLE LAFAYETTE IN 1916

June 1, 1916

This flying is much too romantic to be real modern war with all its horrors. There is something so unreal and fairy-like about it, which ought to be told and described by poets, as *Jason's Voyage* was, or that Greek chap who wandered about the Gulf of Corinth and had giants try to put him in beds that were too small for him.

Yesterday afternoon it was bright, but full of those very thick, fuzzy clouds like imaginary froth of gods or genii. We all went out. All but the captain and I got lost and turned back, so we two flitted about over mountains of fleecy snow full of shadow and mist. He reminded me of the story of the last fly on a polar expedition as I followed his black silhouette. I went down to a field near the Front and flew again at five o'clock. Then it was marvellous. At 3000 metres one floated secure on a purple sea of mist. Up through it, here and there, voluminous clouds resembling those thick water plants that grow in ponds; and far over this ocean, other white rounded ones just protruding, like strands on some distant mainland.

Deep below me I could just distinguish enough of the land now and again to know my whereabouts—the winding Meuse in its green flood banks or that smouldering Ætna, Douaumont. But off to the north, hovering and curvetting over one of the bleached coral strands like seagulls—not Nieuports, surely! They were the modern harpies; the German machines for the chase. In the still, gray mist below now and again I caught sight of a Farman or Caudron sweeping over the corner of the lines to see some battery fire. But as I peered down, a liv-

The "Popote"

id white object moved under me going south, with the tail of a skate. "There is my fish and prey," I thought as I pointed down after the German *réglage* machine, "but prudence first" So I searched the waterplant clouds. Yes, sure enough, the venomous creatures are there, as dark specks resembling the larvae one sees in brackish water—three of them moving the same way. Those are the Fokkers. I did not want to have them fall on my neck when I dived on the fat, greasy Boche.

This morning we all started off at three, and, not having made concise arrangements, got separated in the morning mist. I found Prince, however, and we went to Douaumont, where we found two German *réglage* machines unprotected and fell upon them. A skirmish, a spitting of guns; and we drew away. It had been badly executed, that manoeuvre! But ho! another Boche heading for Verdun! Taking the control stick between my knees I tussled and fought with *mitrailleuse* and finally charged the *rouleau*, all the while eyeing my Boche and moving across Vaux toward Étain. I had no altitude with which to overtake him, but a little more speed. So I got behind his tail and spit till he dived into his own territory. Having lost Norman, I made a tour to the Argonne and on the way back saw another fat Boche. No protection machine in sight. I swooped, swerved to the right, to the left, almost lost, but then came up under his lee keel by the stern. (It's the one position they cannot shoot from.) I seemed a dory alongside a schooner. I pulled up my nose to let him have it. *Crr—Crr—Crr—*a cartridge jammed in the barrel. He jumped like a frog and fled down to his grounds.

Later in the morning I made another stroll along the lines. Met a flock of Nieuports and saw, across the way, a squad of white-winged L.V.G. How like a game of prisoner's base it all is! I scurry out in company and

A CAUDRON AMONG THE CLOUDS

they run away. They come into my territory and I, being alone, take to my heels. They did come after me once, too! Faster they are than I, but I had height, so they could but leer at me with their dead white wings and black crosses like sharks, and they returned to their own domain.

This afternoon we left together, it being our turn for the lines at 12.30. The roly-poly, cotton-wool clouds were thick again. Popping in and out of them, I ran upon some blue puffs such as one sees when the artillery has been shooting at aeroplanes. "Strange phenomena, perhaps there exist blue puffs like that." Yesterday I had fruitlessly chased about such puffs to find the *avions*. More smoke balls! There above me, like a black beetle, was the Boche! But well above me, and heading for his lines. For twenty minutes I followed that plane ever in front of me, and inch by inch, almost imperceptibly I gained in height and distance. He veered off to give me a broadside; I ducked away behind his tail; he turned off again; I repeated, but I did not have enough extra speed to manoeuvre close to him, though I temporarily cut off his retreat. After three passages-at-arms he got away. Then like a jackass I went on to Verdun and found no one.

On my return what tales were told! The Boches had come over Bar-le-Duc and plentifully shelled it; two of our pilots had their reservoirs pierced and one had not returned. The town, the station, the aviation field, all shelled—forty killed, including ten schoolchildren. (And we had word this morning that Poincaré has formally forbidden bombardment of every description, even on arms factories—it might kill civilians.) Yes, this is what comes of getting notoriety. There were disgusting notices about us in the papers two days ago—even yester-

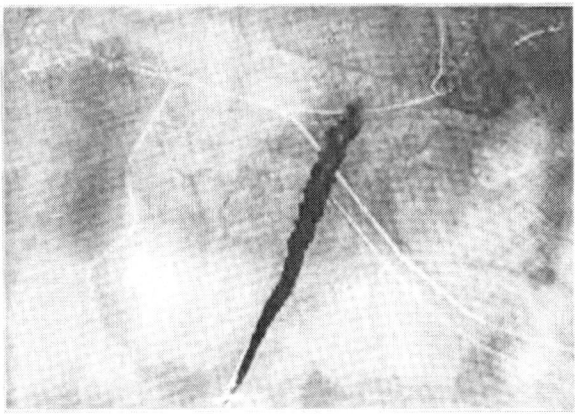

BOELKE SHOOTING DOWN A VOISIN
Boelke's plane appears above upper end of smoke near top of cut

day. I am ashamed to be seen in town today if our presence here has again caused death and destruction to innocent people. It would seem so. That Boche at Luxeuil, by the way, came again after we left, on the day and at the hour when the funeral services were being held. But through telephone they got out a Nieuport *escadrille* and cut off his retreat, bringing him down in the French trenches. By the papers on him he was identified as a one-time waiter in the Lion Vert, now, of course, a German officer.

With the N 124s

June 16, 1916

The last two days have seen a lot of action in the air, but none of us have had much luck. I myself was caught by surprise twice yesterday, although I was watching for it and being very careful in what I was doing. The only reason that I didn't get brought down was that the Boches shot poorly. I was attacking machines all the time, but they were always too many. Victor has been a little too courageous, and got me into one mess-up because I couldn't stand back and see him go in alone. He was attacking all the time, without paying much attention to what went on around him. He did the same thing this morning, and wouldn't come home when the rest of us did.

The result was that he was attacking one German, when a Fokker, in which we think was Boelke (the papers say he is dead, but we don't believe it), got full on Chapman's back, shot his machine to pieces, and wounded Victor in the head. It is just a scratch, but a miracle that he wasn't killed. One of his *aileron* controls was shot in two, but he landed by holding it together with his hand. The Germans came over yesterday and today to bombard us. I didn't see them yesterday. Today I went up, but my motor didn't work when I left the ground; one of the *bougies* was broken, so I was unable to continue. There were four machines in this *escadrille* that didn't work, because we had been doing too much flying beforehand. The others had fights with the Germans, but didn't bring any down. Navarre was wounded today.

I saw a pilot and his passenger burned up in a machine; the fault of the pilot. I had thought beforehand that yesterday and today I would try my darnedest to kill one or two Germans for the boys who got it this time last year; but, as I say, I had no luck. Am tired out now. Have been out four different times today, and all the time going up and down. Once I dropped straight down from 4050 metres to 1800 metres on a Boche, but he got away. It tires one a lot, the change in heights.

The Escadrille Américaine at Luxeuil, 1916

June 18, 1916

Yesterday was a bad day for us. You know we thought Balsley rather young and inexperienced, but ever since he came to the *escadrille* I have liked him better and better each day, as I saw he had plenty of good work, and was not afraid.

Yesterday we left for an offensive *barrage* over the lines. We were posed to follow the captain: but only Prince, Balsley, and I did so. We four were over the lines when we ran across about forty Boches in one little sector, flying at different heights. At the top where we were there were twelve or fifteen little *Aviatiks de chasse*, which go just as fast as we do, and in addition carry a gunner. The pilot shoots as we do, but the man back of him has a second gun, which can cover the rear and sides.

We were only four, and over the German lines, but we stayed close together, and for ten or fifteen minutes circled around the Boches, who were shooting at us nearly all the time. Finally we saw our chance. One of their machines crossed over between us and our lines, while all the others were to the rear of us. Suddenly I saw either Prince or Balsley go over in a regular death-drop, and thought to myself that he was killed. Then I lost sight of another of our machines, and only the captain and I were left. He signalled to me, so we turned back and finally came home, thinking the other two were killed. Prince came home soon after. He had had to drop straight down, owing to a Boche getting the upper hand of him and putting a bullet through his *casque*.

Poor Balsley seems to have dived on one Boche, got close to him, and had his gun jam after one shot. He turned off, and as he did so a bullet caught him in the hip and exploded on hitting the bone. Balsley fell straight down, but luckily had his feet strapped to the commands and was able to redress his machine and land, using one foot. He landed just inside our lines, and really had a close call. His machine was completely smashed. At present we are not sure about his wound. It may turn out to be only a slight thing, but several pilots have died from being wounded and getting blood poison. He has been proposed for the *Médaille Militaire*.

June 23, 1916

I feel very blue tonight; Victor was killed this afternoon. I was the guard here today, so didn't go out over the lines. The captain, Victor, Prince, and Lufbery went out this afternoon. Inside the German lines they attacked five German machines. The captain, Prince, and Lufbery came home all right, but Victor didn't show up. We were beginning to feel uneasy, when a Maurice Farman pilot telephoned. He said he saw one of the Nieuports suddenly dive straight down, and then break to pieces in the air. I figure that Victor was probably hit by a bullet, and that also some of the cables of his machine were cut by bullets. When he was hit, he probably fell forward on his "broomstick" (or whatever you call in English the controller); that would cause the machine to dive.

He fell inside the German lines. We are trying to notify his parents in America. I would like to see every paper in the world pay a tribute to Victor. There is no question but that he had more nerve than all of us put together. We were all afraid that he would be killed, and I, rooming with him, have begged him every night to be more prudent. He would fight every Boche he saw, no matter where or at what odds, and I am sure that he wounded and killed several of them. I have seen him twice right on top of a German, shooting; but it was always far in their lines.

Victor's head wound was not healed, yet he insisted on flying anyway, and would not take a rest. Since the war he never received anything in the way of decorations; yet for the one month here he was proposed for two citations, *à l'Ordre de l'Armée*, and for the *Médaille Militaire*.

July 23, 1916

Friday, had a very interesting day; flew six hours, and attacked four different machines. The first one certainly had a lot of luck. Right over the lines I attacked him first; when within ten or twenty metres I shot forty-four shots into him. Lieutenant de Laage then dove in just as close and shot over eighty shots into him. Then came another pilot with about twenty shots more, but the damned Boche went on as if nothing had happened.

In the middle of the day, another pilot and I went out alone. I found an *Aviatik* and dove on him; then two Fokkers dropped on me. My comrade dove on the two Fokkers, and two more Fokkers went for him. In that line of battle, we went down through the air for about two thousand metres. I got within ten metres of my *Aviatik*, shot all my shots into him, and saw him fall into the clouds, just as the mist closed in on me. I thought I had got the *Aviatik*, but a ground observer, who saw the fight, said that it redressed. My comrade shot all his cartridges at one Fokker; then the two others got right on his back.

They came very close to getting him; plugged a lot of bullets around him in the machine, but he was not touched.

Yesterday I flew for over eight hours. One machine, attacked by Lieutenant de Laage, Hill, and myself, was forced to land in the German lines. We gave Hill the credit for it, as he was nearest to the German and more likely to have hit him; it does not count anything officially, but may help him toward a citation.

A Caudron in Combat

I meant to get this letter off yesterday morning, but it is just as well that circumstances interfered, for yesterday afternoon I had a fight in my old G 4, with a Boche over the lines, and I want to tell you about it. It happened about three o'clock. I was circling over an enemy battery, spotting the fire of our guns and keeping a sharp eye out for any Boche machines that might try to interfere. Away back behind our lines I could see three or four machines zigzagging back and forth. I cast a curious eye on them from time to time, trying to distinguish of what type they might be. All of a sudden I saw one of them detach itself from the group and come toward us. The machine, at first a speck, grew rapidly larger as it approached. Its outline was soon distinguishable. It was a type I had never seen.

I leaned forward and rapped on the hood that separates me from my observer. He turned and asked me what was up. I pointed out the airplane ahead. He took just one look and jumped for the forward gun. *Ta-ta-ta!* Three shots to limber her up. I knew what that meant. We were about to exchange the time of day with a Boche. He was some speedy boy, that Boche. In no time he came within our range, a two-seater biplane, snowy white, with the big black crosses showing up plainly under his lower wings.

We went for each other nose to nose, the Boche having the advantage of position, about a hundred yards above us. Just before the machine guns got going, the antiaircraft guns of the Allies spotted him and the air all around him was dotted with beautiful white puffs and wreaths where the shells burst. I steered my course straight for the enemy until we got into range. Then the fun began. I shall never forget the real beauty of those ten short seconds while we gave each other hell: that graceful white machine with the black crosses showing up against the bright blue sky; the racket a the shells bursting all around us; my observer crouched behind his gun; the *staccato* of the wicked little Lewis as it spurted a stream of steel into the teeth of the

Caudron G 4

Lufbery (Luf)

other airplane.

In the twinkle of an eye it was over. The Boche shot over our heads with three times the speed of the wind, and instantly dived for his own lines. My observer whirled around and let loose at him with our stern gun, firing over my head; but by the time he had shot half a dozen rounds, the Boche was far beneath us and hidden by our tail, scuttling, as fast as the Lord would let him, for home and fireside.

It's funny. I can scarcely believe it myself, but the only impression I had during the fight—and the only impression that I retain of it—is one of beauty. It was the most beautiful sight my eyes ever feasted upon. Throughout the brush the idea of danger and imminent death never occurred to me for an instant. Even the shells bursting seemed to add only an additional touch to the general *mise-en-scène*. All I thought throughout the little brush was: Gosh, what a beautiful sight this is!

It was only after I came down and looked over my machine that I realised what might have happened if there hadn't been, as the French say, *un Dieu pour les aviateurs*. We had a bullet-hole in our car just beside the observer's leg, two shell-holes in our left propeller, and a shell-hole in the end of the left upper plane. But never mind; I was tickled to death.

Un Biplace Abattu

Escadrille Lafayette, April 27, 1917

Does this good news please you? Yesterday evening at half-past six I shot down a large two-seater German plane. It fell to the ground inside the enemy lines, southeast of Saint-Quentin, and was confirmed officially this morning by artillery observers. The captain will propose me for the War Cross with palm today, I think. Yesterday Chouteau Johnson also shot down a machine, which has been confirmed; that makes six sure ones for out *escadrille* in the past ten days. Lufbery got two and Lieutenant de Laage two last week as well as two doubtful ones.

We are having a good bit of action about here of late and are makin

A Costly Mistake

Hôpital Auxiliaire, June 29, 1917

No doubt you are wondering what happened, listening, meanwhile, to many I-told-you-so explanations from the others. This will be hard on you, but bear up, son. It might not be a bad plan to listen, with the understanding as well as the ear, to some expert advice on how to bag the Hun. To quote the prophetic Miller, "*I'm telling you this for your own good.*"

I gave my name and the number of the *escadrille* to the medical officer at the *poste de secours*. He said he would 'phone the captain at once, so that you must know before this that I have been amazingly lucky. I fell the greater part of two miles—count 'em, two!—before I actually regained control, only to lose it again. I fainted while still several hundred feet from the ground; but more of this later on. Couldn't sleep last night. Had a fever and my brain went on a spree, taking advantage of my helplessness. I just lay in bed and watched it function. Besides, there was a great artillery racket all night long. It appeared to be coming from our sector, so you must have heard it as well. This hospital is not very far back and we get the full orchestral effect of heavy firing. The result is that I am dead tired today. I believe I can sleep for a week.

They have given me a bed in the officers' ward—me, a corporal! It is because I am an American, of course. Wish there was some way of showing one's appreciation for so much kindness. My neighbour on the left is a *chasseur* captain. A hand-grenade exploded in his face. He will go through life horribly disfigured. An old *padre*, with two machine-gun bullets in his hip, is on the other side of me. He is very patient, but sometimes the pain is a little too much for him. To a Frenchman, "*Oh, la, la!*" is an expression for every conceivable kind of emotion. In the future it will mean unbearable physical pain for me. Our orderlies are two *poilus*, long past military age. They are as gentle and thoughtful as the nurses themselves. One of them brought me lemonade all night long. Worthwhile getting wounded just to have something taste so good.

******

I meant to finish this letter a week ago, but haven't felt up to it. Quite perky this morning, so I'll go on with the tale of my "heroic combat." Only, first, tell me how that absurd account of it got into the *Herald?* I hope T—— knows I was not foolish enough to attack six Germans single-handed. If he doesn't, please enlighten him. His opinion of my common sense must be low enough as it is.

We were to meet over at S—— at 3000 metres, you remember, and to cover the sector at 5000 until dusk. I was late in getting away, and by the time I reached the rendezvous you had all gone. There wasn't a *chasse* machine in sight. I ought to have gone back to the balloons as T—— advised, but thought it would be easy to pick you up later, so went on alone after I got some height. Crossed the lines at 3500 metres, and finally got up to 4000, which was the best I could do with my rebuilt engine. The Boches started shelling, but there were only a few of them that barked. I went down the lines for a quarter of an hour, meeting two Sopwiths and a Letord, but no Spads. You were almost certain to be higher than I, but my old packet was doing its best at 4000, and getting overheated with the exertion. Had to throttle down and *pique* several times to cool off.

Then I saw you—at least I thought it was you—about four kilometres inside the German lines. I counted six machines, well grouped, one a good deal higher than the others and one several metres below them. The pilot on top was doing beautiful *renversements* and an occasional barrel-turn, in B——'s manner. I was so certain it was our patrol that I started over at once, to join you. It was getting dusk and I lost sight of the machine lowest down, for a few seconds. Without my knowing it, he was approaching at exactly my altitude. You know how difficult it is to see a machine in that position. Suddenly he loomed up in front of me like an express train, as you have seen them approach from the depths of a moving-picture screen, only ten times faster; and he was firing as he came.

I realised my awful mistake, of course. His tracer bullets were going by on the left side, but he corrected his aim, and my motor seemed to be eating them up. I banked to the right, and was about to cut my motor and dive, when I felt a smashing blow in the left shoulder. A sickening sensation and a very peculiar one, not at all what I thought it might feel like to be hit with a bullet. I believed that it came from the German in front of me. But it couldn't have, for he was still approaching when I was hit, and I have learned here that the bullet entered from behind.

This is the history of less than a minute I'm giving you. It seemed much longer than that, but I don't suppose it was. I tried to shut down the motor, but couldn't manage it because my left arm was gone. I really believed that it had been blown off into space until I glanced down and saw that it was still there. But for any service it was to me, I might just as well have lost it. There was a vacant period of ten or fifteen seconds which I can't fill in. After that I knew that I was falling, with my motor going at full speed. It was a helpless realisation. My brain refused to act. I could do nothing. Finally, I did have one clear thought, "Am I on fire?" This cut right through the fog, brought me up broad awake. I was falling almost vertically, in a sort of half *vrille*. No machine but a Spad could have stood the strain. The Germans were following me and were not far away, judging from the sound of their guns. I fully expected to feel another bullet or two boring its way through. One did cut the skin of my right leg, although I didn't know this until I reached the hospital. Perhaps it was well that I did fall out of control, for the firing soon stopped, the Germans thinking, with reason, that they had bagged me. Some proud Boche airman is wearing an iron cross on my account. Perhaps the whole crew of daredevils has been decorated. However, no unseemly sarcasm. We would pounce on a lonely Hun just as quickly. There is no chivalry in war these modern days.

I pulled out of the spin, got the broomstick between my knees, and shut down the motor with my right hand. The propeller stopped dead. I didn't much care, being drowsy and tired. The worst of it was that I couldn't get my breath. I was gasping as though I had been hit in the pit of the stomach. Then I lost control and started falling. It was awful! I was almost ready to give up. I believe I said out loud, "I'm going to be killed. This is my last *sortie*." At any rate, I thought it. Made one last effort and came out in *ligne de vol*, as nearly as I could judge, about 150 metres from the ground. It was an ugly-looking place for landing—trenches and shell-holes everywhere.

I have no recollection of the crash, not the slightest. I might have fallen as gently as a leaf. That is one thing to be thankful for among a good many other things. When I came to, it was at once, completely. I knew that I was on a stretcher and remembered immediately exactly what had happened. My heart was going *pit-a-pat, pit-a-pat*, and I could hardly breathe, but had no sensation of pain except in my chest. This made me think that I had broken every bone in my body. I tried moving first one leg, then the other, then my arms, my head, and my body. No trouble at all, except with my left arm and side.

I accepted the miracle without attempting to explain it, for I had something more important to wonder about; who had the handles of my stretcher? The first thing I did was to open my eyes, but I was bleeding from a scratch on the forehead and saw only a blur. I wiped them dry with my sleeve and looked again. The broad back in front of me was covered with mud. Impossible to distinguish the colour of the tunic, but the shrapnel helmet above it was—French! I was in French hands. If ever I live long enough in one place, so that I may gather a few possessions and make a home for myself, on one wall of my living-room I will have a bust-length portrait, rear view, of a French *brancardier*, mud-covered back and battered tin hat.

Do you remember our walk with Ménault in the rain, and the *déjeuner* at the restaurant where they made such wonderful omelettes? I am sure that you will recall the occasion, although you may have forgotten the conversation. I have not forgotten one remark of Ménault's *apropos* of talk about risks. If a man were willing, he said, to stake everything for it, he would accumulate an experience of fifteen or twenty minutes which would compensate him a thousand times over for all the hazard. "And if you live to be old," he said quaintly, "you can never be bored with life. You will have something, always, very pleasant to think about." I mention this in connection with my discovery that I was not in German hands. I have had five minutes of perfect happiness without any background—no thought of yesterday or tomorrow—to spoil it.

I said, "*Bonjours, messieurs*," in a gurgling voice.

The man in front turned his head sidewise and said, "*Tiens! Ça va, monsieur l'aviateur?*"

The other one said, "*Ah, mon vieux!*"

You know the inflection they give to this expression, particularly when it means, "This is something wonderful!" He added that they had seen the combat and my fall, and little expected to find the pilot living, to say nothing of speaking. I hoped that they would go on talking, but I was being carried along a trench, and they had to carry me shoulder-high at every turn, and they needed all their energy. The Germans were shelling the lines. Several fell fairly close, and they brought me down a long flight of wooden steps into a dugout to wait until the worst was over. While waiting, they told me that I had fallen just within the first-line trenches, at a spot where a slight rise in ground hid me from sight of the enemy. Otherwise they might have had a bad time rescuing me. My Spad was completely wrecked. It fell squarely into a trench, the wings breaking the force of the fall. Before reaching the ground, I turned, they said, and was making straight for Germany. Fifty metres higher, and I should have come down in No Man's Land.

For a long time we listened in silence to the subdued *crr-ump, crr-ump*, of the shells. Sometimes showers of earth pattered down the stairway, and we would hear the high-pitched, droning *V-z-z-z* of pieces of shell-casing as they whizzed over the opening. One of them

INSIGNIA OF FRENCH ESCADRILLES IN WHICH MEMBERS
OF THE LAFAYETTE FLYING CORPS SERVED.
PLATE 6

would say, "Not far, that one," or, "He's looking for someone, that fellow," in a voice without a hint of emotion. Then, long silences and other deep, earth-shaking rumbles.

They asked me, several times, if I was suffering, and offered to go on to the *poste de secours* if I wanted them to. It was not a heavy bombardment, but it would be safer to wait for a while. I told them that I was ready to go at any time, but not to hurry on my account; I was quite comfortable.

The light glimmering down the stairway faded out and we were in complete darkness. My brain was amazingly clear. It registered every trifling impression. I wish it might always be so intensely awake and active. There seemed to be four of us in the dugout; the two *brancardiers*, and this second self of mine, as curious as an eavesdropper at a keyhole, listening intently to everything, and then turning and whispering to me.

The *brancardiers* repeated the same comments after every explosion. I thought: "They have been saying this to each other for over three years. It has become automatic. They will never be able to stop!" I was feverish, perhaps. If it was fever, it burned away any illusions I may have had of modern warfare from the infantryman's viewpoint. I know that there is no glamour in it for them; that it has long since become a deadly monotony, an endless repetition of the same kinds of horror and suffering, a boredom more terrible than death itself, which is repeating itself in the same ways, day after day and month after month. It isn't often that an aviator has the chance I've had. It would be a good thing for us if they were to send us into the trenches for twenty-four hours, every few months. It would make us keener fighters, more eager to do our utmost to bring the war to an end for the sake of the *poilus*.

The dressing-station was in a very deep dugout, lighted by candles. At a table in the centre of the room the medical officer was working over a man with a terribly crushed leg. Several others were sitting or lying along the wall, awaiting their turn. They watched every movement he made in an apprehensive, animal way, and so did I. They put me on the table next, although it was not my turn. I protested, but the doctor paid no attention. "*Aviateur américain*" again. It's a pity that Frenchmen can't treat us Americans as though we belonged here.

As soon as the doctor finished with me, my stretcher was fastened to a two-wheeled carrier and we started down a cobbled road to the ambulance station. I was light-headed and don't remember much of that part of the journey. We had to take refuge in another dugout when the Huns dropped a shell on an ammunition dump in a village through which we had to pass. There was a deafening banging and booming for a long time, and when we did go through the town, it was on the run. The whole place was in flames and small-arms ammunition still exploding. I remember seeing a long column of soldiers going at the double in the opposite direction and they were in full marching order.

Well, this is the end of the tale; all of it, at any rate, in which you would be interested. It was one o'clock in the morning before I got between cool, clean sheets, and I was wounded about a quarter past eight. I have been tired ever since.

First Combat—First Victory

July 9, 1917

I am writing to give you a bit of news which I know will interest you. I had my first real combat the day before yesterday, and was fortunate enough to get my first Boche. He is not yet official, but is reported as *probablement abattu*, and I am waiting for the confirmation from the *observateurs* in the *saucisses* and from the *fantassins* in the first-line trenches. I was reported brought down just as the Boche attacked me, having fallen into a *vrille* doing some acrobatics to mix up his aim. He evidently did the same thing, because, just as I was redressing, he shot past me in a vertical dive, and I went after him about fifteen to twenty metres from his tail. We dropped like that with full motor for 1500 metres and I had him right in my *colimateur* every second with my gun going full tilt. My oil radiator broke at this point and I had to quit and beat it for home. The last I saw of him, however, he was still going down and was only about six hundred metres from the ground. He probably fell back of their line, but not very far, and I have every reason to believe he will be homologue. Four of our pilots saw the combat, but they were too occupied with some other Germans to see the result.

Guynemer

Saint-Pol-sur-Mer, September 16, 1917

You will have seen in the papers, long before you get this letter, that Captain Guynemer, the greatest of them all, is gone. He and another officer went out on Tuesday morning to hunt the Hun. They were flying fairly high, somewhere around 16,000 feet, I think, and Guynemer went down a little way to attack a two-seater while the Lieutenant who was with him stayed up to protect his rear. About that time eight Boche single-seater machines put in an appearance and the lieutenant was kept busy trying to worry them and keep them from going down on the captain. He succeeded and none of the Boches dove down, but in the general mix-up he lost track of Guynemer and he has not been heard from since. He must have fallen in the Boche lines and I am afraid he was killed without much question. The place where the fight occurred was over the Boche territory, but close enough to our lines to have allowed Guynemer to have reached them if he had been merely wounded. Also, if the Huns had taken him prisoner, we should certainly have heard of it before now. They would be proud to get him and I am surprised that they have as yet made no announcement of his having been found.

The loss of this man is very great, as he was by all odds the greatest aviator and individual fighter the war has produced. I am awfully sorry, for if ever a man had won his spurs and deserved to live it was Captain Guynemer. He had fifty-three Hun machines to his credit officially and I hoped that he had become so skilful that he would never be killed. As I have already written you, he was small and of a frail appearance. I believe his health was very far from good and the high altitudes sometimes made him so sick he had to come down. He would fly for a week and then go away for a rest, as he was not strong enough to stand any more. In the course of several hundred fights he had been shot down seven times and twice wounded. To keep at it under such circumstances and after all he had gone through, a man's heart has to be in the right place and no mistake. He certainly deserved to live the rest of his days in peace and one hates to see a man like that get it.

The evening before he disappeared, I was standing on the field when he landed with a dead motor caused by a bullet in it. There were three others through his wings. He had attacked another two-seater; something went wrong with his motor at the crucial moment and this gave the Boche a good shot at him and spoiled his own chance of bringing down his opponent. A little episode like this, however, rolled off his back like water off a duck, perhaps a little too easily, I fear. Long immunity breeds a contempt of danger which is probably the greatest danger of all. Guynemer's loss naturally throws more or less of a gloom over everyone.

It is clear again this evening, so I am going to close this letter before I have to start for a dugout. We were out in quest of the elusive

Boche this afternoon and got up as high as I have yet been, between 19,000 and 20,000 feet, but had no luck. Saw a couple of them, but they were above us and by the time we had got up to where they were they had run for home while we were still too far away to catch them. Reminds me of the old days when I used to chase what you were wont to call the "invisible duck."

THE FIRST OFFICIAL VICTORY

October 24, 1917

I think you will be pleased to hear that I have been cited *à l'Ordre de l'Armée* and have been awarded the *Croix de Guerre* with a palm. The reason for my being so honoured is as follows: On the morning of October 17 I officially shot down a large German two-seater aeroplane which had been making some observations in our lines southwest of Nieuport. The combat was witnessed by our artillery observers and they plainly saw my Boche dive down and smash to pieces several miles south of Dixmude, just inside the German lines. I really had some very good luck in getting him, because all of the fifty shots which I fired at him were from a minimum distance of 450 feet. I think I must have hit the machine-gunner first, because he quit firing at me at the very start; and then one of my bullets must have laid out the pilot, as the machine shortly after dived out of control and smashed to bits on hitting the ground. When I spotted this Boche, I was leisurely returning from a chase after a Boche *monoplace* (he got away) which had led me quite far into *Bochie*. I was at 13,000 feet and, though I had nearly regained our lines, I kept my eyes "peeled" and was looking all about to avert a possible surprise attack (so dangerous when alone).

Suddenly, about 6000 feet below me I saw the white puffs of smoke which our anti-aircraft shrapnel makes. I knew they must be shooting at a Boche, so I looked carefully and presently caught sight of him. I dove vertically. It took me about twenty seconds to go down those 6000 feet. I placed myself about 700 feet behind and a little below his tail. Putting on full steam so as to catch him closer, I started firing. Our gunners, meanwhile, had seen me attack and had ceased shooting, so there was no danger of my being hit by mistake by shrapnel meant for the Boche. Well, after firing fifty shots in three volleys, he was done for and I beat it home. He did try to escape by diving, but as I was flying a 180 horse-power Spad, I was always able to keep my sights on him. He was taken by surprise by my plunge at him from above and couldn't escape.

I have had quite a lot of battles, but this is the first time I have succeeded in actually killing an adversary. I hope I can get some more. Some of the crack French pilots have twenty-five and thirty such victories, and that poor kid Guynemer (he was only a year older than I) had fifty-three before he got killed. Well, I'm going on a ten days' vacation now to rest up and enjoy the fruits of victory. My captain congratulated me and said he thought I might turn out an A1 pilot, especially as I had started to bring down Germans after such a short experience of handling aeroplanes and fighting at the Front.

INFANTRY CONFIRMATION

I have brought down another German. We were out on patrol, and were attacked by three Boches. The captain and I were together. First they made an attack on the captain. He immediately went into a *vrille* to get out of danger. The three Boches dove down after him, and left me entirely alone. I dove on the one nearest me, and missed him with my first few shots. I swooped up to gain a bit of altitude, and then dove on him again. He had gone down quite a way, so it gave me an excellent chance to train my gun on him. This time I got him. He fell in a *vrille* and smashed to pieces in a farmyard below. I came down a bit lower in a long spiral to make sure that my eye hadn't deceived me, and then beat it for home, and before I landed I did every acrobatic stunt I knew to advertise the fact that I had downed another Boche.

The next day the captain and I went up to the Front to see if the Boche had been seen by the observation balloons. Sure enough, the combat had been seen, not only by the observer in the balloon, but by the men in the trenches. We visited the trenches for four hours. I prayed most of the time that the Boche wouldn't pull off an attack while we were there. It was quite interesting, walking over reconquered ground. We had to walk, because the car could never have gone over those roads, torn up by shells. We went in the captain's staff car, a big eight-cylinder Renault.

The soldiers we passed saluted continually, and it was worse when we had to walk, saluting the whole time. We very rarely salute around the camp of aviation. After we had visited the terrible battle-ground, we rode back to a big town a few miles behind the lines and had our dinner, which was mighty good. I bought the captain the most expensive wine in the place, which was not very expensive, nine *francs* a bottle. He certainly did like it, and after the meal I called for the bill.

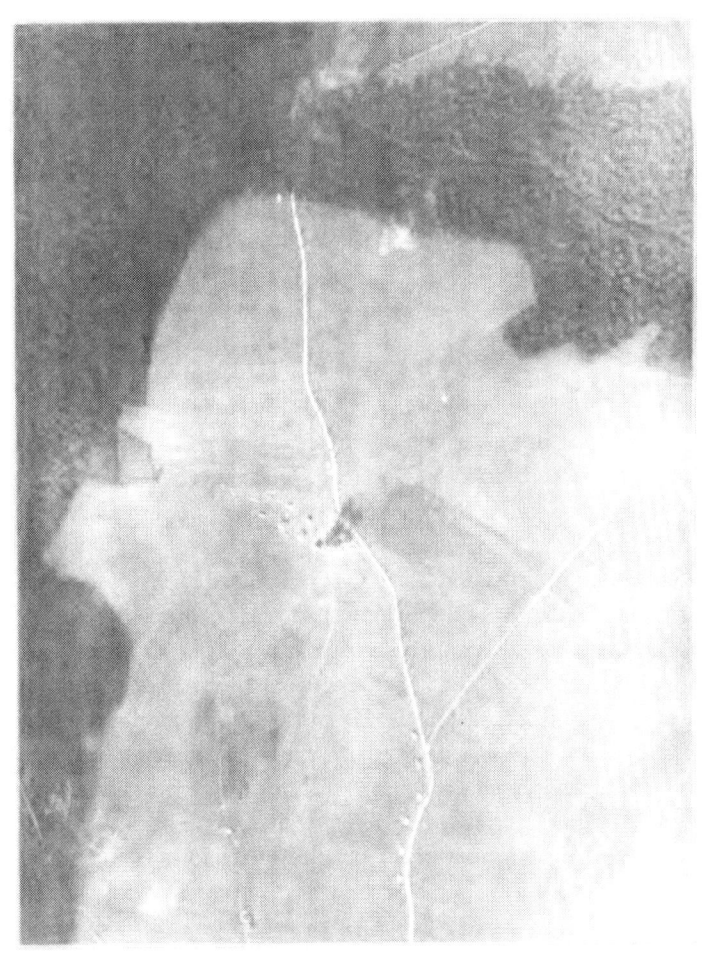

Soin chez les Boches—A German aerodrome

It came, but the captain wouldn't let me pay a cent. I insisted so much that my French gave out and so he paid it after all. He said it was his treat to me, on account of my second victory and of being made a sergeant.

AT CLOSE QUARTERS

January 9, 1918

Although it is late, and the lights are going out soon, I will have time to write you about the big day I had last Sunday. Sent you a cable saying I had brought down an Albatross, but all communications are so rotten I don't know whether you ever got it, so this may be the first you know of it.

On January 6 three of us were to make an hour and a half morning patrol. One of the Frenchmen had magneto trouble, and couldn't go up, so Lieutenant Parizet and I started off together to patrol the sector. There was nothing doing. Not a Boche in sight. So far as that goes, I haven't seen a Boche on our side for two weeks. We crossed the lines a bit at 4000 metres, and soon saw three Albatross *monoplaces* sailing along at about 3300 metres. I didn't wait for Parizet, who was leading, to start for them, but *piqued* on one of them immediately. Parizet made a slight detour, then dove on one from the side, leaving the third, the leader, free. My Boche made a quick turn, so I redressed and began manoeuvring to get behind and above him.

Finally I got him where I wanted him, and *piqued* steep, shooting all the time. Parizet was then just ahead of and above me, and I saw him shooting at a Boche who was manoeuvring to attack me. He over-*piqued* eventually, and the Boche fired about twenty shots at me from the side and a trifle below. He got so close I could see his face, and for a second I hesitated whether to turn on him or continue with the original one. He fell over on his side, though, so I let him go; I put my machine in a vertical nose dive, gaining tremendous speed, then redressed, and quickly overtook my fleeing Boche. Got within one hundred metres of him, and sent in a steady stream of bullets.

When I was so close to him that I started to redress to avoid colliding with him, I saw him slowly slip over on the wing, then go into a slow *vrille*, and after a few manoeuvres to keep him always under fire, I saw he had been hit, and made a vertical spiral to watch him *vrille* down to the ground. I was now at about 2500 metres, and the other two Boches about 1000 metres below. Parizet had remained at 3000 metres, but I decided to take my chances with the other two, so threw my machine over on her side, and dropped 700 metres like a plummet in a couple of seconds. Both Albatrosses immediately continued their piquing. I followed one as low as 1000 metres, but dared go no farther after him. Then the fireworks began. One thousand metres is extremely low for five kilometres inside the German lines, and the air became black around me with their anti-aircrafts. I couldn't go in a straight line, and, as there was a heavy head wind, it took me ages to get inside our lines again.

That is all the description I can give of my first fight. It was very thrilling, and the most wonderful sport I have ever participated in. I was in danger only for the time when the Boche fired at me, and then somehow it seemed so funny I burst out laughing. I had always rather dreaded my first combat, but there's nothing nervous or rattling about it. It was more like practice at target shooting than anything else, as the aim has to be very carefully timed and corrected. There is a tremendously exhilarating thrill about it, however, and the passion of the hunt.

Had another scrap in the afternoon, and if I had not been so pressed I could have brought him down easily. Was on a rather large patrol in a concentrated area, as we had reason to believe the Boches were going to make a *coup de main* there. Everything was perfectly quiet, however. There wasn't a Boche to be seen in the sky. I got kind of bored at this stupid empty flying, so left the patrol, climbed to 4400 metres (I was a little sick with the cold) and crossed over to ten kilos in Bocheland.

Still nothing to be seen, so I came down to 3600. At last I saw an

A LONE NIEUPORT

avion coming in my direction, so I turned to meet him, both of us climbing at the same time. He looked like a Nieuport, and I was sure he was. When he was 800 metres from me, he turned, throwing up the bottom of his wings to show, as I thought, that he was French. I made a quarter turn, then decided to follow him, thinking all the time it was a Nieuport. Overtook him, and then pulled what is probably the dumbest, bonehead stunt in the war's aviation history. By this time I had taken it for granted he was a Nieuport, so had got in position to patrol with him.

He apparently was just as positive that I was an Albatross, and I don't wonder, for a Nieuport is practically never seen now, especially alone, so far inside the German lines as I was. Well, for three minutes the two of us made a patrol together, I swerving from side to side and looking keenly above, below, behind, and on both sides for any enemy machines, and all the time I was 150 metres behind and 50 metres above one, thinking he was French! Then suddenly I saw the Maltese crosses on his wings, and the sight of them hit me like a blow. I couldn't believe my eyes. For a second I thought I must be in a dream. Then I made in my haste a big mistake. Had I taken my time I could have closed in, dived beneath his tail, and shot him down from directly underneath. I was a little upset by the startling discovery, however, and acted a little hastily. I immediately *piqued* on him, firing my gun.

At the first shot he glanced back, and immediately dove, then put his machine in a *vrille*. At first I thought I had hit him, and was feeling pretty jubilant at the thought of bagging two in one day—a rare feat. The beggar had just been too yellow to fight, though, and dove without making any effort to put up a scrap. I saw him redress at about 1000 metres, and I was pretty sore, for if he had stayed I might have got him, as the Albatrosses are too clumsy to manoeuvre well, and I can spin my little Nieuport around into any position. Fritz is frightened to death in this region, though, and the two of us in the morning were too much for their three.

Had quite a time getting home. The head wind was still blowing hard. I had a long way to buck it, was all alone in enemy territory, and the "Archies" were shooting all around me. I didn't care to zigzag back, but preferred to take a chance on a more or less straight dash, which would bring me home quicker, but at the same time make me an easier target for the "antis." Got through their fire all right, though it was pretty uncomfortable. Then, just before I had regained the lines, they threw up a perfect *barrage* directly in front of me. I veered off

EARLY MORNING *ALERTE*. A BOCHE IS SIGNALLED

at right angles just in time. You see, they can get the range almost perfectly, but have difficulty in laying angle of direction. I was feeling perfectly safe now, so near our lines, so decided to have a little fun with them. I made no effort to go through their continued *barrage*, but commenced a vertical spiral just in back of it.

When the first couple of shots broke near me, I made a dart parallel to the lines, then before they could alter their aim, turned sharp, and gave full speed in the opposite direction. Before they could alter, I changed again, and did this six or seven times, laughing at how mixed up they must be. Finally they became so bewildered that they ceased firing altogether, not knowing where to aim. Then was my chance, and giving full juice I dashed back into French territory before they could put up another shell at me. If they had a good telescope, I hope they could see me turn in my seat and thumb my nose at them.

That was all for the day. I was awfully sorry I hadn't got my Boche, but I didn't deserve to on account of being so dumb as to mistake him for a Nieuport. The two machines look very much alike, but I should have been more careful. In the evening the commandant of the group called me to his office, and after congratulating me for the Boche, said that we had broken an order in crossing the lines with less than three Nieuports, and strictly forbade me ever to cross alone again.

It was foolish of me to do it, but it was the recklessness of ignorance and a little unlooked-for success. I shall be much more prudent in the future.

Unfortunately there was a mist and poor visibility in the morning, so no *saucisses* were up, and the C.A.'s could not follow the Boche to the ground, so, although my Boche is recognised, it is not "homologated" and I can't get a citation out of it. These are always rather disappointing. As a rule, on the average, only two thirds or three fourths of the machines descended are homologated. Thus Guynemer had some twenty-five victims unhomologated. Lufbery has at least a dozen.

A Fight with an Albatross

January 20, 1918

We started off on our patrol with me hugging the lieutenant's tail as tight as I dared. You can imagine how hard it is to watch the ground, keep your place in formation, and watch the German *contre-avions,* all at the same time. Being up there for the first time, with very little flying experience, I was all for sticking with the leader. We made the beat once without incident; saw some Germans, but they were well within their lines, so we did not bother them: turned around at last, and were about halfway back when the lieutenant's machine started rocking from side to side and up and down; the signal to get ready for an attack. I looked around and saw, well-above us and to the left, three German machines, surrounded by a lot of shell-bunts.

The lieutenant started climbing so as to get above them, and between them and the sun, but they saw us coming and turned back. We did not follow them, but continued our patrol, and soon the lieutenant started wiggling his tail again. I looked around, but failed to see any Boches, so thought he was just trying to find out what kind of a pilot I was. I kept with him for a while and then he went up on one wing and into a terrific wing-slip straight down. I did my best to follow him, but did not make a very good wing-slip, so went into a nose dive. By this time he had dropped at least 1000 metres and I had lost him. It seems that he had seen three Boches and had piqued to attack. I did not see them. It is hard to realise how fast you are going, especially when you drop like that. If you wing-slip correctly, it flattens you against the side of the machine.

Well, I started back toward the lines and saw a machine flying alone which I thought was the lieutenant. Headed straight for it, but as I came up it had an odd dark look, so I mounted above just to play safe. It banked, and as the side of the fuselage turned into the sunlight, I saw the old black cross on a silver background staring me in the face. By this time I knew that I had made a mistake, but there was nothing to do but to attack. I took a couple of deep gulps and a firm hold on the stick and tried to figure out the next move. He had seen me and was coming at me on a diagonal, but I was above, and when he was almost underneath I *piqued* on him and squeezed the trigger. I thought I had him, for he was only 100 metres off and my luminous bullets seemed to be streaking right for his head. But they didn't seem to bother him, and the next thing I knew he had turned up and was *piquing* on me. I heard his *mitrailleuse* go *tac-tac-tac*, and sort of pulled my neck in, but nothing happened, and I banked off and *piqued* again, but with no better results. This time my gun jammed, and by the time I had cleared it he was almost directly over me in a beautiful position.

Nothing to do but fall in a *vrille* to get away from him. I came out of it and started to climb again until I was even with him. We passed each other again and exchanged a few shots and my *mitrailleuse* jammed again. Then I noticed three Germans above us and a little way off, who were coming up as fast as they could; furthermore, one of

AN ALLIED AERODROME

the stays holding my elevator was flapping in the wind, and I decided it was high time for me to get home. By this time we had worked well over the German lines and home looked a long way off, but I opened the motor wide with a short prayer and pulled the stick into my stomach, with four Germans on my tail. They were faster than I, but I could climb faster. From then on it was a case of "get out of the way and let someone run who knows how." They did not go very far over our lines, and, believe me, I was glad to see them call it off. I took one peep at my elevator, saw it was still there and started a very gentle descent to our aerodrome.

INTERRUPTING ENEMY *RÉGLAGE*

February 1, 1918

The weather has eased up and the past week has been like spring. As a consequence we had patrols over the lines every day, and a few days ago had the good fortune to bring down a Boche machine. We were flying in formation, the lieutenant ahead as *Chef de Groupe*; Ferguson and myself just behind, on his right and left respectively, and another behind us. As we approached the end of our sector, we saw the Boche plane about 2000 metres below us. It was a large biplace, probably a Rumpler, regulating artillery. The *chef* signalled to go after it, so down we went, weaving in and out, trying to get into a good position to dive. When he was about 200 metres over it, the lieutenant dove and opened fire. I was 150 metres behind, so dove immediately I got in position, which happened before he pulled up.

After he got out of the way, I opened up and pulled out of the dive just above him—the Boche. We then looked around to see what had happened—but we couldn't have hit him very seriously, as he was flying all right. The other two stayed above us to protect us from any stray Boche who might have come unexpectedly on the scene. We worked around again for position and repeated, this time with better luck, for on the way down I saw my tracer bullets going into the fuselage, and, as I pulled up, he fell off into a *vrille*. A moment after, we saw him crash into a forest. I doubt whether it will be counted officially, as he fell eight kilometres within the lines.

HIS FIRST COMBAT

March 15, 1918

Yesterday and today I did not fly, on account of magneto trouble, but Wednesday I had enough excitement to last me for two days. It was my first combat. Lieutenant Ronalet, Bollinger, Cavieux, and I were booked for a photo protection mission. We followed, in V-shaped formation, the two slower photo machines for an hour or so over the lines. Just as we had returned to the lines I saw the *chef de patrouille* turn and dive. I was directly behind him on his right and followed suit. As soon as I dove, I saw a group of six Albatross D III's circling around like a bunch of hornets directly below us. I aimed my machine at one and it seemed as if I could see my tracer bullets go right through him. I pulled up, dove again, and fired. The other Spads were close to me on right and left and one down among the Boches.

After I had fired three times, I looked up and saw two more machines, evidently German and coming at us. They had the advantage of altitude, but believing I could climb fast enough I turned toward them. Lieutenant Ronalet had seen them too, and I found him beside me at 4200 metres.

The last two Boches turned and flew away. I don't know how near I came to them with my bullets. I might have hit the machine, but all I know is that I fired 200 rounds and I did not see my man fall. You have too much to figure out in aiming, the speed of the machine— which changes as it climbs or dives—the direction it is going, and the distance between you and your target. To help, there is the tracer bullet which leaves a flame, but even at that, you cannot count much on them.

I shall never forget those few minutes, the sight of the gray Al-

CLIMBING

batrosses with the big black crosses and the excitement of trying to shoot them down. The Germans have one trick that they continually use, just as they did the other day. They send out about five or six small fast *monoplaces* at 3000 metres and then several big *triplaces* at about 5000 metres to attack any French planes that may wish in combat the lower planes. Height is always an advantage, for one has speed and better control over the machine. One can lose height rapidly, but it takes time to regain it. A machine is not so steady and requires more attention in a climbing position.

Une Panne de Moteur in No Man's Land

March 31, 1918

Have been so terribly occupied for the past ten days that it was impossible to write more than a few lines. Huns advanced twenty kilometres, pushing English and hundreds of refugees before them. At noon on the 26th we thought it best to leave; getting rather too warm. Five hours later Huns occupied our aerodrome, burned hangars and a machine; fortunate to get them all away except that one. Lost two trucks and quantities of belongings.

We flew six hours a day; mostly reconnaissance, flying very low over the enemy, shooting the troops in the trenches, the cavalry on the roads, and detachments of cannon and *ravitaillement*. Three men were brought down, including myself, and all had close shaves.

I will tell you now what happened to me—regular dime novel affair. Flying at 1000 feet and six kilometres in the Hun lines, on the forenoon of the 28th, I saw a double-seater Boche toward the lines at 600 feet. Banked and attacked. Fired three balls, when my motor stopped; a ball had cut magneto wire. Managed to land directly between French and Boche first lines, 60 feet from a large Hun detachment and 150 feet from French. Took my watch and altimeter and ran as fast or faster than I ever ran before in all my life. An approaching Boche (three of them, as a matter of fact, came out to welcome me in their midst) was nearly to my machine when he was killed by a Frenchman in the first line.

Huns took great delight in potting at me with machine guns as I was running in. Made our lines unhurt and reported to the colonel. Several Huns in meantime advanced on machine and with rifles demolished wings, and ignited debris. Spent the night in first-line trench. The following morning was taken to the general, where means of conveyance were produced and I motored back to my *escadrille*.

Decorated

May 2, 1918

Yesterday was a very proud day for me; I'll tell you all about it. Miserable weather we have been having; nothing whatever to do. Go into Beauvais for dinner and loaf around enjoying the sights. I was in my room yesterday afternoon puttering around when the orderly came in, saying I was wanted by Lieutenant Raymond. Hustled out in old duds; an old pair of flying-boots on my feet. Imagine my surprise when I was presented to the general in charge of Aviation, a nice old duffer who pinned another citation on Fonck and on me; then embraced me on both cheeks. Quite an affair; troops marched by and the drums beat. I was flustered as a kid. That was my fourth official Hun. I have been proposed for another medal, and, I believe, a lieutenancy in the French Army.

Now I have some more good news: This forenoon, the first good day for a long while, I cranked up Mon Lion, as the mechanic proudly calls my Spad, and went to the lines. Loafed about with another chap, looking around for any lurking Hun, but nothing in sight. Turned around and started home. Thought I'd look back over my shoulder just once before bidding lines farewell, when directly over my head I saw three double-seater Rumplers (*chasse* type).

They had not seen me. I turned and started climbing. Number one passed directly overhead; the second was vertical. I pulled back on my

THEIR LAST RIDE

stick, stood the Spad on its tail, and let the Hun have the benefit of two perfectly working, well-regulated machine guns. He didn't have much to say; went down without a minute's hesitation. Fell out of control, hit the ground an awful blow, and lay there a crumpled mass of debris. (Poor devils, their last ride. Still, you have the consolation of knowing that they'd get you if they could.) Turned around to attack the second, but both guns jammed.

This evening out again. Hadn't been over the lines five minutes before I spied five Hun double-seaters, out for a few photos. Dove a thousand feet on the last and shot at him as I passed, but missed. Came up again under his tail—*ta-ta-ta*—and the Hun was no more. Called it a day's work and came home for dinner. Landed just as the sun was setting. Douched myself with cold water, changed my shirt, and ate like a person famished. You have an appetite like a bear. Well, that makes six Boche machines accounted for.

These Frenchmen are fellows to be proud of. After four years of it, fed up and weary, they fight like maniacs. The Hun is good, we'll all admit, but for individual efficiency and initiative give me a Frenchman; he'll wipe up the ground with the Hun. Practically all air combats of today are fought in the German lines. If they won't come over our lines, we go over theirs. Lieutenant B———, an old pilot of the *escadrille*, attacked a Boche, just as the Fritz shut off his motor to coast down to his field. That's delivering the goods into their hands; not so far to go to clean up the debris.

Fair Play

May 28, 1918

I imagine the papers at home are full of the terrific attack that is raging; as usual we are in the midst of it.

This morning enjoyed very interesting few moments with four Huns at close quarters—incidentally managed to save one of our machines. For about an hour I had been watching the battle that was raging so fiercely below, dodging shrapnel, and looking for a stray Boche, when all of a sudden, about three miles in their lines, I saw two of our photo busses being attacked by four Huns. One of our machines, by clever manoeuvring, managed to elude the Boches, but the second was not so fortunate. He fell out of control; observer seriously wounded. I dove on the first Boche, and when within a hundred feet, opened up with guns. Down he went, and I saw him crash bang into the ground. The other three, needless to say, hastened away—probably discovered they were late for lunch. The *biplace* fell 3000 feet out of control, redressed, and came home badly shattered; seventeen holes. Pilot came this afternoon and thanked me; very nice chap. This morning's Hun makes my tenth official, and I have five unofficial besides.

Twelve Hits for Fritz

April 14, 1918

Three mornings ago we were on early morning patrol; four of us. We had gone fifteen or twenty miles inside the enemy lines, when we were attacked by ten Boches. The leader of our group was 300 feet under me. (That is the way we fly on patrol, like an inverted V—each machine 300 feet higher than the one in front.) I looked on my left suddenly and a Boche went diving past me, shooting at the leader of our patrol. The enemy machines were all Albatrosses, painted black, with black crosses on a white background. I dived down after him, with full motor. I could see his incendiary and explosive bullets flying pretty near our leader, and I also saw mine going into the Albatross, until at last I saw it go out of control, fall into a *vrille*, and burst into flames. It fell 12,000 feet, and smashed into a forest. I pulled my machine up, and directly in front, about a hundred feet higher than I, were three more machines, Boche; I let go again with my machine gun, and it popped once and jammed.

I began to think that home was a long way off. They were attacking another member of our patrol, when they saw me under them. I put my machine into a *vrille* and dropped a few thousand feet. All the time I was in the *vrille* I could see their tracer bullets going by. I straightened out, and sure enough, when I looked up, one of them was still after me, but I fooled him by diving for the nearest cloud. I got my direction again, and finally landed at our hangars, when I found that I had twelve bullet holes in my machine. Soon after, the other three landed, and one of them had also brought one of the Boches down. Another fellow had thirty-five holes in his machine, one of them just missing his gas-tank.

We were congratulated by the officers, and I was kissed several times on the cheek. That is about all there is to tell about the combat, but while it lasted it was hot.

A Victory Chez Eux

I had my first fight this morning at 11.30. I shall describe to you my morning's flight from beginning to end; it is the biggest thing that has happened to me since I came over here. I cannot realise, as yet, the greatness of my luck. At about 10.30 I went up from our field at Lunéville with two other Nieuports to guard an A.R. which was going to take some photos. After circling around over our field for a while, waiting for the A.R. to get altitude, we started off toward the lines. It is not much fun guarding a slow machine, because one has to make S's to stay with it, and it is very easy to lose when the camouflaged wings blend with trees. Well, anyway, I got up too high, so that I got only an occasional glimpse of my ward. Finally I saw no more of him, but my attention was attracted by some French anti-aircraft guns that were shooting at a German plane quite a way off from me and much higher.

I then abandoned the search for the A.R. and tried to gain altitude and approach the Hun, who was only a speck in the distance. My machine never seemed to go slower, but finally, after about fifteen minutes (seemed like fifteen hours), I got a little above the other machine at 5200 metres. The German pilot suddenly turned and made for his lines; by cutting the corner thus formed I arrived about 200 metres from him and still above. The machine-gunner immediately opened fire. I could hear distinctly the *rat-tat-tat* of his gun. I dove and tried to get under his tail. He kept making spirals to prevent me, his machine-gunner firing away all the time. After about two circles I got pretty close to him and under his tail. He then made a sharp turn to disclose me to the gunner, so I decided it was time to start shooting.

Now here is where the luck comes in. My gun hadn't gone off six times before the Hun went into a spinning nose dive. I shouldn't have thought I hit him if it had not been for a tracer bullet that seemed to go right where the pilot was. Anyway, I was not going to take any chances, so I started down after him. It is a common trick to pretend you are hit and redress just above the ground. Gee! I have never gone down so fast before! At about 2000 metres he seemed to come out of his nose dive and go into a steep spiral. I caught up to him and took a couple of shots. They were wasted, however, because he spiralled right into the slope of a hill in the Vosges Mountains. I circled around low over him to make sure he was down. There was no mistaking the machine, nose down in the hill. I was in a stupor; some women ran out of a little house near by and I shouted at them at the top of my lungs, waving all the while.

I had rather an abrupt awakening; I thought it was the 4th of July, but instead of being on the ground watching the fireworks I was the goat, for a swarm of luminous bullets went tearing past me.

It was Germany I was over, not friendly France! Black puffs of smoke began breaking around me. I took several good looks at the place so as to be able to identify it on the map when I got back. The small map on the plane did not include that sector. Then I started home with very little gasoline left in my tank. There was another German plane far above me; after taking another look at my gas I decided that discretion was the better part of valour and beat it for what I thought was home. I could see the Alps clearly on my left; to my right and ahead of me low clouds covered most of the ground. Finally, after much anxious waiting and wondering when the motor would stop, I saw some hangars, and machines flying about. Diving on one of them, I found it to be a French Sopwith.

This was good news; France and a good place to land. My last drop of gas, however, was gone, so when I tried to catch my motor to make the field, nothing doing. I made a forced landing not far from it in too small a field, and rolled off it over a road into a ditch. There my Nieuport stood, straight upon its nose with me hanging by my belt. It is now being fixed at the aviation field, but will not be ready for several days. I go back to Lunéville by train tomorrow. I do not yet know if my German will be official or not. He fell pretty far in their lines, but he was a long way up and came down in quite a spectacular manner. Someone may have seen him. If so, I get a *Croix de Guerre* with a palm. If not, the reputation of being a big bluffer. In either case, the German won't be any more bother, and that, after all, is the main thing.

A Victory Chez Nous

94th Aero Squadron, April 17, 1918

I doubt very much if anybody was ever more happy than I am now. I tried to cable you the news, but found it practically impossible from here; so I wrote Paul immediately and asked him to do it for me. But I suppose you already know something about it, for in the last two days I have been interviewed by nine reporters.

Here is the story:

On Sunday morning, April 14, I was on *alerte* from 6 a.m. till 10 a.m.; that is, I, with Lieutenant Douglas Campbell, of Harvard and California, were on emergency call duty. We were sitting in the little *alerte* tent, playing cards, waiting for a call. Our machines were outside, ready at a moment's notice. I was patrol leader. At 8.45 I was called to the 'phone; told by the information officer, who is in direct touch with all batteries and observation posts, that two German aeroplanes were about 2000 metres above the city, which is only a mile or so from here. We were told they were going east. We were rushed down to our machines in side-cars, and in another minute were off in the air. Doug started ahead of me, as I was to meet him above a certain point at 500 metres, and then take the lead. I gave him about forty-five seconds' start, and then left myself, climbing steeply in a left-hand spiral, in order to save time. I had not made a complete half-turn, and was at about 250 metres, when straight above and ahead of me in the mist of the early morning, and not more than a hundred yards away, I saw a plane coming toward me with huge black crosses on its wings and tail. I was so furious to see a Hun directly over our aviation field that I swore out loud as I opened fire.

At the same time, to avoid my bullets, he slipped into a left-hand *renversement*, and came down, firing on me. I climbed, however, in a right-hand spiral, and slipped off, coming down directly behind him and on his tail. Again I opened fire. I had him at a rare disadvantage, due to the greater speed and manoeuvrability of our wonderful machines. I fired twenty to thirty rounds at him and could see my tracers entering his machine. Then, in another moment, his plane went straight down in an uncontrolled nose dive—I had put his engine out of commission. I followed in a dive, firing all the way. At about six feet above the ground he tried to regain control of his machine, but could not, and he crashed to earth. I darted down near him, made a sharp turn by the wreck, to make sure he was out of commission, then made a victorious swoop down over him, and climbed up again to see if Doug needed any help with the other Hun:—for I had caught a glimpse of their combat out of the corner of my eye.

I rose to about 300 metres again, to see Doug on the tail of his Boche; his tracer bullets were passing through the enemy plane. I climbed a little higher, and was diving down on this second Hun, and about to fire, when I saw the German plane go up in flames and crash to earth. Doug had sent his Hun down one minute after I had shot down mine.

Mind you, the fight took place only 300 metres up, in full view of all on the ground and in the near-by town; and it took place directly above our aviation field. Furthermore, my Boche dropped about one hundred yards to the right, and Doug's one hundred yards to the left, of our field. These are remarkable facts, for one of our majors, who, with the French Army since 1915, has shot down seventeen machines, never had one land on our side of the lines—and here we go, right off the bat and stage a fight over our aerodrome and bring down two Huns right on it. It was the opportunity of a lifetime—a great chance.

When we landed, only our respective mechanics were left in the drome, to help us out of our flying clothes. The whole camp was pouring out, flying by on foot, bicycles, side-cars, automobiles; soldiers, women, children, majors, colonels, French and American—all poured out of the city; in ten minutes several thousand people must have gathered. Doug and I congratulated each other, and my mechanic, no longer military, jumping up and down, waving his hat, pounded me on the back and yelled: "Damn it! That's the stuff, old kid!" Then Campbell and I rushed to our respective Hun wrecks.

There was a huge crowd around mine, and the first man I ran into was our major—the C.O.—and he was the happiest man in the world outside of me and Doug. After him, everybody began shaking my hand. It was an awful time for me. A French and an American general blew up in a limousine to congratulate me—colonels, majors, all the pilots, all the French officers, mechanics—everybody in the town and camp. All had seen the fight. One woman, an innkeeper, told me she could sleep well from now on, and held up her baby for me to kiss.

I looked at the baby, and then felt grateful to my major, who pulled me away in the nick of time. I had my mechanics take off everything available—the machine was a wreck—but I got some splendid souvenirs. The big black German crosses from the wings, his rudder, pieces of canvas with holes from my bullets in them, all his spark-plugs, his magnetos, his mirror, clock, compass, altimeter, his clumsy signal revolver, etc.—it is a great collection. After I gathered all this stuff, and had my mechanics take it back to camp, the photographers began to arrive, and then there was another awful time. When that agony was over, they wheeled what was left of the Hun plane back to our field, and then the photographers got excited all over again. Nevertheless, they got a wonderful lot of interesting pictures—the duplicates of some I will send you under separate cover, for I don't dare trust many to the mail. I will keep all the films.

Doug returned from similar experiences, and then they worked on both of us all over. He had set his Hun machine on fire at 300 metres, and it had fallen in flames, rolling over three times, and then completely burning up. There remained but a charred wreckage, like the sacrifice of some huge animal. The Hun pilot had been thrown

"ABATTU EN FLAMMES"

out and was badly off. His face, hands, feet, nostrils, and lungs were all burnt, while his leg was broken. He is now in hospital and my Boche is probably commencing his job of ditch-digging for the rest of the war.

They got much valuable information from my man—the other couldn't speak. But I can't, of course, give that out. However, he was a Pole, said he was not an officer because he was a Pole, although he had been an "aspirant" and a pilot at the Front for two years. He said to me, with a sort of sigh of relief, throwing up his hands at the same time, "*Alors, la guerre est finie pour moi!*"

That afternoon my wrecked Hun plane and the charred result of Doug's good work were exhibited in the public square of the town, surrounded by an armed guard, and overlooked by a French military band. Not only was it a great day for me, Doug, the major, and the whole squadron, but it also was a great day for the townspeople, and has had a good m can imagine it, when you realise it took place above their roof-tops, at only 300 metres, and that they were able to see the whole fight. The Americans are, indeed, welcome in the town now, and Dong and I can buy almost anything at half-price.

An amusing incident: the fight was so near to the earth that bullets were flying dangerously all about. No one was hurt, save a French worker in a field, who received a hole through his ear from one of my bullets, and is very proud of it.

Two days later was another happy day, for Doug and I were both decorated by the French colonel (*aide* to the general of this army) with the *Croix de Guerre* with a palm leaf. That is equivalent to two *Croix de Guerre,* and you can well imagine I am proud—that was the proudest moment of my life. Also, I have received a fine letter from the Chief of the Air Service, and have been mentioned in the General Orders. Likewise the General of the Division of the American Army in this sector came to pay me a visit Furthermore, I have been proposed for the American Distinguished Service Cross, and for a promotion. Isn't that all splendid?

The ceremony of giving the *Croix de Guerre* was very impressive. The whole squadron was on parade, all the near-by French officers attended, and the French Colonel made a speech. I was a little nervous, but passed it off and everything went smoothly. The official staff photographers were there, with their movie camera and took the whole thing. Then we had to make fools of ourselves for the movies, after it was all over, by putting on our helmets, climbing in and out of our machines, and trying not to be embarrassed. It was awful. Those pictures are to be shown in America as official war photographs in about four to six weeks, so you might look out for them.

A Shot at a Boche

April 30, 1918

I hardly know what to say, as we have had nothing but rotten weather for the last week. I have accomplished nothing in the way of flying. As you see by the date above, I started this note on the 30th, but I knew that it was going to be so uninteresting that I stopped trying to write. Today is the 2nd of May and the weather continued bad until this morning. At five o'clock this afternoon the captain and five of us went out on patrol. We floated along in a beautiful clear sky about three miles and a quarter up, the highest I've ever gone, and I thought I was going to have the same uneventful trip as I had had so many times before.

Suddenly, from my position at the back of the patrol, I saw the captain *pique* down on a *biplace* machine. None of the other machines followed him; we were just making a turn and it happened that nobody saw his dive except me. I was supposed to follow the man immediately ahead of me, but I wanted to see what was going on, so I broke formation and went shooting down after the captain. He swerved off some distance from the *biplace*, which confused me for a moment, as I thought perhaps he had only dived down to take a look at the passing machine. However, I continued my descent on it and got close enough to see the gunner standing up in the back seat and distinguished the black crosses on the wings. I knew that I was going to have my first real shot at a Boche. Well, I swerved away and kept on diving. One is not supposed to attack a *biplace* from above and behind, as the gunner has a direct bead on you, which is liable to be unhealthy.

To make a long story short, I came up behind, but under him and began firing. It was difficult shooting, as I was too far behind him. Anyhow, the pilot swerved his machine, uncovering me to his gunner. I dove and swung around under his tail again. By this time I had gained on him and was not more than 600 feet behind. Well, I pulled the machine up in a climbing position until she was at an angle of forty-five degrees, and just as I got a bead on him, the motor stopped and I flopped off on a wing. Of course he pulled away from me while I caught my motor. I made the same manoeuvre again and the same thing happened. Of course, I was losing distance all the time. I made one more effort and when the motor failed the third time, I was so damned mad that I swung away.

THE DREADNAUGHT OF THE AIR

July 18, 1918

In the last few days we have had quite a little excitement. To begin with, on the 15th of July I went up with Sitterly just before dinner; we had just got the necessary altitude and were starting for the lines when one of our motors began to fall to pieces. I was in the front seat, and as I turned around, I saw some of the pieces flying out and almost hitting the *mitrailleur* in the rear. We came down all right and Sitterly was given another machine.

The second time we started out, we were supposed to have three other machines with us. Owing to motor trouble, two of them couldn't go. Three Bréguets started out just then to take photographs, so our machine had to protect them; it was very cloudy and the worst day we have had. When we got over the Boche lines, they started shooting with cannon at us, and I turned around to tell Sitterly. When I looked in front again, only a second afterwards, there were several Boches *piquing* on us—fifteen of them, and nearly all attacked our machines. One of the first bullets went through the stock of my Winchester and a piece of this bullet went through my combination: the Winchester is the only thing that saved my leg.

The fight lasted fifteen or twenty minutes, I think. Lacassagne, the French machine-gunner with us, was wounded quite badly in the beginning of the combat, but continued to fire. Bullets were going all through our machine, and the next thing I knew, I got a piece of steel in my back. The wires that control the wings were cut, and when Lacassagne changed his magazines, he let one fall on the wires that control the rudder, causing a jam there. After this there was no way of turning the machine at all, and then one of the motors got on fire. Our gasoline tanks are fixed so that by pulling a lever they can be dropped: Sitterly was right on the job and pulled the lever. The one that was on fire dropped, but the other stuck until we landed. After dropping the tank, Sitterly started down, and the Boches followed us until we landed.

They were only 300 metres over us when we landed and we were both shooting at them. At that moment one of their lucky shots put a hole through my magazine, so I couldn't shoot any more, and Lacassagne finished his last drum. When Sitterly was diving, I was shooting over the top wing and I glanced behind and saw a wood under us. It flashed through my mind that we were landing on top of the trees. Just beyond this wood there was a little field about a hundred metres square, and Sitterly came down in this, making a perfect landing.

There was an *infirmerie* a few yards away, so we were able to get at-

A CRASHED TRIPLACE

"Ground Flying" at the Chatham Bar

tention at once. We were brought down at 4.45 p.m. My wound was very slight, and I didn't want to stay in the hospital; every time I saw the doctor I asked to be let out. On the 17th I was discharged.

Sitterly certainly is a good pilot and he didn't lose his head for one minute; he has been flying every day since and has had a fight every time. The day we had our fight there were at least sixty bullets that went through the machine. There were two Boches brought down, but only one is official; I believe another machine has been given credit for this, but I honestly believe the machine-gunner with us brought it down. A general told a lieutenant in our *escadrille* that he saw the fight and was very pleased with the way we worked.

Today Sitterly went over the lines again, and had another fight. On the way back both of his motors stopped when he was over a village, and the only place he could land in was a wheat-field. The wheat caught in his wheels and the machine turned over on its back; he had two American officers with him who are attached to our *escadrille*. One of them hurt his arm and the other got a bump over the eye. Sitterly was strapped in and had to wait until the American could crawl out and take his belt off.

Since coming back to the *escadrille* I have asked the captain four times to let me go back to work; he said at first that he wanted me to take a rest, but tonight he said I could go tomorrow sure. I think he said that so I wouldn't bother him again. This big battle is on now and I would like to do my share in it.

Sitterly tells me that the other machine-gunner and I have been proposed for the *Croix de Guerre*. I think Sitterly should have it just as much as we; because if he hadn't been such a good pilot, we shouldn't be here now. Yesterday our best machine-gunner and one of the best fellows in the *escadrille* were killed; the other machine-gunner and pilot were wounded. I guess I could write a book of the things that have happened in the last week.

Single Combat

August 4, 1918

I have answered your last letter, but decided not to wait for another one before writing again. Probably one will come today at twelve o'clock. We have had rain for the past two days and consequently no flying. I expect it to clear up tomorrow, however, in which case we will get at it again. Day before yesterday I had my first real combat, but I am sorry to say I did not get the Boche. Five of us went out on patrol in the morning. I was high man and had been instructed to stay high in case of a scrap, to keep any one from dropping on us from above. After about an hour up and down the lines, the leader spotted two Boches quite a distance inside their lines. He went after them and attacked. I was watching the fight and circling around when I ran into a plane above. It was a black machine with big iron crosses painted in white. I was so excited that I never stopped to think of any rules of combat, but just pulled around slightly above and behind him and opened up. It was a foolish thing to do, for the machine was a *biplace* and his gunner had a beautiful shot at me. I should have dived down behind and come up under him.

Anyway, I didn't. I got him in my sight and started to pour lead at him from my machine gun. I could see my tracer bullets going all around him as he twisted and turned to get out of range. Another pilot who saw the fight said that his bullets were also flying all around me, but I never saw them at all. In all I fired 150 balls at him. One time I came so near that I almost ran into him and then I could hear his gun going like mad. We kept at it for about five minutes, getting farther and farther into the enemy lines. Perhaps I killed the gunner; I don't see how he missed me if he was alive and able to man his gun.

After things had gone along, as I say, for about five minutes, he suddenly disappeared, and I, finding myself all alone, decided it was about time for a speedy return to our lines. The others had long since started back, but I had lost them. The Boche anti-aircraft batteries opened up as I went back, but by turning and twisting I managed to avoid them easily. When I got home I found that not a bullet had touched my plane. I was disgusted not to have downed the Hun, and can only attribute it to the fact that I went crazy with excitement. I can still see that black body with the big white crosses, and my tracers flashing around it. The next time I get into a mix-up you can bet I'll go at it more sanely.

I am glad my first experience in a close-up fight is over. I have been in scraps before, but never so near and alone with just the one other plane to contend with. In the fight below me one plane was brought down. I don't know what got into me in my scrap. I just thought: here is my chance, I've got this man; and throwing all caution to the winds went after him. It gives me confidence, though, to have been in the fight. I had wondered before how I would act and feel. Well, I did not use my head as I should have, but at least I felt no fear. I never thought of getting hit.

We run into something almost every patrol up here, and the next time I think I can do something. My new machine, with two machine guns and 220 horse-power motor, is ready now. Until now I have been using a 180 motor and only one gun. If that one gun could make the Hun so eager to get away, what would two guns have done to him? You can simply pour out a stream of lead.

We are still in the same sector and it rather looks as if we would remain here for some time. It's good to be with the Americans. They are wonderful soldiers, as the Allies can testify. All the United States now knows what they did at Château-Thierry and thereabouts. The Boches are well aware of their prowess too.

A Raid on Ostend

August 13, 1918

August 11 proved to be a great day for me; one which I shall not forget for some time. We went to Ostend. I was sighting to drop bombs when I saw a German machine right under me—I was sitting right above the town and let go on a warehouse near the railroad. The bombs, however, nearly hit the German. I turned out toward the sea with the rest of the formation, to get out of the *barrage* which was bursting all around us. I looked up—the *barrage* had stopped suddenly—and four small, very fast planes were speeding down the coast toward us from Zeebrugge. At this moment my engine began to lose power very rapidly—so fast that I could not stay with the formation, which began to pull away. I stuck the nose of the machine down a little and in this way increased my speed so that I was able to stay under the formation. The four Boches came closer and closer.

A slight mist, through which I could barely see, now came between the formation and myself. I kept watching my tail, and sure enough the Huns had picked me out for their meat; just as I had expected, I was to be the goat. Alone, twenty miles behind the lines, and with a bum motor, the scrap started. I began to manoeuvre just as soon as one was within range of my observer's gun. Three of them came at me—they were Pfalz scouts, very fast, and handled very well. George Lowry, my observer, kept up a continual fire at them, shooting each time I manoeuvred him into position.

All three Germans came within one hundred yards of me, shooting continually. I manoeuvred constantly, changing my direction at the moment I saw one of them getting in position to fire. It was great work sitting there, shaking the stick and foot controls back and forth while my observer emptied pan after pan of bullets into the Huns. I could not shoot or do anything but sit still, watching and wiggling the controls, while the *tac-tac* of their machine guns was going behind me and the *zip-zam* of their explosive bullets passed. I let out my wrath by yelling. I was trying to encourage George, yelling encouragement, but not knowing or remembering what I said.

The noise of the German machine gun makes you try to pull in your neck, but when an explosive bullet enters the machine, two inches from your arm, and explodes on the cartridge container right in front of you, believe me, you do some tall thinking! The bullet went through that box, making a hole as big as a silver dollar, passed through my bomb-carrying gear, pierced my gasoline-tank, and finally hit the engine, taking off one of my magnetos. I never heard before of an explosive bullet going through a gas-tank without setting the plane on fire.

In this fight, Lowry thinks he brought down one of the Germans, as he saw the machine go into a spin soon after he had fired a burst into it, but as it was 'way back in Germany and no one saw it but ourselves, we are not sure. Anyway, we saw our tracer bullets going through the Hun machine just as he was going to dive on us. The machine turned over on its back and went into a spin, disappearing below. We were not able to watch it, as the other two kept us busy, and so do not know what happened to him. At any rate, he did not come back and join the fight.

Well, to make a long story short, I manoeuvred for twenty minutes, with that bad engine coughing away in front of me. By the end of that time I had arrived at the lines; I came out under the bank of mist and was seen by the formation. Two of our planes dove from above on my two persistent friends, firing as they came, and the Germans beat it back to Germany. As soon as I had support, I wanted to turn and get a few shots in on my own account, but on looking around at George I changed my mind. He had been swinging the gun turret from side to side so rapidly that he was all in. Big drops of perspiration were all over his face. He watched the Huns as they disappeared, and then turned around and patted me on the back.

I hurried home, landed, and found that the machine was badly shot up by explosive bullets; a complete wreck. The captain, who dove to help me, told me afterwards that he was afraid that it would be all up with me before he could get there. I thanked him for coming, but you should have seen his face when I told him the fight had been going on for twenty minutes!

ABOVE THE DOUGHBOYS AT SAINT-MIHIEL

September 15, 1918

At last I've got some interesting news to write about, but, as it happens, not much time to do the writing in, for we are very busy, this being the fourth day of the American attack, and orders likely to come in at any minute. However, if I am interrupted, I will continue on the instalment plan.

Of course the papers at home are full of what the army has been doing in the last few days. The attack started on the morning of September 12. We were told what was coming off the day before, so that the squadron could make all preparations possible. We knew the line of battle: where the American Army would be and the points the French hoped to take. The morning of the 12th we were up soon after daybreak; told to remain on the field with machines ready to get off at ten minutes' notice. Each pilot warmed up his motor and saw that his guns were working properly. Then we stood around and listened to the heavy artillery fire, speculating as to what was happening. It was a very windy day. The clouds were at 400 or 500 metres, and rain was falling pretty much all the time. We thought there was a possibility of not getting into the fight on account of the wretched weather.

About noon the orders came. Every aeroplane in our *groupe* was ordered to get out quickly. We were told that the Huns were retreating as fast as they could; that all roads leading from the lines were congested with traffic; that troops were being rushed up to reinforce the men being driven from the trenches, and that we were to fly at 500 metres from the ground, shooting up all traffic and all massing of troops. This is an extremely low and dangerous altitude at which to fly, for we are targets for all machine guns and anti-aircraft batteries from the ground as well as from enemy planes above.

Within seventeen minutes we had fifty-one planes in the air. They were all Spads, one-man fighting planes with two machine guns, as I have described in former letters. I was told to lead my flight to a certain junction of roads some twenty kilometres behind the enemy lines and attack the traffic and troops that were reported to be congested there. I had seven pilots in my flight, besides myself. I showed them the objective on the map, told them the course we would take, and then we were off. It was the worst weather I have ever flown in. The wind was terrific and the field so muddy we had to exercise great caution in leaving the ground. But we got together in the air, flying in a V formation. Sometimes we had to go as low as 350 metres, dodging under clouds.

ABOVE THE BATTLE

Starting out toward the lines we could see other formations going on like errands, which the aviation reports call special missions. We headed straight toward our objective. As we crossed the trenches we were so low that we could see what had gone on. The American infantry had been at work since five o'clock that morning, and they had completely swept away every bit of enemy opposition there. We saw the network of trenches, and even the barbed-wire entanglements, but very few soldiers. They had all advanced. On we went until in the distance we saw the town which marked the beginning of our objective. Up to then we had not, so far as I know, been shot at. No anti-aircraft shells, everything serene. I dove down on the road, but the reported congestion was not there. Hardly a vehicle was to be seen. We fired a few shots, anyway, attacked a railroad depot, where there were a number of freight cars, and then turning came back along the road to make sure that nothing had been overlooked. We still had a lot of ammunition left in our guns, so I began to look for other targets. It was not long before they began to appear on all sides.

Despite the clouds, our formation had kept together in the best of shape. We were flying very low, and soon began to see signs of the enemy, and of the great disorder that prevailed. We saw lines of wagons and auto trucks passing toward the rear; men hastily loading things on other conveyances and troops moving this way and that—mostly toward the rear, however. At one place behind a wood I saw a large assemblage of wagons being loaded. I dove down on these firing with both machine guns, and all seven followed. We could see the men leave their work and run in every direction: some throwing themselves flat on the ground and others ducking into the forest. It was impossible to know what actual damage our bullets did, for we were travelling at better than 120 miles an hour, and had little time for careful scrutiny. Then we passed on and caught what I estimate was a brigade of infantry all assembled behind another forest nearby. Here we all dove down again. I could see my bullets going right into the mass, and when I turned to make a second attack, saw all the other pilots going at them. They looked like a school of fish bobbing up and down. By this time the Germans were scattering as fast as they could, and as our ammunition was pretty well spent we started homewards, still in formation.

No sooner had we got under way, however, than we saw the best sight of all. Not three kilometres distant from where we had attacked the Germans we saw the first wave of Americans advancing in a perfect line, open-order formation. They were walking at a slow gait, I supposed timed to fit in with the artillery preparation that was paving the way for them. All my men returned, and that ended our work the first day. The machines were in bad shape, the mechanics working all night to get them ready for the following day.

September 13, the second day of the attack, the weather improved somewhat. There were intermittent showers, but the sun came out every now and then. At about 10.30 in the morning our Squadron was ordered to do the same kind of work as on the preceding day. I had six pilots with me and we started out to attack other roads that were farther back than those we attacked on the 12th. But things were more difficult. The weather made it possible for the Boche to get busy with his anti-aircraft cannon. Also he had posted machine-gun companies at frequent intervals all along the roads and in every village. When we got to our junction of roads, we found things as reported. German traffic toward the rear was very heavy.

There were two lines of it converging in a village and passing from there farther toward the rear. But we found something we had not expected, for there was a whole company of German infantry with rifles and machine guns on hand to keep aeroplanes away. They opened up on us the minute we were in range. I did not attempt to attack them, but passed right over their heads to get at the heavy traffic on the roads. Other pilots in the formation got busy on the infantry while the first three of us gave our attention to the roads. We could see our tracer bullets going all along the line of vehicles, men jumping from their seats, running away as fast as they could, other wagons coming from behind and jamming up against those that had stopped in the front, and before we left, traffic at those roads was in a perfect muddle, which I'll bet took some time to straighten out.

All this helped, inasmuch as our infantry was advancing very fast, and the more we could delay things, the more prisoners and property would fall into our hands. (Last night the colonel commanding our "wing" told our commanding officer that it was estimated a third of the great number of prisoners and material taken was due to the efforts of the Aviation.) Then we started back into our lines. We were met by an attack from the anti-aircraft and from countless machine guns from the ground. During the whole of the trip back, the shells were exploding all around us and we could see the tracer bullets from the ground machine guns coming right at us, into us, and all around. I felt one go into my machine with a clank, and could hear many others snapping around. Almost immediately the temperature of the engine began to go up, and I knew that the motor had been hit. However, it kept going all right. Soon the oil from the crank case began to flow out into the cockpit on the floor around my feet. When I got home I found that the bullet had pierced the cam shaft, and broken a bearing-bedding. It was necessary to put in a new engine. Three of the other pilots had been hit. One of them was forced to land just after reaching the American lines.

Pilots who worked later in the day reported a great concentration of German aviation which apparently had been rushed to this sector after the attack started. Two of our twenty-three men in this squadron were missing. Today word came from one that he is wounded and in a hospital, but the other missing from my flight has not yet been heard from.

The third day of the attack was bright and sunshiny. We were taken off "ground strafing" and made patrols over the new lines and into Germany to keep the Hun machines away from our troops. Most of the aeroplanes in my flight were out of commission; I had only two pilots to take with me when orders came for a patrol at 2500 metres over the new sector. This is called the intermediate altitude, a mean position, because it is only "halfway up," and the enemy can easily attack with great advantage from a higher position. All the time that we were flying we could see their formations about us. There were American planes up there, too, and frequent fights were taking place between them. After we had been flying for about an hour, I saw something painted red flying several thousand feet below us. As many German planes, belonging to what are called "circuses," are painted in red and other bright colours, I thought it best to look it over. So I gave the signal "on guard" to the two pilots following (a flapping of the wings) and started to dive down. We dove almost vertically.

I didn't want to start shooting until sure the plane was not one of our own. But suddenly the black crosses became plainly visible. I took careful aim and fired, as by this time we were at very close quarters. I could see my tracer bullets going right into the German machine, and just in front of it, which indicated that the burst was accurate. While firing I saw another burst come at him from another direction, another pilot getting into the scrap. The Boche flew straight for a few seconds, then fell over on his right wing, went into a spin, falling out of control to the ground, which was only a few metres below him at that time. The third pilot shot at him as he spun down to make sure that he was not playing some kind of a trick to escape. When it was over, we could see other Boche planes from above, coming toward us, so we got out as quickly as possible. When I got home there was one bullet hole through my wing. It must have come from the ground.

A Dog-Fight over the Argonne

September 29, 1918

Well, things are picking up around here. At the time I'm writing you will be reading about the Franco-American attack going on on both sides of the Argonne Forest. As this forest is right in the middle of our sector, you can imagine we are getting a bit of work.

This afternoon we wandered rather far beyond the German lines. It's impossible for us to tell the exact limit of the two armies now, because the French have advanced so much in the last couple of days. We were flying along looking for Boche machines to attack and ran into a scrap between eight or ten Fokker *monoplaces* and five Spads. There were four in our patrol and we jumped into the fight; in a couple of minutes about twenty more Boches and as many more Spads appeared. It was what the English call a "dog-fight." I steered right over the middle of the *salade* and was about 500 metres above the rest when I first attacked. I picked out a green-coloured Fokker, with white-bordered crosses, and dove almost vertically on him, using both machine guns.

I don't know how many bullets went into his machine, but if he got home alive he's lucky. He dove when he saw the bullets going through his wings and all around him, and after I pulled up he continued to dive and went on down through the layer of clouds below us (which hid the earth completely), so I can't tell whether he went clear to the ground or not. He may have redressed under the clouds, but I think not. I think I shot the pilot, although I can't tell. I was using tracer bullets in one gun and incendiary bullets in the other, so I could see them easily.

When I pulled up, I had a terrific speed, so I went upwards in a spiral and found myself on the tail of another Boche who was shooting the tar out of a Spad below. I started my guns on him, but only fired a few shots when one gun ran out of ammunition and the other jammed, so I had to come home. The scrap broke up and in the end we found that two Boches had gone down and one French machine. Rather a lucky fight for both sides, considering the numbers engaged. From what the observation posts reported, there were forty machines in the fight.

They report three machines brought down. Five of us reported firing on Boches to good advantage, but only two of them fell, so we can't tell to whom the two belong. In a fight like that, the machines will be credited to the patrols and not to the individual pilots. I was the only one in our patrol who got in any good shooting, so it was sent in on the report that "Sergeant Paden" probably brought down one of the two that fell. The French pilot who was shot down was from another *escadrille*.

I forgot to say I've been made a sergeant. My nomination came in the other day after just twenty days at the Front. That's pretty good, I think, in that short time.

The man just came in with the *service pour demain* and I've got a patrol at 6 o'clock tomorrow morning, so I must stop and go to sleep. I'm going to try for a Boche *saucisse*, or observation balloon, if I get a decent chance tomorrow morning.

The Argonne Offensive

October 3, 1918

Believe me, I'm working these days! I've been six hours over the lines today and had two combats. It's very hard work out here now, as the French have advanced on one side of the Argonne and the Americans on the other, and the line is so confoundedly crooked that we never know when we are flying over German or French territory. The old trench system can be seen, but we are away past that now and as yet the new lines are not distinguishable from the air. We find the front by going forward until the Boche antiaircraft guns begin firing at us. I went on three patrols to-day; two hours each. I was the leader of two of them. Twice while I was *chef de patrouille*, I started combats, but both times it was so far in the German lines that we didn't dare continue long enough to get any Boches. One of our group was killed today, and another, who was with me in the first patrol, was wounded in three places by bullets from a Boche machine. It is not serious, however, as they are all flesh wounds.

Two or three days ago I wrote telling of a combat I got mixed up in, in which from all appearances I got a Boche. The next day I got another! A *biplace* this time. I was flying at 10,000 feet or so and I saw him at about 5000. I dove for him and he dove for his lines. I caught him, however, and filled him full of lead. I waited until the observer turned his guns on me and then I opened up. He was a rotten shot because I saw all his bullets pass below me. He must have shut his eyes when he shot because we were only about fifty yards apart. I was straight behind him in his line of flight and a little above, so neither of us had any correction to make for firing. He was using two machine guns strapped parallel—movable, of course. He stopped firing after a few moments because he probably stopped one of my bullets and after that it was cold-blooded murder for me to shoot the pilot down; but I did it all the same, and he continued his dive into the trees.

I pulled up out of that dive and found myself clear at the Boche end of the Argonne Forest, so I crossed our lines just over the treetops. Under 15,000 feet I always go as close to the ground as possible so the anti-aircraft guns can't shoot at me. It's not the anti-aircraft shells we are so afraid of, but the Boche gunners start those big black bursts all around us and the patrols of Boche *monoplaces* can see us from a long way off. We find Boches the same way. The French anti-aircraft gunners have signals for us which change every day. They usually put up a certain number of bursts just between us and the Boches and in that way we locate their patrols or single machines. It's very hard to see another machine in the air, especially if it's below you, but you can see the anti-aircraft shells in the air; they make a cloud of smoke as big as a barn.

LATE PATROL

Au Front, October 11, 1918

We have been doing some pretty exciting and important work, helping in the attack the Americans are pushing through. The other day one of the finest fellows in the Squadron went on patrol with a couple of others and became separated. Nothing has been heard of him since. It is strange how things move on just as usual—some come and some go—yet the work is carried on as though nothing had happened. I have had little time to write because of the work, and besides I have found it difficult to come down from patrol and re-live the experiences in writing. At the time the action takes place, I feel as calm as possible, but afterwards the reaction affects me more than it used to, probably due to the letting-down of my nervous system.

Since I last wrote you I think I have bagged two more Germans. My fourth one has been officially credited, as I told you last time, and I hope these last two will eventually be confirmed. Besides having some pretty good fights, the other evening just at dusk I led a bombing expedition which was rather exciting and which received a nice little write-up in the Headquarters report. We were on *alerte*, that is, waiting to be called out on special mission. About four o'clock word came in that all available planes were to bomb and machine-gun a road between towns just inside the German lines. By the time the bombs were in place and we were ready to take off, it was quarter to five and getting rapidly darker. To make matters worse, a cloud of mist about 900 metres high was cutting off all the remaining daylight. Just as we left the field I saw an American balloon go down in flames, the Boche evidently having crossed the lines above the mist, surprising the balloon. The gun-flashes were getting more distinct as we approached the lines and the darkness fell. The five of us pushed on, heading for the burning town I saw ahead.

Flying at 600 metres we could hear the reports of the guns below us as well as feel the concussions of the blasts. The whole line was a mass of spouting flame. On the German side as we drew near, the artillery reply seemed to be just as great. As far as the eye could see the ground was flashing red and yellow fire. Then we came to the old lines, shot to pieces—nothing but shell-craters and desolation. Out of the valleys the evening mists were rising. We passed over several balloons nestling in their beds. Ahead the burning town blazed brighter than ever. In different places signal flares showed. On the German side of the lines, gas-shells were bursting with a greenish glare. Off toward the west, signal rockets were falling from a Boche artillery plane. It was pretty dark by this time. Finally we reached the burning town; and turning up the road we were to bomb and machine-gun, I dove, followed by the others. I dropped my bombs and began shooting at some dark, irregular objects on the road. What a flare the machine guns made in the darkness! I could see my tracers bouncing off the road. By this time I was at 400 metres. The others were firing and dropping their bombs at the same time.

Then my motor stopped. I had a terrible, gone feeling, I can assure you. I put the motor on the auxiliary tank and it took again. I then wheeled and headed for home. I could see the others blazing away at the road. There was a strong west wind, which made slow going, and I had only fifteen minutes of gas. By the time I started for home, the woods all back of the lines were full of little camp-fires twinkling like fireflies. I made poor time against the wind. Ahead of me were fires and landing-lights on the different Allied aviation fields, burning as beacons for the pilots still away. I did not think I could make our field, though its four lights became brighter and brighter every minute.

After fifteen minutes were up and I had not reached the field, I thought I had better land. I started to come down at one field, but found it was a dummy. A few seconds later I saw another. There were no lights, but I took off my goggles, and made two turns of the field, trying to draw the attention of the mechanics so they would put out some lights for me. When they failed to do this, I landed, anyway, in almost pitch darkness. I still had two bombs, as I discovered when I got out, which had stuck in the rack. I returned to the field in a motorcycle a little later. All the other fellows returned safely.

Yesterday morning I was leading a patrol when I sighted a Boche *biplace* coming toward our lines. I waited until he came closer, then attacked head on. He fired at me as I passed over him. The two others followed me closely, firing at the same time. I turned and attacked again from under his tail. This time he went into a vertical nose dive. There were five Fokkers above, and eleven others coming toward us, so we could not follow the *biplace* any farther. I am sure the Boche was brought down, as he fell so steeply. A few minutes later we three attacked the patrol of eleven Boches, firing whenever we got a chance. They would all come piling down upon us when we could get near, then we would hover just in front of them teasing them on. I saw a patrol of five Spads coming, so I kept up the game of tag, hoping the Spads would help us out. They did so, going around behind unobserved and attacking after a few minutes. A dog-fight followed which had no apparent result so far as I could see.

The other day a pilot attacked a Boche and was jumped by five others and sent down in flames. He dove so fast that the fire was blown out and he managed to land in our lines. It was a most remarkable happening.

The group has done mighty well, getting something like forty Boches since it was formed. Yesterday we got seven, our squadron getting three of them. The American Aviation is covering itself with honour. The other day 300 planes went to bomb a large concentration of enemy troops massing for a counterattack. Just think of that number—300! I saw 110 pass over the field. I tried to join them, but had the misfortune to blow a spark-plug. I never saw so many planes together at one time in all my life. When they came home together at sunset the sky seemed to be filled with bugs, they were so thick.

The lines have advanced steadily over most difficult ground. The advance on the western end of the American attack has been very difficult and necessarily slow. The doughboys have done mighty fine work, showing the spirit and stuff that will make Germany ask for peace.

Airman's Luck

October 12, 1918

Our squadron has now moved to another sector. We are taking part in the push, and if you look in the newspapers of this date and see where the American Army is, you will know on what part of the line we are fighting. So far, since joining the Americans at the Front, I've had about sixty hours of flying over the lines and have been in five aerial combats. In my letter to Father I told of shooting down one German aeroplane at Saint-Mihiel. The other day I had a fight with another German and succeeded in getting a number of good shots into him from very close range. He went down out of control, but as yet I have not got official credit for him, because the combat took place about twenty kilometres behind the German lines and none of the balloon observers were able to see it. However, the Group Operations Office called me up and said they thought that I'd get credit for it when the next observation reports come in.

This took place while I was with a patrol which had been sent out to protect a number of American aeroplanes on a bombing mission. While we were waiting for them I looked down and saw a German plane somewhat lower than we were and off to one side. I dove down to him and fired about one hundred shots from above and behind. He tried to manoeuvre, but didn't seem to know just what to do. One of the pilots who was with me saw him fall.

Several days after that, twenty of us (all of the available pilots from two squadrons) were sent out to bomb some troops. For this we carry four very light bombs, charged with a high explosive. We were flying in a big formation, and just as we reached our objective a patrol of seven German planes stumbled onto us through a break in the clouds. Before they could escape we were all on them. It was a regular "dog-fight." There were planes bobbing up and down everywhere. We shot five of them down, and the other two escaped by diving into the clouds and out of sight. In a fight like this you have to be very careful not to run into another plane; if this happens it is "goodnight." These odds of twenty to seven were hardly fair from the enemy standpoint, but sometimes the odds are one way and sometimes another.

The day before yesterday they worked out just the opposite. I was sent to lead a patrol of six planes to meet some large American bombing machines—those with the Liberty motors. We are supposed to escort them across the lines, where the danger of attacks from enemy aeroplanes is greatest. We went to the designated place, and were "sitting" there waiting, when all at once a formation of German pursuit planes appeared out of the clouds right over our heads. Two of my pilots had been compelled to leave us on account of motor trouble, only four remaining. The Germans in this instance not only had the advantage of numbers, but had the best position also, because they could have kept above us all the time, firing at will, while it would have been impossible for us to get our guns on them at all.

Under the circumstances there was only one thing to do, to dive away from them as quickly as possible. I gave the signal of "attention," which is made by shaking the wings of the aeroplane up and down so that all the pilots in the patrol can know you want to call their attention to something. Then I started to dive. But the Germans were already on our tails. They were shooting at us with more speed than accuracy, and we could sec tracer bullets flying all around. I guess an incendiary bullet must have hit the plane next to me, for it burst into flames with a big explosion as it plunged toward the ground. I could see that the others got free of the scrap all right, but when I pulled out of the dive there was only one machine remaining with me. The two of us started back to finish our mission and see the bombers through, but suddenly my plane began to vibrate as though it would fall to pieces, and I saw that in the steep dive a part of the engine had come loose from the base. There was nothing to do but glide down back behind our lines. The squadron commander came out in his car to bring me back while the mechanics started work getting the plane into shape.

SHOT DOWN IN FLAMES

I learned that the pilot who had gone down in flames was a young boy named Richard Phelan, who had been in my flight since the squadron was founded. He always flew on my left and we had worked up a lot of team work in manoeuvring. I felt badly about it, of course, especially to lose him in a ghastly way. When we got back to the squadron all the pilots who had taken part were discussing the fight, each telling his own experience and how he had got away. There was general gloom at the loss of Phelan, but didn't last long, because it wasn't half an hour later when an automobile stopped at our billet and out he jumped! He told us that his machine had been hit by a number of incendiary and explosive bullets. His gasoline tank had been set on fire, but by some freak of fortune it had exploded and blown clear of the machine. Also while he was going down he was able to shoot down one of the Germans. How is that for an experience? Our mechanics, who went out to get his aeroplane, learned from the infantry stationed where it had fallen that they saw him dropping down all in flames, smash up in a shell-hole, and crawl out of the wreckage without so much as a scratch.

We have lost five men during the attacks. One fellow fell behind our own lines and was killed in the crash; another was wounded, and three are missing.

SHELLED BY FRENCH BATTERIES

Au Front, October 18, 1918

Each day brings better news from all along the Front. Though the past week has been exceedingly rainy and misty, the victorious advance of the Allies has been pushed home in most convincing style. Work has been held up in our line because of this bad weather. However, the moon is changing and the sun is shining, so we are hoping for an improvement.

The past week has been rather a severe one on our squadron. The two pilots who disappeared the other day have not been heard from. One was an intimate friend of mine and an especially fine fellow. No one can understand what happened to them. The day was bad with low mists. They were last seen headed for the lines.

I started this letter just after lunch, but was interrupted by a call for a patrol. It was a special one, the whole group going out to protect some Bréguets and Liberty bombers. Another pursuit group was to bomb and shoot up roads in the same neighbourhood. I was to lead two of our squadrons, to act as protection for the high bombers. Sharply at the appointed hour we were off, forty planes leaving the ground in the space of a few minutes. The clouds at 1000 metres interfered with our rendezvous, but twenty strong we started off, meeting the other squadron on the way. There I was, at the head of a giant V of some thirty-odd planes. It was a great sight looking back on either side to see them lined up in a great ladder, stretching away as far as I could see in the hasty glances I cast backwards now and then.

We passed over the field so the major could see us. Then climbing steadily and easily, we passed over the designated point where our departure was to be observed by some U.S. officials. Here we picked up a Liberty formation, flying very close together, not more than ten or fifteen metres separating the planes. We ran parallel to each other, crossing the lines at about 400 metres. We accompanied them to their objective, about ten kilometres inside the lines, seeing only a few Hun planes flying around at a lower altitude.

By this time, for various reasons, the patrol had lost in numbers. We were only ten, yet we cruised up and down, just behind the German balloon waiting for the bombers to arrive. Off to one side we saw French shrapnel bursts, indicating German planes. But because our special business was to protect the high bombers, we stayed up. A few minutes before the appointed time, the bombers showed up. Only five, by this time, we nevertheless went to their objective with them, driving off two patrols of four Fokkers besides scaring several isolated fellows who were trying to attack the end men of the bombing formation. All the bombers got away safely, but directly they had left the air was alive with German Fokkers. I have never seen so many in all my life. They came from their own lines, in groups of ten. But they were too late, because we had accomplished our mission and were away.

On the way out my patrol attacked four Fokkers who were getting pretty close to the bombers, each one of us singling out a Boche. Mine dove away and I could not follow him because of the many others above me. One of the latter went into a *vrille*, but he came out of it, so I guess we got none of them. Below, close to the ground, we could see Spads and Fokkers whirling around in a mad scramble. One Boche fell in flames just as we headed for home. I never saw a wilder half-hour. I was bothered the whole time by a rotten motor which was missing and firing unevenly. It is just luck. It ran for forty hours before with never a miss. Now it isn't worth a continental!

A little later I managed to be almost hit by French anti-aircraft guns while chasing a German two-seater who was a thousand metres above me. I couldn't catch him, to save me. All I could do was to take pot shots at him at long range. The French shells meant for him were bursting all around me. I have seldom been shelled as badly by the Boches as I was today by our own guns. They all missed the German a mile, and missed me by feet. Behind, seven Fokkers were trailing me. I sure was sore.

The major has just told me that three men are missing from the group, one being from our Squadron. But the group got ten victories today; quite a goodly number, I should say. Tomorrow, if all goes well, we shall get more.

Le Bourrage de Crâne at a French aerodrome.

The great news from the Flanders Front continues to thrill us more each day, but I doubt more and more the German peace sincerity. They are trying to fool us, and President Wilson's latest answer is a knock-out. I am all for him, as is everybody over here. Certainly he is a wonder.

I remember when Armentières was a long, long way "in." And to see Lille was an unusual experience, except on the clearest of days. But even now I think peace still eight months off.

Escorting Liberty-DH Fours

Au Front, November 4, 1918

I suppose you have been reading of the latest American push toward the German border. It has been a most remarkable offensive, starting in the rain, yet going forward for ten miles, endeavouring to overtake the Germans with motor trucks and the like and losing comparatively few men. We are all mighty glad to have made substantial progress where it was as important as it was difficult.

The past few weeks have been wonderful, with the encouraging news of the Austrian capitulation as the very latest. Things are breaking up for the Central Powers all along the line, and if this winter does not end their resistance in occupied territory I shall be greatly surprised. These are wonderful days to be living in. Last spring's nightmare of losses still lingers in my memory. Those were dark days, but these are bright and hopeful ones, praises be! What cause for gratitude we are likely to have this coming Thanksgiving!

Today I sent one man, and probably another, to the unknown future. I saw him fall for 15,000 feet, swerving and *vrilleing*, slipping and diving, until he was merged with the brown of the autumn fields. In the twinkling of an eye such things are over and done with. I am no longer stirred or exalted over them. They are a part of the day's work.

A few minutes later I saw a plane fall 3500 metres like a blazing meteor. I watched it fall, wondering where it would strike and whether it were friend or foe. One is better off to disregard the thought that a human life is thus going out.

High and low bombing have been our special work during this latest drive. We have met many Germans and still they come at us in great numbers in the air. Today I led a patrol to go back about twenty-five kilometres for the purpose of bombing an important railroad centre and at the same time to act as protection for the regular bombing planes. Naturally we flew high, at 4500 metres. We were to meet over our objective at a specified time, the entire bunch making the rendezvous. Eight of us started, but for various reasons three dropped out before the lines were reached. As we approached the new lines I looked eagerly for fresh landmarks which would establish their exact position. Over the lines of yesterday swung an American observation balloon!

High above us four enemy planes waited for unwary prey. Off to the west eight Spads—probably Frenchmen—approached the lines. Along the edge of a forest swung a line of half a dozen French balloons, indicating the advance of the lines. Suddenly an ammunition dump blazed up dead ahead. I wondered if it were Boche or American. It seemed to be the former. There was little artillery action to reveal the new positions.

Off to the northwest the enemy were making the sky dark with shrapnel hunting for some trespassing Allied plane. On our right the same thing was going on. A patch of forest, made up of rather precipitous slopes, was being sprayed with white bursts from our own artillery.

Being a few minutes ahead of our schedule, we gained height by circling just back of our lines, being careful to give no warning of our approach to the enemy. Between us and our objective, a patrol of eleven German planes circled around above the clouds only a few hundred feet below our level. I hoped they would disappear before we crossed. I watched the black shelling grow heavier off to the east. We described another circle, and upon returning to our starting-point the Boches were no longer visible.

It was now time to proceed upon our mission, though the heavy bombing planes had not arrived. We headed for Montmédy. When a dozen kilometres or so inside I saw the Boche patrol of eleven Fokkers coming for us from the south. I headed straight on waiting to see what would happen. We had some height on them. Three came directly up at us and the others began circling us. I observed the altitude they were gaining, and because we were loaded with bombs, I thought best to head for a small town. Accordingly I dropped my bombs there and the others of my patrol did likewise. Then we turned and jumped four of the Fokkers. My right gun jammed and I had to pull up to fix it. The other chap followed the Boche down several hundred metres and saw him disappear in *vrille*. I found another Boche and promptly dove on him, getting in some pretty good bursts. Another was following me with a steady stream of fire. I was not conscious of it and only learned of the fact when I got back. The plane I was attacking pitched up on one side and went down in a straight dive falling off first on one wing and then on another. I watched him descend about 2500 metres until he disappeared.

A few seconds later I looked down and saw a band of about eleven Liberties passing with one lone German diving on them. He went on past, pulling up below them, then doing a *renversement* and diving away toward home. I couldn't go for him on account of the Germans surrounding me.

In the meantime another Spad had come along with a Boche on his tail. One of our fellows disposed of this pursuer, allowing the Spad to escape.

Then a formation of five Liberties passed under me, one solitary Boche above them. I dove on the Boche and got in a burst of about forty shots at a distance of twenty-five metres. He went off on a wing, out of control, falling about 500 metres, when I lost sight of him. I was so close I nearly rammed this fellow and I could see my bullets entering his plane. These planes had white rudders with black crosses and dark-blue stabilizers with lighter blue edges. They maneuvered none too well, unlike those of the previous day who had out-manoeuvred and out-fought three of our best pilots besides wounding a new pilot in the leg.

After this fight I saw no more Germans, so escorted the bombing formations as they came to and from the objective. Results must have been excellent, for I observed a great conflagration in a railroad yard. As my gas was running low, I came home, the others of the patrol having been separated from me in the "dog-fight." It was a most satisfactory day and each succeeding one will surely bring even greater results.

Nearing the End

November 10, 1918

Today is Sunday, November 10, and by tomorrow morning at eleven o'clock, I am sure the war will be over so far as fighting is concerned. None of us in my group see how the Boches can possibly fight on. We are all curious to know just what the end will mean for us; how we'll be mustered out and when; what the United States will look like when we return, etc. I don't believe the A.E.F. will be pleased to see a "dry" America. Every man over here swears that he'll never work again. Of course, not one of them is serious.

However, the end may not be here at that. I wish they'd either end the war or end the peace talk. The latter is very demoralising to the forces. Personally, I would just as soon keep on fighting. It has been the greatest thing that could have happened to me. Besides being a wonderful adventure, it shows you what you're made of and brings out the best in every one who fights on the right side and plays the game in a sportsmanlike way. The worst part of it all is the loss of friends. In our squadron of twenty-one pilots we've had fifty *per cent* casualties since the drive at Saint-Mihiel. Eleven of them are dead, wounded, or missing. This is rather heavy, but I think we have done our work pretty well.

Now for a little bragging. Since I wrote last, I've shot down another plane and a German observation balloon. This brings my total victories to four. I need one more to be classed as an "ace" and hope to get it before hostilities cease. The combat in which the plane fell took place a couple of weeks ago. We were patrolling over the sector for the purpose of protecting aeroplanes employed in regulating the fire of our artillery. I was leading a patrol of five or six and at an altitude of 7000 feet saw a group of four German single-seaters coming toward our lines. They were a little higher than we, and just behind them was a second German patrol of nine or ten machines. I figured that we could attack the first four and get out of the way before the others could catch us at a disadvantage. There was one German a little ahead of the rest, so I picked on him. We were going, head on, at one another at a rate well over 100 miles an hour, and, naturally, it didn't take long to get into action. Both of us started shooting at the same second. I expected him to get excited and try to turn out in front of me, and he probably expected me to do the same thing.

He didn't turn, but kept coming right on. We were shooting as fast as the guns would work. I could see my tracer bullets going into and all around his machine, and out of the corner of my eyes could see his tracers going all about me. A man who was flying near by said there was a solid column of smoke from the bullets stretching between our machines, and he didn't see how either survived it. We passed by so close a margin that it looked as though the German's wheels missed my top plane by a fraction of an inch. The second he was past I tried to swing my plane around so as to "get on his tail." I looked up and saw that he was swinging about, too. We were doing vertical turns almost on the same axle, figuratively speaking, he so close above me that I could see his face. While watching him I paid too little attention to what I was doing, with the result that I "missed the turn" and my machine fell for a few turns of a *vrille*, out of control.

But when I stopped this and looked about again, I saw that the Hun was falling. My bullets had taken effect, for down he went, landing inside our lines.

While I had been having my personal scrap with this fellow, a regular "dog-fight" had been going on behind during which two others in the patrol accounted for a German each, one of which fell in flames. All our men returned home unscratched. My bus had been hit by three or four bullets, one of them going right through the main spar of the right-hand lower wing, which weakened it so that it had to be changed. Two other bullets had ripped a hole in the tail, but had done no other damage.

The observation balloon was shot down two or three days ago. We were on a strafing expedition, flying very near the ground and looking for troops to shoot up. The balloon was at about 1200 feet, apparently fastened to a motor-truck base, for it was being towed farther back when we attacked it. A couple of small bombs dropped at its base stopped all activity below and a few bullets set the bag on fire. No observer jumped with his parachute, as is usual in the case of balloon attacks. I don't know whether he had been killed by the bullets, was afraid to jump, or whether the balloon had been sent up without any one in it. Just after the balloon fell in flames, we found a battery of artillery going along a road. We attacked this and chased all the Germans into the woods.

AFTER THE ARMISTICE

Toul, November 12, 1918

It is hard to believe that the whole show is really over and that we shall probably never have to fight again. Yesterday morning they called me up from Headquarters and said that no more patrols were to go out—as the Armistice went into effect at 11 a.m. I hung up the receiver with a sort of a "Well! What do we do now?" feeling. It is a wonderful relief to have it over, but it does leave you with a very much let-down feeling, as though one had suddenly lost one's job. Having been at it so long, it almost seems as though one had never done anything else and that one's reason for existing had suddenly ceased. I wish I could simply drop everything and come home, but I fear that time is still a long way off. With 125 officers and about 950 men on my hands, I shall be mighty busy devising means to keep them well and amused and out of mischief.

Then, again, this being only an armistice, the formation of the group, gathering of supplies, planes, etc., goes on as usual as though the war were to last forever, so that I shall be just as busy as if nothing had happened. Our days of air fighting are over, I guess, but the administration and organisation work goes on as usual and I am mighty sick of it. We shall be a sort of international police for a while, but here's hoping they hurry up with the peace confab so that we can all close up shop and come home. It will be immensely interesting, though, if we should be sent up to the Rhine for a while.

What do you all think of the Armistice terms? If they go through with them, they do not leave the Germans much chance to start the war again, do they? There does not seem one chance in a thousand that there will be any more fighting outside of what the Boches may do to each other if there ration. When one thinks of the critical situation in which we were last June, it seems nothing less than a miracle that this wonderful change should have come about and the war be over in so short a time. I suppose Full will be considered the world's greatest general and he certainly deserves it. No man ever had as difficult and stupendous a job handed over to him, and it is hard to see how he could have handled it better.

I wish I could get off for a few days and go to Paris, for there are a number of people there I should like to see, to say nothing of the tremendous celebration they must be having. I ran over to Nancy last night in my car, and if the spree in Paris was like the one there, it must have been a wild night on the *boulevards*.

ON THE BOULEVARD DES CAPUCINES

Am afraid, however, that I shall have to miss it all, for there seems to be little prospect of my getting away just now. Perhaps a little later I can arrange it. I hope so, for I feel pretty stale and think a few days' change would do me good. I will admit now that there have been days recently when I did not want to fly a bit; the losses in the squadron were so heavy that it was hard not to let it get on one's nerves. Twelve pilots in three weeks is pretty hard on the morale of the ten who are left. I am speaking of the original members, for a squadron is, of course, kept up to strength by replacements. Things went much better afterward, however, and for a month we had no losses at all and the squadron did some good work. A couple of days after I left it seven of them jumped on seven Fokkers and shot down six without any of our men even getting their planes shot up. That is a clean-up which is hard to beat; in fact, the most successful fight I have ever heard of and I certainly hated to miss it.

Now the open season for Huns is over and you can't half guess how glad I am. Tonight the moon is shining and we admire it instead of swearing at it and taking to the dugouts. It is almost too good to be true to think that before very long we shall be home again. There have naturally been a good many days when the chance of ever getting back again seemed a bit slim, and it is hard to realise that I shall some day be shooting ducks on the river once more. The losses in the 13th Squadron were pretty high, but recent reports received through the Red Cross make things look brighter. Of the eleven men who went down inside the German lines up to the time of my leaving the squadron, six were not killed, but are prisoners, some of them wounded, but just how badly we do not know. During offensives such as we have had in the last couple of months considerable losses are, of course, to be expected. I remember that in my old French squadron during the four months of the battle for the Passchendaele Ridge, we lost nine out of the original fourteen, but of these nine two were killed in accidents.

8
Prisoners of War

SHOT DOWN IN GERMANY

1
My capture was the result of a series of bizarre accidents which happen only in the air. Three of us, Eddie Rickenbacker, Edward Green, and myself, all of the 94th, had gone out in answer to an *alerte* from an infantry observation post. An enemy formation had been sighted approaching our lines in the region of Pont-à-Mousson. After a twenty minutes' search we saw them, five Albatross single-seaters, north and cast of the town. At that period the 94th Squadron was equipped with a new kind of craft, the Nieuport, type 28, a single-seater with rotary motor, built by the French Nieuport Company. It was a splendid little bus for pleasure purposes. It manoeuvred well, climbed rapidly, and was better than a Spad for acrobacy. But it had been rejected by the French Government as being too flimsily built for combat.

The U.S. Air Service had just started work at the actual front, and had been compelled to accept these Nieuports as plane equipment for the 94th; for the French were not then able to live up to their agreement to furnish American pursuit squadrons with Spads, their best type of combat machine. All of which explains one of the "series of bizarre accidents," for had we been flying our trusty old Spads, I should not have had to cool my heels in a *kriegsgefangenen Lager*, "ground-flying," after the fashion of aviator prisoners of war.

The combat started at 14,000 feet. Having the advantage of the enemy in altitude, we attacked immediately, they being compelled to dive farther into their own lines because of their inferior position. While dropping vertically upon the enemy nearest me, the fabric covering the upper surface of my upper right plane, burst along the leading edge, throwing my machine completely out of balance. Compelled to leave the combat immediately, I turned toward our lines which I could see in the distance, but, oh! so very far away! The wide rent in the fabric of the wing increased in size under the steady encouragement of the wind. Other strips ripped loose and flapped and fluttered out behind. Enemy anti-aircraft fire was brisk and increasingly accurate during that precarious journey homeward.

Owing to the damaged wing, I was unable to manoeuvre. It was a moment of intense excitement. All airmen have known similar ones when their hopes of safety hung in a balance jauntily swaying back and forth, with old Godfather Chance jiggling the scales in a purely vindictive mood. Looking behind me, I saw my former quarry become huntsman, climbing toward my level for all he was worth. Occasionally he would pull up and fire a burst in my direction. But he was yet too far distant and too far below me to make accurate practice.

The bark of the "Archies" was really ominous. When those dogs are on the scent, and one's old bus is worn out and incapable of swift flight, how vicious they seem, and how they snap at one's heels! Suddenly I felt my plane give a violent lurch. The motor spilled forward, wrenched partially loose from its bed, and down we went, plane and pilot, toward that inhospitable land bounded by German trenches. It was not until afterward that I learned the reason for the sudden descent. A small incendiary shell from a quick-firing gun had struck my engine. It stuck there, and failed to explode, but ended for all time the delicate functioning of that marvellous little Rhone motor. I have never heard of a more remarkable hit. Somewhere in the archives of the German Aviation Service there is a large photograph taken close to my motor, showing the shell wedged into it. The officer of the German anti-aircraft battery which made the lucky shot, showed it to me a few days later at Jarny where I was in a hospital.

I wondered, in that peculiarly objective way which is the most amazing thing to reflect upon afterward, what the result of this adventure was to be. I believed, at the moment, that I didn't much care, for I had read many stories of the treatment by the enemy of Allied prisoners of war. Death seemed a preferable fate.

The suspense was not long drawn out. Aerial troubles bring intense anxiety, but they have the merit of passing almost with the swiftness of thought. I remember the elemental roughness of Mother Earth's welcoming embrace, a shock of pain in legs and head, and then, despite my fear of German prison camps, the great surge of joy at the consciousness of being alive. After all, life is sweet, and a few moments of illuminating experience taught me how much more truthful one's instincts are than one's professed beliefs. I thought that I wanted to be killed, but Nature knows what is good for us and doesn't take any stock in our melodramatics. At any rate, she very effectively overruled my impulse, if I really had one, to let matters take their course. She merely gave me a fleeting but very vivid glimpse of a green field, spinning up to meet me. And I gave a violent pull on my control stick in an effort to save myself from a too hasty contact. The result was that I did not crash hopelessly, and now have behind me an experience which was, in a melancholy way, some compensation for the loss of freedom.

Seeing German soldiers rushing from all sides toward my machine, I expected rough usage, and scowled in what I thought must be true Hauptmann fashion, hoping to overawe them. This was a needless effort. One of the first men to reach me said, "You are hurt, sir-r-r?" in good German English. I told him that I was, a little, whereupon he immediately called two others. They lifted me gently out of my seat, and carried me to a dugout at the edge of the wood. It is a temptation to digress here, and give a description of that underground officers' mess-room, but this is beside the story. It was a wonderful place, though, beautifully and strongly built, and as neat inside as a New England kitchen.

A good many soldiers followed me down into the dugout. I felt uneasy when I saw no officers among them, thinking: "This is where I lose my few possessions, and Lord knows when I'll get a new outfit of clothing." However, although they could have taken everything from me in the absence of their officers, and no one any the wiser, not the slightest attempt was made to do it. Instead of that, an elderly German orderly brought me a cup of hot coffee from a compact little kitchen adjoining the mess-room. Or, to be more exact, it was the German substitute for coffee, made, I believe, of roasted nuts and grains. It was not good, black, but with milk and sugar, furnished later by a wonderful American Red Cross, one can drink it with pleasure.

An ambulance man came, and in a jiffy he had my right leg in splints and carefully bandaged, and my head bound up. Then I was given a German cigarette and began to think: "This is not going to be so bad as I thought." The soldiers cleared out in a hurry upon the arrival of an officer. He saluted with a stiff little bow from the hips, as Germans always do, told me in English that he was sorry, but "for-

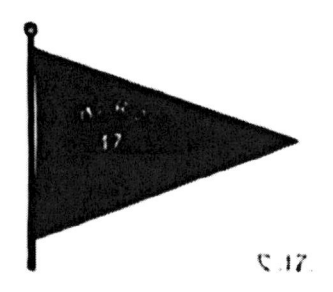

C. 17.

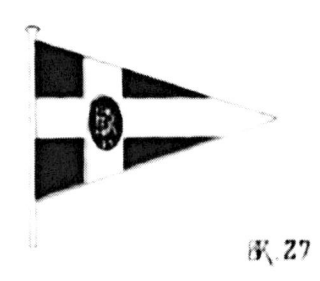

BR. 27

Spa. 24

Spa. 30

C. 74

BR. 66

INSIGNIA OF FRENCH ESCADRILLES IN WHICH MEMBERS
OF THE LAFAYETTE FLYING CORPS SERVED.
PLATE 7

tunes of war," etc. Then he asked if I would let him see my papers. Luckily I had nothing but 800 *francs* in money—it was the first of the month—and my identification card. At least I thought I had nothing else, although later I found a typewritten sheet of squadron orders in my trousers pocket. In a moment of unguarded leisure I chewed this up and swallowed it, my stomach receiving the morsel not gladly, but in a spirit of admirable resignation. The officer kept the card, returning my pocketbook and money, accepting my word for it that I had nothing else.

About half an hour after this, several other officers—aviators—arrived. Each of them saluted and bowed in the same smart, soldierly, but rather odd way. Then one of them said that they had had the honour—a nice way to put it, I thought—of fighting with my patrol that morning, and that my two comrades had returned safely. Without any apparent bitterness, he added that, as a result of the combat, a pilot of their squadron had fallen in flames and was burned to death. (This machine was brought down by Eddie Rickenbacker, needless to say a fine *chasse* pilot.) He inquired about my injuries, and told me that the nearest hospital was at some distance. If I could endure the delay, they would be glad to have me lunch with them at their squadron headquarters which was not far out of the way. I accepted with a good deal of reluctance, not feeling in a company mood, but brightened a bit at the thought of what had just been happening. This might have been a conversation among friends in front of the Café de la Paix in Paris.

As they carried me to their car, I felt more like a pampered Back Bay baby, going for an airing in the Boston Public Garden, than a prisoner of war. They left me in the car at the side of the road, while they went over to have a look at my wrecked machine. This gave me a moment of leisure for collecting my thoughts. I had often been warned that a prisoner must be very much on his guard. I had heard that a favourite German ruse with a captured aviator is to take him to a squadron mess, wine and dine him, particularly the first, so that he may forget his caution. Then, when he is sufficiently mellow, they pump him dry of information and send him on his way, feeling well repaid for their liberal expenditure of good Rhine wine. Sometimes, so I had been told, they try brow-beating, a good deal depending upon their estimate of the captive.

I hoped that this latter would be the method chosen with me. It is hard to be suspicious of courteous and hospitable treatment; but one can easily meet an attack which is a straightforward attempt at "bulldozing." I knew, of course, that prisoners have their rights and cannot be forced to talk.

I had a homesick moment while sitting there, thinking of the uncertain future, aware that, for me, even an attempt at escape was out of the question for months to come. Far in the distance I heard the faint drone of rotary motors, a sound high-pitched, familiar, terribly saddening under those circumstances. It could come, I knew, from the machines of only one squadron, the 94th. Very soon I saw them, flying very high, almost directly overhead. Shrapnel was bursting in their vicinity with the far-off plopping sound, drowsy, hardly audible from a point more than two miles beneath them. They were moving unconcernedly on, tipping up now and then in a steep bank, making jaunty earth-scrutinizing changes of direction which told me that they were perhaps searching for some trace of me. I wanted to shout, to wave my hand, to pull myself by my boot-tops, away from the solid earth. If only I could have reached up far enough to tighten my fingers around a tail skid, I felt that I could hang on long enough to be carried across that little strip of enemy ground.

Then I could have dropped into the Moselle where it flows through friendly territory. But they were miles above me, and so I sat there watching them, helpless and sick at heart. Presently they turned westward and disappeared in the morning haze. They were not more than ten minutes' distance from the old aerodrome. They would be landing there before the smoke from the shrapnel bursts had been ravelled out by the wind. My own distance from that green, secluded, sunlit field, I made no attempt at that time to compute.

It was a ride of about fifteen kilometres to the aerodrome of the German squadron. I learned that these officers belonged to a combat group lying directly opposite our own sector of the Front. The town near which they were stationed had been a place of considerable interest to us. We had often talked among ourselves about this very group of German pilots, wondered how they lived, what they did between patrol times, what they said of us. Evidently they were equally curious. Had it not been war-time, and had I been in a more comfortable frame of mind, we might have had a very interesting chat, comparing notes as to time and place of combats. Some of them spoke French and others English.

But I had to keep clear of the subject, lest I should disclose, even approximately, the location of our squadron. My German hosts, or captors—I hardly knew in which light to consider them then—respected the difficulty of my position and asked no embarrassing questions.

They were quartered in a comfortable old house in the town, much better accommodation, in fact, than any we had ever had on our side of the lines. But, of course, we were not living in invaded territory. We could not commandeer any dwelling which pleased our fancy and order out the rightful owners. The enemy had the better of us there. While we were waiting for lunch, one of the men sat down to the piano and played some French music, songs which I had heard in our own mess at Tours only a day or two before. For a moment I was tempted to let my preconceived notions of the Germans go to the deuce, and talk as one human being likes to talk to another. I wanted to let down the barrier of reserve as they seemed ready to do. Then came the suspicion: "This is doubtless a part of the game. First the mellowing influence of music, then that of wine, and then the indiscreet disclosures." It is far better that a prisoner of war be too cautious than not cautious enough. Furthermore, American aviators were rarities on the German side of the lines at that time, and I knew that the enemy were mighty curious about the plans and the organisation of our Air Force.

Well, the wine proved to be *café au lait!* First we had a roast, then a salad, dessert, and the coffee to wind up with. No wine, no liqueurs of any sort. I felt rather relieved, of course, and amused as well. Although they did not know it, they were quieting my fears with a vengeance. I could not have objected to one glass of wine, and a Benedictine with the coffee.

Everything was open and aboveboard in so far as I could judge. None of the officers felt it his duty to act as a self-appointed intelligence officer. I was even informed beforehand that one acting in that capacity was coming soon to see me, so that I was ready for him when he did appear. He was a man of about forty-five, erect, soldierly looking, with a pleasant face, not at all the Prussian type of official I had expected to see. He greeted me in a jovial sort of way with "Well, H——, tell us all about it. What are you people doing over there?" I thought to myself: "Watch your step! That hearty, last-name sort of greeting does very well in America, but it isn't a German practice." However, it certainly seemed natural enough, and I decided that I could meet apparent friendliness with apparent friendliness without damaging the Allied cause greatly. So I said: "All right, major. You know how we Americans love to brag. Ask me whatever you want to know."

He began by asking me what my belief was about the treatment I should receive at the hands of my captors. "Now tell me frankly," he said, "haven't you expected that your ears would be cut off, or your tongue slit—something of that kind?" I said that I had heard some pretty damning things relative to the German treatment of prisoners of war, but—oh, subtle flattery!—but I knew that there were good Germans as well as bad ones, and that I was delighted at finding that I had fallen into the hands of the decent ones.

We talked of this and kindred matters for some time, and I got the following information applicable to my own situation: Much would depend, in so far as my welfare as a prisoner was concerned, upon the German officer in charge of my particular camp. Some of them were decent and some bad. The best camps, the intelligence officer thought, were in the south of Germany. "You may consider yourself lucky," he said, "if you are sent to the south."

Thus far I had done a good deal of the quizzing. It was now my turn to answer, or to refuse to answer, questions. However, I was first told by this officer what he knew, or thought he knew, of the movements of our troops, the organisation of our Air Force; what squadrons were on the Front, what others were soon to be there, etc. He told me also of the movements of British and French squadrons, and showed me splendid photographs of Allied aerodromes along the Meuse and Toul sectors. While some of his information was wrong, a good deal of it was, to my knowledge, quite accurate. However, of course, I made no comment one way or the other at that time. And when, among other photographs, I saw a beautiful one of my own aerodrome, I believe that I successfully registered only polite interest. This cost some effort. I had seen that view of our field many times when going out on patrol or upon returning home, and the thought that I might never see it so again was a bitter one.

He told me he knew exactly where my squadron was located and how long it had been there; but evidently he did not, for he was anxious that I should either confirm or deny his statements. Finally I said: "I'll tell you what I'll do, major. I will leave the matter to these officers. Supposing that one of them is in my position as a prisoner, being questioned by one of our intelligence officers. If any one of them will honestly say that under these conditions he would be willing to give the location of his squadron headquarters, I'll tell you where mine is."

It would have been awkward not to have fulfilled this promise had there been occasion for doing so. But those pilots were gentlemen. All of them said that in my place they would do as I was doing.

The major was a decent old fellow, and didn't question me any further. On several occasions he sent greetings on to me by other American aviators who have passed through his hands.

After the examination, my airmen hosts—they had proved to be hosts after all—ordered their car, and the major, and an officer from Group Headquarters went with me to the war hospital at Jarny, not far from Metz. The pilots of the squadron were on patrol duty, and when leaving the town, we passed their aerodrome just as some of them were taking off. It gave me a strange thrill to see those Albatross and Pfalz single-seaters, with their provocative black crosses, so close at hand; and a terrible feeling of homesickness, to be sitting there, impotently watching them, knowing that for me the war was over, at least for a long time to come.

"A SNAPSHOT OF MY WRECKED MACHINE"

I must not forget to speak of another courtesy extended me by the pilots of this German squadron, one which, I believe, cost the pilot who did it his own freedom. It is a practice among airmen of whatever nationality, in case of the capture of an enemy pilot, to drop a message giving this information on his own side of the lines. I had asked if this might be done for me, adding, for caution's sake, that they might throw it out anywhere between Verdun and the Vosges Mountains. They replied that they would willingly deliver such a message, and they did. Some Americans from my own group, captured later, told me that the note was dropped, and received, and that the German pilot who carried it was shot down in our own lines and made a prisoner.

On the way to the hospital I discovered that I had left my flying helmet and gloves in the dugout near the field where I fell. I spoke of this in some by-the-way fashion. I think I said that the helmet had a sentimental value which made me sorry to lose it. Two or three days later one of the pilots came to the hospital to see me, bringing both helmet and gloves. Not only that: he also brought me some snapshots of my wrecked machine, souvenirs which are very precious to me now. In order to get my helmet and gloves he had had to make a journey of about thirty-five kilometres—a pretty decent thing, I thought, for one's enemy to do.

2

Paris, December 20, 1918

Now that I am a free man again I will tell you how I was persuaded to land in Germany last summer. We left the ground at just 10.30, fifteen Spads in two patrols, one group to fly at 2500 metres and the second at 3000. I was on low patrol, but because of the clouds we were never higher than 1500 metres. West of Rheims we had to fly still lower, and then became separated in the mist. I saw that I was falling behind the Spad nearest me, and had just opened my throttle a few notches, when I heard a machine gun directly behind me. Just as I turned to locate the German, he dove past me, so I got on his tail and let fly. I saw my tracers going all around him, then he made a sharp turn and kept going down as if to land, so I pulled up to start climbing, hoping to find my patrol. I found at once that something was wrong with my controls. The rudder wouldn't respond at all, and I kept going around to the right.

I heard more machine guns very close, making a great racket even above the sound of my motor. I hated to look behind me, for I expected to see at least a dozen Boches coming down full tilt. But I looked just the same, mighty quickly. There wasn't a machine to be seen anywhere! Then I understood. I was being fired at from the ground. I was very low and coming down all of the time, for my controls were useless, and the only thing I could do was to keep from falling in a spin, no very great satisfaction. I thought, "if I can only keep going a little longer!"—for I knew that I was in German lines. I remembered Frank Baylies and Steve Tyson, landing in No Man's Land. An hour before that kind of an experience would have seemed bad enough, but I now should have welcomed it with joy.

Well, I came down at last, in an orchard, smashing beautifully, and although I was pretty badly dazed, I realised that the coal-scuttle helmets which came bobbing toward me covered Boche soldiers. They lifted me out of the wreckage, and in less than three minutes had a first-aid dressing on me. Then they carried me to a battery of "seventy-sevens" a short distance away where there was an officer. They laid me out on a blanket behind the guns and gave me a large cup of champagne and a cigarette. I replied to the officer's questions in German, which seemed to surprise him a good deal. While we were talking, another officer, the observer for the battery, called our attention to a solid sheet of flame which was falling out of the clouds about three miles away. He said that it was a German machine which cheered me up a good deal. That made the result one and one.

These two officers were very anxious that I should admit that they shot me down. I was grateful for the champagne and the cigarettes, and so I said that I supposed they had. They immediately rushed to a telephone and reported that their anti-aircraft machine guns had brought down a Spad. One of the officers told me that this would mean a citation and five hundred *marks* for him. He was pretty happy and I was pretty miserable, although I didn't let him know it. But at any rate I was a good deal luckier than the poor devil we had just seen falling in flames; and now that the show is over I'm glad I had the experience; for as Chuck Kerwood says of Germany and the Germans, "Wonderful people, wonderful country, and, oh! such exquisite soup!"

Kriegsgefangenen Sendung

1

Kriegsgefangenen-Staumlager, Lazarett 4. Trier
September 1, 1918

First let me tell you of the fight. I was leading a large patrol of our machines on July 31, and gave battle to an equal number of German aeroplanes at an altitude of 18,000 feet. I picked out one man who hovered above the rest for my adversary. We fought for fifteen minutes without touching each other with our machine guns. Suddenly a third machine swooped up from below, and before I could turn fully upon him, he had opened fire and unluckily wounded me severely in the left arm. My engine also was put out of commission. Nevertheless, I had plenty of altitude to make France and started to glide. But my opponent wanted to make sure of me and followed, firing all the while. This caused me to zigzag and lose distance, in order to avoid his bullets. Finally I landed safely—Lord knows how—in a shell-shot field, crawled out of my machine, saw strange uniforms on soldiers, and fainted. I was a lucky man to get down alive—18,000 feet with one arm. I don't clearly remember much that passed in the next three days, until I found myself being well cared for in a German hospital.

The wound in my arm was very serious. The upper arm was practically all shot away. I had a compound fracture, and my hand was riddled. There was no articulation. For three weeks they tried to save my arm, but it could not be done. At the end of that time, with my consent, my arm was amputated, about six inches below the shoulder.

A little later I was moved farther into Germany to this hospital. Here I am excellently cared for. I am in a ward for Allied officers only. I am in a bed next to an English lieutenant, who is a peach, and there are also two splendid French officers—just the four of us. We have an excellent time together, and are all very content. We eat very well, and the doctors and nurses are first-class and sympathetic. My arm is coming along with no trouble at all. Today the doctor told me that in a week I should be up and walking around and that in three or four I would be entirely well. I am in splendid health, outside of my wound, with good colour, good spirits, and appetite. I eat enough for two men.

This letter is most badly written, as I am in bed. We are allowed to write two letters a month from this hospital (or from anywhere I go) and these I will send to you. In all cases, I suppose, they will not get through, but some will. Of course they will take time. Also, we are allowed four postcards a month. These I will save for Paul in France, or my captain, because they will be received quicker and the news can be cabled to you. You can write me, *via* Holland, care of the address on the envelope.

What a time you must have gone through, mother dear, for the first few weeks when you didn't know whether I was killed or prisoner. But I knew you would be brave, and would patiently wait for definite news. I informed the International Red Cross as soon as possible, so that the news of my being alive must have been out soon. But there is no need to worry any more at all.

Furthermore, in all probability, when I get well, I shall be sent back to France by way of Switzerland. This is done to all soldiers and officers who have had an amputation, or who are otherwise no longer fit to wage war. In that case, I should, upon arrival in France, go as soon as possible to America. Of course it will take some time, and one is not sent as soon as one is well, but, mother dearest, in all probability I shall be home for Christmas. Think of it! Of course it is not sure, but darn near.

Don't worry about me. I am coming along fine, well cared for, and in splendid health and spirits. Be brave and cheerful, mother, as I know you will. Think of how lucky I am—only my left arm. It might have been one hundred things worse—and any other limb would have been worse. So cheer-o: as my English neighbour says.

2

Kriegsgefangenen Lager
Landshut, Bayern

I am still at Landshut: in the best of health and getting a lot more cigarettes. They are nothing much to boast of, but still they are a smoke. I am supplied with enough money.

There isn't much news to write about here. The weather has been rainy for the past week, so I have missed the sun bath in the morning, but the shower baths are still the greatest advantage of the camp. I think that we Americans may be here for quite some time. There are several of us here now; Whitmore, McKee, Hitchcock, and others in the U.S. Service. We can buy sardines, beer, canned peas, beans, and jam, so we are not badly off for food.

I don't think I have told how I was brought down. Two of us were attacked by at least ten German machines. I got a bullet through my gasoline tank and it caught fire. I did a wing slip and kept the flames away from me until I reached the ground, where I landed all right and jumped, but without being burnt a bit. It was certainly lucky that I wasn't high, only about 800 metres. I landed a couple of kilometres behind the front line. Just after I jumped out, I saw the other fellow, who was with me, coming down in flames also. He crashed behind some trees and I ran over to see how he was. He was killed in the air, I think, and had smashed all to pieces in landing. He was a French-

AMERICAN AVIATOR PRISONERS AT LANDSHUT, BAVARIA, SEPTEMBER, 1918

man who had recently joined the *escadrille*, a good pilot, too, who had brought down four Germans. A German came up then and I had to leave him. I walked back several miles and then they put me in s car and drove me to a town quite a way from the Front. There I joined some other French pilots and we took the train back into Germany, spent two days at the camp at Giessen, and then about three weeks at Darmstadt, a French camp, and finally came here, where there are no French at all, so I suppose I shall stay with Americans from now on.

TRAUSNITZ CASTLE, LANDSHUT, BAVARIA
A prison camp for American Aviators, summer of 1918

3

Here I am at my next camp. Arrived a week ago from Stralsund, where I was sent with the two Royal Flying Corps officers with whom I escaped from Landshut. There are no aviators here except myself and a Frenchman, and he is in the hospital with a wounded foot. The prisoners are English, French, and Russians. I am quartered with the English. I am getting food from the French Committee.

A few days before I left Stralsund I received a package from the American Red Cross in Berne which helped tremendously. It contained ten boxes of crackers, too cigarettes, soap, rice, two tins of corned beef, and three tins of pork and beans. Hope I receive another one soon, mainly on account of the cigarettes, for I am not so badly off for food. A British corporal who came with me from Stralsund

PRISON CAMP FOR ALLIED OFFICERS, KARLSRUHE, BADEN

OFFICERS' MESS AT KARLSRUHE PRISON CAMP

gets stuff from the British Committee and with my supplies from the French we get along all right. I received 225 *marks* from Stralsund yesterday, where I had written out a cheque, so I have enough money for the present.

I don't think this is a bad camp, there is only one roll-call, at eight in the morning. Everybody cooks in little braziers out in the middle of the square. We get our wood from the Russians, who keep two big charcoal braziers going all the time. They charge two cents for making tea and three cents for cooking rice or potatoes or other vegetables. I have sent a postcard to the American Red Cross to let them know of my new address. The French are giving a show tonight at nine o'clock. It is a translation from an American play, *Baby Mine*.

Escaped

Bellevue Palace Hotel, Berne
August 30, 1918

I am free! Thank God! Ever since I arrived in Lechfeld two months ago, and my wound was well, I have been training and planning to escape. I had found some good comrades among the French prisoners there, and another American, McKee, four Frenchmen, and I had worked out a plan so that the six of us could leave together. It was very advantageous for McKee and me, as three of the Frenchmen were old prisoners and had been several times to the frontier only to be caught by the guards. However, they knew the road and the various tricks of the trade, so we stood a fair chance of passing. The camp was a very hard one to get out of, as it was well guarded, and also surrounded by three rows of barbed wire. However, we had found combinations, which at the last minute failed, and left us still there.

On the 19th of August three of us were going out under some potato peelings, and three more by another method, but there were not enough peelings to cover us, so we had to put it off again. The next day McKee, Whitmore (another American), and I were told we were leaving for another camp that afternoon. Imagine our disappointment, after two months of preparing and planning, to have everything spoiled at the last moment and all our carefully prepared equipment, such as maps, compasses, and sacks, endangered by the search on leaving the camp. That was about the lowest point of my captivity, I very nearly burst out crying. You must understand that I was quite nervous at the time, and this sudden overwhelming depression just knocked the stuffing out of me.

Well, I pulled myself together as best I could, put all my carefully saved food in my sack, hid my compass in a piece of bread—the maps were so big that I did not dare try and get them through—packed up the rest of my stuff, and the three of us, McKee, Whitmore, and I, started out for another camp. Things began to look better the moment I left the camp. There was only one guard for the three of us, and he had the simple, good-natured face of a Bavarian farmer. Our destination was Rastatt in Baden. The guard had a large railroad guide and timetable that he kept looking at. We started talking with him and asking about the different towns, when we got there, etc.; he gave me the book to look at and in it, lying loose between the pages, was a map. I asked to look at it. He said "Sure," and I found it to be an excellent railroad map giving rivers and small towns reaching to within twenty miles of the Swiss frontier. Those last twenty miles I knew by heart. I handed it back, and he put it on the seat beside him on top of two packets, one containing our money and the other our *dossiers*.

Well, to make things shorter, we all three decided to leave just before reaching Ulm, the nearest point to the Swiss frontier. At 11.20 we were to arrive in Ulm, so it was agreed that from 10.30 on we would be ready to go. At about 10.30 the guard was dozing, so I changed the position of the map and money from beside the guard to my pocket. As luck would have it, at the next little station he awoke and looked out for the name of the station. Then he looked in his time-table. He missed the map, then he looked down, and the money was gone. I thought it was time to be going, so I left and reached Switzerland eight days later.

Across the German-Swiss Frontier

(*Note*: Harold Willis, of the Escadrille Lafayette, was shot down in combat behind the German lines on August 18, 1917. After several unsuccessful attempts at escape, he finally succeeded in crossing the German frontier into Switzerland by swimming the Rhine. Four simultaneous attempts were made to break out of the prison at Villengen by four groups of American aviators and Lieutenant Isaacs, of the U.S. Navy. The lights of the camp were short-circuited, whereupon each of the four groups followed prearranged plans for getting outside the camp. Willis was provided with a wooden gun and a prison-tailored uniform somewhat resembling those of the guards. His plan was to rush out of the camp with the German sentinels when the

Temps Aéronautique

alarm was sounded. He made the cross-country journey to the border with Lieutenant Isaacs.)

Isaacs and I had a light dinner and spent the early evening greasing our bodies, rearranging our packs and clothes, and trying to remember that most important article which we knew we should forget.

At 10.30 the lights in the rooms were turned out. The first three teams were in their places ready for action. My lot sauntered out, trying to hide guns under coats, and edged over toward the point we were to attack. At 10.35, zero hour, everybody at his station and quiet. But one of the inner guards was in a bad position. The boys watching him must have done their work well, for he soon disappeared. The boss of the inside men gave a signal. Black night dropped on the camp, with the exception of one circuit, which flickered on account of the chain swinging. In a few seconds that fuse blew also. When the first circuits went out, in spite of the flickering, Isaacs and Puryear bent back the bars of their windows, making considerable row. Thanks to German stupidity, nothing was noticed while the light on their side was flickering. Isaacs held back the men in charge of sliding on his bridge until complete darkness, then out she went. "Tiny" Tucker reached across on his hands and knees, and swung off at the feet of two guards facing each other. Isaacs was on his heels, and Battle behind him in order of weight. The bridge held like a dream. The Germans, after the first forty seconds of stupefaction, started to cry "Halt," and then to fire.

During this time Puryear had dropped out of his window and worked his ladder stunt with complete success. There was a guard on the other side. An absurd game of dodge ensued, which became a bit too hot when a second one approached. Puryear took to his heels up the sloping meadow. I heard a fusillade from the camp. From where I lay on my stomach, quietly cutting my way into the German quarters, it sounded like a glorified 4th of July. I had visions of at least half a dozen Americans shot down in their tracks. The firing died down somewhat and the *Feldwebel* of the guard rushed into the court of the men near where I was lying, shouting, "*Heraus!*" "*Heraus!*"

The outside guard had already been tripled by the men from the guardroom. The guards tumbled out of bed, grumbling and cursing and reaching for their guns and boots. One, two, three ran out of the door of their barracks at a jog. I slid along the wall of the building to their doorway and also started off in a dog-trot for the guardhouse.

Arriving at the gate, we found it closed. I had hoped to find every-

American aviator prisoners at Karlsruhe, with Lieutenant Isaacs seated on righ

thing wide open and the men streaming out on the hot foot. A patrol was being formed and being instructed in the guardroom where there was a light. I dared not go in with my crude disguise, and the only thing to do was to stall about outside. One of the guards I had passed was evidently vaguely suspicious. He came up to me and said,

"What are you doing here?"

Fearful of my bad accent, I mumbled something about being half asleep. I thought the game was up.

At that instant the patrol which was being formed in the guardhouse filed out, went to the gate, unlocked it, and started out. I sidled over behind the last man and was out.

My patrol started on a run to the left, a dangerous direction, for it was toward the *casernes* of the instruction battalion.

I cut around to the right and along the back end of the camp behind the pigsties. The guard outside had already been trebled, for where there were posts for two guards, I found six. However, holding my gun high over my head, I ran past them without question. On the back corner, with the clear slope of the hill in front of me, I no longer dared keep close to the camp, and cut away at an angle. One of a group of sentinels on the back end challenged me, once, twice, and fired.

That started the fusillade, which seemed to keep up about fifteen minutes while I dug for it up the slope of that hill, loaded down with heavy underwear and shoes, and three or four pounds of food. That was worse than the finish of any crew race. Finally, my wind gave out completely, and I went over the crest on a walk, with painful visions of hundreds of men close behind me.

Unbuttoning everything and getting the cool night air on my chest I reduced my distress a little bit, and then the way was clear. A thin layer of clouds over the stars produced a dim, luminous light everywhere, and the way across country we had so carefully memorized on our walks was easy to follow.

Lieutenant Isaacs and I had planned our first rendezvous at the foot of a great mound called the Hun's grave, situated at the top of the second high ridge. Toiling up the slope, and full of hope of finding him there, I called my name in a low tone. We had agreed, in case of an encounter, to speak our own names. There was no reply. Louder and louder again, and still no reply. I was doomed to continue the long trail alone.

Trying to encourage myself by the thoughts of good men that had made much harder and longer journeys without the help of a comrade, I swung on along our predetermined route.

About a mile farther on, as I was skirting the edge of a small wood, I suddenly heard voices close to me calling. The battalion had cut me off. I realised the ignominy of escaping clear and being recaptured three miles away. I dove under a young pine tree. Again the call, but it was Isaacs! We fell on each other's neck. I am sure neither of us ever had as much joy in meeting any one as then. He had waited for me at several points along the road, and had finally heard the swish of my rubber raincoat behind him. Knowing the Germans did not possess such garments, he took a chance and called. We held each other's hand for mutual support when we stepped in ditches and holes, and things went well enough for a while. Then we tumbled into our first unforeseen unpleasantness, a swamp. Fortunately, there was not much mud. As soon as we could pull ourselves out of one waist-deep water-hole, we would fall into another.

By the time we had blundered out of that we were soaked to the skin. Every time we crossed roads, we carefully killed our trail with pepper, but the pursuit was not within hearing. Twice rabbits gave us horrible frights, and a startled deer made us think for a minute that all was lost. On the brow of the hill, above Thannheim, we took our first breathing spell, and nibbled a bit of chocolate. The mania that the Black Forester has for crowing, ringing clocks helped tremendously to locate villages. The sound of their bells striking the quarters enabled us to get a fairly accurate compass bearing of all the unseen villages about us.

By this time we were far enough on our road to risk using a little path through the woods which gave us delightful walking, after clumping for so long a time through ploughed fields. As we approached the more densely populated country about Donaueschingen, we cut southwest across the Thannheim brook, and eventually the state road, Brege River, and railroad above Wolterdingen. This latter valley was a nervous place for us, for it marked an excellent position for them to cut us off. We crossed it as noiselessly as possible, and gave the ground a good looking-over. Had any one been there, he would have certainly heard us splash across the power canal and the swift but shallow river. We didn't see a soul.

The first dose of clawing through forests at night was ahead of us, and it was no joke. A lumbering road one can follow by watching the split in the sky-line overhead, and big trees can be avoided by looking up and locating their trunks against the sky. But low brush is hopeless.

You push ahead, get your eyes full of twigs, pine needles, and finally in desperation you turn around and push yourself through backwards. Fortunately, we were soon in the open again and skirting the edges of woods which we located on our chart. For the first time we saw our pursuers after us—soldiers on bicycles with bright headlights following along a nearby road. It didn't worry us much, for no cycles could follow us across those rough fields.

An unpleasant ten minutes with a barking dog (fortunately well attached) near a forest guard's house decided us that it was time to make westing deeper into the wooded region, and by picking logging roads through the dense pines, which appeared to follow our compass course most closely, we worked our way to within hearing of the little village of Unterbrand. We stumbled upon a cross-roads, and we decided that such points should be avoided as dangerous spots where sentinels might be posted, but a careful examination of the locality on tiptoe from the edge of the wood showed everything to be safe. Isaacs standing on my shoulders was able to read the letters of the signboard, partly by starlight, partly by feeling with his fingers. We crawled into the shelter of the woods and under cover of my coat checked up the information we had gained. The needle of light to which we had cut down our pocket flashlight, worked out splendidly, giving very little glare.

The hours were slipping by; it was time to begin to think about shelter for the day. We skirted around the village to the north, and crossed the Brand River into a perfectly impenetrable evergreen swamp. The first gray of dawn forbade us to go much farther, though we were pretty close to houses. The trees were so thick and close together that the only way we could make our path into the thicket was by crawling up the bottom of a drainage ditch. It looked pretty safe.

After some discussion we chose a little opening where there was space to lie down and commenced our preparations for the day. First trousers and underwear came off and were wrung out as best we could; then we very carefully washed each other's feet with carbolic soap we had brought for that purpose, dried and greased them, and put on dry socks. During the whole trip we carefully repeated this performance every morning, and this is certainly the reason why we did not develop blisters or sore feet: the greatest bugbears of escaping prisoners.

Having no warm coat to put over us, we cut a great heap of evergreen branches; crawling under these, cuddled as close together as possible, with our arms about each other, we were able to get two or three hours' good sleep before the damp cold of the morning had penetrated our bones. Then, of course, we both awoke trembling and goose-fleshed all over. Sitting up, we tried rocking forwards and backwards from the hips, which gave us enough exercise to keep circulation going.

The mist of morning slowly dispersed and a few days of yellow sun gilded the tops of the trees above us. What wonderful good fortune! We would really be able to warm and dry ourselves! The warmth crept slowly down through the branches till finally the long-awaited sunlight touched the bottom of our clearing.

The rest of the day we lolled about on the ground like old cats, only moving when a shadow crept out upon us. It would have been a perfect day had not the sound of dogs and children in the woods about us kept our nerves tense most of the time.

Isaacs was sure that the dogs were after us. We had certainly attracted a certain amount of attention at the forester's house five miles back, where the dogs had worried us. It was also certain that the first day after a big break from an officers' camp would see the whole countryside roused and out.

Sometimes the dogs seemed excited about something and approached; then just as we clutched our clubs for action, they would string away to another quarter. Perhaps the last hundred metres up the bed of the ditch saved us, for toward noon the dismal bay died away for good.

Not so the children. All day long they seemed to be within a hundred feet of us; all day long we could distinctly hear their voices, what they said, the sound of their feet as they stepped on dry twigs.

Their labors of stick and acorn gathering did not carry them to where we were hidden, but it worried us tremendously. One of the most peculiar things that we noticed on our little walking trip through the Black Forest was the enormous number of children there seemed to be about. In a mountainous heavily wooded country, one might well expect that lying hidden in thickets miles from the nearest village or house, there would be but few people passing by. At least you would not expect to hear children all day long within a couple of hundred feet of us. The reason was, I suppose, that the crops were in and the children were sent out to go over every square foot of ground and carry home everything that could be burnt or eaten.

With the lengthening shadows and the first chill of the late autumn evening, our sufferings from cold recommenced. One of the principles we decided to hold to at all costs was to run no unnecessary risk in order to be more comfortable. This included not leaving our shelter of the day until 10.30 in the evening at the earliest, for several of our friends had been recaptured on account of venturing on roads too early in the evening.

We snuggled up together again as best we could and waited, shaking with cold, for the long early hours of darkness to pass. Finally the moment came when we dared start on our night's journey. The first few miles consisted of a compass course directly through the forest. Unfortunately, here, none of the old logging roads led in the right direction; we had to buck our way through a great deal of underbrush, dead trees, and the like. By the time we arrived at the wood crossroads for which we were aiming, Isaacs had lost his hardwood dog protector, and I something infinitely more important—a good-sized piece of my trousers.

Things looked quite deserted, and we indulged ourselves in the comfort of walking along the edge of the roads for several miles, keeping to the soft-ground side so that we might hear people coming before they should hear us, and watching carefully, in front and behind all the time, for bicycles. Happily we did hot meet anyone.

The next two hours were wasted in making good a blunder of direction. When the time came to leave the road on which we were walking, we took a bee-line course across the fields checking our compasses by the north star, which was plainly visible.

We had planned to leave Dittishausen far to our left and strike the railroad somewhere between Rotenbach and Löffingen. But, after painfully crossing a very deep ravine, we found ourselves above what must have been Dittishausen, for it was a fair-sized town with no railroad. We were so annoyed by the lost miles that we forgot to steal some fine cabbages which we had passed. There was nothing to do but change our night's route and work our way round Dittishausen and Löffingen. That was the most exhausting setback of our whole trip. The country here was divided into fields of an acre or two, around the borders of which for generations the peasants had thrown flints, making dykes five or six feet high of sharp, loose stones.

An especially prickly kind of thorn apple had chosen to grow most exuberantly on these dykes. We had to cut across country through these natural hedges, and it is easy to imagine the state of our tempers after a couple of miles of this work.

Two cedar trees about the size of men on the edge of the railroad valley gave us a great scare. We certainly waited fifteen minutes for them to change position. We crossed the open meadow at the valley bottom just north of Seppenhofen, and succeeded in scrambling up the opposite slope without attracting attention. After a few more thorn hedges we found ourselves in the open and on the road to Goschweiler. Three miles of easy walking brought us to within sound of the clocks of this village.

From all indications on our maps the Wutach River which barred our route to the south was nothing more formidable than brooks we had previously encountered. We certainly had the wrong dope. As we turned south from the edge of Goschweiler, the fields started to slope toward the south, at first gently, and then pitching off to a 45° angle. Everyone who has wandered about much at night knows how difficult it is to judge heights, depths, and angles of slopes by starlight.

We cheerfully stepped off the edge of something, and were startled to find ourselves up to the knees in mud eight feet lower down, when we had confidently expected to find a slight upward slope!

The valley kept caving away before us; every line of bushes we would think was a brook, we found to be the edge of a terrace; finally everything pitched down in a wooded slope which was little less than a cliff, and we could make out dim mist-filled depths below us and the distant roar of violent waters.

A well-graded road to our left seemed to offer the only possibility of going out without risk of a dangerous fall in the dark, although it was strictly against the rules we had set down for ourselves. We looked carefully down, making no noise and listening frequently, but had several soldiers come along this way we should have been in a very bad position, with a steep cliff on one side of the road, and a sheer drop on the other. Our good fortune held true on the whole venture, however, and we were thankful for our success. No one was on the road that night.

As we tiptoed our way toward the bottom of the canon, we could see that getting across the stream by wading would be a tough proposition; a large volume of water roared down a deep rock channel with sheer sides. Even if it were possible to get down to the water, we should be certain to find deep falls that might prove fatal, heavily loaded down as we were. We decided to take a chance on the bridge, and so, creeping by the buildings of a waterpower plant, we sneaked up toward the edge of the bridge. There did not seem to be anyone on our side. We started to cross, feeling that we were making a mistake, and prepared to turn and run if challenged.

Our precautions proved to be needless. It was strange that such a point should not be guarded. For a distance of twenty-five kilometres this almost impassable valley, running at right angles to one's route to Switzerland, has only three bridges. A score of men could have held the whole thing.

Of course, our theory was to travel through the rough country rather than by the easiest way, and to follow a course that had never been used before. As we commenced to breast the dreary switchback incline up the opposite wall, which towered high above us, it began to drizzle.

Isaacs took the rubber slicker and I buttoned up the collar of my waterproof sheepskin coat. Four kilometres of this even, steady climbing took it out of us pretty well, although we made a practice of resting ten minutes or more every hour. In spite of fatigue and approaching dawn, the lack of cover in the high-rolling plateau to which we had climbed forced us on, always following the edge of the road. Our good fortune and weakness were beginning to make us a little careless. The gray of dawn at last forced us to leave the road and take to the big woods, but the carefully cleaned-up spaces between the boles of the great towering spruces offered no safety to us. In almost full daylight we found a thicket of young trees, somewhere to the south of Gudenwalden. It was a night of risks. Not twenty minutes after we had crept into cover of the dense foliage, we heard woodmen commencing their day's work near by.

Perfectly exhausted, we ate a piece of chocolate and threw ourselves down on the ground regardless of the drizzle, where, in turn, one enjoyed an hour of oblivion, while the other kept watch. Unfortunately, the warmth from the day's ration of chocolate was soon exhausted, and we awoke chilled through. Dry branches were hard to find, for the night's drizzle had soaked everything. Isaacs hit on the scheme of giving the less wet under-branches of trees a hard shaking that got rid of most of the little drops of water at least, and, making an Adirondack bed to lie on, we piled a great heap of branches on us, and topped everything with a waterproof.

The drizzle continued all day, and though worried by the voices of woodcutters about us, we lay huddled together during all its trying hours.

Several trains passed on the Bonndorf branch, close enough to us to enable us to see the steam of the locomotives. This gave us an exact check on our location.

Toward evening, the damp chill simply could not be endured any longer, immobile as we were. We crawled out from under our mound of sodden branches and did Müller exercises for fifteen minutes, to start the blood going again, and after taking our evening biscuit, it being dark, we worked our way out through the forest to the edge of the railroad, where we waited a later and safer hour.

A wood road following the railroad toward Bonndorf did not appear to be frequently used, and we risked following it for several miles, crossing the railroad and descending toward the southwest into a deep, heavily wooded valley. We passed several houses with lighted windows and continued always down into the depths of that great ravine. Had we met any one we could not have left the road, but we had begun to see that an encounter in such a position would not necessarily be fatal, though we should not be able to take to the brush. We looked enough like farmhands for our appearance not to attract attention, and we could speak German well enough to grunt the "*Nacht*," the familiar greeting.

In case we ran across a *gendarme* or soldier who was suspicious and wanted to make trouble, the chances would be that he would not be well armed, and certainly not so desperate as we were; we always carried two nicely balanced clubs to give us a feeling of security.

Coming to the last steep slope before the bottom of the valley, we saw that there was a large building at the side of the road brilliantly illuminated, throwing great shafts of light across our route. We could not make out what it was, until coming closer we discovered that it was an electric light plant. We heard no one, so we walked deliberately through the light and past the place; it was an uncomfortably critical moment. The bridge spanned another roaring stream—quite as impossible to wade as the one of the previous night. Some planet or other which had just arisen gave us light enough to see that the place was deserted, so we slipped over.

There it again became necessary to pass a building with lighted windows. Thinking that it must be some sort of a mill, for it was well toward midnight then, we kept on by. Whatever the place was, they were supposed to keep watch upon the road. Just as we were opposite the building a dog started barking, a window slammed open, there was a shout, but the danger was over. We took to our heels up the side of the road and in a few seconds were in the shelter of the woods.

The next hour and a half was without incident; there was a long, steady ascent out of the valley and through the forest to Rothaus.

We had a very amusing time going around this town. We thought that it was like most Black Forest villages, a well-defined group of houses and fields all about, but this village seemed to have some kind of a suburb. As we were scouting its outlined gardens, bothered somewhat by a very powerful electric light in the centre of the place, we found ourselves all at once walking through the garden passage of a very pretentious house. A lot of hedges and walls made going around the back of the house impracticable, so we kept on through a rose-garden into the cabbage patch and down the front walk. Luckily there were no dogs. Our next road took us due south through great open plains. The whole region was evidently owned by some of the local nobility, for agriculture was carried on on a great scale.

There were groups of well-built barns and granaries every few miles, with little squalid huts all built in the same design for the peasantry. It reminded me a good deal of the mediaeval order of things in Mecklenburg.

Soon a number of little field roads, not marked on our maps, confused us. Picking one by compass that led in the right direction, we headed into the woods again.

A queer incident took place that evening. We heard some one approaching and decided to brazen it out. Good luck was making us imprudent. It proved to be a man carrying a great bundle under his arm. He was more frightened than we were, for he gave a start on seeing us and hurried by without speaking, an unheard-of thing for a German to do. A couple of kilometres farther on, we came to crossroads; none of the places mentioned on the signboard meant anything to us, though we again picked a road by compass which led us into what seemed to us a great monastery farm where Isaacs spotted some very fine cabbages. We each took the biggest and best one we could find, and continued on into the woods on the other side. The road led into a small clearing in a very dense woods. Though we went all around the edge of the place, we could find no other outlet than the way we had come in.

Retracing our steps, we tried another branch of the road, and about the same distance away we pushed into similar difficulties. The way emptied into a big clearing, without a break in its walls. It was very discouraging.

We sat down for our early rest and dug into one of the cabbages. I never tasted anything so delicious in all my life, and we munched away like rabbits until the greater part of one of them had disappeared.

During all our trip we had never felt really hungry. We had to restrain ourselves from eating more than the daily ration, but the nervous strain seemed to take away our appetite somewhat. However, those cabbages really did touch the spot.

Going back to the crucifix, we took the road leading west. It was the right one. We soon started in zigzags down the slope of the Mettema Valley, and for once there was no power house or tavern at the bottom of the valley.

We found a solid lumberman's bridge across the torrent and a little back road to help us up the slope on the other side. This valley was not so deep as the previous one, and a half-hour's walking brought us within sight of a little village on the edge of the plateau. Nearing the houses, we saw that there was a fork in the road just at the entrance of the village—a little place of perhaps fifteen or sixteen cottages. One of the roads led by the church and through the middle of the village, while the other branched off toward the northwest. Our plan named Hausern as the next town on our route. It was necessary to see the sign-board at that cross-road, although it was altogether too close to the village.

We had no more than reached the post when an enormous black dog dashed out of the village barking furiously. We were both so startled and frightened that we ran up the northeast road without bothering about where it led as long as it took us away from that hound. Although it meandered about a good deal over the high plateau, it led us in the right direction. We circled two or three other small hamlets, dogless (it was toward about four in the morning), and dropped over the western edge of the plateau down the wooded slope of the next big north-and-south valley. The long night's journey was beginning to tell on us, on me especially, but as the route was downhill, we still had a good hour of darkness, and Isaacs urged that we should continue.

After a half-hour or so, down through the evergreen forest, we found an old sign-board, on which we finally deciphered Hausern, which checked up the dead reckoning of our compass course. Five o'clock found us at a point where the slope of the valley shelved a little bit, and there seemed to be fields and perhaps houses below us. One could see that there was a magnificent view there in daytime, for from the height where we stood one looked down the great trough of the valley toward the Rhine, and at our left could dimly be made out,

PRISE D'ARMES

against the starry sky, the highest peaks of the Schwartzwald. But we stopped only long enough to swallow delicious water from a wayside spring and dive into the forest to find a safe thicket for the day.

There did not seem to be any patches of young trees, and so we curled up on the ground quite done in, for the hour's sleep we always had after our morning's ration of chocolate.

In the gray of dawn, we discovered a beautiful fir tree whose thickly matted branches swept down to the ground. When we had camouflaged some of the holes from branches cut from other trees, we were perfectly protected from view of people outside as we lay on the ground, in the centre.

We built our bed as before, Isaacs cutting branches and I arranging them, weaving a sort of a wattle mattress to go over us. The sun did not come out during that day either, but it did not rain and it was not too cold. On the whole, we were fairly comfortable till children commenced to bother us in the early afternoon.

We were certainly five miles from the nearest village, but the woods were full of children all day long. At one time one lone youngster came within a few feet of our tree. Isaacs was down the hill cutting more branches, and fearing that he might make a noise and give himself away, I crept out on the opposite side and came down to him. For half an hour that boy kept us crawling about to avoid him, and all ready for a dash; finally he wandered off without having seen us. As the result of these alarms, we always kept our shoes and coats on and our food packed about us, even when sleeping.

That evening our bed proved well enough made for us to brave the cold until 10.30. For the first half-hour's walk the wood road pitched steeply down; we had not been as near the bottom of the valley as we had thought. When we at last came to the opening at the bottom, we found another one of those annoying mills. Placed beside the roaring waters of the mountain torrent, it endangered our crossing, but it was a back wood road we were on which led toward the west, and not toward the frontier, and it again seemed better to risk the bridge than the whirlpools and deep holes of that stream. However, we had to tiptoe across pretty carefully, for every step resounded on the planks, and the millers house was at the other end of the bridge.

We even fooled an old stupid dog, for we heard him snort the "*wuff-wuff*" that a dog first makes when he is suspicious; then as we froze in our footsteps he finally put his head down and went to sleep again. We tiptoed away and started to breast the steep slope through a sweet-smelling forest of balsams. All this time we were wondering where Hausern was. We thought it would be at the bottom of the valley. When we left the woods for the cold wind of the upper plateau we found it in a sort of a pass, between the river valley we had just crossed and the one to the west. To the north and south the hills domed up 2000 feet higher. The difficulty was that Hausern quite filled the bottom of this pass from one mountain wall to the other. To cross it we should have to go between the houses.

As at Rothaus there was a question of stealing through back gardens and garbage piles, with prayers that the dogs had all been eaten. However, we did not care much, and so risked taking a long pull of delicious spring water at the pump.

A short tramp due west of Hausern brought us to a point overlooking Saint-Blasien and the great horseshoe belt of the Alb River which was to guide us southward to the Rhine and liberty!

From above we were able to spot a small lumberman's bridge which we tiptoed across in safety after a tedious half-hour working down the almost perpendicular east wall of the valley.

A grass-grown wood road led southwards along the west bank of the river. The main highway followed the east bank. We chose the former, for main roads directing toward the frontier were sure to be watched for several miles.

The valley was so narrow and the side slope so precipitous that there was barely room in places for the roads and street. When a farmhouse or lumber mill was placed in the valley bottom, we were forced to pass right under the windows of the buildings; twice we had to slink directly through farmyards under the picturesque overhanging balconies and wooded gables of the great Black Forest farmhouses. The dogs seemed to be anything but alert. Only once did we hear one snort at us, and a few minutes of immobility quieted his suspicions. Again the brilliant lights of a power plant caused us a good deal of worry. Like night animals, the only places which seemed kindly and friendly toward us were the deep woods. We hated to approach that beam of white light from the open dynamo window. Walking across that illuminated patch gave us the same sort of shock an ice-cold shower would have done. Holding our breath, we continued boldly but quietly on. No one had seen us.

Beyond one of the farms we stumbled upon another vegetable garden. We loaded ourselves down with turnips, potatoes, and cabbages. Most serious discussion arose as whether to attempt to cross the bed of a roaring tributary or to cross it by a bridge which was lighted by a lamp in front of a mill straddling the torrent. We made a reconnaissance of the ground and could see or hear no one, but Isaacs did not like the idea of going into the light, while I did not at all like the look of the water. Much against his will, he finally came with me, and as luck would have it we were not seen, although we passed along fifty metres of lighted road. Fatigue and good fortune were causing us to take risks we had planned not to incur under any circumstances.

It was time for us to quit the valley and take to the rough cow trails and steeply sloping banks of the uplands. The climb proved that my legs were not as strong as my partner's. He could take a faster pace with less frequent rests. It was a little humiliating to be the weaker sister.

Emerging from the rough, wooded slopes we came out on the same sort of a windswept plateau we had traversed on previous nights. Fall ploughing made walking heavy, but we could take a direct course across the open field. Wolpadingen we encircled to the right, and headed for a patch of woods about three miles away, which we could dimly see in the starlight. By the time we had dragged ourselves across the mucky fields, we were pretty well all in, but we had to continue for a half-hour or so, to find shelter from the cold, piercing wind which seemed to blow from all quarters. We stood on a sort of promontory made by the main river valley, an important tributary from the west. Finally we lay down on a pile of stones behind a tree and took our customary early morning snooze.

With the first light we cut enough baby firs and spruces to build a tent around our hiding-place to keep the wind off. Then we constructed our bed and mattress of branches. The day was anything but restful. A draft of cold air leaked in through our fortifications and our bodies were cold except where they came in contact. In addition, the inevitable children were all about us keeping us continually on the alert. After our late afternoon biscuit, Isaacs made his way down the face of the promontory to find a good ford for the evening.

He came back with the information that we should have to make our way down the face of the gulch before nightfall. Twilight saw us on our way; the descent was tedious enough and consisted of letting one's self down from one tree to another. The delicate thing was to avoid starting the stones rolling down, and despite all our precautions this happened once or twice.

Crossing the deserted valley road just in time to miss an ox-team hauling logs, we made our way down through an alder thicket to the tributary; to cross this proved easier than we had expected. We were even able to do it without a wetting by taking off our shoes and lower garments. We almost immediately found a wood trail which took us about a hundred metres above the valley. Then we entered one of those chutes used by peasants in the Black Forest for sliding logs from the plateaus to the valleys. They are made by cutting the trees and brush vertically up the sides of the cliff. The tumbling logs themselves scour them smooth. We started up it on all fours. The place was a pitch-black tunnel and we met with all sorts of annoying obstacles—old legs jammed across the way, outcrops of rock, and, worst of all, rolled-up balls of dead blackberry vine, which had caught under roots. I had to fight one of these for five minutes before I could get clear of it.

As soon as we had climbed the steepest slope and were at the top, we found a good-sized village at the entrance of a gully on our left. This seemed to check with my hand-made map. At any rate, it was the last point we thought we recognised, until we arrived at the Rhine Valley itself. This village was strung out along a road for an infinite distance, and it did not seem too dangerous to pick our way through a line of the outlined houses. For several miles away it led across open ploughed fields. A cold wind prevented us resting long anywhere, and we made good progress.

All this time we had not heard the whistle or the rumble of the railroad train, and as there is a line on both banks of the Rhine, this was to be our final proof that we were in the neighbourhood of our goal. Soon a vast, mist-filled valley barred the road. We had certainly walked long enough to be at the Rhine. Somewhere in the distance the report of a gun came faintly up to us. It was time to play safely and carefully, keeping well off sky-lines and making no sound. We continued to the thick evergreen thicket marking the edge of the valley. By this time it was a little after midnight, and it seemed best to wait until dawn gave us a chance to get our bearings. We found the most uncomfortable night's lodging imaginable. Evidently the peasants had flung the stones from the field down the slope since the time of Attila. There was not a place to be found where one could sit on the soft earth. There was nothing to do but sit on a pile of nigger-heads with our arms around each other's shoulder and start our rocking exercise to keep warm. This could not be kept up long; we would fall asleep, stop our exercise, wake up with a start, and commence again.

Five o'clock was a long way off. How we finished the night I do not clearly remember. I know we came to bitter words once because we had fallen asleep and pulled the rubber coat from each other. Then I awoke. Isaacs was shaking me and it was the dawn. I had the impression that my lungs and stomach were cold from breastbone to backbone.

Isaacs leading, we made our way cautiously into the valley, letting ourselves down from one tree hand-hold to another. It seemed too quiet for the Rhine Valley; there was no sound of a railroad and there did not seem to be enough width to the place to include a large river, two railroads, and two roads. When we got to the lower edge of the wood we discovered only a fair-sized brook with a little sloping meadow on each side. Our long and uncomfortable night on the rock-pile above had been lost to us. We had not even had a decent rest. It was still very early and it seemed the best plan to go on for a few miles before the country people came out to work in the fields.

The only thing to do was to take a compass course, south by a few points east, which is the most direct route to the Rhine. The country here was broken up into a welter of winding valleys and rounded knolls. By keeping just inside the woods either near the top or the bottom, we could make safe progress and at the same time keep a lookout toward the fields. About six in the morning we had to cross a little grassy interval at the intersection of two brooks: three women were just starting to work hoeing potatoes in one corner of it. As luck would have it, a sort of a hedge ran across the place which permitted us to continue and at the same time to be screened from their view.

We kept on much too late that morning. But the five hours we had lost made us impatient. All at once we were startled at hearing children's voices near by. Instantly stepping into the bushes from the wood road we crawled on ahead and took a look about us. We saw two little girls playing and probably picking up sticks by the side of the road. A forest lane crossing our path and well within their field of vision made it awkward to continue. We walked down to the very edge of the lane and, watching their heads until they were both looking away, stepped across into some small pines. No sooner had we done this than two cows hauling a load of wood came up our road from behind us. The greaseless axles gave us good warning, however.

It was becoming a warm corner, for the hillside thicket in which we lay hidden was surrounded by open fields. Directly below us was the little settlement of Tiefenstein. The only thing to do was to lie low. It was just as well that we did so, for other lumber teams followed the first; people walked up the hill from the village with dogs, and more children appeared, to collect beechnuts and sticks. I took advantage of this forced rest to have Isaacs lace the crevasse in my trousers which threatened to come apart in two pieces. Using spare shoe-laces he made a very neat, sailorlike job of it.

At noon there was a good opportunity to make a shift. We retraced our steps and made our way through the woods to the top of the slope. There we saw a great expanse of cultivated fields with the campanile of Gorwihl in the distance. The peasants had not all left their fields, for there were several old men and women ploughing with cattle not far off. Toward 12.30, they too left. We went on. The edge of the upper fields was bounded by a natural hedge of ferns and weeds. Crawling behind this hedge in the field, we were able to avoid being seen from the houses of Tiefenstein. About halfway across this open region, Isaacs spotted some more cabbages which, of course, we nitched.

The next two miles we walked along paths in the welcome shelter of the woods. Then we found ourselves near a water-mill where the woods narrowed to a mere strip of trees. Just as we were wondering what to do, a small boy came around a corner at a run. We got under cover a fraction of a second before we should have been seen. This incident showed us how imprudently we were going, and we concealed ourselves in a spruce thicket for the rest of the day. The sun shone for a while in the afternoon and we were able to dry our clothes for the first time in four days. When we had finished, and had eaten our two biscuits, sausage, and chocolate ration in the late afternoon, there remained food enough for just one day more. The day's rest enabled us to lie quietly until late in the evening.

About an hour after midnight, while steadily following lumber roads to the southeast, we heard the sound we were longing for—a distant whistle and the unmistakable rumble of a train along the Rhine Valley.

As we had had no definite information as to the location of the frontier guards, it again seemed the wisest thing to stop and spend the next day looking over the land. We curled up in a well-concealed nest, ate a bit of chocolate and fell asleep for an hour or so. The rest of the night was passed rocking forward and back to keep warm. When the blackest of the night had passed, we set out again at a rapid clip. Narrow valleys ran in all directions. We kept within the shelter of the woods all day, sometimes at the valley bottom, sometimes along the edge of the upper fields, always making toward the south.

The first people we saw were harmless enough—two old peasant women in their quaint local costume. We kept far enough behind so that we could just make out their silhouettes in the mist, but they walked so slowly that it was rather irritating. Finally their path turned off to the right and we continued southwards along the edge of the woods, which gave excellent cover. A nearby turnip-field was not to be resisted, and we made our last vegetable raid. Looking out through the foliage we saw German soldiers pushing milk-carts down the road. They were certainly of the frontier guard.

Eventually our woods tapered to a half-acre patch of alder and blackberry bushes. Ahead of us to the south we could dimly see a great mountain wall towering into the mist. Our compasses told us that it ran northeast, southwest, the direction the Rhine should have at Hauenstein. It must be Switzerland! Still we had so often been mistaken that we did not dare be too hopeful until we had made sure of the presence of the railroad line.

We pushed our way to the very southernmost corner, where we cut out enough brush to give us a place to lie down, and constructed with green branches a sort of an observation post. Then we waited for the mist to lift.

It rose slowly, and at last, far down the valley we saw a moving white streamer vanishing, reappearing, changing position constantly. It was a train in Switzerland. Soon after a roar and a white plume of smoke, rising out of a deep cut five hundred metres to the south, located for us the German railroad. Of the river, there was nothing to be seen. Apparently Holstein Station was very near to us, for the trains stopped shortly after passing in front of us, and we could distinctly hear the whistle as it started again.

Near to us there was a path, a short cut across the fields, which passed directly in front of our hiding-place. A good many people went by; a short-winded, fat woman in a hurry to catch a train, small boys dragging baby-carriages full of potatoes, two well-dressed men who dunned an old woman for forty marks right in front of us. We had filled all the holes in the screen of foliage so that, although we could see them, there was small chance that they could see us. Toward noon the sun came out splendidly. Standing guard in turn, we each took cat-naps sprawled out in the warm sunlight. Then occurred what might well have been the disaster of the trip: a farm labourer burst through the bushes so suddenly that we did not have time to move; he threw some implements which he had, under a tree, glanced at us without much curiosity, and disappeared. He had not appeared to be startled. Isaacs was wearing the German hat which I had made because it was more comfortable than his own, and his black coat and trousers vaguely resembled a *Landsturmsmann*. Nevertheless, we crept out of the place and down the road where the woods were fairly wide and we would have a chance to run for it. Evidently the man had not suspected us, for there was no pursuit.

Shortly before sunset we ate our last biscuit and chocolate, and prepared for the most trying part of the whole adventure, crossing the frontier.

Stripping first one part of our bodies and then another, we greased ourselves thoroughly with lard we had brought for the purpose. I discarded all my clothing with the exception of trousers, sheepskin coat, and socks. Isaacs did the same, except that he made a sort of swimming suit out of his shirt and underwear. We had quite a discussion about that, for it seemed to me that the additional ease one has in swimming naked was not to be overlooked. What matter how we should arrive in Switzerland so long as we were free men!

The early hours of night, until the setting of the new moon, were passed cuddled up to each other and rocking as usual. Once the twilight had completely passed, we crawled out into the fields. We agreed to keep together, not to hesitate to use our clubs if there was need, and to stick it out whatever happened.

For the first five hundred yards we were perfectly certain of our route, so we took only the precaution of keeping off the sky-line. We reached the edge of the railroad cutting where the light from the windows of a passing passenger train showed us that there were no fixed guards in the vicinity.

We went through the wire fence down the embankment to the rock-bed right-of-way, and crossed it not a moment too soon. We had barely gotten into the bushes on the other side when a patrol passed behind us up the line. This was the moment to go slowly and carefully. We crawled on hands and knees with occasional long halts to listen. A heavy fog had formed at the bottom of the valley and the grass was wringing wet. We did not mind much, although by the time we had got to the jumping-off place above the river we were soaked through. We peered down through a break in the trees and could make out the water slapping against the gravel. The river-bank was fifty feet below us and at a steep angle. As we lay there listening, we heard someone walking, crunching through the gravel, five short deliberate steps in one direction and five back.

We worked along the brink eastward, letting each other down over the side again and again, without finding a foothold. If anything, we were going upward, and the cliff becoming higher. All this was done so slowly and carefully that it was after midnight before we resolved to find another way down. There was a road at the foot of the cliff where there seemed to be sentinels every hundred metres or so. This sort of thing might continue for miles. Then we remembered the brook we had followed the previous morning, which led under the railroad and through the town of Hauenstein. We struck inland again to the railroad, and then worked eastward along the embankment. Once I touched the signal wires which twanged and sang for an infinite time. Isaacs was wild, but he was decent enough not to say what he thought. We arrived at the railroad station at the outskirts of the village; every window was dark and the town asleep. A hundred feet beyond the station was the guarded bridge over the gorge, so we left the railroad and slid down the slope of the embankment toward the bed of the stream. Suddenly we came to the coping of a retaining wall.

We looked over. There seemed to be a thirty-foot drop to the road below. We worked along the edge of it toward the river, and then back toward the bridge. I was leading and stepped on a dead branch which snapped. There was a scurry of feet on the bridge and a circle of white light appeared against the slope of the gorge on the opposite side of the bridge. It studied one place carefully, moved up and down, back and forth slowly, found nothing unusual, and darkness closed in on us again. We did our usual freezing act for a good quarter of an hour—it was certainly that, for I was standing on one foot, which went to sleep and gave me a terrible time afterwards. Then we left the vicinity with as little ceremony as possible and made our way back to the railroad station. Going still farther inland, we found a place where the land sloped down to the bed of the stream at a gentler angle.

There we took to the water and headed for the Rhine.

Our stream ran over the bed-rock with occasional loose boulders and patches of gravel. This time there could not be any mistakes, and we made every step a study—first feeling with our hands to insure that we would not step on any loose rock which might grind or roll under our weight. The roar and gurgle of the water helped a good deal. Step by step we made our way under the railroad bridge and deeper into a little canon spanned by bridges connecting the streets of the town, through a tunnel and finally through another where the bed of the stream rushed down a series of great natural steps to the level of the Rhine.

As there was certain to be a guard on the rocky point above us, we kept our bodies well under water, and we crept down the bed of the stream to where dark, swirling lines and eddies showed its junction with the river. The opposite shore we could dimly make out, for the mist seemed to be less dense on the surface of the water; at least there would be no danger of our losing our way in the fog.

We dared not slip off our clothes, for our white skin would have been visible from above. Looking back, I saw Isaacs slipping into the water a few steps behind me. All at once, the tug of the current caught me, rolled me over and over across the shallows into deep water. I could slip out of my heavy sheepskin coat quickly, for I had left it fastened with only one button, then I struck out. It was like a nightmare. Though I swam my hardest, the current kept swirling me back toward the German shore. We had been forced to enter the water on the outside of a great bend where all the force of the river was driving in from the centre of the river.

I saw that I could not keep on with my heavy trousers. They were commencing to drag me down. While I swam with one hand, I snapped my belt buckle and pushed them down over my knees with the other. That was a bad moment. In those eddies and whirlpools it is impossible to keep above water with one hand, and as I went under, the trousers clung to my feet. I finally worked them over my heels and my limbs were free.

Swimming easily, I touched bottom on the Swiss shore more than a mile below where we had gone in. I went up and down the bank shouting for Isaacs, but had no reply. He had not spoken very confidently of his swimming, and I had fears for his safety, hampered as he was with clothing.

The bank was steep, but I pulled my way through the bushes to the railroad line. The place was lonely enough. What with worrying about Isaacs and my own troubles, I confess that I did not feel the thrill at the thought of freedom which I should have felt in the early months of my captivity.

A cold wind blowing down from the mountains warned me that with a wet skin and no clothes I must keep moving. That morning we had thought we could make out a Swiss town toward the west. I set out in that direction at a dog-trot down the middle of the track. Traprock ballast is about the last thing one would pick to run over with bare feet, and after three or four hundred yards I came to the conclusion that even cross-country through the brush was better.

As luck would have it, I found a good highway about one hundred yards farther inland. Shuffling down this road for about a kilometre, I came to a railway station. I banged on the doors and shutters hallooing and shouting, but there was no response.

I went on till I came to a great stone building, where beating on the massive front door roused a dog which commenced barking ferociously.

In a few minutes a head in a night-cap appeared at one of the upper windows and demanded *"Was ist los?"* in German-Swiss. I told briefly what the trouble was, but my chattering teeth were hard to master. The head was sympathetic and hurriedly withdrew.

Those good people hurried, I am sure, but it seemed to me that I waited for hours on that cold stone doorstep.

At last a young lad unbolted and unchained a great door and let me in. The smell of stale red wine and syrup was unmistakable. It was a country inn. I was taken up the back stairs along a long corridor into a clean, large bedroom where they helped me, wet and muddy as I was, into a feather bed. Then the *hausfrau* appeared and would not let me speak a word until I had spooned down a formidable glass of *schnapps*. She was a kind, motherly old soul who took a joy in playing the role of most efficient Samaritan to me. Long live the Swiss!

On my appeal she packed off her son with a lantern to search the bank for Isaacs. I did not have much hope, though. This done, two little strawberry-and-cream daughters appeared with a great tray loaded down with hot milk, chocolate, and home-made bread and butter. They stayed with me until the boy came back. There was no news of Isaacs.

I must have fallen asleep before they left the room, for the next thing I remembered some one was shaking and pulling me violently. Coming to, I saw before me a plump, jolly chap, some sort of a frontier guard. He was grinning from ear to ear. Isaacs was safe!

It all seemed too good to be true.

In a moment he came in with the sergeant of the frontier guards, who had an armful of clothes and shoes for me. The sergeant, who was a little jollier and plumper than any of his men, had placed his entire mufti wardrobe at our disposal. Isaacs was already dressed. The coat went around him once and a half, and was pinned under his arms. A wide-brimmed soft hat and flowing necktie made him look like a

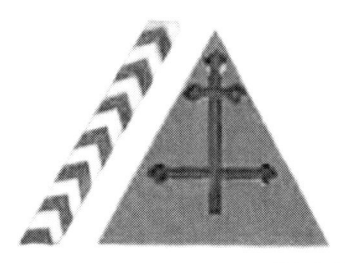

INSIGNIA OF FRENCH ESCADRILLES IN WHICH MEMBERS
OF THE LAFAYETTE FLYING CORPS SERVED
PLATE 8

Bolshevik. Neither of us had suffered any serious hurt, although that two-hundred-yard dash on the railroad track the night before kept me from enjoying a walk for some time.

Isaacs's experience in crossing the Rhine had been quite like my own. He was carried a little farther down the river, and upon reaching the shore had come upon a Swiss frontier guard, from whom he received the kindest possible treatment. After a couple of rounds of *schnapps* with Madame and her daughters, we said goodbye to these kindly people, who would not take a penny from us. A few days later we crossed the border into France.

CERTIFICATE OF SERVICE IN THE LAFAYETTE FLYING CORPS

Lightning Source UK Ltd.
Milton Keynes UK
UKOW04f1846141214

243094UK00001B/51/P